Women of All Nations

A Record of Their Characteristics, Habits, Manners, Customs and Influence

BLACKFOOT INDIAN GIRL.
DRAWN BY NORMAN H. HARDY.

FRONTISPIECE -- 1

Women of All Nations

A Record of Their Characteristics, Habits, Manners, Customs and Influence

IN TWO VOLUMES

Edited by

T ATHOL JOYCE

N W THOMAS

Fellows of the Royal Anthropological Institute

With 647 black and white and 24 colour illustrations

VOL. 2

GYAN

GYAN PUBLISHING HOUSE

NEW DELHI

Women of All Nations
(Women's Studies, Sociology, Anthropology, Culture, History)

ISBN : 81-212-0002-4 (Set)

ISBN : 81-212-0158-6 (Vol-II)

Published in 1997 in India by
Gyan Publishing House
5, Ansari Road,
New Delhi-110 002
Printed at Goyal Offset Printers Delhi

CONTENTS

LIST OF COLOUR-PLATES

strict observance of rules. Not only were a long list of actions *tabu* to her, but she was also the same to others, not only to human beings, but to the spirit and the animal world. The awful influences that went out from her affected inanimate objects, such as tackle or gambling sticks, and she could heal by her touch.

being that it has been chiefly through the women. The half-castes everywhere are chiefly the children of Indian mothers. It is a rare thing for a white woman to marry one of the other race. Also the industrial activities forced upon the Indians were not men's, but women's.

Intermingling of Aboriginals and Whites.

Photograph by Scott.

MEXICAN WOMEN (STATE OF OAXACA) SPINNING.

Her period of seclusion ended with feasting or public ceremonies, and some changes in her dress or adornment. The Hopi girl in Arizona, who wore her hair formerly in whorls imitating the squash flower, one over each ear, after marriage changed her *coiffure* to a simple braid. All these ceremonies and *tabus* were in the nature of a consecration and protection to the incipient woman. This close connection between social customs and the tribal cult will at once recall Cicero's assertion that all the artificialities of human life have a common bond, and are associated by a kind of fellowship.

In each area there has been blood and industrial mingling, the most significant fact

Bloody massacres have followed governmental efforts to compel the men to engage in farming. Not so the women. Gardening, sewing, weaving, household cares under better shelter and protection, were not tabooed nor irksome. The women therefore are the saviours of those that survive.

Father Morice suggests, as a motive why the Indian woman more easily becomes a part of our civilisation than the man, that her lot was so terribly hard that she had everything to gain and scarcely anything to lose by the change.

Ethnologists are wont to speak of stages of culture as though they resemble the distinct stories of houses. Cultures and tribes grow and decline just like individuals by insensible degrees. It is not true to the facts to regard the peoples of North America as possessing separate cultures. They all belong to one culture the qualities of which fade into one another. As in the individual woman's life its current at certain points has shallows and falls, so in North American primitive peoples Mayan or Aztec women will seem to be on an elevation quite above that of the Utes. But a comprehensive view reveals innumerable connecting links. The question will often occur whether, after all things are considered, these Indian women were nearer in tune with Nature. Has the artificialising of human life improved the air breathed, the water drunk, the food eaten, the raiment worn, the care of the skin, the sunlight enjoyed, work and exercise, rest and sleep, the pace and stress of life, the personal habits ? Since life is longer, on the whole, yes. It happens, however, that elevation and depression are related. The greatest virtues are shadowed by the greatest crimes, the greatest successes are neighboured by the deepest miseries.

The advent of the white man has brought radical changes into the life of the native, and many customs and beliefs are rapidly fading into disuse—in fact have disappeared over large areas. Still they are typical of the life of the people of this continent, and so cannot be passed over without mention. For the sake of uniformity the present tense is used throughout this sketch, but the reader must bear in mind that in many localities the old ceremonies have become obsolete.

Having taken a bird's eye view of North America in association with aboriginal women, a few of its environments or culture-areas may now be scrutinised one by one in the following order :—

1. Arctic area, Eskimo women.

2. North-west Coast insular area—Tlinkit and Haida women.

3. California-Oregon area — Hupa and Maidu women.

4. Interior Basin desert area—sedentary tribes and unsettled groups.

5. Plains area—Siouan and other women.

6. Atlantic slope area—Algonquian, Iroquoian, and Muskhogean women.

7. Tropical North American area—Mexican and Caribbean women.

II—THE ESKIMO

The Frozen North—Physical Characteristics—Language and Industries—Clothing—Food and its Preparation—Eskimo Household Arrangements—The Importance of the Lamp—Eskimo Women Potters—The Woman's Knife—The Woman's Boat—Tattooing and other Forms of Adornment—Hair-dressing and Ornaments—Decoration of Clothing—Eskimo Games—Songs and Dances—Social Life of the Eskimo—Birth Customs—Parental Affection—Eskimo Girlhood—The Marriage Question—Divorce—Old Age—Exchange of Wives—Eskimo Education—Religion

The Frozen North.

ESKIMO women formerly lived along the border of Arctic America chiefly north of the 60th parallel, from Eastern Greenland to Eastern Asia. Their settlements also extended to Newfoundland, if not to Maine, to the southern limit of Hudson Bay, and to the farthest Aleutian Islands. But their range is now much curtailed. Their environment was the home of the Frost King, of six months' night, of snow and ice for building material. It was the lamp-land, and woman was the vestal. Most of it was treeless, compelling her to make her utensils of bone, horn, and ivory. Vegetable diet was limited to a few berries, and her food supply was chiefly the flesh and fat of sea mammals, fish, reindeer, bear, muskox, birds, and a multitude of smaller creatures.

In physical characteristics the Eskimo differs from the Indian woman. She is much lighter in colour and shorter in stature, has a long head, a flat, pinched nose, and somewhat Mongolian eye. Murdoch speaks of her small hands and feet, but is not as pleased with her carriage as he is with the man's. Although possessing a good physique, she is singularly ungraceful in her movements, and walks with a sort of shuffling half trot, her toes turned in, the body leaning forward, and the arms hanging awkwardly.

Physical Characteristics.

This air and gait are not affected by her in order to attract attention, but are caused by the exactions of her snow life and dress.

A remarkable thing about the Eskimo women is their flexibility of body and limbs. They will endure for a long time the stooping posture, and that assumed by them in dressing skins of the larger animals, without great fatigue.

ESKIMO MATRON, PORT CLARENCE, ALASKA.

The language spoken by the women of this interminable coast of ice is remarkably similar throughout, while that of the Indians southward varies greatly from place to place. When it is remembered that their narrow strip, if straightened out, would be 5,000 miles in length, this homogeneous speech is surprising.

Language and Industries.

The industries of Eskimo women are especially the outcome of the environment from beginning to end. They will be found associated with man in those occupations where weapons are absent—in all sorts of manufactures, in transportation, and in training the dogs. Besides, there are a multitude of crafts that are their own, such as furnishing the house, making the dress under the most exacting circumstances, and preparing the food.

The Eskimo have to dress in furs, caribou in winter, and sealskin in summer, and there are ever so many processes for under-garments and over-garments, for haired and unhaired work, for softest down and waterproof soles. Women do every bit of this work, and have their styles and fashions in each locality.

Both sexes wear long stockings, boots, trousers, and a hooded jacket, all of which are double. The inner part is worn with the fur side next the skin, the outer with the fur side exposed.

Clothing.

The married woman's jacket has a long hood extending far down the back, and a belt around the jacket under the hood sustains the infant borne inside on the back of the mother.

In her exacting climate the demands on the Eskimo tailoress are great and continuous. Her materials in former times were abundant and varied, including the skins, intestines, sinews, bones, horns, teeth, and hoofs of reindeer, seal, bear, fox, wolf, dog, marten, ermine, lynx, whale, walrus, goose, duck, and many more, if her exacting taste demanded. All of these skins were dressed, cut out, sewn, and adorned by women. Their costume differed somewhat from that of the men, and consisted of frock with hood and girdle, inner frock, often without the hood, mittens, tight-fitting breeches, long stockings with hair inside, slippers lined with dry, soft material, and outer boots. On the woman's frock the hood is larger, while the front and back extend downward in longer flaps. Boas* intimates that artistic ideas were not highly developed among the Eskimo. But with better needles and new ideas to inspire them, these Northern tailors turn out beautiful work, both in the East and the West.

The food of Eskimo women is almost wholly animal, being derived from the land, the air, and the water, not forgetting the

* "The Central Eskimo."

ice and snow. It is eaten either raw or cooked, usually the latter. Neither is there

YOUNG ESKIMO WOMAN, PORT CLARENCE, ALASKA.

particular choice of parts—indeed, certain portions, which in England would be considered offal, are special dainties with them. The capture and gathering of these creatures is the duty of men, though women are not excluded from the hunt. But the moment the dead animal is secured, woman's many tasks begin—hauling the game home, skinning animals, dressing hides, cutting up and curing meat, preparing it for consumption, purveying, and general housekeeping. They have no regular hours for meals, but eat whenever they are hungry and have leisure. The women keep a supply of cooked food on hand ready for emergencies. When the men are working together, the women at intervals through the day prepare dishes of meat which the men eat by themselves or are fed until gorged by the women. When a family returns from the spring hunt, with plenty of venison, they keep open house.

Food and its Preparation.

Boas tells us that Eskimo women live in tents in summer, and two kinds of winter houses—the underground permanent home, and the snow hut. The former is semi-subterranean, the sides being of stone and whalebones, and the roof of poles and bones, over which is stretched a cover of skin. Outside of this may be a layer of small shrubs and another layer of skin, weighted down with stones. In other localities earth and moss are used. The doorway and front hall consist of a subterranean passage, lower at the outer end, as may be imagined, to keep out the demon of cold. For the houses of snow, blocks are cut out with long, thin knives of ivory or bone, and fitted into the tiniest of domes, the only mortar being the frost. Bedroom, kitchen, dining, and sitting room are all one; but storage rooms, especially for the snow houses, are built apart. The beds are on a bench of earth, or snow, overlaid with brush and skins. The lamps with all their accessories are on the side. Just as soon as the sun returns, after the long winter, the Eskimo women dwell in tents set up on poles, where Nature is kind enough to furnish them; but it is most interesting to see how they lash together short bits of bone, narwhal tusks, wood

Eskimo Household Arrangements.

ESKIMO WOMAN, AGED 23, PORT CLARENCE, ALASKA.

from whaling ships, and drift, to form the support of a shelter of skins.

Household utensils are reduced to the lowest terms, noteworthy specially for omissions rather than variety. Vessels of wood, bone, baleen, and animal integuments answer many purposes. The most serviceable is the lamp with its accessories.

Women must have invented the lamp; at any rate, without it there would have been no Eskimo. Lamps are illuminators, heaters, dryers for wet clothing, and cooking stoves, especially in the six months of darkness and cold. They are shallow dishes, straight along one side like a turnover. The wick of moss or fibre is spread along the straight front edge, and the cavity is filled with seal blubber, which furnishes the fat. Obtaining this, setting up the lamp and trimming it constantly develops much knack and skill. As the soapstone of which lamps and cooking pots are usually made is not found everywhere, it is a great factor in Eskimo commerce, which extends sometimes as much as a thousand miles. Failure of soapstone stimulated the Eskimo women about Bristol Bay to make their lamps of clay.

The Importance of the Lamp.

Of the influence of the lamp, Dr. Walter Hough remarks: "The extent to which the lamp has entered into Eskimo life as a social factor is very great. It is essentially the care and possession of the women, peculiarly the sign of the social unit, and though several families may inhabit the same *igloo*, each maternal head must have her own lamp. 'A woman without a lamp' is an expression which betokens, of all beings, the most wretched among the Eskimo. The lamp is placed in the woman's grave."

By courtesy of Dr. George B. Gordon.

ESKIMO WOMEN AND THEIR CHILDREN, KING'S ISLAND, ALASKA.

Showing tattooed patterns on the arms.

Eskimo Women Potters.

Women were the potters among the Eskimo, their ware being restricted to lamps and the requisite cooking vessels. Clay from the tundra was reduced to a smooth paste by mixing with walrus blood and kneading it with the hands. Sand from the beach was added, together with fine feathers. The vessel was built up with the hands or by means of a paddle. Compared with the Indian pottery of the Pueblos, this ware is very plain; however, some ornamentation was effected in the form of lines made with a pointed stick, a pitted surface produced by means of a roughly carved paddle, or by wrapping the unbaked vessel in grass matting which left its impression.

The Woman's Knife.

A word about the woman's knife. Hundreds of them may be seen round the kitchens of civilisation as hash cutters, called "chopping knives"; but you must visit the saddler and watch him cut leather to understand the tool in its most primitive function. In old times the blade was of slate or harder stone, but the trader and the whaler have substituted a far better one of steel. With this knife-of-all-trades the women prepare hides and cut out garments.

The Woman's Boat.

The woman's boat in Eskimoland, like its namesake, is the burden-bearer, and quite unlike the *kaiak*, or man's boat. It is practically an open coracle, or scow, with framework of wood or whale ribs, over which the covering of seal or walrus hide is tightly stretched. A dainty sail—made of thin intestines—is sometimes added. The steering is done with a long paddle.

Tattooing and other Forms of Adornment.

The æsthetic life of the Eskimo woman is made up of adornment and enjoyments. The women nearly all are tattooed, and in some localities the designs are quite elaborate. They are chiefly marked on the chin or about the mouth with one or more stripes, but the arms, breast, and back are also brought into service. The original motive seems to have been fashion or social rule, but it is related of one that she tattooed whale marks in the corners of her mouth to show that she was the wife of a successful hunter. But Eskimo women, in company with their husbands, had a more barbarous fashion than tattooing, called by Dall "labretifery." So far as is known, it was practised only by those living west of the Mackenzie River; indeed, the habit prevailed much more widely among the men. Captain Cook says that in Cook's Inlet the under lip was slit parallel with the mouth, the incision being commenced during infancy. "In adults it was often two inches long. In it was inserted a flat, narrow ornament, made of a solid shell or bone, cut into little narrow pieces like small teeth, almost down to the base or thickest part, which has a small projecting bit at each end, which supports it when put into the incision. . . . Others have the lower lip perforated into separate holes, and then the ornament consists of as many distinct shelly studs, whose points are pushed through these holes." But the number of studs, their location in the lip, their materials, size, and form were matter of fashion from place to place.

Hair-dressing and Ornaments.

The usual custom of dressing the hair is to part it in the middle from the forehead to the nape of the neck, and to gather it into a club on each side behind the ear. The club is twisted or braided and adorned, not with gay ribbons, but with leather strips, beads, brass buttons, and the like. The marrow of the reindeer is sometimes used for pomatum. The women are tidy in arranging the hair, and Murdoch* never saw one of them bald.

Earrings, says Murdoch, are worn by nearly all the women. In olden times these were little hooks of walrus ivory, but trade has long since added cheap jewellery in abundance. Gordon† adds to earrings necklaces of glass beads and bracelets of the same materials.

Besides the adornment of the person, the Eskimo woman's taste runs riot in the

* "Ethnological Results of the Point Barrow Expedition."

† "Notes on the Western Eskimo."

decoration of clothing. Here she has the advantage, because there is so much of it; and she busies her fancy and skilful fingers quite as much with the male attire as with her own. Skin, haired and unhaired, furs and feathers and down in all procurable colours, in masses and tasteful patchwork, gives her all the opportunity.

Decoration of Clothing.

The enjoyments of Eskimo women are derived from play and from the higher art of song and the native traditions, which are fosterers of art. The supple bodies of Eskimo women do not wear out all their energies in dressing hides. They join with men in their athletic sports. The girls play with dolls, have small models of domestic utensils for playing housekeeping and at woman's work. Storm-bound much of the time, there are house games as well as games in the open, all of which were studied by Nelson during a five-years' residence about St. Michael. Among them may be mentioned :—

Eskimo Games.

Toss the dart.—A block, 6 inches long, is sharpened at one end, and has a flaring cup at the other, 3 inches in diameter, with a deep hole in the middle. It is set up in the floor of the hut, the players squat around, and the game is to toss up a dart so that it will turn in the air and fall with its point sticking in the middle of the cup. Small sticks are used as counters.

Jackstraws, or spillikins.

Ring the stake.—A kind of quoits, played during the long twilight nights of June.

Top-spinning.—Girls and boys engage in this game. The moment the top is spun the owner runs out through the entrance and tries to encircle the hut and return before the top falls. Each successful round counts a score.

Football.—The ball is made of leather stuffed with moss and deer hair, and is about six inches in diameter, and there are four players, who stand each at the corners of a square facing inward.

Handball.—Played with a rounded rectangular leather bag filled with sand. The young men of the village form one side, and the young women the other. The game is for one side to secure the ball and keep it going among themselves.

Blind man's buff.

Hide and seek.—Played in summer in the long grass.

Ring around.—Played by men and women, together or separately. There are two rings which circle about swiftly.

Tossing on walrus hide.—Like tossing in a blanket, but the Eskimo get more fun out of it.

The tug of war.—Played by women as well as by men.

The Eskimo women are fond of tricks with the fingers, and have many devices in cat's cradle, making parts of the body, things of daily use, and well-known animals. Dolls and children's games in great number are included in Nelson's* lists.

The Eskimo are fond of singing, but the men do the most of it, their musical instrument being the drum. In their dances the women remain with their feet planted squarely on the floor, and, swaying the body and slowly gesticulating with hands and arms, go through the figures, always keeping time to the music. They carry a long feather wand in each hand, which they wave as they move. In certain religious festivals they use finger masks.

Songs and Dances.

Of course, what will be said of the Eskimo women and their social life must be looked at in its environmental settings, which will explain all and condone much. As the woman all her life carries an infantile face, so all her arts and activities bear the stamp of, and voice the childhood of mankind.

Social Life of the Eskimo.

The Eskimo social unit is the family and not the clan, and is built about the mother, who, with father, children, and a relative or two, make up the household. Descent is reckoned in both paternal and maternal lines. Children after marriage may continue to reside at home, either with the

* "The Eskimo about Bering Strait."

husband's or the wife's family. The political unit is not strong. The households in the same locality do not form a social organisation.

The treatment of Eskimo women was for this reason somewhat different tribally from that of Indian women. They seem to be a good-hearted people, and writers speak well of personal treatment of women among them. Parry says that the women were treated as equals of the men, and the wife was always consulted by the husband when a more important bargain than usual was to be made; and Murdoch says: "The wife is the constant and trusted companion of the man except in the hunt."

Birth Customs.

When a babe is about to be born, the Eskimo mother either builds for herself a hut or tent apart, or is secluded from contact or association with her people or their accessories. Even her husband is under *tabu*, as he cannot go seal-catching or even use the common industrial tools for a certain season.

The babe is carried about naked on the mother's back under her warm fur clothing, made fuller for the purpose. Around the mother's waist, high up, a girdle is tied for support. When she wishes to nurse the little one, the mother loosens the girdle and slips the babe round to the breast, without bringing it out into the freezing air. Children are carried in this way until they are able to walk. The precise style of this unique baby-carriage varies from place to place, and the surprising thing about it is that the woman is not inconvenienced, but rather happy at her work, and the child takes its shaking up as a matter of course. Little girls also play mother as with us, and carry infants around on their backs in the same way as does the mother.

Parental Affection.

The diet is so hard for adults that children are nursed until they are three or four years old. Infanticide is rare, infant mortality great, and children usually much prized. Everybody speaks well of these Arctic children, and it is a glowing tribute to the patient little mothers that it is so. Murdoch sets this forth so appreciatively that his words are quoted freely: "The affection of parents for their children is extreme, and the children seem to be thoroughly worthy of it. They show hardly a trace of the fretfulness and petulance so common among civilised children, and though indulged to an unusual extent are remarkably obedient. Corporal punishment appears to be absolutely unknown, and the children are rarely chidden or punished in any way. Indeed, they seldom deserve it, for, in spite of the freedom that they are allowed, they do not often get into any mischief, especially of a malicious sort, but attend quietly to their own affairs and their own amusements."

Eskimo Girlhood.

The little girls grow up just as they do everywhere. In all industrial employments they associate freely with their elders, catching fish, fetching drift wood, driving dogs, so that by the time they are in their teens they are sober little women.

The Marriage Question.

Murdoch has gathered the data for studying Eskimo woman's domestic life. His opinion is confirmed that the marriage relation was entered upon generally from reasons of interest or convenience, with not much sentiment about it. The woman looked for a man who was a good hunter and industrious—a bountiful provider. It is not alleged that prudential motives do not have a share in civilised match-making, nor is it denied that Cupid had found his way to the Frozen North. Child betrothal, by which very young persons are set apart for each other in tender youth, is said to have been practically universal among the Eskimo. Marriages were arranged by parents. Murdoch knew of a young man of about twenty-two who offered himself as the prospective husband of a girl of eight or ten when she should reach a marriageable age, and quotes Simpson as follows: "As soon as the young man desires a partner and is able to support one, his strict observance of rules. Not only were a long list of actions *tabu* to her, but she was also the same to others, not only to human beings, but to the spirit and the animal world. The awful influences that went out from her affected inanimate objects, such as tackle or gambling sticks, and she could heal by her touch.

Photograph by Scott.

MEXICAN WOMEN (STATE OF OAXACA) SPINNING.

Her period of seclusion ended with feasting or public ceremonies, and some changes in her dress or adornment. The Hopi girl in Arizona, who wore her hair formerly in whorls imitating the squash flower, one over each ear, after marriage changed her *coiffure* to a simple braid. All these ceremonies and *tabus* were in the nature of a consecration and protection to the incipient woman. This close connection between social customs and the tribal cult will at once recall Cicero's assertion that all the artificialities of human life have a common bond, and are associated by a kind of fellowship.

In each area there has been blood and industrial mingling, the most significant fact being that it has been chiefly through the women. The half-castes everywhere are chiefly the children of Indian mothers. It is a rare thing for a white woman to marry one of the other race. Also the industrial activities forced upon the Indians were not men's, but women's.

Intermingling of Aboriginals and Whites.

Bloody massacres have followed governmental efforts to compel the men to engage in farming. Not so the women. Gardening, sewing, weaving, household cares under better shelter and protection, were not tabooed nor irksome. The women therefore are the saviours of those that survive.

Father Morice suggests, as a motive why the Indian woman more easily becomes a part of our civilisation than the man, that her lot was so terribly hard that she had everything to gain and scarcely anything to lose by the change.

Ethnologists are wont to speak of stages of culture as though they resemble the distinct stories of houses. Cultures and tribes grow and decline just like individuals by insensible degrees. It is not true to the facts to regard the peoples of North America as possessing separate cultures. They all belong to one culture the qualities of which fade into one another. As in the individual woman's life its current at certain points has shallows and falls, so in North American primitive peoples Mayan or Aztec women will seem to be on an elevation quite above that of the Utes. But a comprehensive view reveals innumerable connecting links. The question will often occur whether, after all things are considered, these Indian women were nearer in tune with Nature. Has the artificialising of human life improved the air breathed, the water drunk, the food eaten, the raiment worn, the care of the skin, the sunlight enjoyed, work and exercise, rest and sleep, the pace and stress of life, the personal habits? Since life is longer, on the whole, yes. It happens, however, that elevation and depression are related. The greatest virtues are shadowed by the greatest crimes, the greatest successes are neighboured by the deepest miseries.

The advent of the white man has brought radical changes into the life of the native, and many customs and beliefs are rapidly fading into disuse—in fact have disappeared over large areas. Still they are typical of the life of the people of this continent, and so cannot be passed over without mention. For the sake of uniformity the present tense is used throughout this sketch, but the reader must bear in mind that in many localities the old ceremonies have become obsolete.

Having taken a bird's eye view of North America in association with aboriginal women, a few of its environments or culture-areas may now be scrutinised one by one in the following order:—

1. Arctic area, Eskimo women.
2. North-west Coast insular area—Tlinkit and Haida women.
3. California-Oregon area—Hupa and Maidu women.
4. Interior Basin desert area—sedentary tribes and unsettled groups.
5. Plains area—Siouan and other women.
6. Atlantic slope area—Algonquian, Iroquoian, and Muskhogean women.
7. Tropical North American area—Mexican and Caribbean women.

II—THE ESKIMO

The Frozen North—Physical Characteristics—Language and Industries—Clothing—Food and its Preparation—Eskimo Household Arrangements—The Importance of the Lamp—Eskimo Women Potters—The Woman's Knife—The Woman's Boat—Tattooing and other Forms of Adornment—Hair-dressing and Ornaments—Decoration of Clothing—Eskimo Games—Songs and Dances—Social Life of the Eskimo—Birth Customs—Parental Affection—Eskimo Girlhood—The Marriage Question—Divorce—Old Age—Exchange of Wives—Eskimo Education—Religion

The Frozen North.

ESKIMO women formerly lived along the border of Arctic America chiefly north of the 60th parallel, from Eastern Greenland to Eastern Asia. Their settlements also extended to Newfoundland, if not to Maine, to the southern limit of Hudson Bay, and to the farthest Aleutian Islands. But their range is now much curtailed. Their environment was the home of the Frost King, of six months' night, of snow and ice for building material. It was the lamp-land, and woman was the vestal. Most of it was treeless, compelling her to make her utensils of bone, horn, and ivory. Vegetable diet was limited to a few berries, and her food supply was chiefly the flesh and fat of sea mammals, fish, reindeer, bear, muskox, birds, and a multitude of smaller creatures.

In physical characteristics the Eskimo differs from the Indian woman. She is much lighter in colour and shorter in stature, has a long head, a flat, pinched nose, and somewhat Mongolian eye. Murdoch speaks of her small hands and feet, but is not as pleased with her carriage as he is with the man's. Although possessing a good physique, she is singularly ungraceful in her movements, and walks with a sort of shuffling half trot, her toes turned in, the body leaning forward, and the arms hanging awkwardly.

Physical Characteristics.

This air and gait are not affected by her in order to attract attention, but are caused by the exactions of her snow life and dress.

A remarkable thing about the Eskimo women is their flexibility of body and limbs. They will endure for a long time the stooping posture, and that assumed by them in dressing skins of the larger animals, without great fatigue.

ESKIMO MATRON, PORT CLARENCE, ALASKA.

Language and Industries.

The language spoken by the women of this interminable coast of ice is remarkably similar throughout, while that of the Indians southward varies greatly from place to place. When it is remembered that their narrow strip, if straightened out, would be 5,000 miles in length, this homogeneous speech is surprising.

The industries of Eskimo women are especially the outcome of the environment from beginning to end. They will be found associated with man in those occupations where weapons are absent—in all sorts of manufactures, in transportation, and in training the dogs. Besides, there are a multitude of crafts that are their own, such as furnishing the house, making the dress under the most exacting circumstances, and preparing the food.

The Eskimo have to dress in furs, caribou in winter, and sealskin in summer, and there are ever so many processes for under-garments and over-garments, for haired and unhaired work, for softest down and waterproof soles. Women do every bit of this work, and have their styles and fashions in each locality.

Clothing.

Both sexes wear long stockings, boots, trousers, and a hooded jacket, all of which are double. The inner part is worn with the fur side next the skin, the outer with the fur side exposed. The married woman's jacket has a long hood extending far down the back, and a belt around the jacket under the hood sustains the infant borne inside on the back of the mother.

In her exacting climate the demands on the Eskimo tailoress are great and continuous. Her materials in former times were abundant and varied, including the skins, intestines, sinews, bones, horns, teeth, and hoofs of reindeer, seal, bear, fox, wolf, dog, marten, ermine, lynx, whale, walrus, goose, duck, and many more, if her exacting taste demanded. All of these skins were dressed, cut out, sewn, and adorned by women. Their costume differed somewhat from that of the men, and consisted of frock with hood and girdle, inner frock, often without the hood, mittens, tight-fitting breeches, long stockings with hair inside, slippers lined with dry, soft material, and outer boots. On the woman's frock the hood is larger, while the front and back extend downward in longer flaps. Boas* intimates that artistic ideas were not highly developed among the Eskimo. But with better needles and new ideas to inspire them, these Northern tailors turn out beautiful work, both in the East and the West.

The food of Eskimo women is almost wholly animal, being derived from the land, the air, and the water, not forgetting the

* "The Central Eskimo."

ice and snow. It is eaten either raw or cooked, usually the latter. Neither is there

YOUNG ESKIMO WOMAN, PORT CLARENCE, ALASKA.

particular choice of parts—indeed, certain portions, which in England would be considered offal, are special dainties with them. The capture and gathering of these creatures is the duty of men, though women are not excluded from the hunt. But the moment the dead animal is secured, woman's many tasks begin—hauling the game home, skinning animals, dressing hides, cutting up and curing meat, preparing it for consumption, purveying, and general housekeeping. They have no regular hours for meals, but eat whenever they are hungry and have leisure. The women keep a supply of cooked food on hand ready for emergencies. When the men are working together, the women at intervals through the day prepare dishes of meat which the men eat by themselves or are fed until gorged by the women. When a family returns from the spring hunt, with plenty of venison, they keep open house.

Food and its Preparation.

Boas tells us that Eskimo women live in tents in summer, and two kinds of winter houses—the underground permanent home, and the snow hut. The former is semi-subterranean, the sides being of stone and whalebones, and the roof of poles and bones, over which is stretched a cover of skin. Outside of this may be a layer of small shrubs and another layer of skin, weighted down with stones. In other localities earth and moss are used. The doorway and front hall consist of a subterranean passage, lower at the outer end, as may be imagined, to keep out the demon of cold. For the houses of snow, blocks are cut out with long, thin knives of ivory or bone, and fitted into the tiniest of domes, the only mortar being the frost. Bedroom, kitchen, dining, and sitting room are all one; but storage rooms, especially for the snow houses, are built apart. The beds are on a bench of earth, or snow, overlaid with brush and skins. The lamps with all their accessories are on the side. Just as soon as the sun returns, after the long winter, the Eskimo women dwell in tents set up on poles, where Nature is kind enough to furnish them; but it is most interesting to see how they lash together short bits of bone, narwhal tusks, wood

Eskimo Household Arrangements.

ESKIMO WOMAN, AGED 23, PORT CLARENCE, ALASKA.

from whaling ships, and drift, to form the support of a shelter of skins.

Household utensils are reduced to the lowest terms, noteworthy specially for omissions rather than variety. Vessels of wood, bone, baleen, and animal integuments answer many purposes. The most serviceable is the lamp with its accessories.

Women must have invented the lamp; at any rate, without it there would have been no Eskimo. Lamps are illuminators, heaters, dryers for wet clothing, and cooking stoves, especially in the six months of darkness and cold. They are shallow dishes, straight along one side like a turnover. The wick of moss or fibre is spread along the straight front edge, and the cavity is filled with seal blubber, which furnishes the fat. Obtaining this, setting up the lamp and trimming it constantly develops much knack and skill. As the soapstone of which lamps and cooking pots are usually made is not found everywhere, it is a great factor in Eskimo commerce, which extends sometimes as much as a thousand miles. Failure of soapstone stimulated the Eskimo women about Bristol Bay to make their lamps of clay.

The Importance of the Lamp.

Of the influence of the lamp, Dr. Walter Hough remarks: "The extent to which the lamp has entered into Eskimo life as a social factor is very great. It is essentially the care and possession of the women, peculiarly the sign of the social unit, and though several families may inhabit the same *igloo*, each maternal head must have her own lamp. 'A woman without a lamp' is an expression which betokens, of all beings, the most wretched among the Eskimo. The lamp is placed in the woman's grave."

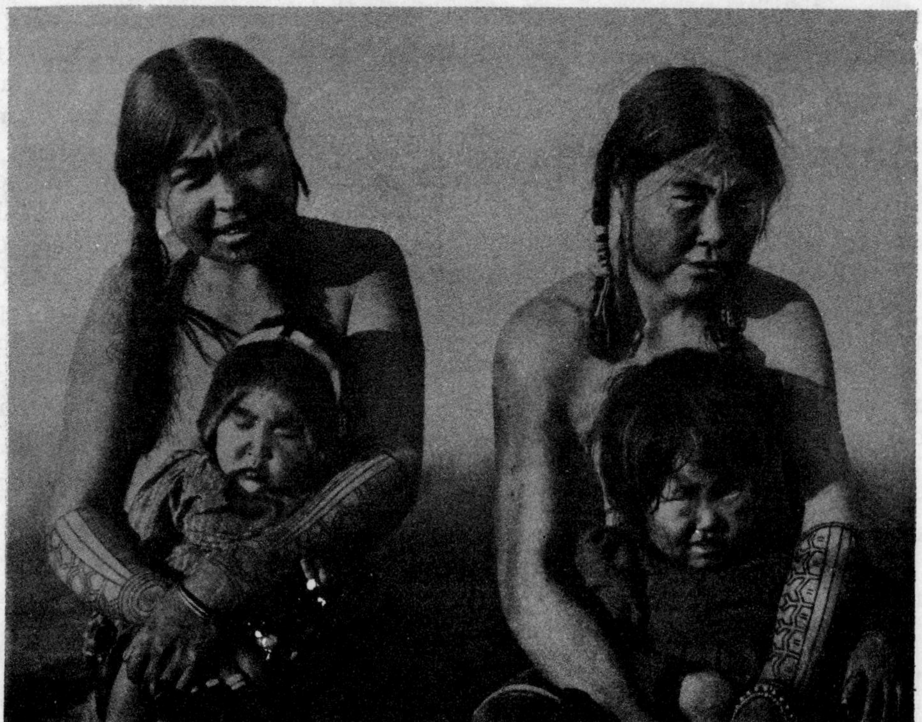

By courtesy of Dr. George B. Gordon.

ESKIMO WOMEN AND THEIR CHILDREN, KING'S ISLAND, ALASKA,

Showing tattooed patterns on the arms.

Eskimo Women Potters.

Women were the potters among the Eskimo, their ware being restricted to lamps and the requisite cooking vessels. Clay from the tundra was reduced to a smooth paste by mixing with walrus blood and kneading it with the hands. Sand from the beach was added, together with fine feathers. The vessel was built up with the hands or by means of a paddle. Compared with the Indian pottery of the Pueblos, this ware is very plain; however, some ornamentation was effected in the form of lines made with a pointed stick, a pitted surface produced by means of a roughly carved paddle, or by wrapping the unbaked vessel in grass matting which left its impression.

The Woman's Knife.

A word about the woman's knife. Hundreds of them may be seen round the kitchens of civilisation as hash cutters, called "chopping knives"; but you must visit the saddler and watch him cut leather to understand the tool in its most primitive function. In old times the blade was of slate or harder stone, but the trader and the whaler have substituted a far better one of steel. With this knife-of-all-trades the women prepare hides and cut out garments.

The Woman's Boat.

The woman's boat in Eskimoland, like its namesake, is the burden-bearer, and quite unlike the *kaiak*, or man's boat. It is practically an open coracle, or scow, with framework of wood or whale ribs, over which the covering of seal or walrus hide is tightly stretched. A dainty sail—made of thin intestines—is sometimes added. The steering is done with a long paddle.

Tattooing and other Forms of Adornment.

The æsthetic life of the Eskimo woman is made up of adornment and enjoyments. The women nearly all are tattooed, and in some localities the designs are quite elaborate. They are chiefly marked on the chin or about the mouth with one or more stripes, but the arms, breast, and back are also brought into service. The original motive seems to have been fashion or social rule, but it is related of one that she tattooed whale marks in the corners of her mouth to show that she was the wife of a successful hunter. But Eskimo women, in company with their husbands, had a more barbarous fashion than tattooing, called by Dall "labretifery." So far as is known, it was practised only by those living west of the Mackenzie River; indeed, the habit prevailed much more widely among the men. Captain Cook says that in Cook's Inlet the under lip was slit parallel with the mouth, the incision being commenced during infancy. "In adults it was often two inches long. In it was inserted a flat, narrow ornament, made of a solid shell or bone, cut into little narrow pieces like small teeth, almost down to the base or thickest part, which has a small projecting bit at each end, which supports it when put into the incision. . . . Others have the lower lip perforated into separate holes, and then the ornament consists of as many distinct shelly studs, whose points are pushed through these holes." But the number of studs, their location in the lip, their materials, size, and form were matter of fashion from place to place.

Hair-dressing and Ornaments.

The usual custom of dressing the hair is to part it in the middle from the forehead to the nape of the neck, and to gather it into a club on each side behind the ear. The club is twisted or braided and adorned, not with gay ribbons, but with leather strips, beads, brass buttons, and the like. The marrow of the reindeer is sometimes used for pomatum. The women are tidy in arranging the hair, and Murdoch* never saw one of them bald.

Earrings, says Murdoch, are worn by nearly all the women. In olden times these were little hooks of walrus ivory, but trade has long since added cheap jewellery in abundance. Gordon† adds to earrings necklaces of glass beads and bracelets of the same materials.

Besides the adornment of the person, the Eskimo woman's taste runs riot in the

* "Ethnological Results of the Point Barrow Expedition."

† "Notes on the Western Eskimo."

decoration of clothing. Here she has the advantage, because there is so much of it; and she busies her fancy and skilful fingers quite as much with the male attire as with her own. Skin, haired and unhaired, furs and feathers and down in all procurable colours, in masses and tasteful patchwork, gives her all the opportunity.

Decoration of Clothing.

The enjoyments of Eskimo women are derived from play and from the higher art of song and the native traditions, which are fosterers of art. The supple bodies of Eskimo women do not wear out all their energies in dressing hides. They join with men in their athletic sports. The girls play with dolls, have small models of domestic utensils for playing housekeeping and at woman's work. Storm-bound much of the time, there are house games as well as games in the open, all of which were studied by Nelson during a five-years' residence about St. Michael. Among them may be mentioned :—

Eskimo Games.

Toss the dart.—A block, 6 inches long, is sharpened at one end, and has a flaring cup at the other, 3 inches in diameter, with a deep hole in the middle. It is set up in the floor of the hut, the players squat around, and the game is to toss up a dart so that it will turn in the air and fall with its point sticking in the middle of the cup. Small sticks are used as counters.

Jackstraws, or spillikins.

Ring the stake.—A kind of quoits, played during the long twilight nights of June.

Top-spinning.—Girls and boys engage in this game. The moment the top is spun the owner runs out through the entrance and tries to encircle the hut and return before the top falls. Each successful round counts a score.

Football.—The ball is made of leather stuffed with moss and deer hair, and is about six inches in diameter, and there are four players, who stand each at the corners of a square facing inward.

Handball.—Played with a rounded rectangular leather bag filled with sand. The young men of the village form one side, and the young women the other. The game is for one side to secure the ball and keep it going among themselves.

Blind man's buff.

Hide and seek.—Played in summer in the long grass.

Ring around.—Played by men and women, together or separately. There are two rings which circle about swiftly.

Tossing on walrus hide.—Like tossing in a blanket, but the Eskimo get more fun out of it.

The tug of war.—Played by women as well as by men.

The Eskimo women are fond of tricks with the fingers, and have many devices in cat's cradle, making parts of the body, things of daily use, and well-known animals. Dolls and children's games in great number are included in Nelson's * lists.

The Eskimo are fond of singing, but the men do the most of it, their musical instrument being the drum. In their dances the women remain with their feet planted squarely on the floor, and, swaying the body and slowly gesticulating with hands and arms, go through the figures, always keeping time to the music. They carry a long feather wand in each hand, which they wave as they move. In certain religious festivals they use finger masks.

Songs and Dances.

Of course, what will be said of the Eskimo women and their social life must be looked at in its environmental settings, which will explain all and condone much. As the woman all her life carries an infantile face, so all her arts and activities bear the stamp of, and voice the childhood of mankind.

Social Life of the Eskimo.

The Eskimo social unit is the family and not the clan, and is built about the mother, who, with father, children, and a relative or two, make up the household. Descent is reckoned in both paternal and maternal lines. Children after marriage may continue to reside at home, either with the

* "The Eskimo about Bering Strait."

husband's or the wife's family. The political unit is not strong. The households in the same locality do not form a social organisation.

The treatment of Eskimo women was for this reason somewhat different tribally from that of Indian women. They seem to be a good-hearted people, and writers speak well of personal treatment of women among them. Parry says that the women were treated as equals of the men, and the wife was always consulted by the husband when a more important bargain than usual was to be made; and Murdoch says: "The wife is the constant and trusted companion of the man except in the hunt."

Birth Customs.

When a babe is about to be born, the Eskimo mother either builds for herself a hut or tent apart, or is secluded from contact or association with her people or their accessories. Even her husband is under *tabu*, as he cannot go seal-catching or even use the common industrial tools for a certain season.

The babe is carried about naked on the mother's back under her warm fur clothing, made fuller for the purpose. Around the mother's waist, high up, a girdle is tied for support. When she wishes to nurse the little one, the mother loosens the girdle and slips the babe round to the breast, without bringing it out into the freezing air. Children are carried in this way until they are able to walk. The precise style of this unique baby-carriage varies from place to place, and the surprising thing about it is that the woman is not inconvenienced, but rather happy at her work, and the child takes its shaking up as a matter of course. Little girls also play mother as with us, and carry infants around on their backs in the same way as does the mother.

Parental Affection.

The diet is so hard for adults that children are nursed until they are three or four years old. Infanticide is rare, infant mortality great, and children usually much prized. Everybody speaks well of these Arctic children, and it is a glowing tribute to the patient little mothers that it is so. Murdoch sets this forth so appreciatively that his words are quoted freely: "The affection of parents for their children is extreme, and the children seem to be thoroughly worthy of it. They show hardly a trace of the fretfulness and petulance so common among civilised children, and though indulged to an unusual extent are remarkably obedient. Corporal punishment appears to be absolutely unknown, and the children are rarely chidden or punished in any way. Indeed, they seldom deserve it, for, in spite of the freedom that they are allowed, they do not often get into any mischief, especially of a malicious sort, but attend quietly to their own affairs and their own amusements."

Eskimo Girlhood.

The little girls grow up just as they do everywhere. In all industrial employments they associate freely with their elders, catching fish, fetching drift wood, driving dogs, so that by the time they are in their teens they are sober little women.

The Marriage Question.

Murdoch has gathered the data for studying Eskimo woman's domestic life. His opinion is confirmed that the marriage relation was entered upon generally from reasons of interest or convenience, with not much sentiment about it. The woman looked for a man who was a good hunter and industrious—a bountiful provider. It is not alleged that prudential motives do not have a share in civilised match-making, nor is it denied that Cupid had found his way to the Frozen North. Child betrothal, by which very young persons are set apart for each other in tender youth, is said to have been practically universal among the Eskimo. Marriages were arranged by parents. Murdoch knew of a young man of about twenty-two who offered himself as the prospective husband of a girl of eight or ten when she should reach a marriageable age, and quotes Simpson as follows: "As soon as the young man desires a partner and is able to support one, his

ESKIMO WOMEN AND CHILDREN IN FULL DRESS.

mother selects a girl according to her judgment or fancy, and invites her to the hut, where she first takes the part of a *kiogak* or servant, having all the cooking and other kitchen duties to perform during the day, and returns to her home at night. If her conduct proves satisfactory, she is further invited to become a member of the family."* In other cases the bridegroom became a member of the wife's family.

ESKIMO UMIAK, OR WOMAN'S BOAT.

"One youth," says Murdoch, "who had had his lips pierced for the labrets just previously to our arrival, was betrothed to a young girl at Nuwŭk. This girl came down frequently and visited her lover's family, staying several days at a time, but we could not discover that she was treated as a servant. She went with them to the spring deer-hunt, but we were distinctly given to understand that the young couple would not be married till after the return from this hunt. When the season came for catching reindeer fawns, the couple started off together, with sled and dogs and camp equipage in pursuit of them, and always afterwards were considered as man and wife."

This matter-of-fact way of marrying seems to have been the rule, to which there were variations in different localities. In one case there was a house full of people, singing and dancing, to celebrate the marriage of the daughter of the house.

Wife capture must have been rare in Eskimo society; it is mentioned in Greenland by Egede and Bessels. Simpson says that a man of mature age frequently chooses a wife for himself, and fetches her home, to all appearances, much against her will.

Polygamy, in the sense of having many wives, is not an Eskimo custom, and Murdoch says that most of the men are content with one wife, and he never heard of a case of more than two wives.

The same author tells us interesting facts concerning the selection of a wife. The man usually picks out one of about his own age, but, as elsewhere, reasons of interest lead to a great disparity of age between the two. He did not recall any case where an old man had a wife much younger than himself, but knew of several men who had married widows or divorced women old enough to be their mothers. In one remarkable case the bride was a girl of sixteen or seventeen and the husband was a lad not over thirteen.

While it is true that polygamy was not the rule among this people, one man in

* Simpson, John (Dr.). "Notes on the Western Eskimo." Arctic Blue Book. Roy. Geog. Soc., Lond., 1875, pp. 233-275.

his time played many parts. As there was no special marriage ceremony, so there were no formal divorce proceedings. Marriage was regarded simply as a contract made by agreement between the parties. It was easily dissolved on account of incompatibility or even of temporary disagreements. Two cases are mentioned where wives left their husbands on account of ill-treatment. One case resulted in permanent separation, each of the couple marrying again. In another case the wife, after receiving a beating, ran away and married another man. Her first husband followed her in a day or two, and by violence or persuasion induced her to return. They afterwards appeared to live together on perfectly good terms.

Divorce.

But men also sometimes abandoned their wives. On the same authority, a young Eskimo had married a widow very much his senior, who seemed to have a bad temper, so he left her and married a young girl. His second venture was no more satisfactory, for the young wife proved to be a great talker. Said he. "She talked all the time so that I could neither eat nor sleep." So he discarded her, and not long afterwards he espoused another old widow.

It is recorded with pleasure, on several excellent authorities, by Murdoch that quarrels and separations happen seldom, excepting between persons in their younger years. "The older they grow," says Cranz, "the more they love one another."

Old Age.

Old women are scarce. The strenuous life shortens existence, but women of advanced years are treated well save in times of scarcity, when they commit suicide or are left to starve.

One does not have to look far to discover that the ills of life are made of the same cloth as its blessings. In other words, this statement means that the legitimate activities of one grade of culture survive as the misdemeanours of higher grades. In

ESKIMO WOMEN OF ST. LAWRENCE ISLAND, BERING STRAIT.
This tribe is almost cut off from the outside world; famine killed over a thousand of them in 1860.

this category might be placed the custom of general exchange of wives in certain Eskimo villages — each woman passes from man to man till she has been through the hands of all, and finally returns to her husband.

Exchange of Wives.

Murdoch suggests that the Eskimo had, in a more primitive form of existence, lived in the state of communal marriage called polygamy, in which each woman is, under prescribed conditions, the wife of each man in the community. He mentions the instance of a man who borrowed his cousin's wife to go with him on a summer deer-hunt because she was a good shot and a good hand with the game, while his own wife went with the cousin on a trading expedition to the eastward. On their return the wives resumed their respective husbands.

The learning of Eskimo women from our point of view would be confined, according to Rink, to some trifling knowledge of medicine, of astronomy, and of the division of the year into seasons according to the movements of animals, the position of the heavenly bodies, and scanty observations derived from experience. In the matter of lore it is quite different, since they are in possession of hundreds of old tales and traditions which were familiar to women, and in which they play an interesting part. From them, in an epitomised and generalised fashion, may be gathered many of the lost manners and customs of the sex.

Eskimo Education.

By courtesy of Dr. G. B. Gordon.

AN ESKIMO WOMAN FROM NINIVAK ISLAND, ALASKA.

There is only a brief space for that most fascinating theme, the religion of Eskimo women, their beliefs and practices respecting the spirit world. In Greenland the traditions unfold the creeds respecting the origin and history of the world, the souls and bodies of persons, the supernatural powers or "owners" of the world and of all things about it. It is Tylor's animism. There are the earth and the other two worlds, the under and the upper. The former is the abode of plenty and warmth; the upper world, of cold and famine. Its inhabitants are called ball players, and it is their game with walrus heads that makes the Aurora Borealis. Among the supernatural powers here of interest is *Arnarkuagsak* (the old woman), having her home in the depths of the ocean. She is the divine providence of the Eskimo, the source of nourishment and supply of other wants. And naturally so, since the ocean is the place for the regeneration of life. She sits in her dwelling in front of her lamp, beneath which is a vessel receiving the oil continually dripping therefrom. From this vessel or from her abode she sends out all the animals to serve the Eskimo. There are good and evil beings everywhere who may be exorcised or implored, and whose favour is won by charms. Women as well as men may become priests or *angakut*.

Religion.

The motives that brought about the dispersive social conditions of the Eskimo deprived them also of imposing rituals.

Boas, who studied them on the spot, gives the following account of their beliefs. Sun and moon are sister and brother, the latter always in pursuit of the former; or, in other traditions, they live in one house in heaven. She is the ruler of the sea mammals. When she was a girl she was given in marriage to a bird. When he maltreated her she tried to escape with her father, who had come to visit her. The birds raised a storm and tried to swamp the woman's boat in which they were fleeing. The father cast her overboard, and when she clung to the gunwale he cut off the joints of her fingers one by one. The first joints became the whales, the second the seals, the third the ground seals. She became mistress of the underworld, and controls the animals that originated from her fingers. The souls of those who die a natural death go to her abode.

In the beginning children were found in the snow: the present condition was brought about by two girls. The narwhal is a transformed Eskimo woman whose braid became the tusk. The walrus and the caribou were parts of a woman's clothes that she had cast away. A woman running along the beach bewailing the loss of her grandson was transformed into a bird.

The Central Eskimo have an important annual festival in honour of the female divinity who protects sea mammals. Every autumn, when the ice forms, she comes to the villages, at which time a ritual is performed to rid her of all the transgressions that are attached to her body and give her pain, and also to send her home appeased. In some places the performance of the *shaman* is accompanied by masked figures, as with the Indians, representing assistants of the deity and other spirits. It is at this time that the queer practice of "swapping wives" takes place.

III.—THE NORTH-WEST COAST

Locality and Climate—Physical Characteristics—Food Supply—Clothing—Personal Adornment—Houses of the North-West—Tlinkit Household Arrangements—Woman's Work—Methods of Counting—Social Life—The Origin of a Clan Crest—North-West Aristocracy—"Coppers" and Women—The "Potlatch"—Maidenhood Rites—Marriage in the North-West—The Ceremony of the Crest—Wives *v.* Blankets—Birth and Infancy—The Cradle as an Instrument of Deformation—Cradles as Treasures—Child Names—Medicine and Magic—Funeral Customs—"The Spirit World"—Influence of Civilisation

Locality and Climate.

On the North-West Coast of America, from Mt. St. Elias southward to Vancouver Island, dwells quite another type of women. The warm currents of the Pacific, breathing over the islands and uplifted shores, have clothed them with verdure and forests of gigantic evergreens. Nature furnished the archipelagos, the climate, the soft tree trunks for canoes and for communal homes, superabundance of aquatic and land food, mountain goats for wool, and excellent fibres for basketry, matting, and other textiles. Here came the Tlinkit, Haida, Tsimshian, Salish, and Wakashan Indians under many tribal names, and behind them were spread out the Athapascan and Salishan tribes over interior Alaska and Western Canada. Canoe intercourse was easy, but, with the exception of inlets and coves here and there, approach to the interior was cut off by the mountains, beyond which woman's life was under new conditions.

Physical Characteristics.

The women of this coast area, like the men, vary greatly in physical characteristics. In stature the difference is as much as four inches, the shape of the head is not the same from place to place, and the women do not look like those of other areas. Boas distinguishes four types on the coast of British Columbia—the

Northern, embracing the Tsimshian; the Kwakiutl; the Harrison Lake (shortest stature and broadest head); and the Salish of the Interior. The life is strenuous, and a bunch of the old women huddled together at some occupation is not prepossessing. All who have visited them are struck with the contrasts shown between them and the Indians of the other areas.

Food Supply.

Food was abundant in aboriginal days, and women had their hands full of work. The animals on the hills—deer, elk, bears, wolves, goats, beavers, otters, martens, mink, fur seals—in addition to their skins and hair for clothing and other comforts, also helped the larder. The staple food was the gift of the sea. Seals, sea-lions, and whales were taken, but the natives depended almost entirely upon salmon, halibut, and candle-fish. Women also gathered clams, mussels, sea-grass, berries, and roots.

The preparation, serving, and preserving of this variety of nourishment called out their industrial life. There was not a piece of pottery in all the region. Basketry of spruce root, grass, and cedar bast, of superb workmanship, served for utensils. The soft cedar and other woods were in greatest abundance for canoes, cooking vessels, and dishes. By means of stones heated in an open fire the candle-fish were "tried out" in a canoe or vessels of hot water, and the oil kept in stems of dried kelp. Salmon and halibut were dried in the sun or over a fire, and in winter the flesh was dipped in this oil and eaten. The women strung clams and mussels on sticks or strips of cedar bark, and dried them for further use. Fish roe, especially of the herring, was collected in great quantities and dried, to be eaten with oil. Special attention is called to the providence of the North-West Coast women for the future. It is a long step forward in culture. Sea-grass was dried into square cakes; several kinds of berries were treated in the same manner, to be soaked afterwards in water and eaten with fish oil, which seems to have been the general lubricant. The wonderful carved boxes in which all kinds of provisions were stored are the treasures of museums.

Clothing.

Dress is woman's care. It is both protection from injury and the framework for adornment. The natives, go bare-legged, the principal part of the clothing being the blanket made of dressed skins, or woven from the mountain goat's wool, dog's hair, feathers, or a mixture of both. In former times the thread was spun on the bare leg by means of the palm and wound on a spindle. Cedar bast was made into soft blankets by twined weaving and trimmed with fur. Since trade came among them woollen blankets are extensively used, and are worked into aboriginal patterns quite ingeniously. At festive occasions will be seen a blue blanket with red binding, set with pearl buttons from the traders. The totemic devices formerly painted on robes of dressed hide are cut out of red flannel and sewed on to the blue blanket. Before the coming of the traders' blanket women wore pretty aprons and petticoats of shredded cedar bast. The most picturesque object in woman's attire was her large water-tight hat of basketry, worn when canoeing or working on the beach. It was of spruce root, twined weaving, and the workmanship was the woman's finest. On the surface was painted the crest of the owner. The women early adopted European dress with the ordinary blanket. Only in the coldest weather are moccasins worn.

Personal Adornment.

The women dress their hair in two plaits. Formerly it was worn long, parted in front, and club-shaped behind. Personal adornment of the women included ear and nose ornaments of bone or abalone shell. Those of the most northern tribes wore labrets (lip-plugs). The lips of maidens on reaching puberty were pierced, and into the slit a wooden or bone pin was set with the point protruding. The marriage of the girl was followed by the wearing of larger and larger plugs, typifying power, respect, and privileges. The custom has now died out, and only old women are seen with this peculiar "ornament."

The dwellings of the women are temporary or permanent.

Houses of the North-West.

In their summer camps, in hunting and fishing excursions, in canoe trips, the former will suffice. Near the mouth of a fresh-water stream, where salmon run thickest, a shelter is set up having a light frame covered with broad strips of bark laid inside and outside alternately upward, and held down with stones and cross-pieces. They may have smoke holes, but usually the fire is built outside, where the smoke assists in curing the strips of salmon and halibut hung on frames above it.

A TLINKIT WOMAN, S.E. ALASKA.
The dress is decorated with common white buttons—traders' goods.

The travelling tent consists of strips of bark carried in the canoes. To erect the tent, two saplings are pointed and stuck in the ground, forked ends up, with a cross pole laid thereon. The bark strips are rested on the cross pole, forming a sloping wall against the wind. Along the water courses, where there is a safe canoe beach, springs of fresh water, shelter from the winds, and good hunting near, these frames are left standing. In primitive times the tent was made with walls of cedar bark, mats, or skins of animals. Piles of wood were left there for belated travellers, on the understanding that all used should be made good. This was far better than scouting about in the rain and darkness.

The permanent houses of this insular and inlet area, which are among the largest of wooden buildings erected by savages, are the work of the men and consume several years in the construction. The women help at every turn, and, what is important in this narrative, the permanent as well as the temporary shelters are erected in connection with them and their demands.

Niblack explains the structure of these marvels of engineering and handicraft, which reached their highest development among the Haida. Further north the houses become mere shelters, and southward they are inferior in artistic construction. There are three kinds: those on the ground, those on a foundation of logs or a slightly raised platform, and those on high posts.

The Kwakiutl are a cosmopolitan tribe, and have several styles of dwelling. Their permanent houses are inhabited by four families, one in each corner, with a fireplace of its own. The corners are divided off by a rough framework of poles, the top of which is used for drying food. On each side of the fire is an immense settee, large enough for the whole family. The sloping back is adorned with totemic paintings. The bedrooms of these queer abodes have the form of small houses built on the platform that runs around the house; though the women here, like their sex on the other side of the Pacific, are born, nurtured, seated, sleep, and die on the floor.

A TLINKIT BASKET-MAKER (S.E. ALASKA)
Making one of their beautiful baskets.

The Tlinkit, living between Mt. St. Elias and Dixon Entrance, usually build the permanent house on a slightly elevated foundation of logs, with three or four raised steps in front. Entering the door, one stands on a platform about 6 feet wide, running around the four sides of the house. Next, one steps down about 3 feet upon a ledge of the same width, also running around the four sides. The next level, 3 feet below this, is the solid ground. In the centre of this the fire burns, the smoke ascending through a square smoke-hole in the roof. The floor is covered with mats and skins, on which the family pass their lives. At one end the diligent housewife, who has sought out wool of the mountain goat and fine bark fibre, has set up the most primitive loom in the world. It consists of two forked stakes driven in the ground, across which a pole serves for yarn beam—that is all. The warp hangs down from this beam, the ends are carefully gathered into balls and securely covered with bladders. The skilful weaver is crouching before the loom, gazing at her pattern board on which are painted the heraldic emblems that she will weave in black and white and yellow in a rude sort of tapestry work. Near her is her husband carving a mask, but we leave him to look at another wife just beyond making a fine, umbrella-like hat in twined basketry. Her material is the long, delicate young root of the spruce. To complete the group, there will be the babe on the floor, snugly tucked into its basket, while another wife is bringing in a carved box filled with hot stew, which she dishes up with a beautiful spoon carved from the horn of the Rocky Mountain sheep. No spot in this barn-like dwelling is vacant. Trunks are carved and painted. Hand-woven rugs and mats cover ugly boards and vacant places.

Tlinkit Household Arrangements.

In front of the house stands the decorative column, the totem post, an immense log or half-log carved from top to bottom with heraldic animals, which proclaim the family of the inhabitants. Sometimes it is close to the building. In that case, a hole is cut in it near the ground for a front door. The erection of the column requires, among the Haida, the co-operation

A TLINKIT INDIAN WOMAN
At work on a basket.

of many hands, the gathering being the occasion of a feast and a *potlatch*, or grand distribution of presents among the participants.

In their active industrial life there seem to be no idle moments for the North-West Coast woman. There are grasses with tough leaves to gather, to dry, to colour, and to fit for their decorative functions. The young roots of the spruce, tough enough and pliable, but far from rattan as a textile material, must be boiled to bring out their good qualities, beaten with sticks to soften them, and shredded for use. Quite as important is the cedar bast or inner bark. When it comes from the tree it is in great sheets, looking more like an immense hide from the tannery. More work! These slabs are soaked thoroughly for several days until they can be separated into strips, ribbons or filaments, as the case may be, for yarn, thread, petticoats, matting, basketry, and many more textile functions. For such work the tool-chest is not large, and was in former days much smaller; but the bones of the whale were adequate for hammers, peelers, shredders, and spinners, guided by nimble fingers. It must not be overlooked also that the young inne most bark of the cedar and other trees was in spring scraped from the trunk for food, when vegetable diet was scarce. No mention is here made of the equally exacting labour of the men in wood, horn, shell, stone, and metal. Niblack gives an excellent account of the work in ropes and cordage. Their simplest lines are of kelp, single, or twisted in two or more strands. The neatest rope and cords are from spruce root or bark fibre, twisted between the hand and the thigh.

Women's Work.

A TLINKIT WOMAN AT HOME.
Showing seal skins stretched for drying.

Mat-work is made principally of bark, in

checker or twilled weaving, plain or dyed, and varying from place to place in texture and ornamentation. Mats are the bedding, floor rugs, coverings for cargoes, and screens for camps when travelling. In the old days, when slavery was in full sway, on ceremonial occasions mats were used as vehicles by slaves to carry the chief to or from the house. Basket-making comes next to mat-working, both being pure handwork.

Most interesting of all the textiles for our women is the wool of the wild goats, which they do not have to shear, for at the proper season the animals obligingly get tired of their overcoat and wander through the brambles and underbush in order to rub it off. It is only necessary to walk about their haunts to gather wool in the greatest abundance. The washing and the spinning with fibre of cedar bark and wild hemp give the women a mixed textile for the world-famous blankets, which are the standard of wealth, as well as the bank-notes with which to buy wives and commodities, and to conduct the all-important *potlatch*.

Methods of Counting.

To serve their purposes in the arts our coast women have their arithmetic and metrics. They count, just as we do, with the cardinal numbers, but these have different uses. Dawson observed that the Kwakiutl have expressions for the first two ordinal numbers, as " first " and " next to first." They are seldom used, and it is difficult to explain the idea to the Indian mind. On the other hand, the names of the numerals are modified to apply in counting flat objects, such as blankets, spherical or circular objects, as balls and money, in counting persons, in making up lots or like numbers of objects, and in distributing, as " one apiece, two apiece."

For standards of measure, after the same authority, the Kwakiutl women are quite up to our English folk. They employ the fathom, measured between the outstretched hands across the chest, as their principal measure; the half fathom, measured from the middle of the chest to the elbow, or from the elbow to the end of the outstretched fingers; the long finger span, reckoned from the tip of the thumb to that of the outstretched second finger; and the short finger span, between the tips of the thumb and first finger.

Social Life.

The social life of the North-West Coast, as elsewhere, will include the family, the village, economics or union in their industries, and ceremonies—all of which have peculiar relations to women and their destiny. The northern tribes of the coast have maternal social organisation, the southern have the paternal, and the middle tribes are mixed or transitional in this respect. The northern have the animal totems, and always marry out of the clan. Boas tells us, however, that these tribes do not consider themselves derived from the totem, as the legends show.

The Origin of a Clan Crest.

The Tsimshian say that a long time ago an Indian hunter met a black bear, who took him home, taught him to catch salmon, and to build canoes. Two years after he returned, but the people did not know him—he looked like a bear and could not speak. One man caught him, took him home, rubbed him with herbs, and restored him. He built a house and painted a bear on it, and whenever he was in want he called on his animal friend. His sister made a dancing blanket, with the design of a bear on it. Therefore her descendants to this day use that animal for their crest.

This story unites the beliefs on this coast to the Manitou dogmas of the Eastern Indians, and accounts for the wonderful intricacy of the clans and crests. The latter are carved on columns intended to perpetuate the memory of deceased relatives, and are used also for decorating personal ornaments; they are painted on house fronts, carved on totem posts in front of the houses, and shown as masks in clan festivals.

To obtain a comprehensive idea of woman's family life here, it is necessary to bear in mind the great, the dominating power of the system of aristocracy that prevailed. Whether descent was counted through the mother, as at the north; through the father, as at the south; or through transitional forms, as among the Kwakiutl, marriage carried with it much of the destiny of the tribe.

North-West Aristocracy.

Instead of seal rings, medals, and other symbols of wealth and station, bound up in the life of these people is a class of objects called "coppers." Along the North Pacific Coast thin sheets of copper are shaped in outline like a broad axe-blade

HAIDA INDIAN WOMAN OF QUEEN CHARLOTTE ISLAND, BRITISH COLUMBIA.

Notice the nose ring and lip-plug.

with a T-shaped ridge on the poll. On the face is painted and engraved the crest animal of the owner. It is like a bank-note—the amount of metal is small, but the "copper" itself stands for the large number of blankets it brings in the festival at which it is sold. The oftener it is sold the greater the number of blankets. The women of the tribes are, as it were, wrapped up in the "coppers,"

"Coppers" and Women.

for both they and these precious objects are standards of value and the mechanism of wealth. Furthermore, their nimble fingers create the thousands of blankets which buy the coppers.

The *dentalium* shell was formerly used as a currency, but, as with other coast tribes, the blanket is now the unit of value. A somewhat inferior quality, known in the Hudson's Bay Company parlance as a "two and a half point blanket," is the standard.

The "Potlatch."

Niblack describes at length the universal custom of gift-making ceremonies among the North-West tribes, usually mentioned as the *potlatch*. The purpose in these imposing functions is to exchange favours and to buy goodwill. As women enter into these not only to enjoy them, but as a motive in many of them, a few words may be given to the custom.

To procure a wife, to retain the medicine man, to become a chief, to get your children into society, to adopt ancestral title, to build a house, to be influential, to atone for a wrong, to resent an insult—property had to be destroyed to show rage, grief, or indifference; or it was given away to secure respect. Getting rich was a necessity, and wealth a subtle basis of the social fabric. In a *potlatch* all sorts of property was given away—blankets and other garments, household and kitchen furniture, weapons, money, trinkets, furs, etc. Discrimination was carefully made in gifts for services, or damages, or marriage *dot*, or the ceremonial self-impoverishment proper. Among the more northern tribes the *potlatch* is a perfect system, "involving," says Niblack, "more thoughtful consideration and balancing of obligations than the giving of a select entertainment by a well recognised leader of society."

Maidenhood Rites.

Dall ("Alaska") told us long ago that the girls of the Tlinkit tribes, on arriving at the age of puberty, were considered unclean, and had to observe a ceremonial cleansing. A girl was confined to a hut apart during a year. Only the mother and a female slave could take her food, and she wore one of the broad-brimmed hats of twined spruce root, which are now so highly prized, to protect the sky from pollution. During this period the girl's lower lip was pierced and a silver pin, shaped like a nail, was inserted with the point outward; the broad head prevented the labret from falling out. This was her mark of freedom and graduation into womanhood. The slave girl was not allowed to wear one. On the release of a rich Tlinkit girl a great feast was given. She was gorgeously dressed, and seated on precious otter skins. The slave that waited on her during her seclusion was set free, and all her old clothing was destroyed.

By and by, when the time of marriage came round, the little nail-shaped lip-plug was exchanged for the large labret, which fitted into the lip like a stud, and was replaced from time to time by a larger one, until the old woman graduated by becoming the most hideous of mortals.

Marriage in the North-West.

If the reader were a North-West Coast woman, this would be her way of getting married. The usual coquetry, manœuvring, and courtship taken for granted, there would be something more than merely "asking father," something less than the modern signing of documents—a plenty of ceremony, but very different from the drama before the minister. Boas tells us that marriage is a purchase, in which the result is not only the woman, but also the right of membership in her clan for the future children. Many political or clan, privileges descend only through marriage upon the son-in-law, who does not use them for himself, but for his offspring. He becomes entitled to them by paying for his wife, who is the first instalment of the goods. The crest and its privileges and property will arrive later on with children. This business conception of matrimony obtains throughout life. There comes a time when the old bargain is called square. If the wife continue with the husband, she does so of her own free will; the husband will then make a new payment to the father-in-law. If a man should have no daughter, in order to save his name and coat-of-arms he performs a sham marriage between his son and one seeking the crest, and, if he has no children, the sham marriage will be with some portion of his body. After the same fashion the crest and privileges of the family were provided with a successor in any emergency.

A chief invited the young men of all the tribes to come to his house, and said to them: "Thank you, my brothers; I want to marry to-day. Invite all the people. Now dress yourselves; there are the paint and eagle down."

Boas gives an excellent account of the traditions concerning the ancient marriages, described as "making war on the daughters of all the chiefs all over the world." The getting together of four hundred blankets, the going to war with them, the landing on the beach, approach to the girl's father's house, the passing through fire, the counting of blankets, the *potlatch* and singing, winding up with the plain statement that "she went to live with her husband."

The Ceremony of the Crest.

The ceremonies connected with the return of the purchase money and the delivery of the family crest to the son-in-law were of the greatest moment. They include the assembly of people in the house of the wife's father, the entrance of the latter with his clan, four of them carrying the mast of a canoe. After they have taken their places, the wife's father calls the son-in-law, who takes his position in the right-hand rear corner. The old man is told that the mast represents boxes containing everything he owes. The son-in-law then asks whether the sheet coppers, house, carved posts, and the old gentleman's names are in the mast also. After an affirmative answer is given, the young wife is then sent to fetch the precious copper, attended by young men of her clan bringing blankets. The young husband proceeds to sell the copper for blankets, which he gives away on the spot. In this way he purchases the right to live in the house. These services are drawn out and varied, but they show how rank and wealth have reduced government of life to an exact science. The fate of woman, not merely in procuring her mate, but in deciding the destiny of the tribe, is sealed.

Wives v. Blankets.

Among the Kwakiutl, when a young man desires to obtain a girl for a wife, he must bargain with her parents, and pay to her father a number of blankets. Owing to the great desire to accumulate blankets for the *potlatch*, and the scarcity of girls, the parents are very exacting in this respect. The young man may have further demands made upon him by his wife, who, at a hint from her parents, may leave him. The parents then exact a further payment of blankets for her return, and so on.

Birth and Infancy.

The ever-recurring wonder at the treatment of the mother during childbirth among savages is here awakened. The Tlinkit mother is ceremonially unclean, her babe is born in the open air, and the mother spends her allotted number of days in a shed apart. But she is from the first able to care for herself and for her little one. Trusting to nature, she is not deceived. She is far ahead of the civilised mother in this respect, but behind the Eastern Continent woman in that she must nurse the child far longer. The North-West Coast mother allows her little one to chew the raw blubber of marine animals, excepting that of the whale, for weaning food. The babe, on beginning to walk, is bathed daily in the sea. As elsewhere, infant mortality is great, but in the primitive stage of culture it is the unfit that die off, and there is no doubt that the rough treatment accounts for the robustness of the Tlinkit.

The cradle, so-called, flourishes in the North-West area, and plays tricks on the physical anthropologists. After one leaves the Eskimo of the entire Arctic coast, where the mother packs her little one in her ample hood, the cradle board of the Athapascan and the cradle trough of the coast are encountered. In each of them the soft, plastic skull of the infant is deformed for life. Either the cradle board or framework flattens the occiput naturally and undesignedly on the part of the mother, or the babe is laid in a cedar trough adapted to the purpose, and a long, soft pad of cedar bark is bound on the forehead to stop the growth there. The result is that the development of the young brain follows the lines of least resistance, and pushes the skull away up behind. Its size, capacity, and vigour are not reduced. As the foreheads of slaves are not so treated, it is a mark of aristocracy to be thus mutilated. When to this is added the rosette of perforations about the ears, the tattooings, the nose rings, and the labrets, the women now under consideration must take the prize as victims of fashion. Some of the deformities of civilisation are much more hurtful in effects on women, but could not be uglier. In the new race-life of the Indian woman the hideousness is laid aside. May it be hoped that the civilised will imitate?

The Cradle as an Instrument of Deformation.

When a Kwakiutl child had grown large enough to leave the little cradle, tied into which it spent most of its earlier days, the cradle, with its wrappings, bed of shredded bark, and appendages, was carried to a recognised place of deposit. The custom is still obligatory as regards the bedding, which is neatly packed in a box or basket and laid away never to be touched again. Every village probably has such a storing place — in the cliffs, behind the village, beneath logs, or other lonely spot.

Cradles as Treasures.

The first name of a child is given by the mother soon after its birth, and is for girls that of a maternal ancestor. Ancestral names, remarks Niblack,* are preserved with the greatest care, being favoured by the custom of erecting mortuary columns and preserving traditions.

This is without ceremony. When a wealthy chief would adopt a son as heir to his possessions, a sister may figuratively take the child as her own and give it some ancestral name. The chief makes her a gift, and, when the boy grows up, it will be his duty to reward her. If the parents are poor, the first name must suffice, for with every new name must go a feast.

Child Names.

Medicine may be administered by friends; but the sorcerer, who may be a woman, devotes himself or herself solely to exorcising the evil principle causing the disease. It is done by singing incantations, the use of the rattle, and vigorous sucking of the parts affected, which may be kept up for hours, frequently repeated, and must be handsomely paid for. The same writer calls attention to the use of charms in bringing good as well as averting harm. A Haida woman wore the figure of a halibut with the face of her chief painted on the tail to protect her and her husband from drowning at sea. Sickness was formerly attributed to the witchcraft of enemies. Certain persons are believed to possess magic power, and to bewitch an enemy go through a series of complicated ceremonies—procuring a lock of hair, some saliva, a small scrap of dress, or a few drops of perspiration of the intended victim. These might be placed with a small piece of the skin and flesh of a dead man, dried and roasted before the fire, and pounded together. The mixture is then tied up in a piece of skin and covered with spruce gum, and placed in a human skull. The whole is placed in a box, tied up, gummed over, and buried shallow. A fire is built near enough to warm the whole. Then the sorcerer beats his head against a tree and names and denounces his enemy. This is done at night or early in the morning, and in secret, and often repeated till the enemy dies. The actor must keep as quiet as possible till the spell has worked. If a person suspects witchcraft, an

Medicine and Magic.

* "Indians of the North-West Coast."

KWAKIUTL WOMEN, NORTHERN END OF VANCOUVER AND MAINLAND OPPOSITE.

The curious shape of the head is produced by pressure in infancy, and is looked upon as a mark of good breeding.

attempt is made to find the box and throw it into the sea, handling it with great care. Formerly the evil person was killed.

Funeral Customs.

Death does not disrupt society—it only changes. When a woman dies the body is immediately coffined before it stiffens. Should death occur at night, the box is set outside till daylight admits of its disposal. The face of the dead is washed, the hair combed, both are painted with vermilion, and the body wrapped in blankets. It is then coffined in any box of suitable size, being doubled up and pressed in with some violence if necessary. The Kwakiutl have two kinds of burial—scaffold or tree burial, and house burial on the ground. In the former little scaffolds, to which the coffin-box has been lashed, are placed high upon the branches of fir trees. Tombs were formerly built of slabs of wood. Small tent-like erections of calico now are substituted, and in both cases the bodies of relatives and friends dying at different times are often placed together. Tree burial may be close to the village, but tombs are generally on some rocky places in sight, which become cemeteries. Graves in trees are festooned with blankets or streamers, and poles similarly decorated mark the house burials. Roughly carved images in wood are sometimes added. After the depositing of the bodies, a fire is built near the grave, in which food is burnt, and all the smaller articles belonging to the deceased. In the division of property, wife, sister, and daughter, come into possession of portions assigned by custom. The women have their share in the mourning. For a season the wife lives in a very small hut apart, eating and drinking alone, using separate dishes. Women cut a small portion of the hair; a widow scratches or cuts her face with a shell, and does not marry again for a year. Father Morice says of the Carriers, who, with their co-linguists, used to burn their dead, that the widow of a deceased warrior used to pick out from the ashes of the pyre the charred bones and carry them on her back in a leather bag until the deceased's clansmen could amass enough food and dressed skins for a *potlatch*.

MRS. TOM, THE RICHEST WOMAN IN ALASKA.

The blanket round her shoulders is worth £100.

"The Spirit World."

The study of women in the last act introduces the spirit world. The results of creeds in the Indian minds are certain organisations or societies, private worship and ceremonials in common, the telling of stories, incense, songs, dances, and sacrifices. These activities are accompanied by special cos-

CHILKAT BLANKET WEAVER.
Showing how the primitive loom is set up and worked.

other races that during the nineteenth century went among them brought them good and evil. And these are to decide their future. Lieut. Emmons has made observations among them as to the result on women, and this is his testimony :—

" In south-eastern Alaska the half-breed Indians are the issue of native women and white men, and poor white men at that—which would greatly simplify the answer to the question why the breed is not a success. I know of no human being that more deserves pity than the result of this union of races. But there are a few cases where better white men have married native women—not simply lived with them—and the children have

tumes and masks, and are performed in places fitted up for the purpose. In them one sees the promise of the great historic religions. The torturing and gashing of their bodies are chiefly men's prerogative, but women are also victims. Sproat and others, quoted by Boas, tell of women slaves being put to death. A Sheshaht woman was stabbed to death by an old man in whose house she lived, and who probably owned her as a slave, and offered her for a victim. The body was then laid out without a covering by the water-side, where it was exposed for two days. Even after the removal certain furious rites took place on the spot where the body had been exposed.

Influence of Civilisation.

One must not judge too severely these dwellers among the islands for their personal habits, nor criticise their morals from too high a standard. In both they are far from perfection. The

CHILKAT (KOLUSEKAN FAMILY) BLANKET WEAVER, LYNN CANAL, ALASKA.
In this tribe are the finest weavers in North America.

had the advantages of care and education. Here I have seen good results.

"Now, in British Columbia, the old Hudson Bay Company men, who were nine-tenths Scotchmen, good, healthy, hard-headed people, more often married full or half-blood women (native), Crees, not Coast women, and heredity in the children was very marked. The males were in most instances indolent, dissipated, or without purpose and initiative, while the women took the good qualities of the better parent. Victoria, among the older families, shows this in a marked degree. The descendants of Sir James Douglas, the Tohnies, and others, all exhibit their Cree blood. The women are cultivated, capable, and Scotch in their virtues and thrift, while few of the males reach the average. The half-breed women more easily accept civilisation, and, when the men are above the average, their intelligence is used for lower ends."

III.—CALIFORNIA-OREGON AREA

A Mountainous Area—The Hupa Tribe—Hupa Clothing—Personal Adornment—The Acorn as "the Staff of Life"—How Acorn Meal is Made—Basket Work—Child Birth—Hupa Legends—Hupa Childhood—A Hupa Girl's Initiation to Womanhood—Hupa Courtship and Marriage—How Divorce is Arranged—A Hupa Woman's Day—Women's Recreations—Hupa Magic—Hupa Widows—Maidu Women's Work—Indian Costumes—Fashions in Hair-dressing and Ornaments—Curious Basket- and Feather-work—The Maidu Dwellings—The Ubiquitous Basket—The Important Acorn—Curious Cradles—Maidu Games—Californian Music—A "Soup Dinner"—Maidu Birth Customs—How Maidu Girls are Named—Maidenhood Ceremonies—Marriage—Curious Courtship—Other Courtship and Marriage Customs—Maidu Mourning Customs

A Mountainous Area.

ALMOST shut off from the Pacific Ocean by precipitous shores, this is a mountainous area, of which the valleys are not conducive to travel and the free movement of its people. The result is a mass of small linguistic families between Puget Sound and Santa Barbara. The Salmon Indians congregate near the coast; the Hupa and Maidu are seed gatherers and basket-makers.

The Hupa Tribe.

The Hupa Indians had their original home on the Lower Trinity River, in Humboldt county, California. They are interesting to students, because they speak the language of the Athapascans, who were spread over the interior, Alaska and western Dominion of Canada. As the strict tribal system did not exist in this polyglot area, the women were not bound by such rigid rules of marriage. Their homes were grouped in villages on the banks of rivers and near springs. The dwelling is peculiarly the home of the women—the men sleep in the sweat-house apart. We are in a land of good cedar, so the house will be made of that obliging wood, about 20 feet square, with an excavation 12 feet square and 5 feet deep in the middle. The entrance to this abode is made as round as possible, to resemble the woodpecker's hole, 18 or 20 inches in diameter, cut in the second plank from the corner on the right. It is closed by a slide on the inside. There is a second wall on the inside across the front end and next to the excavation, leaving a space 3 feet wide. A second doorway through this wall opens on the stairway, which is merely a plank in which steps are cut. This corner of the pit has a wall built in diagonally. The fire is in the centre, in a small hole bordered with stones, and above it are poles for smoking fish and venison. The furniture is limited to stools carved out of the section of a tree. Of the banks of earth on three sides the women make a storehouse, where the winter's supply is kept in baskets of their own handiwork. Here also are the materials of their industries—skin-working, embroidery, and basket-making. In the front, between the outer and the inner wall, the wood for the fire is stored. The space behind the fire is the post of honour, reserved for the men and for guests; to the women belong the places on both sides; the section next the stai way is for slaves and menials. At night the women sleep about the fire on their deer-skin robes or tule mats.

Hupa women wear more clothing than the men. The costume consists of skirt, apron, beads, blanket, cap, head-dress, and moccasins.

The body of the skirt consists of a buck-skin without hair, about 26 in. long and 30 in. wide. It is adorned at the bottom with a fringe about 16 inches deep, formed by attaching many narrow strips of buck-skin to the margin. The top of the skirt is often a work of art. It is folded over and slit into a fringe about six inches long, which is divided by cross-twined weaving, The strands of the upper band are neatly wrapped with brown fern and golden yellow grass. For dances the skirts are beautiful, and are among the most attractive objects in ethnographic collections. The lower fringes might be strung with glossy pine nuts, and the ends of the upper fringe finished off with shell beads, pieces of abalone shell, and flakes of obsidian.

By courtesy of the Hon. John Daggett.

KLAMATH RIVER INDIAN WOMAN PREPARING TO POUND ACORNS.

The skirt is tied about the waist so as to be open in front, where hangs the apron underneath. This consists of many long strands of buck-skin attached to a belt, commonly hung with shells of *Pinus attenuata* and wrapped or braided with leaves of *Xerophyllum tenax*. More gaudy examples have the strands strung with pretty shells and pendants cut from abalone shell. Beads of dentalium, olivella, pine seed, and viburnum fruit are worn about the neck. Blankets of skin from the deer, wild cat, and civet cat are worn with the hair next the body, except in rainy weather. A close-fitting cap of exquisite twined and overlaid basket-work is worn not only as dress, but as a pad for the band from which is suspended the baby and the burden basket.

Personal Adornment.

The women, when necessary, wear a high moccasin of soft deer-skin like the men's. The hair is worn long, except by widows, brought in front of the ears in braids, and adorned with shell pendants, strips of mink-skin, woodpecker crests, and stems of *zerba bruna* to impart perfume. Ear ornaments are discs or oblong pieces of abalone shell. The Hupa women tattoo their chins with vertical marks for ornament, the process beginning with quite young girls. It is done by pricking in soot with a sharp flint or a splinter of bone.

The Acorn as "The Staff of Life."

Among the Hupa food is plentiful—meat from the forests and fish from the waters. Men gather it, women cook and serve it. The meat not needed is cut into strips by the women, and cured over a fire. They roast it before the fire or boil it in a basket by dropping in hot stones.

But it is in the plant world that the Hupa woman is at home. And acorns are her staff of life. These are gathered in a conical basket, and carried home on the back by means of a strap which passes round its middle, over the woman's shoulders, and across the top of the head. The acorns are dried, shelled, and stored in immense baskets which hold nearly a barrel. The basketry associated with this acorn harvest is as much a marvel as the varied treatment of the nuts. When the stored acorns are needed the women grind them into flour. The milling outfit consists of a buck-skin or cloth for catching the meal, a flat slab for the nether mill-stone, a pestle of stone for pounding, and a basket hopper.

The next process is to leach the bitter taste from the meal, which the woman does with clean sand in a saucer-shaped hole. Water, heated in a basket vessel by means of hot stones, is poured over the meal with a basket cup until it loses its acrid quality. The mass is lifted out, and the adhering sand washed off.

To cook the acorn meal it is placed in a tight basket, a little water is added, hot stones placed in, and the whole stirred vigorously. The mush is eaten by the men from individual baskets with spoons of horn or of wood. The women use for spoon the valve of a mytilus shell, and often eat direct from the basket vessel in which the mush is cooked.

The Hupa woman adds to her vegetable supplies nuts, seeds, bulbs, fresh shoots, and seaweed. Some of the same baskets are used as in the acorn industry.

Governor Daggett, who has lived for some time among the acorn eaters, writes as follows: 'Old Mary (*see* p. 429) is making acorn soup. The conical depression at her side is made of sand, and the acorn meal, having been formed into a paste, is plastered on the side of the hole for about half an inch in thickness. Mary then fills the cavity with water, which percolates through the mixture into the sand and the element

By courtesy of the Hon. John Daggett.

INDIAN WOMAN POUNDING ACORNS.

How Acorn Meal is Made.

of bitterness departs with it. In order to recover the paste, she strikes the flat of her hand against it, and a portion adheres. plate is rapidly vibrated by thumb and fingers, which causes the coarser particles to roll down into the mortar, while the finer

By courtesy of the Hon. John Daggett.

A KLAMATH RIVER INDIAN WOMAN MAKING ACORN SOUP.

Holding it out, she washes off the adhering sand with water thrown by the other hand.

"On one occasion Mrs. Daggett thought she would like to know how acorn soup tasted, and found 'Old Mary' at the camp pounding acorns (*see* p. 428). The woman is seated on the ground, having between her legs a flat rock upon which she has placed a mortar basket, and is holding it down with her limbs.

"While she uses the pestle with one hand she deftly pokes the coarse particles of acorn underneath the pestle with the other. When the pestle hand gets tired, she spits on the other, which does the pounding, while its neighbour looks after the particles, and so the process goes on. And that is the reason why my wife and I have taken the Indian's word for the sweetness of acorn bread. The sifting of the material is not done with a sieve, but with a disc 8 or 10 inches in diameter, upon which the coarse meal is placed by the handful. The adhere and are brushed off with a little broom made of soap root. The operation of shelling the acorns is as good as an exhibit of legerdemain. When the nuts are gathered the caps are removed and left on the spot. After 'carrying' home the day's picking in her conical carrying basket, the woman sits down and proceeds to shell the result. Placing an acorn, point upward, into her mouth with one hand, she gives it one bite, and the shell cracks in two and is removed. With the other hand she takes away the kernel. This process goes on with such quick and uniform motion as to be quite interesting."

Basket-work.

The women on the Pacific coast of North America, more than any others in the world, find pleasure in illustrating story and myth by their basketry. This the Hupa women do by using plants of various natural colours, by dyeing, and by working in designs. These are, by the exigencies of weaving, geometric in detail, and are named after some characteristic in the weaving as "sharp and slanting," "set on one another"; or they bear the name of some well-known object, as "rattlesnake's nose," "bear's hand," "worm's stairway." Among other tribes stories are hidden in these designs. It may be that men of the tribe use the same designs, reading into them quite different meanings.

Childbirth.

The prospective mother during the first four months of her term makes medicine, and observes certain practices that the child may be "small but strong at birth." When her time draws near, the woman carries in her basket, as she goes for wood, a stone knife, and may return with the child. For ten days the mother remains apart. If the child is a boy, she eats by herself for forty days; if a girl, for fifty days. Just why the little girl should add ten days to the mother's solitude is not known.

Hupa Legends.

Evil spirits are believed to haunt the infant during its first ten days. To counteract them, three kinds of medicine are prepared, to make the child grow fast, to make it grow strong, and to make it reach old age. The preparation, brought by a doctor, is boiled in a basket-pot, and the child, tied in an open-work plate, is held over the steam and nearly suffocated. These steamings insure a veritable survival of the fittest, for it is said that many children die during the ten days of medicine-making. Next, the infant's hair is cut off and put into the fire. The divinities thus are made cognisant of the child's existence.

Hupa Childhood.

The baby for the first year is under the spell of ceremony in which the dear old grandmother comes on the scene. At the end of the first ten days it is put into the pretty openwork basket cradle, looking for all the world like a slipper. The pocket at the bottom is for absorbent material, and the back is lined with sweet-smelling herbs. The child is wrapped in a blanket, arms and all, but below the knee the lower limbs are free. At first the little one is confined to the cradle, and is not quite emancipated until it is about three years old. The child usually weans itself. It receives a daily bath, and goes through a daily kneading and pulling into shape.

The little girls grow up under the direction of mothers, aunts, and maternal grandmothers, conning lore while they twine baskets or cradles for their realistic dolls.

A Hupa Girl's Initiation to Womanhood.

The dawn of womanhood is awaited with great solicitude. The girl is then under the care of her grandmother or some other female relative. Bathing and carrying burdens are a part of the cult. During ten days of seclusion she must not look up, or at any one's face. She dons the long fringed skirt, fasts, and keeps her hands from touching her hair. She must be careful not to use improper language or tell an untruth. If she does she will remain untruthful throughout life. While she is undergoing her ordeal, dances are held in her honour, and other ceremonies in which she takes part. She is then marriageable.

Hupa Courtship and Marriage.

Courtship often extends through a summer and a winter. The marriage takes place during the summer season. It is really a matter of purchase. A relative of the young man offers to the proper relative of the young woman a sum of Indian money suited to her standing and attainments. She may or may not be consulted. Woodpecker scalps and shell money, valued from \$30 to \$100, being paid, presents are assembled, and on the appointed day the bride is conducted to her husband by a band of maidens and young men from her village. There is a great feast, and on the third day the convoy returns, carrying back gifts from the groom's family.

If the man cannot pay all the woodpecker scalps and shell money, he may pay half, and go to the bride's home to serve

A KLIKITAT WOMAN,
With specimens of native baskets.

Photograph by Gifford, The Dalles, Oregon.

Photograph by Gifford, The Dalles, Oregon.

A CHINOOK WOMAN
Carrying pack with head-band.

her father in return for the balance. A writer familiar with this people has recorded that a child for whose mother nothing had been paid was called "a babe in the woods." He grew up a social outcast, and was usually a slave; he could not enter the sacred sweat-house, might marry only with his kind, and his children, it was believed, would be bad.

How Divorce is Arranged.

A man may send his wife back to her people for stinginess, bad temper, "big mouth" (scolding), and the like. He receives again the price paid if there are no children, and half the price if there is one child, so that it might not be left without endowment. The woman is obliged to accept her fate.

A Hupa Woman's Day.

The Hupa woman rises at break of day and takes her bath in the river before the men are astir. She serves two meals a day in the family house, a light breakfast, and the principal repast in the evening. The traveller already quoted thus describes this meal:—

"The men ate very slowly, looking about and talking after each spoonful of soup. The women sat in silence, with uncovered heads and hidden feet to show their respect for the men. They passed a basket of water after the supper that the men might wash their hands. After that, the latter retired to the sweat-house."

Women's Recreations.

The Hupa women have a dice game, played with four shell discs, two smaller than the others, which are dropped from the hands held palm against palm. The score is kept with small sticks for counters. They also make several varieties of cat's cradle.

Hupa Magic.

In his chapter on "Medicine of the Hupa," Goddard explains in great detail the Brush dance, the doctor of which might be a man, but at present there is only one old woman who knows it. It is esteemed the remedy for delicate constitution, chronic trouble, or the loss of children, and is performed when the parents wish to safeguard a child. The first part of the ceremony consists in going in search of the "medicine," in which the "doctor" washes and paints her body. She then goes forth with a virgin to gather pine bark for bathing the patient, and pitch wood, which is cooked and tied into bundles. At night they go to the dwelling where the healing ceremony is to be held. Early in the evening the people come together, the women and children sitting on the bank of earth inside the house. The doctor pounds the pine bark in a basket mill (singing the proper songs the while), and boils it in a basket vessel. The child lies with its mother by the fire, and the "doctor" takes up her position at its feet and the girl assistant at its head. Each takes one of the cooked pine sticks, lights it and waves it for some time over the child. The "doctor" then takes her place by the fire and repeats prayers, while burning incense. Then follow ceremonial dances about the fire, which last all night, and are repeated on the following night. To accommodate spectators the roof and walls of the house are removed. Dancers from different localities compete. On the morning of the third day the dancers dress in gay attire, the women wearing their basket hats and shells. Special dances close the ceremonies. The child is bathed with the medicine, and a little is put into its mouth. The doctor woman closes the services towards morning with a song as she dances, with the medicine held above her head. The visitors remain to a feast served at the expense of the child's father.

Hupa Widows.

At the burial of a Hupa husband, the widow may release herself from her marriage vow by standing between her dead husband's legs, otherwise she is bound as widow for life. The Hupa widow has her hair cut short, and wears it so as long as she lives, or until she marries again. Nearer relatives cut the hair as a sign of mourning, and all members of the household wear necklaces of braided grass to prevent their dreaming of the dead.

A second view of this Babel of Indian tongues is given by Dr. Roland B. Dixon in his studies on the Maidu, occupying the area drained by the Sacramento River.

Maidu Women's Work.

The Maidu skin-dressers are, as a rule, women. They remove the hair with scrapers of bone or stone; they soak the skins and rub them with dried deer brains, wringing and rubbing until dry and soft. They seldom smoke them.

The women are also skilful in making cordage and netting from milkweed and wild hemp fibre. Seines and dip nets are in use, made with a primitive needle formed by lashing two slender sticks together. For netted caps the makers have gone up a step on the ladder of invention, for they use a forked stick.

Indian Costumes.

In the Sacramento Valley the women wear two bunches or tassels of grass or shredded bark, about sixteen inches long, suspended from the waist, one in front and one behind. Neighbouring tribes make aprons of buck-skin thongs, strung or tipped with pine nuts and deer hoofs. Women, as a rule, go barefoot, but on the mountains wear moccasins, and also robes of deer-skin or mountain lion skin in cold weather. A basket hat flat on top forms their head covering.

Photograph by Gifford, The Dalles, Oregon.

WARM SPRINGS INDIAN AND SQUAW.

Fashions in Hair-dressing and Ornaments.

The women wear the hair long, either loose or tied by a band passing over the top of the head and under the chin. They cut the hair in most primitive fashion with a sharp flint on a stick, and burn the ends with a glowing ember. They wash the hair frequently, using soap-root for the purpose. Combs are formed from pine cones, pine needles in bunches, and porcupine tails. Personal adornments are adapted from shell, bone, feathers, and wood. These take the form of beads, cylinders, pendants, and tufts, in great variety, and are worn on the breast, about the neck, and in the ears.

Tattooing is more elaborate and more common with women than with men. It consists of vertical lines on the chin, marks on the cheek, and dots with lines on the hands. There are no ceremonies connected therewith, but it takes place at about the same age as with young whites, seeming to mark the growing consciousness of coming womanhood.

Curious Basket- and Feather-work.

Maidu women are the basket-makers, using redbud, peeled and unpeeled, for bright brown effects, peeled willow for white or wood colour, grass for overlaying, maidenhair fern for black, bracken-roots for bright red, and hazel for the warp in burden baskets. The Maidu are fond of feather-work. Beautiful creations of this material are the feather belts worn by women in dances. A strip of soft deer-skin of the proper shape is covered with woodpecker's scalps, varied with those of ducks and wild canary to form patterns. Plume sticks, to the ends of which are tastefully attached pretty feathers, are used. The variety of ways for mounting the feathers is a pleasant study in technique, and it adds to the effectiveness of their decoration.

Maidu Dwellings.

The Maidu woman's home is an earth lodge or a brush shelter. The principal structure is a large circular, semi-subterranean, earth-covered dance or "sweat-house," used also as a regular dwelling. There are also less carefully made conical huts, with little excavation, and summer shelters of brush. In the earth lodge, on each side, is a low platform of willows covered with pine needles and skins. It forms a lounging place and bed, the inmates sleeping with their feet toward the fire. A pole along the edge serves for a common pillow, or an old basketry plaque supports the head of an individual. In the ruder lodges are no platforms, but only pine straw and skins, the latter rolled up at the ends for pillows. The bed coverings are woven robes of rabbit fur or of bird skins, when any are needed, but ordinarily the sleepers are quite naked.

Food and other property is stored in baskets about the edge of the walls, or under the platform, or in an apse-like cellar, or in willow basket-like granaries, or in hut-like structures. In the floor of the hut flat stones are sunk on which the women pound acorns in stormy weather. There are also pestles for the mortars, and *metates* and mullers for the preparation of acorns and seeds. Baskets there are, appropriate to every use.

The Ubiquitous Basket.

These women have few vessels of wood or stone, and rely on the ubiquitous basket for everything. Wood is often kept on large coiled trays, and smaller baskets of this type are used as plates to eat from; dried meat or fish is served in open-work twined trays. Cooking is done in bowl-shaped baskets by means of hot stones, which are handled with two sticks for tongs. These Maidu women have not risen to the spoon age. They use any common stick to stir their mush. Mussel shells serve for spoons and ladles. Mush is eaten with the index and middle finger of the right hand, illustrating the saying that fingers were made before forks. For napkins, bunches of grass serve to wipe the hands and face after eating.

The acorn harvest furnishes an example of the division of labour among the Maidu and other central Californian tribes. The men and larger boys climb the trees and knock off the fruit with long poles. The women and children gather the nuts in their burden baskets, carry them to the village, and place them in the granaries and storage baskets. The women also at the proper time crack the nuts, separate the shells with their teeth, and spread the halves in the sun to dry. They also grind and sift the meal and make the mush.

The Important Acorn.

The bitter flavour is removed by means of hot water, as among the Hupa. To make acorn bread, the dough is made into a loaf six inches in diameter, which is flattened, a hot rock rolled in oak leaves is placed in the centre, and the dough folded over and pressed all around. The mass is wrapped in oak leaves and placed in the ashes or under a pile of hot stones to bake. The bread is solid and heavy, and, like the soup and mush, almost tasteless. Sand and ashes get mixed with them all. The cedar sprigs give a little taste, and mint or bay increases the flavour; but surely this comes very near to giving a stone when asked for bread!

The women are also the primitive farmers, gathering roots with the digging stick hardened in fire. They, at the same time, unconsciously till the soil for the next crop. Roots are eaten raw, roasted, boiled, or dried, pounded fine, mixed with berries, and baked in small cakes. Berries are eaten raw, dried for winter, made into cakes, or crushed for cider. Pine nuts are a great luxury, gathered with much labour, and used also in trade. Grasshoppers, locusts, angle worms, as well as eels, fish, deer, and other meat, complete the dietary. The capturing of the animals is man's work, but woman's mind is developed, her hands made skilful, and her body rendered more vigorous by the multiplicity of her varied employments. The change for her to civilisation, therefore, is not so abrupt, and her race is being perpetuated by this means, for nearly all the Indians of mixed blood are through white fathers. They glide easily into the family life of the dominant race. In some places the Indians are thus increasing in number.

For land transportation the freight is carried on the backs of women as well as men, in baskets. Goods of all sorts, and even old people or invalids, are borne thus. But the chief passengers are the babies, and they are carried on cradle frames of basketry set up on a forked stick. The lower end of the Y-shaped frame is sharpened, and when the mother is gathering roots or berries, is thrust into the ground. The babe is thus held upright and protected from harm.

Curious Cradles.

The life of the Maidu women is not all work and no play. In one of their games each player has a stick about 5 feet long, with which she tosses a plaited rope of buck-skin a foot long, or a couple of sticks 6 inches by 2 inches tied to a buck-skin cord 4 inches apart, or a bundle of frayed cotton-wood bark. The game, between sides, is to toss the rope or sticks from one goal to another. This is excellent for the development of health and skill. Guessing games and cat's cradle are among their amusements. The men are confirmed gamblers, and the women play with bones or pebbles, concealing them in the hand and guessing.

Maidu Games.

As an art of pleasure the women of California cultivate music with the deer-hoof rattle and singing. There are many types of songs, such as love songs, puberty songs, dance songs, and basket songs.

Californian Music.

"An eye for an eye" is the law in the punishment of crimes. If a woman is killed in an encounter between two parties, the aggressors usually give one of their women in exchange to prevent further reprisals.

The great event in the social world is the "soup dinner." The invitations are not cards but cords, with as many knots tied in each as there are days before the dinner. Each day one of the knots is untied by the head of each family, and on the day all things are ready. Abundant supply of acorn soup and mush, with other viands, is provided, and two days are spent in eating, gambling, and merry-making.

A "Soup Dinner."

Dixon's account of central Californian customs most closely connected with woman's existence is so admirably told that his words are closely followed.

A CAYUSE GIRL.

Maidu Birth Customs.

Most strange but widespread is the rule that during the period of pregnancy both husband and wife must be careful in all they do. Towards the last neither may eat meat or fish, the husband must not hunt, and the woman stays much at home. When her time arrives the woman goes to the hut of seclusion, and is there delivered, generally assisted by two old women. In the foot-hills the woman merely goes off with an old woman to help her, giving birth to the child at some distance from the village.

Both husband and wife observe strict regulations at this time. In the Sacramento Valley both must fast five days. After that both go to the river to bathe, then return for five days more. Then after a second bath their purification is over. These restrictions vary from place to place, but in principle they are the same. Twins, in the foot-hills, are a bad omen. The mother, it is said, is often killed, and the babes either buried alive with the mother's body or burned.

How Maidu Girls are Named.

The naming of girls in the Maidu country, and, indeed, in all Indian tribes, is interesting. At first they receive no name, but are addressed as "baby," "child," "girl"; but in a year or so they acquire names from some habit, such as "Runner," "Climber," etc. The family term for a girl varies as she grows older, changing first at puberty, then at giving birth to a child, and finally in old age. There is a sacredness and certain *tabus* connected with names, and those of the dead must not be mentioned for a fixed period. After that they may be given to children.

Maidenhood Ceremonies.

At the important time when the girl enters upon womanhood she notifies her mother of the fact, who tells all the relatives and friends. In the evening they all, men and women, assemble at the girl's house. The fire is covered with ashes, and all sit down around the fireplace, each one holding two stones for beating time to the songs sung. The girl sits apart at the north-west corner of the house covered with mats and skins, and no man or boy may come near her. The whole company sings, beginning with the "grasshopper song," followed with others, in which food products gathered by women are mentioned. The songs are kept up through the night, and at dawn all go out on the roof and sing "On Manzanita Hill the dawn shows first." After that they return to the interior, where a breakfast is served *en règle* by the parents. This goes on nightly, perhaps, for a week. Except during these ceremonies, the girl must remain in a small separate hut. She must eat no flesh during five days, and must be fed by her mother or some other older woman.

A separate basket, plate, and cup are set apart for her use, and she must not scratch her head with her fingers but with a scratching stick. On the sixth day she takes a warm bath, and though she must remain in her separate lodge, now feeds herself, but still uses the scratching-stick. On the twelfth day she bathes in the river and her parents give a big feast, at which a guest may ask for anything that pleases his fancy. The parents must grant these requests even to giving a daughter in marriage. At the feast the new woman dresses in her best and great display is made.

In the foot-hills the girl has five vertical lines, alternately red and black, painted on her cheek. A ring of pine needles about a yard in diameter is prepared, and in it stands the novice, with another who has been through the ceremony. The heads of both are covered with skins, and the pine needles are set on fire. Upon the word they uncover their heads, and run a short distance. On returning to the place they find a crowd of women, who greet them with laughter, while some of the older ones sing. A circle of earth, similar to that used in leaching meal, is filled with warm water, and the young women are washed. All the women and girls repair to the home, and at nightfall a dance of women only is performed out of doors—of which men and boys are allowed to be spectators. This being over, singing is generally kept up by the women till morning, when one mark is removed from each cheek of the initiate. The rules of abstinence from meat, of being fed, of remaining quiet, of dancing

A KLIKITAT MAIDEN IN GALA DRESS.

and singing, are enforced until the fifth day. The girl is then considered ready to marry.

Marriage.

Marriage is the one event in the Maidu Indian woman's life the interest of which is perennial. In the Sacramento Valley, when a man wants to marry, he sends a friend with a gift of beads to the family of the young woman. If the father and other relatives consider the gift large enough and the match desirable, the old gentleman keeps the beads; if not, they are sent back. Or he may hand the gift over to his brother and demand a second one. It is delightful to read that the consent of the girl is always necessary, and precedes the sending of the gifts, though this upward ethical move is far from universal in Califo nian tribes. If the wife is of the man's village, he usually goes to live with her family; but if of another village she goes to live with him. For some months at least he hunts and fishes for her family. Often, if the bride is from another village, the pair dwell with her family for six months after the marriage.

Many of the men are monogamous, but those who can afford it have two or three wives, the chief being the only one who has as many as four. All have equal rank and rights. The unfaithful wife must be taken back and the strings of beads refunded. If a husband dies the brother usually takes the widow. Mother-in-law and son-in-law do not speak when they meet, the woman always covering her head.

Curious Courtship.

The Maidu of the foot-hills has a kind of "Barkis" courtship. The young fellow goes to the girl's lodge and sits there for a week or so. He then exerts himself and goes a-hunting. The spoil is brought to her house, and, throwing it down, the swain says, "I give you a deer," or words to that effect. If the present be accepted, that is all the encouragement he wants. So he goes on hunting and bringing, but not entering the house. When he has delivered a sufficient amount he comes into the house. A bed is prepared for him, and he takes his place as a member of the family. The pair live thus until the girl is old enough to manage a house, if she has been married young, or till the husband can provide a house for her. Girls are often given as wives when only six or eight years of age. Old men often have four or five wives ranging from ten to fifty years or more. "Many wives, much discord," is the rule, and the moral status is low.

Other Courtship and Marriage Customs.

In the North-Eastern area occupied by this people the courtship is less sentimental. The young man goes to the house of the girl's parents, and if she accepts him they are married; if not, that ends it. A man who is a good hunter will have a wife sent to him by her father, and he must accept her. If one of two brothers marries one of two or more sisters, the other brother has the first right to marry the remaining sister or sisters, if the first brother does not. Divorce is simply an agreement to separate, and both can re-marry at once.

Maidu Mourning Customs.

Mortuary customs differ among the Maidu tribes. Inhumation and cremation are both practised. How the last act is performed for women, and what share the living have in the ceremonies for the dead, will be here told. In mourning the widow cuts her hair short and covers her head, face, neck, and breast with pine-pitch and charcoal, a gloomy mourning which she is obliged to preserve until it wears off. Indeed, there are long periods set, and the anointing is renewed. The widow must remain in the house in the day time, but may come out after dark, until the time of the "burning." During her stay in the house she makes baskets and other objects for the ceremony, in which she is aided by relatives. A necklace of beads strung in peculiar fashion is worn until she stops mourning for the deceased.

The dead are doubled up and tied into a ball, the body is decked with beads and feathers, wrapped in skins and laid on the back in the grave, or, in other locations, placed in a sitting posture. The body is sometimes put into a large basket. Food and water are placed in the grave, which is then filled in. The houses are generally burned—a good sanitary measure at least—and personal property as well. When a mother dies leaving a very young child, it is buried with her lying on her breast, as if still being nursed, or burned with her.

IV.—WOMEN OF THE INTERIOR BASIN

Tribes of the Interior Basin—Woman's Influence—The Widespreading Athapascan—The Shoshonean-Nahuan Race—The Great Desert—The Pueblos—How the Desert People Secure their Food—Pueblo Cookery—Dress in the South-West—Navaho Houses—Ute Dwellings—Cliff Houses—Woman as House-builder—Home Arts—Women's Work—Women as Potters—Social Customs in the South-West—Zuñi Courtship and Marriage—Zuñi Birth Customs—Position of Navaho Women—Men as Spinners and Knitters—Indian Co-operation—Woman's Influence on Commerce—Man's Use "to Fetch and Carry" for Woman—Burial Customs—A Loitering Ghost—The Power of the Pueblo Woman—Characteristics of Pueblo Women—Woman as Heroine—Pueblo Religion's Influence on Woman—Pueblo Mythology—A Zuñi Legend

THE area known as the Interior Basin is a well marked, arid, but elevated and healthful region, situated chiefly in Arizona and New Mexico. It included formerly the drainage area of the Colorado and Upper Rio Grande Rivers.

Tribes of the Interior Basin.

Tribes of the Shoshonean, Athapascan, Piman, Yuman, and small Pueblo families were its inhabitants. Cultures fostered there were in both the hunter and the sedentary stage. The first two families mentioned form a long chain of tribes connecting the Yukon and the Mackenzie drainage with the State of Costa Rica. It is a mixing ground of the nations, covering over a hundred thousand square miles.

Woman's Influence.

Two sets of women and their lineal descendants were, in course of time, the pupils of all the environments along the Pacific coast between Alaska and Costa Rica—namely, the Athapascan and the Shoshonean-Nahuan. They jointly occupied a large part of the South-West, helping to develop its sedentary *pueblo* life and its unsettled hunter life. The Pimas, Yumas, and a few smaller linguistic families filled up the rest of the area. Arts are practised in common, but in other respects the tribes are as wide apart as possible in woman's share of culture. But the most charming part of the study is that concerning the play and struggle always going on between the settled and the roving life.

The Wide-spreading Athapascan.

The Tinneh or Athapascan language, says Matthews,* stretches from northern interior Alaska down into Sonora and Chihuahua, more than four thousand miles, extending diagonally over forty-two degrees of latitude, like a great tree whose trunk is the Rocky Mountain range, whose roots encompass the deserts of Arizona and New Mexico, and whose branches touch the borders of Hudson Bay and the Pacific and the Arctic Oceans. But the same writer makes it clear that the Navaho and Apache of the South-West speak a mixed language. Under such conditions the people may have killed off a great many men, but they saved the women, together with their arts and skill. So the women of this area have much to tell of their struggles with environments.

A similar story would be told by that immense group of women, the Shoshonean-

* "Navaho Legends."

Photograph by C. C. Pierce, Los Angeles.

AN APACHE INDIAN GIRL CARRYING NATIVE BASKET.

Nahuan. A look at the Powell map reveals them in the Interior Basin north of the 45th parallel. In the South-West they almost disappear from the *pueblo* country, to become in southern Mexico the distinguished Aztecs. Six of the Hopi or Moki towns in northern Arizona are of this family. They, as well as the Navaho, claim to have been cliff-dwellers ; but most of the Pueblo dwellers are of different stocks, small islands in the northern end of an Athapascan sea around which stretches the Shoshonean family. Further on the family organisation of these tribes will be shown.

The Shoshonean-Nahuan Race.

The country inhabited by the Pueblo and non-Pueblo women mentioned—which has been their home from time out of mind—includes almost the entire area of Colorado, Utah, New Mexico, and Arizona. It was, before the days of railroads, called the Great American Desert, and was thought of as a place of utter desolation, thirst, and starvation—shunned of mankind or entered with foreboding. Some parts of this land are not suitable for human habitation, but in others there are fields of corn, melons, squashes, beans, peppers, etc., and orchards of peaches. There is often a system of irrigation, and dams are built for the storage of water for irrigating and domestic purposes.

The Great Desert.

It is a country where good things do not stand out obtrusively as in the fertile Mississippi valley, but are hidden from those who do not have the anointed eyes to see them, discerning minds to appreciate them, courage against inhuman and non-human enemies, and skill in primitive handicrafts. Whether it was that those specially gifted survived there, or that the environment was fitted to make men and women of the right stamp, it is certain that one of the most specialised groups of human beings made their homes and prospered in the South-West. From the point of sex, the region

Photograph by C. C. Pierce Los Angeles.

A NAVAHO INDIAN SQUAW

Wearing a native blanket.

was bi-sexual, in that men and women were made to share the destiny, "In the sweat of thy face shalt thou eat bread." The mutual bearing of the burden suited the size of the body to the region—an environment which said to its tribes, "Go ye near the sources of water and help ye one another."

Photograph by C. C. Pierce, Los Angeles.

A NAVAHO INDIAN SQUAW WEAVING NATIVE BLANKETS.

The Pueblos.

Thus came the communism of the Pueblos, and thus was their advancement promoted. The life is one prolonged sigh for water. The serpent is worshipped because it reminds men of lightning, thunder, rain, and bread. Woman appears with the pad upon the head and the water-jar on the top of that, because she is bringing the one thing needful. Even the wild tribes there must yield to the environment, and if they are not potters they must learn to make water-tight basketry. Old things pass away. The Navaho becomes a weaver, other tribes practise commensalism in many ways.

What did the people in this South-West eat, and what connection had women with alimentation? Though the region looks small on the map, it covers many thousands of square miles, and its regimens are varied.

How the Desert People Secure Food.

The Apache or Ute woman is a hunter's wife, with duties just like those elsewhere belonging to that estate. She cannot have pottery: it is too fragile for her unsettled life; nor vessels of wood—there are no large trees of soft grain from which to carve them; so Necessity stepped in and suggested baskets dipped in pitch. The Ute woman, in addition to her function as a preparer of meat, is a gleaner of wild grass seeds, which she beats from the stems in the field by means of a basketry wand looking for all the world like a rude tennis racquet.

The receptacle is a conical basket, which also serves for carrying purposes. But the most interesting of her implements is what answers to the modern fan mill. It is a twined basket in the shape of a large, shallow scoop, and serves for winnowing and toasting at the same time. The harvest is placed in the basket tray with hot stones, and shaken skilfully and quickly. Charred spots on old specimens in the museums tell of an occasional laggard. The roasted seeds may be eaten whole or ground and made into Indian bread.

The Pueblo women have a still more generous larder. The cornfields belong to the men, and as fertile patches are not always close to safe places for homes, the walk is long to and from work. Here also are their other crops of gourds, beans, etc. It is the Pueblo women's duty to care for the crops and make them into food. Let us see. For this purpose they need water, which often must be carried up long and winding trails. This ever-crying need made them the best potters in North America. As they live in settled habitations, there can be more than two women grinding at a mill. This is not of a circular pair of stones, like the old-fashioned mills of the Orient, but a long box of stone slabs set into the floor. It is divided into compartments, in each of which is a slab—the nether mill-stone, about the size of a small washboard. This rests at an angle away from the miller, who grasps the flat muller, resembling a thin brick, with both hands, and, kneeling down, rubs away after the fashion and with the energy of the old-time washer-woman. The meal is ground very fine, and as a result of the many coloured grains—white, yellow, red, purple, and black—the meal is dark in colour.

Pueblo Cookery.

To cook it a smooth slab is laid on two stone rests over, and near to, the fire. The woman takes wet meal in her right hand, and quickly spreads on the hot griddle a cake not much thicker than a postage stamp. This is quickly peeled off and piled on a pretty basket tray. A dish of the grey result looks very much like a hornet's nest. It is probably the best product of culinary work attained by North American savage women, who have also other ways of cooking, into which the chile, or Mexican pepper, enters obtrusively. It goes without saying that people who do not depend on the daily success of hunting and fishing for a living remove themselves that much farther from starvation and its demoralising consequences. It is true, however, here as elsewhere, that the South-Western Indians had exhausted the search for edibles.

Dress in the South-West.

The next want to observe is that of dress and adornment. There are Ute women, Apache, Navaho, and Pueblos. On occasion they are fond of dress, though the legends say that before the whites came the Navaho were poor. The word Ute suggests to the ethnologist buck-skin. Both men and women recall the colours of new chamois skin. In the old dress all the display of gaudy beads is absent. It is quite characteristic. The Apache and Navaho, under Spanish influence, were dressed in wool, and the women, as well as men, of the latter are among the finest of Indian weavers. In the southern groups of the South-West little clothing is needed, but the body is washed with clay water, which wears off as the day grows warmer.

But to be dressed up constantly does not accord with the practical mind of the Pueblo woman ; rather, she prefers going barefoot to wearing moccasins, and keeps her best for occasions of ceremony. Her dress, designed as it is for service and freedom of action for her body, is appropriate and picturesque. She wears as the principal garment an oblong, rectangular creation, made from one piece of strong, dark blue woollen stuff of Hopi weave, which her white sisters might term a meal-sack, coming to the middle of the calf, belted at the waist and held on the left shoulder by stitches joining the edges. The right shoulder in the ancient pattern was left bare, but usually at present an under tunic of cotton clothes the bust and arms.

Photograph by P. G. Gates.

NAVAHO WOMEN SPINNING AND WEAVING.

These women seem to inexperienced eyes to be dressed alike, though some little feature, such as shoulder stitching of coloured cord, tassels at the corners, or other touches of fancy, no doubt give them individuality. At Acoma the skirt is a mass of gorgeous embroidery, but, as a rule, no ornament—except sometimes the skilful stitches of the weaver—relieves the surface of the cloth. Colour enters the costume with the oblong shawl, which is a length of tasselled stuff drawn over the shoulders, or the flaunting mantle of bright cotton affected by the younger people, and the woven belt. On ceremonial occasions the bride may display her white cotton mantle with its border of brilliant embroidery and its huge vari-coloured tassels, but not often does she wear this costume, which marks the heyday of her life.

Photograph by C. C. Pierce, Los Angeles.

A YOUNG HOPI GIRL OF ARIZONA IN NATIVE DRESS.

The Pueblo woman's foot-wear consists of the tiny moccasin, to which is sewn a loose flap consisting of half a white tanned deer-skin, to be wrapped around the calf with many turns, forming a cumbrous, but not uncomely bulk. Jewellery she affects, of strings of precious sea-shell and stone or silver beads, and earrings fashioned by the silversmith or worker in turquoise. In a word, this paragon of the South-West may lay claim to being the most picturesquely and the best dressed of her Indian sisters.

With all the occupations that seem to fill such a major portion of her life, the Pueblo woman still finds time to make herself neat and attractive, showing that there is even here the common sentiment called fashion. Rightly, the blossoming of *coiffure*, costume, and ornaments is displayed by the maidens, whose modest prettiness gives an indefinable charm to the many-celled villages—none the less do the mothers of families array themselves in befitting costume; while the aged, gradually being weaned from life, are careless of its forms and gauds.

Navaho Houses. The habitations of the Navaho women, according to Matthews,* vary somewhat, but are simple in structure. The "hogan" is a conical lodge of poles, with an opening on one side for a doorway. The frame is covered with weeds, bark, or grass, and earth, except at the apex, where is an opening for the escape of smoke. The doorway is like a dormer window. Then there are lodges of logs built up in polygonal form, covered with earth, with a doorway at the corner, screened with blankets; and again huts built partly of stone, with a conglomeration of brush and earth for covering and fencing. The corrals are contiguous to the huts, where the family cook and spend most of the time in fair weather, and the summer-houses are erected in a few hours. A couple of forked sticks are set upright, and a pole laid across. Slanting poles against this, in the direction of the prevailing winds, form a windbreak, and this is covered with grass, weeds, and earth. The medicine lodge is like the hogan, though of much greater size, and the "sweat-house" is a diminutive hogan, without smoke-hole or storm door. Stones are heated outside and placed on the floor, the entrance is covered with blankets, and the heat thus raised causes a

* "Navaho Legends."

violent perspiration. Dr. Matthews observes that a few progressive Navaho are building stone houses with flat roofs, glazed windows, wooden doors, and regular chimneys. They have Mexican and Pueblo examples before them for centuries, but, believing that a house is accursed in which a human died, they abandon it, so they hesitate to erect permanent dwellings. The venturing of these pioneers away from superstition is in a line with many changes that are silently working their way into the old life.

Ute Dwellings.

The Ute branch of the Shoshonean family are tent dwellers. On the east they are in immediate contact with the Siouan, Algonquian, and Kaiowan tribes. The woman's housekeeping life also resembles that of these tribes. Only quite recently have they abandoned their old ways.

Cliff Houses.

The sedentary people of the South-West, whatever their blood or linguistic family, have also had a variety of domiciles, some of which are ages old. Guessing that the conical house came from the north, it would be only natural to look southward for those of stone and adobe. The cliff houses were, says Farrand, "stone buildings containing from a single room to more than a hundred, and were sometimes three or four storeys high. The largest of these, known as Cliff Palace, is estimated to have one hundred and twenty-five rooms on the ground floor alone." There were also cave dwellings, cavate abodes, immense pueblos on plateaus and in the valleys, adobe structures, Casa Grande being the best known, and large ditches for irrigation.

Farrand rejects the theory of a cliff-dwelling race, and attributes the structures to the ancestors of the present sedentary tribes. The stone and adobe structures of the South-West could be stood in a row, beginning with the oldest cave dwelling and ending with the latest pueblo, in such order as to leave not a break in the thoughts that planned them.

Woman as House-builder.

The Pueblo woman builds her house of stone or adobe. Her agile hands are the whole kit of mason's tools for fitting the materials and smoothing the walls. Who but the potter would have the feeling for this? Men do the heavy work, and the women are like the wasps clustering their rooms together like the cells of a honeycomb. Two motives first impelled them to do this—the environment and their neighbours, the hostile tribes. Since the whites came, more eligible sites have been chosen, and the lower storeys have doorways on the ground floor. The clay and stone also were unconscious organisers, which in all ages ensured the largest co-operation.

Home Arts.

When the house was finished it was in truth the woman's, for here, more than in other areas mentioned, were concentrated the home arts, and here were gathered the means of cultivating these arts. The home was the basket-maker's workshop, and the pottery-maker's *atelier*. Here were worked out the milling slabs, cooking slabs — stone griddles, they might be called—and pot rests. In the walls were made the ovens, and on the spot was manufactured the furniture for the diversified cooking practised there. In the lowest stages of handicraft its products are worked out on the spot, but as culture advances the materials are carried to the factory. The pueblo is a primitive factory village, where the home and shops of a hundred or more are under the same roof. All speak the same language, produce the same artifacts, are moved by the same symbolism, tell the same marvellous stories of nature, and worship the same spiritual beings in the same way.

Women's Work.

Women's arts in the South-West, in addition to those relating to dress and house, are associated with food, water, transportation, and trade. Here the basket-maker revels in many types of the art, and the potter is at her best. The former has to put up with desert materials. There are no long spruce roots as at the North, but the toughest of desert fibres and twigs of abundant shrubbery. As soon as the Spaniards came, the Navaho eagerly adopted sheep, while the Apache held on to the basket art. Matthews says that the Navaho excel all the finishing labour. For the various harvests of fruits, seeds, grain, and other vegetable products there is a time for each. They are ever busy with details, leave nothing to chance, and their work develops the individual. Their hard conditions have been blessings in disguise.

Photograph by C. C. Pierce, Los Angeles.

A HAVASUPAI SQUAW MAKING POTTERY.

other Indians of the United States in the art of weaving, and, curious to tell, they knit stockings with four needles. Leggings of human hair, knitted with wooden needles, have been found in the cliff dwellings on the Navaho Reservation.

Every season of the year has its own special handicraft for the women of the pueblo. Should the cornfield, with its accessory crops, need them, they lend a helping hand with the hoe, or on occasion drive away animal enemies. The calm summer days are the time to burn pottery against the year's breakages. Then also they gather roots, stems, and leaves for basket materials, and prepare them for

The two classes of women, sedentary and unsettled, make two kinds of receptacles for water their eternal problem. The Apache woman weaves strong basket bottles and jars, and dips them in piñon gum. That is the best for wanderers. The sedentary women of the pueblos are best served by pottery. The demand is immense, the motives for having the best are the strongest, and the material is unsurpassed. Holmes relates that after the passage of a storm and the disappearance of the flood, the pools would retain a sediment of clay two or three inches thick, whose consistency was perfectly suited to the hand of the potter.

Women as Potters.

Photograph by C. C. Pierce, Los Angeles

A HOPI INDIAN WOMAN GRINDING CORN IN HER HOUSE.

Sand, pulverised shards, and mica are used in tempering. The ware is built up in several ways. There is no potter's wheel, and yet the narrative would lose a part of its interest if it failed to note that shallow earthen vessels, baskets, and sections of gourds turn easily as the coiling process goes on. The processes are shaping with the fingers, pressure into a mould, or slowly building up by coiling, as in basketry, and pinching the turns together, sometimes with basketry effects in mosaic patterns, but more often in rubbing the surface down and smoothing it with a slip "that takes the place of the enamels used by more accomplished potters, and being usually white, gives a beautiful surface on which to execute freehand designs in colour. The firing is not nearly as successful as the making—the ware is soft, smoke stained, and never glazed. The ancient ware is superior to the modern, and occasionally, through accidents of firing, a piece will have the ring and hardness of stoneware."

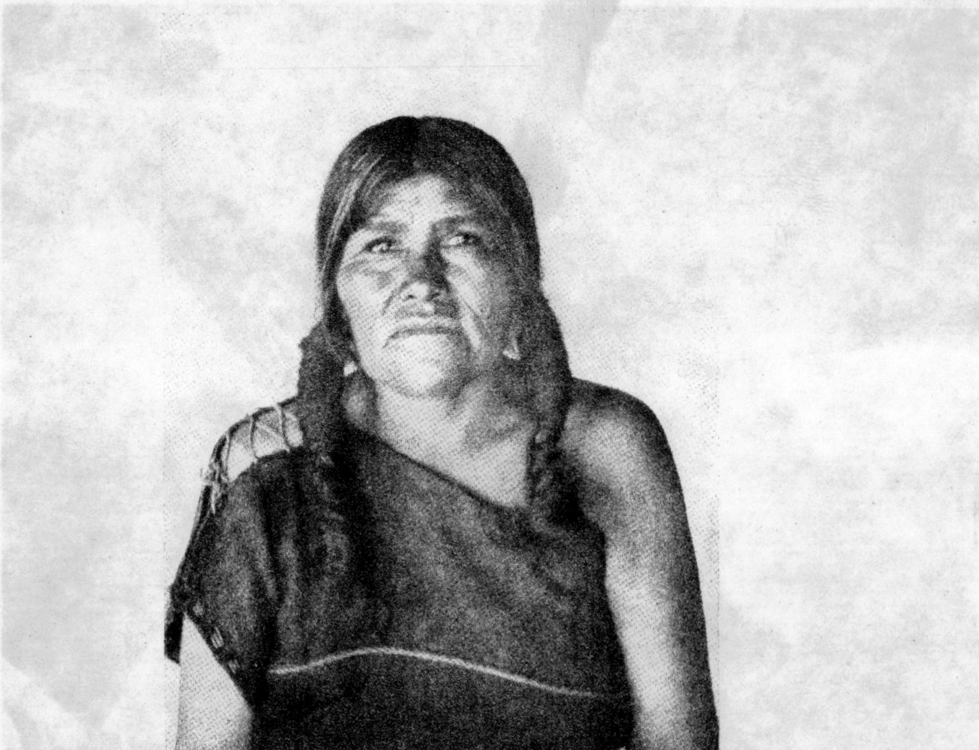

Photograph by C. C. Pierce, Los Angeles.

A HOPI WOMAN.

A splendid type of the matron.

Both Holmes and Cushing dwell upon the profound influence of the textile art on pottery. The former calls attention to the fact that "basketry was practised from remote antiquity, and within modern times the manufacture of baskets has been the most important industry of the tribes of the Pacific slope. Ceramic shapes in this region coincide with textile outlines."

Social Customs in the South-West.

The sociology of the South-West must take into consideration the family life, the community life, and the ceremonial life of sedentary pueblos and dwellers in frail structures. In this varied environment it is quite clearly set forth that blood-kinship, speech, art, and industry, social structures, and functions are distinct problems, and yet they are inseparable factors in the whole life. When a woman is called an Athapascan, it must be added "in speech," for in blood she is far from being the same as her Alaskan namesake.

The South-Western tribes arranged for the marriage of their daughters in various ways. Among the Pueblos and the Navaho people, mother-right prevailed—that is, maternal clans were the rule—but the more usual law of paternal descent governed the Yuman tribes living about the lower Colorado; while the Shoshonean or Ute tribes, except the Hopi, and the Piman tribes in north-western Mexico, were without true exogamous divisions. There the young folks not too closely related could fall in love and marry like civilised people.

In the twenty-third annual report of the Bureau of American Ethnology, Mrs. Matilda Coxe Stevenson gives a faithful account of the Zuñi family in its formation, with references to other Pueblos. Some of their houses have as many as eight rooms, and a few have only two. Ledges, built with the house, form seats and shelves. The household works, eats, sleeps, and entertains guests in the living room. Wardrobes are hung from poles suspended from the rafters, while more valuable things are carefully placed in the storage rooms. The mills for grinding may also be set up in the living room. "The domestic life," says the authoress, "might serve as an example for the civilised world. The husband lives with his wife's parents, often several families under the same roof. These are not large, and the members are deeply attached to one another. The living room will show the mothers caring for their infants, or the fathers fondling them. The grandmother will have one of the younger children on her lap, and maybe the head of another resting on her shoulder. When a legend is told great interest is manifested in the recital. The children are rarely disobedient, play the livelong day without a quarrel, and are seldom punished. Girls join in some of the pleasure dances. The older ones seldom go about the village unattended. The only place they are free to visit alone is the well, where the youths watch for them in the early evening. The love-making is in good form, the swains must make the advances, and, while parents look after the marriage of their children, there are many love matches in Zuñi."

Mrs. Stevenson has worked out minutely the coming-of-age customs among the Zuñi.

Zuñi Courtship and Marriage.

Marriage usually occurs at very tender years. Should a girl not be married when she arrives at womanhood, there is a great *pow-wow* between the mother, aunts, and grandmother, to know the reason why. When a man loves a girl, he tells her, and

COCOPA (YUMAN) WOMAN.

A PAIUTE WOMAN OF KURATU, UTAH, IN FULL DRESS.

asks permission to go to her house. She usually says, if she favours the suit, "Wait till I ask my parents." If all goes smoothly he calls on her. The mother asks him to be seated, and orders the daughter to set food before the guest. Should the girl hesitate from lack of interest or from coquetry (Zuñi maidens are all coquettes), she is admonished by her elders. After serving, she takes her seat facing the visitor, and the parents talk about his duties. After the repast, the father calls the young man to him, the girl remaining on the other side of the room, and says, "You are to marry my daughter; you must work hard, watch the sheep, help to cut wood, plant the grain, and harvest it." The mother tells him to be good to his wife. The young man works for the family five days, sleeping in the living room, and on the sixth morning goes to his home. He tells where he has been, and that the girl's parents are willing. If his people like the match they say, "It is well." On his return during the sixth morning, he carries a dress as a present from his mother to her intended daughter-in-law. The bride then grinds some flour, and the next day returns with him carrying the meal in a basket on her head and giving it to his mother, who says, "My child, thanks; be seated." The mother hands bread to the girl, who takes a few mouthfuls. The father-in-law lays a deer-skin before her, saying: "This is for your moccasins." The girl then returns to her mother's house with the groom, bearing on her head the basket, filled with wheat, and the folded deer-skin lying on top. They make their permanent home with her mother. They do not sleep in the living room with the rest of the family until after the birth of the first child.

The Zuñis are monogamists, polygamy being abhorred; but divorces are quite common. They would rather separate than dwell together inharmoniously.

Previous to the birth of a child, if a daughter is desired the husband and wife visit the Mother Rock. The prospective mother scrapes a small quantity of the rock into a tiny vase made for the purpose, deposits

Photograph by C. C. Pierce, Los Angeles.

YUMA INDIAN GIRLS.

Photograph by C. C. Pierce, Los Angeles.

CHEMEHUEVI GIRLS MAKING THE NATIVE DRINK OF THE MESQUIT BEAN IN A NATIVE POTTERY BOWL.

it in one of the cavities, and they pray that the daughter may grow to be good and beautiful, possess all virtues, weave beautifully, and be a skilful potter. If the prayer is not answered, it is because the heart of one or the other is not good. At another shrine bits of rock are powdered, put into water, and the mixture is drunk by the woman. Two facts are prominent in the Zuñi birth customs—the cruel sufferings of the young mother, and her wonderful recuperation as compared with civilised women. There will be tribal differences of detail in courtship, marriage, inheritance, the future abode, and the occupation of the groom; the Shoshonean women will have one fate, the Apache or Navaho another, the Yuman and Piman another. But there seems to be no difference in this fact of recuperation.

Zuñi Birth Customs.

"The social position of the Navaho women," says Matthews, "is one of great independence; much of the wealth of the nation belongs to them; they are the managers of their own property, the owners of their children, and their freedom lends vigour to their physiognomies."

Position of Navaho Women.

Here is a good place to call attention to the division of labour in the community life. The men among the sedentary groups are the farmers, but those who are used to seeing tailors sitting and sewing garments will not be surprised to hear that Pueblo men have always been good spinners, knitters, weavers, and seamsters. It is said that the very finest blankets are their handiwork. At present these textile tribes are in the commercial stage of industry. Garments are made for barter; division of labour and selection of the fittest have begun.

Men as Spinners and Knitters.

Pueblo life has not only introduced division of labour but developed co-operation to a high degree. The scheme provides for no idlers; even little girls just out of arms are taught to play at what will come in time to be their daily tasks. Willing hands make lighter work, so that much is accomplished every day. Special proficiency in pottery-making, basketry, or belt weaving, because it is the way to extra income, often relieves a woman from household duties that are taken up by others. The older girls care for the younger children and play the parental part well. Young women toil before dawn at the hand-mills and bake and sew; able-bodied matrons carry water, cook, weave, and superintend; and old women, bent and grey, do such light tasks as they may be able to perform, unless the vicissitudes of life have taken from them their helpers and decreed that they shall bear the heavy burden till the end.

Indian Co-operation.

Primitive trade, with companion activities, has progressed in this heterogeneous environment. The industries dominated by the Pueblo woman have given her as a producer as high a place in the political as in the domestic economy, and it is through her efforts that these features of society have risen from the rudimentary stage, and have become of importance. As long as there has been any history this has been the land of barter, and all the floating tribes from the points of the compass came here to trade with the thrifty ones. Here they met the Pueblo woman merchant, and learned that her mind was intent on getting the better of the bargain—she was persistent, hiding craft with guile and enjoying the play of wits in the game of trade.

Woman's Influence on Commerce.

Let no one believe that the Pueblo woman is a simple-minded savage. She trudges long miles to bring her wares for sale, and as carefully guards her profits as she does the corn laid away sacredly against a bad year when no crops are gathered.

Through Pueblo commerce in times past her fame as a cook went far and near, and the tribes out on the plains eagerly

A NAVAHO INDIAN SQUAW.
DRAWN BY NORMAN H. HARDY.

Facing on page 452

traded for her breadstuffs, and sometimes they would even journey to the Pueblos to taste of delicacies fresh from the baking slab or underground oven.

there is a bunch of them, showing their vitality by luring into them separate linguistic stocks. In pre-Columbian days the lure was still more potent, drawing hundreds

Photograph by C. C. Pierce, Los Angeles.

CHEMEHUEVI INDIAN SQUAW WITH HER PAPOOSE.

of Athapascans from the north, the Apache and the Navaho, to continue their wild Canadian life here.

Man's Use, "To fetch and carry" for Woman.

The ultimate use of man there is to fetch and carry for woman, because in the constitution of society he is the chief person served by so doing, call his motive selfish or self-preservational, as you like. The community life is above all, and the individual sinks out of sight in the village and whole people. This instinct of social self-preservation has shown itself in the clan systems of each area, and after separate fashions in all. There were in this arid region genuine oases, and the social life organised itself around them. On the upper Rio Grande

Burial Customs.

Mrs. Stevenson, in the report beforementioned, gives the mortuary customs of the Zuñi, a few of which are here stated. The dead are buried—not burned. The body is placed with its head to the east, bathed in *yucca* suds, rubbed with corn meal, and dressed in the best. A gash is cut in each garment for the escape of the spirit. The body is next wrapped in blankets and buried soon after. A death is announced by the women to the clans. The mourners are also women, who during the preparation "set up a hideous howl," which continues with slight intermissions until after the burial. In the cemetery women are buried on the north side just as they sat in the living-room.

A Loitering Ghost.

After a burial the body of the surviving spouse is bathed by female relatives. The planting of plumes and drinking warm water as an emetic for purification follow. The ghost of the dead is thought to hover about the village, and on the fifth morning to start on its journey to the judgment seat of the gods. During its stay in the village the door and hatchway of the Pueblo must be left open night and day, or the ghost will be troublesome. Mrs. Stevenson tells of a woman sword-swallower whose spirit so haunted the family that she had to be smoked out. During the four nights of the spirit's remaining, parents or sisters of the deceased sleep at the side of the spouse. A grain of black corn and a bit of charcoal are put under the head of the mourner to prevent dreams of the lost one.

When a wife belonging to the Ant fraternity dies, the survivor goes with others southward to an ant-hill, and, facing west, sprinkles prayer meal. The spirit is fed daily with meal thrown into the fire, and on the fifth morning different foods are cast therein for its use on going to the underworld. Much grief is shown for the dead.

The Power of the Pueblo Woman.

The graces of the Pueblo woman are docility, modesty, sweetness, and fortitude. Strength of character is behind her softer qualities, and her great love for her offspring does not make her foolishly neglectful of their training and education. Her silent power is that of a hidden ruler —the council may sit, but she does much to mould their deliberations, and they reckon ill who leave her out. She is a devoted wife, but her spouse must be on good behaviour, or as judge and executioner she thrusts him from her dwelling.

Characteristics of Pueblo Women.

She loves gossip, is sometimes garrulous, and occasionally, according to report, oppresses her husband; and her rights are not allowed to slumber when the necessity comes to assert them. Nowhere else, however, are found fewer of the asperities of life than among the Pueblos.

In contrast with the gentler side of the Pueblo woman, it seems strange that there should be exhibited at times extreme effrontery, and actions that fill the beholder with astonishment. During some of the winter ceremonies, staid matrons and erstwhile shrinking maidens enact parts that, according to civilised standards, are the reverse of dignified; in fact, a saturnalia as of classic times appears to reign. Paradoxical as it may seem, the women are none the less modest—actions that seem unbefitting are merely in conformity with the demands of a religion that frankly and without false notions looks with veneration upon the welling forth of new life and its varied phenomena.

Woman as Heroine.

There is little in the surroundings of the Pueblos to elicit feminine heroism, so that a historian would only chronicle the simple heroics of starvation and disease instead of the glamour of combat and great deeds. Yet if one could reconstruct the history of this people he would find in the movements of villages from one water to another, in the periodical visits of grim want and sickness, tales of sublime heroism and primitive fortitude, in which Pueblo womanhood shone with brilliant lustre. There is a pictograph on the cliff under the high town of Walpi, which records the heroic act of a Hopi woman, who, aided by a faithful dog, beat off some Navaho who sought to seize her while she was guarding the fields. Other examples might be given, though these are necessarily rare, because the Pueblo woman is a home body, and is not accustomed to wander far from the village without escort.

Photograph by C. C. Pierce, Los Angeles.

A WALLAPAI (OR HUALAPAI) INDIAN GIRL

Wearing the civilised dress supplied to the pupils of the Government schools. She has a basket of native manufacture.

In one great field of social intercourse the Pueblo women never attained pre-eminence. In matters religious they defer women have some parts in every ceremony, and even have a few which are their particular province, and these are appropriately

Photograph by C. C. Pierce, Los Angeles

A PIMA INDIAN BASKET-MAKER OF ARIZONA.

to the men, who from their mobility and freedom from small cares had doubtless more time to think on questions of origin and destiny, and ways to cajole the beings of the other world. Most of the complex Pueblo ceremonials are man-made and man-controlled, though the burden they entail on the women is tremendous, since on them falls the brunt of extra preparations for the feastings which accompany religious rites, and the withdrawal of the services of the men for long periods. Yet the harvest festivals. Beyond this they are represented in the pantheon by beings of the first importance, such as the goddess of germs, the corn-maidens, the spider woman, culture heroine, the dawn woman, and other divinities of the Hopi and Zuñi.

Pueblo Religious Influence on Woman.

This is in accordance with the fact that the duality of nature and the origin of life have made a profound impression in Pueblo mythology, and woman in the scheme takes the high rank that is a reflection of her earthly position.

The religious life of the desert women has evoked a charming literature, written by Bandelier, Cushing, Fewkes, Matthews, and Mrs. Stevenson. It must be picked out from the general accounts of these writers. In his introduction to Cushing's "Zuñi Tales," Powell sets forth the rationale of this religion. The gods of the Zuñi, as of all other tribes, are animals. "All entities are animals—men, brutes, plants, stars, lands, waters, and rocks—and all have souls. The souls are tenuous existences — mist entities, gaseous creatures inhabiting firmer bodies of matter. They are ghosts that own bodies, which they can leave and take possession of bodies that can be vacated. Force and mind belong to souls; fixed form, firm existence belong to matter, while bodies and souls constitute the world. The world is a universe of animals. The stars are animals compelled to travel around the world by magic. The plants are animals under a spell of enchantment, so that usually they cannot travel. The waters are animals, sometimes under the spell of enchantment. Lakes writhe in waves, the sea travels in circles about the earth, and the streams run over the lands. Mountains and hills tremble with pain, but cannot wander about; but rocks and hills and mountains sometimes travel about by night. These animals of the world come in a flood of generations, and the first-born are gods, called the 'ancients' or first ones; the later born generations are descendants of the gods, but alas, they are degenerate sons and daughters."

Pueblo Mythology.

Photograph by C. C. Pierce, Los Angeles.

MERCEDES NOLASQUEZ BASKET-MAKER.

The last story in the Cushing volume is that of "The maiden the sun made love to, and her boys." In the course of the narrative, the natural and the supernatural are intertwined. The maiden weaves the pretty wicker plaques, common in all collections, the little stems dyed in the colours of the corn. But the corn, in turn, owes its hues to spaces in the cosmos—yellow to the north-land, blue to the west-land, red to the south-land, white to the east, variegated to the zenith, black to the regions below. So, throughout the narrative, which sets forth in myth the origin of strife. "Perhaps had men been more grateful and wiser, the Sun-father had smiled and dropped everywhere the treasures we long for, and not hidden them

Zuñi Legends.

deep in the earth and buried them in the shores of the sea."

In the frontispiece of his Navaho Legends, figure 4, Matthews shows a *yébaad*, or goddess, as she is represented in the dry paintings. While the men's arms are painted white, the goddess has yellow arms in obedience to the universal colour scheme, above and below, which gives the yellow corn to woman.

Matthews says that celibacy is not practised by the Navaho gods; every deity has his mate, and she must also be propitiated. The correspondence of the sky-world with the mundane world is brought out by the same writer in the story of "The marriage of the Boy made of White Corn to the Ground-heat Girl, and the Mirage Boy to the Girl made of Yellow Corn." In the Navaho language personification of things resembles the classical languages, in applying feminine names to the finer, weaker, and more gentle—for example, the placid Rio Grande is Female Water, the turbulent San Juan is Male Water, a storm is male rain, a shower is feminine; mountain mahogany (cigarette wood) is male, the cliff rose is female.

Photograph by C. C. Pierce, Los Angeles.

AN OLD WALLAPAI (OR HUALAPAI) SQUAW OF ARIZONA.

V.—WOMEN OF THE PLAINS

Locality—Dwellings of the Plains—The Indian Cradle—Household Implements—Indian Methods of Transport—Indian Women and Decoration—Courtship and Marriage—Polygamy—Divorce—Strict Etiquette of Indians—Indian Childhood—Widows and Widowers—The Sugar Camp—Indian Games—Treatment of Aged Indians—Present Condition of Indians

Locality.

THE Plains women live chiefly in Assiniboia and in the United States west of the Mississippi River and north of the Arkansas. They were originally mainly Siouan, but the ample food supply also enticed Algonquian tribes, Pawnees, Kaiowas, and others to share with them in Nature's bounty.

Nature made fine women on the Plains—tall, robust, and strong. The prominent cheek-bones, Roman noses, and gross mouths of the men were much toned down in the females. Nature also gave them the buffalo and the dog; but the former absolutely withheld its aid from them, either to furnish a drop of milk or to carry a pound of their loads. The dog was more responsive, lending its back for the burden and its shoulders for the sledge.

Dwellings of the Plains.

The homes of the old Plains women were earth lodges, bark or mat lodges, and tents of skin, called usually teepees (tipis). The villages were so arranged that kindreds dwelt near one another.

The Omaha earth lodges were made by the women chiefly for summer use, when the people were not moving about. The roof was supported by two rows of vertical posts, forked at the top for cross pieces. The wall was formed by setting upright slabs behind the outer row of posts. They were not over six feet in height, their tops resting against the cross timbers. Stems of willow a few inches in diameter rested with their butts on the tops of the upright slabs and extended on the inner cross timbers nearly to the summit. These rafters were very close together and formed a cone. They were covered with grass a foot thick, and over the whole earth was piled from one to two feet in depth. A hole at the apex served for chimney, and in the earth at the centre was a depression for the fire. A covered way, 10 feet long and 5 feet wide, formed the hall way entrance, which was closed at its inner and outer end with two buffalo hides for doors, their inner edges overlapping. A notched log served as ladder or stairway. Earth lodges were generally used for feasts, councils, and dances, and were sometimes 75 and 100 feet in diameter.

The bark and mat lodges in which the Plains women were home-makers were elliptical in shape and little over seven feet in height. The poles were planted in opposite pairs, the small ends bent over and lashed together, the series forming wall posts and rafters, which were covered with mats or bark. They were used for summer residence by a number of tribes. There might be one or two fires and smoke-holes in each.

The tipi or skin tent, on the other hand, was the home of migrants and tribes in search of buffalo. It was a favourite abode in winter, also, as the earth lodges were erected in exposed places for summer comfort. Tipis could be pitched in the timber or down in wooded ravines, where the cold winds never had full sweep. The tipi was made of ten or a dozen dressed buffalo hides sewed together, the tanner and tent-maker putting no small skill and energy into her task. The tent was in the shape of a sugar loaf, 10 to 12 feet high, 10 to 15 feet at the bottom, and open a foot and a half at the top for the smoke. A shallow pit in the centre was for her fire, and a forked post alongside served for suspending the kettles. Around the fireplace was a circular space where the people sat on grass mats, or hides rolled up, toasted their shins, and chatted. Couches were arranged about this space, formed of two or three winter buffalo hides with the hair on, and the sleepers covered themselves with similar robes. Their pillows were of unhaired deer-skins stuffed with hair or feathers, and they served as seats also during the day. Behind the couches and next to the tent poles, the spaces served for closets, larders, presses, granaries, and a general "place for everything."

SYBIL CONGIN,
A Sioux Girl of Yankton, South Dakota.

The Indian Cradle.

The cradle was a board a yard long and a foot wide. No pillow or other coddling was allowed. A piece of soft skin covered with dense hair was fitted on the board, and upon this the infant was lashed. To the cradle was attached, just over the child's face, a stout bow of wood, to protect it if it should fall, to serve for the suspension of beads, and other pretty objects. There was a head band on the back of the board, indispensable for carrying or suspension.

Household Implements.

Among the furnishings of the lodgings the brooms must be included, both the stick broom for keeping the space around the front door tidy, and the goose or turkey wing or feather brush for dusting about the fireplace.

The mortars and pestles of the Plains women were of wood, and were used for pounding corn and dried meat. The mortars were small, hollowed at one end by burning, and sharpened at the other for driving in the earth.

Pottery was far from universal among the Plains women, but they had vessels, dishes, and spoons. Spoons were of horn, wood, shells, or pottery. Those of buffalo horn were the favourites, and were often ornamented.

Before the coming of the Whites, the hoe, rather than the axe, was woman's industrial implement on the Plains. It was made from the shoulder blade of the buffalo, which was bound with thongs to the end of a stick.

ROSA WHITE THUNDER,
A Sioux Girl.

The Plains woman made fire by means of the reciprocating drill, consisting of two pieces of soft wood or two stems of very coarse grass. It is done by those who know how in a few seconds. Flint and tinder were also employed by some tribes.

To help in transportation, the women of the Plains were familiar with carrying bands and staves. The "bull" boat was of buffalo hide, and very near to the most primitive. It was a bowl-shaped crate of willow stems, over which the hide was stretched, and it was used in crossing streams.

Indian Methods of Transport.

Over the prairies, where trains are flying at the rate of a mile a minute, freight and passengers were transported by women and dogs before the coming of the horse. Mrs. Eastman describes the travelling methods of a hundred years ago. The hunter with his weapons rode ahead. Next came the furniture waggon—two poles, about fifteen feet long, strapped to the horse's neck, the large ends resting on the ground. Saplings were lashed to the poles with rawhide thongs to support the baggage. The wife and mother jogs along behind with her burden, the larger children are enjoying themselves Indian fashion.

Indian Women and Decoration.

Women of the Plains had their arts of pleasure—play, gambling, feasting, and other diversions, of course. In the absence of clay for art pottery, fine textiles for pretty basketry, and the materials for choice hardware, necessity made them the most picturesque of savages through animal tissues. Whoever wore the gaudy raiment, it was woman's sphere to make it. There were hides of every size and hue, pilous and depilated, hoofs and horns of the buffalo, feathers of the eagle for war, bonnets trailing from crown to the feet, quills for matchless embroidery. These women were also good painters. Their colour scheme was quite varied, as shown by their curious trunks made by folding depilated rawhides together and tying them with thongs. In the museums of American ethnology, by far the most picturesque exhibits of North American Indians are the ornamental handicraft of the Plains tribes. There the monotonous sky and prairie called aloud for colour, and it appeared. The traders grasped this fact by instinct, and the many coloured beads were forthcoming.

Courtship and Marriage.

Coming now to the sociology of the Plains, we find that the ancient family guardianship of females was much disturbed after the discovery of America. A girl was the especial care of her elder brother and her mother's brother. A young girl or even a married woman would not walk or ride alone, and no woman would be seen abroad with any other man but her husband or some immediate kinsman. She generally got some other woman to accompany her, unless her husband went. Young men were forbidden to speak to girls, if they met two or more on the road, unless they were kindred. When girls went to the dances, their mothers accompanied them, and husbands went with their wives. After the dance the women were taken home.

A KAIOWA INDIAN WOMAN AND CHILD.
Showing form of cradle.

A man had to marry outside his blood relations. To facilitate matters the young men grew up with a knowledge of whom they must not marry, and hence they wasted no affections on their own kin. Indian girls marry earlier than formerly—between fifteen and seventeen, and even younger—when they waited till they were twenty. In some Plains tribes girls were betrothed from their infancy.

It is said that the men court the women, but everybody knows what that means. Mr. Catlin describes an ingenious flageolet used on the Upper Mississippi, and called the Winnebago courting flute, playing which the young men of that tribe meet with signal success in wooing their sweethearts. They blow the instrument for hours together, from the bank of a stream, some favourite rock or log, near to the wigwam that contains the object of their tender passion, until her soul is touched, and she responds by some welcome signal that she is ready to repay the young Orpheus for his pains with the gift of her heart.

The proposals were either directly or by proxy. Dorsey makes the quaint assertion that "women used to weigh the matter well, but now they hasten to marry any man they can get." Sometimes the girl told her kindred and took advice, but parents did not force their daughter to marry against her will. If she refused, they could not compel her. As was human, they might say, "Here is a good young man. We want you to marry him." Or they might scatter hints that they had a marriageable daughter. Then men would drop by to look at her and leave presents for the old people. If they thought the donor would not make a good alliance or a good husband, they returned the presents. Suitors curried favour with the old folks in this way, but parents did not sell their daughters. This was rather the fashion with old men, but with the young it was the old story—presents were given and taken *ad libitum*.

Polygamy. With regard to the question of polygamy, the maximum of wives was three, or at most four. They would be, for example, the first wife, her aunt, and her sister or niece, if all be consanguineous.

When a man wished to take a second

SPOTTED TAIL'S SQUAW,
A Brule Sioux.

wife, he would say to the first, "My dear, I do not want you to work so hard. I am thinking of taking your sister, your aunt, your niece to wife." Should the first wife veto the proposition, that would prevent his marrying the other woman. Generally, there was no objection if the two women were kindred. Indeed, the wife would sometimes make the first move, and say, "I wish you would marry my niece; we are kin." The first wife was never deposed. She always retained her right to manage affairs, controlling the distribution of food, and giving to the other wives what she thought they ought to receive. If one of the wives was active and a good hide-dresser, the husband would leave the others with the parents when he went on a long hunt and take the handy woman. Jealous women played their *rôle* here as elsewhere, making life a burden to both husband and their female colleagues.

Divorce. Among the Santees, says Dorsey, a wife's mother could take her from her husband and give her to another man. Among other Plains tribes, if the man was kind, the dreadful mother-in-law never interfered. But if he became unkind, the wife herself would say, "I have had you long enough—begone!" Or the father or elder brother would suggest to the husband, "You have made her suffer; you shall have her no longer." If she married him in spite of warnings, they punished her by making her live with him. There seems to have been no need for divorce-suits and expensive proceedings. When parents separated, law—or rather custom—had a provision in every case. The children might be taken by the mother, by her mother, or by the father's mother. The husband might lay claim to them, in which case she had no redress. Each consort might re-marry, though the parties were not always delighted to hear of each other's re-marriage.

Strict Etiquette of Indians. Etiquette was dreadfully exacting between the sexes among the primitive folk of the Plains. A man did not speak to his mother-in-law except under the direst necessity. He went a step farther and avoided his wife's grandmother—indeed, in the good old days he "cut" both her parents and grandparents. The right way to converse with either of them was by requesting his wife or child to procure the desired information—the reply would flow back through the same channel. A woman would not speak to her husband's father in the presence of the family, and she never passed in front of her daughter's husband. Just a remnant of this survives here and there in the country. If a man were visiting

CROW INDIANS: BEAR-WOLF AND HIS SQUAW, SE-TA-PIT-SE, OF SIOUAN FAMILY

his wife during her stay at her father's, his mother-in-law presented food to him through his wife; in the absence of the daughter, the old lady set it on the ground and retired to give him a chance to eat it.

Men helped women and children to alight from horses, and carried them over streams on their backs, when there was one to ford.

Indian Childhood.

With regard to maternity, Dorsey gives the women of the Plains a good name. The Sioux are fond of children, and sometimes the husband treats the girl infant better than the boy. Large families were, however, the exception; the death-rate was large, and in many cases couples had no children at all. For reasons elsewhere stated, weaning was greatly prolonged among these Indians; cases of the same mother suckling two children were not rare. The little girls were dressed from the first more than the boys. They were in subjection to the mother, whom they helped in her work. At five the girl could go for wood or water; at eight she was taught to make up a pack and fit it to her back; if she were unruly, the mother's hand was ready and versatile in little punishments. As she grew older she cut wood, cultivated corn, and graduated as a young woman. At six the method of dressing the hair was changed. The women did their apportioned tasks willingly, men joined women at their work when it was necessary, and there was always redress in the clan, if one of them was oppressed.

Widows and Widowers.

A widow remained single four to seven years, and if she broke the custom she was likely to be punished. After forty they did not re-marry. If a stepmother should be cruel, the husband might separate from his wife, or some of the children's kindred would take charge of them. A widower also waited several years, and his dead wife's kindred would take his ponies from him if he married too soon. On the other hand, a man who had loved his wife dearly would remain single so long that some of her female kindred would say, "Poor fellow, he has no one to sew his moccasin; let's hunt him out a wife among us." No sooner said than done, and he would be induced to marry again. The student of similarities in culture will find here an excellent example of independent origins.

The Sugar Camp.

The sugar camp of the North-West was woman's enterprise. It was a strenuous season—cutting wood, collecting sap in birch bark vessels of their own handiwork, boiling sap in kettles in later times, straining it through their blankets, and putting the sugar away in other birch baskets, kept the women busy. Indians all loved sugar—men, women, and children; and they got plump from eating it.

CHEYENNE SQUAWS.

No account of the women among any tribe of North American Indians is complete without a study of their games. Walker gives the shinney, foot bones, dice, and bowls for the Teton Sioux. The shinney of the women is every whit as lively as that of the men. It is played with a skin-covered ball or one of wood and with the well-known hockey sticks, straight in the shaft, crooked at the lower and larger end, and long enough to allow the player to strike on the ground with it while standing erect. The game was played between two goals by two parties or sides, equally divided. Each goal was bounded by two stakes set 50 to 100 feet apart, and the goals themselves were from 300 yards to a mile apart. The players arranged themselves in two lines about half-way between the goals, those on one side on one line, and each facing its own goal, the lines being thirty feet apart. After the ball was placed on the ground, at a given signal each side attempted to put the ball across its goal. The side that accomplished this won.

Indian Games.

The Teton women play a gambling game that even men and boys like to play for fun. It is similar to our cup and ball, and called "game with foot bones," because the objects caught are the astragali of deer or antelope, cut into hollow cones to fit on one another. They are pierced on the apex and strung, four to six in a set. The borders are also pierced and loops tied on the outer end of the joining thongs, at the other end of which is the pointed bone on which the cups are caught. The game is played by any number of women sitting, and consists in catching the cones one by one on the end of the bone or in thrusting its point through a loop in the end of the thong or through one of the holes in the border of a cup.

Teton old women also play dice, at which they sometimes become inveterate gamblers. The dice are made of plum-stones, one side plain, the other carved with figures or marks, which count whatever is agreed on. Six constitute a set. They are shuffled in and thrown from a shallow wicker basket of willow. The tally sticks are rods of wood, about a hundred in a set. The game is played by women in pairs on opposing sides, who throw in turn all the dice from the basket and draw as many counters as they are entitled to. When these are all taken the game is finished, and the side that has the greater number of sticks wins.

Girls play with the horned javelin, dolls, and toy tipis. A wooden javelin is tipped with elk-horn and slid on the snow or ice. The one whose javelin goes farthest wins the game.

The Teton maidens are just like all other girls in their love for dolls. They may be made of wood or buck-skin stuffed, much is left for imagination, but they are correct in detail of male and female attire and accoutrements. They tuck them into regular models of baby carriers and bear them on their backs like the mothers. Finally, the girls play house and take on matronly cares in miniature tipis, or skin tents, from a few inches in height to examples large enough for a well-grown girl to enter.

Some writers speak of the abandonment of old women on the prairie, but when the Omahas and Poncas went on their long hunts they left the aged woman at home, provided her with shelter, food, water, and fuel; set her to watch the cornfields, and in winter placed a home for her near the village.

Treatment of Aged Indians.

There are many thousands of Indians in this area, offspring of white men and Indian women. They are in every walk of life, some of them adorning the learned professions. A visit to one of the Government schools is the best witness of this. It is charming to hear the class prophets laying down the future prospects, all of which are bare of wildness and ring with progress.

Present Condition of Indians.

Photograph supplied by M. L. Bradford, Avery Island, La.

OLD CLARA DARDEN, OF THE CHETIMACHA INDIANS OF LOUISIANA.

At work splitting the reed cane, of which she makes most beautiful baskets.

VI.—THE EASTERN AREA

Woman's Important Position—Chetimacha Basket-work—An Indian Educational Difficulty

IF this work were concerned with the women of America as they were in the pre-European days, there would be no more important chapter in the whole work than that on the Iroquois, who, with the more numerous Algonquins, the Muscogees, and other stocks, inhabited this part of America.

Woman's Important Position.

Among the Iroquois the supremacy of woman was far more than a mere phrase; she enjoyed the right of sending mere man upon the warpath whenever she pleased, and at her behest he had to stay at home, however bellicose he might feel. Among the Wyandots the tribal council was composed of four women to one man, and if among the Oneidas the men were actually the councillors, they had to consult woman as to their plans, at least in theory; but Charlevoix tells us that the men rarely told the women anything which needed to be kept secret, and seldom communicated to them any matter of consequence, though all was done in their name. It has, in fact, been said of the tribes east of the Mississippi that among them women constituted the tribe, transmitted the nobility of blood, kept up the genealogical tree and order of inheritance, and perpetuated the family. They possessed all actual authority, owned the land, and the fields and their harvests; they were the soul of all councils, the arbiters of peace and war; they had the care of the public treasury; slaves were given to them; they arranged marriages; the children belonged to them, and to their blood was confined the line of descent and the order of inheritance. The men, on the other hand, were wholly isolated and restricted to their personal affairs; their children were strangers to them, and when they died everything came to an end, as it was only the women who could keep up and perpetuate the family. If there were only men in a household, no matter in what number or how many children they might have, it was doomed; and although by courtesy they were made chiefs, and public business was transacted by a council of old men, yet they acted merely as representatives of the woman and to aid her in those affairs in which it was not becoming for her to appear and act for herself.

But of course this picture does not apply to the present day. The tribes are many of them extinct; others are represented by only a remnant; and though the Iroquois stock is still relatively strong and not yet converted to Christianity in many cases, a picture of their life to-day bears no resemblance to that of the old tribal life.

In other tribes the survivors are fewer, and as an example we may take one of the southern area.

Chetimacha Basket-work.

The illustration on p. 466 is of a Chetimacha Indian woman, Clara Darden, engaged upon her work of basket-making, which is a survival of the ancient double weave. The inside basket has been finished, while the long ends of cane are to complete the outer one. In the early days of Louisiana this group was an independent linguistic family in the Mississippi River delta. In recognition of their services to the colonists, France and Spain granted to them a large tract of land on the Bayou Teche, surrounding one of their villages where the tribe had dwelt from time immemorial. The United States confirmed the grant to them in the Treaty of Paris. When Mrs. Sidney Bradford, of Avery Island, La., began her work among them, she found only one woman—old Clara Darden—who could make a perfect basket. Many of the older women had learned when young, but, having no sale, they had ceased to make them for many years. Mrs. Bradford found that in all the tribe there was only one who could read and write, Christine Paul, the daughter-in-law of old Chief Joken Paul (since dead), and his son Benjamin Paul, now chief. The little thin woman had been taught in the convent when she was a child. Prizes were offered for perfect baskets, and Mrs. F. N. Doubleday gave the first. Soon Clara Darden had gathered about her all the women and young girls; she taught them what kinds of reed cane to gather, how to split and cure them, what roots were needed for the red, black, and yellow dyes, how to stain the canes, and last, but not least, how to weave the beautiful baskets, with their

Photograph by Park & Co., 72, Colborne Street, Brantford, Ontario.

AN INDIAN GRANDMOTHER.

Photograph supplied by Miss Cora M. Folson, Hampton Institute, Va.

ADELE QUINNEY,
Stockbridge Indian girl.

many wonderful patterns. She taught the names and meanings of the patterns and of the roots for the dyes. Now the basket-making is quite an industry among them. There have been sold several thousand dollars' worth for them, and they owe it all to the teaching of old Clara Darden, who is now nearly a hundred years old, with only one eye and one tooth—and they split their cane, or rather peel off the outer part, of which they weave their baskets, with the teeth. When asked how she could do this with one tooth, old Clara said, "Oh, my gums are hard now." And without Christine Paul they could never have sold their baskets, for she is the only one who can write, and she offers her mite of learning for the service of all. She measures and marks the prices on the baskets, and writes the letters to Mrs. Bradford and her sister, who in turn send the cheques to Christine, and she pays them all.

An Indian Educational Difficulty. The Chetimachas are without education, as the white people would not allow the Indian children to attend their schools, and the Indians would not send their children to negro schools. As an illustration of their helplessness without education, several years ago they were in great trouble about their lands. A white man claimed to have paid taxes on parts of them, and wished to seize them. Christine was ill in bed, her eyes were sore, so she could not see to write, and there was no one else to write to Mrs. Bradford. So the chief, with the six head men of the tribe, came about forty miles to tell her their troubles and ask for help.

VII.—TROPICAL WOMEN

Locality and Environment—Central American Tribes—Position of Primitive Women—The Food Question—The Importance of Maize—Primitive Intoxicants—Dress—Typical Houses—House Furnishings—A Curious Bath—Indian Weaving—Pottery—Indian Method of Travel—Indian Trade—Indian Women as Artists—Woman and Indian Architecture—Indian Music—Mother-right—Position of Primitive Woman—Marriage—How Children were Named—The Aztecs—A Mexican Tradition—Religion

THE tropical environment of North America furnished to women a new set of problems to solve. To them were committed the Caribbean Sea, with its numerous islands, and Middle America, beginning at the north with the Tropic of Cancer, and including the celebrated culture areas of the Valley of Mexico and the peninsula of Yucatan. The Aztecs of Mexico were far embracing and inclusive; the Maya, of Yucatan and Guatemala, strangely exclusive and refined. These two were the Romans and the Greeks of the Western world. This narrowing strip of land extends to Panama, the gateway of another continent and of new harmonies between women and Nature.

Locality and Environment.

Cosmic characteristics were at play there that had great influence in the moulding of woman. The days and nights were equal the year round; there was no lamp needed to give light or heat, or to demand the care of women. In all accessible places no ice or frost or snow demanded so cramped and exacting a home as in the Arctic, but abundance—superabundance—of rain fell, making the low places and coasts not only *tierras calientes*, but *pestilentes*. Navigable waters were almost wanting in and about the Isthmus, while the Antilles were the home of the canoe. One associates women with water craft almost everywhere in the north save in the Isthmian tribes, and the southwest. On the mainland there were the choicest obsidian and other materials for domestic utensils to wait on women and sharpen their wits, as well as good friable stones for materials, and tough stones for tools—civilisers of men—in developing architecture and sculpture. These were also the necessary aids of millers and cooks, who were women. Clay also obtruded itself into woman's life and made the potter, the *adobe* worker, and the cook. It associates itself through her with springs and water-courses, the location of the home, the trails among the hills, the *cenotes* or underground springs, and the higher thoughts of art and religion.

Animal life was not specially favourable to woman's exaltation. The Antilles offered marine food, but the getting and serving of this was not quickening to their wits. The western half of the area gave flesh for food, together with feathers and fleece for textile art; but it had not a domesticable animal to help women to bear a burden, to draw a load, or offer a drop of milk to prolong the life of infancy. The corresponding region in South America was the Peruvian highlands, which produced the Auchenias, capable of carrying weights of fifty pounds and yielding one of the finest textile staples in the world. The effect of this absence upon woman's life will be seen later on.

But the vegetable kingdom was more helpful to the sex, with its nutritious, sheltering, and textile plants, in great variety, and of fine quality. In the tropical climate it was never out of service, ennobling and stimulating women and yielding its fruits every month. One of the most interesting facts in woman's culture here, as elsewhere, is the thorough way in which she has

Photograph by Pittier.

A NICOYA INDIAN GIRL; COSTA RICA
Sitting outside a Palm-leaf House.

employed every useful root, stem, and leaf, flower, fruit, and seed, seeking aid or tracking enemies. It is quite in harmony with other areas that the women here, walking in the trails of greatest economy, had accomplished this thorough exploitation of the vegetable world.

Central American Tribes.

Summing up the "pros" and "cons" of resources, the result was a rather small race of women, but possessing a fair amount of beauty and vigour. There is no way of knowing their productiveness or average longevity. In the Archipelago were the native Arawakan Indians and the intruding, fierce Caribs, who had also found their way into coastal portions of Central America. Other families of Southern Mexico and Central America had their lines fall in pleasant places, and they had a goodly heritage, not the least of which were food and drink and salubrious air. These were the progressive areas, if such a term may be allowed; while others were decidedly regressive, making their women retrogressive.

Twenty-three linguistic families were spread about this tropical North American region :—1. Arawakan (Great Antilles); 2. Caribbean (Caribbean Sea); 3. Chiapanecan (Chiapas); 4. Chibchan (Costa Rica); 5. Chinantecan (Oaxaca); 6. Cunan (Panama); 7. Doraskean (Panama); 8. Huavean (Tehuantepec); 9. Leucan (Guatemala, Honduras, San Salvador, Nicaragua); 10. Matagalpan (Nicaragua); 11. Mayan (Guatemala); 12. Nahuatlan (General); 13. Otomian (Central Mexico); 14. Payan (Honduras); 15. Negrandaro (Nicaragua); 16. Tarascan (Michoacan); 17. Chontalan (Oaxaca); 18. Totonacan (Vera Cruz and Puebla); 19. Ulvan (Nicaragua); 20. Xicaquean (Honduras); 21. Xincan (Guatemala); 22. Zapotec-Mixtecan (Oaxaca); 23. Zoquean (Tabasco).

Of these some are extinct, others have dwindled; and the picture presented in the following pages is often rather of what was than of what is.

Not all of them were of great importance. Nos. 4, 11, 12, 18, and 22 have been the best known in history. The perpetual mystery will be the source of so many peoples and tongues that can understand scarcely a word of one another's speech. The same confusion obtains all up the Pacific Coast as far as Mt. St. Elias.

Quite as puzzling as the languages has been the question of advancement. Among the twenty-three peoples some were at the acme of American civilisation; others almost at its lowest ebb. It must not be forgotten, however, that these phenomena were for good and sufficient reasons, which must be sought out, if they have not been destroyed.

Position of Primitive Women.

Authors who have written about these women, both those of the time of the discovery of America and of more recent periods, have not agreed in marking their grade in advancement. With the more enthusiastic writers, the Aztecs and Mayas were civilised, with others they were savages, possessing not one excellence or virtue worthy of preservation. Neither extreme is correct regarding their rank. Their speech was still agglutinative. Their industries were yet dependent upon hand skill; the spindle and the drill were revolving tools only, without machine bearings. Fine art was greatly advanced, but still barbarous in motives and methods. Social structures were rising out of savagery, but not emancipated. Their explanations of Nature were childish. Religion was exalted fetishism.

The different effects of varied environments within a narrow compass are shown here in the appearance of the women generally. One people show woman delicate in form and graceful, with handsome features. The Zapotec women, "though of small stature and bizarre in their carriage, are truly graceful and seductive." Other tribes are spoken of as remarkably ugly. The Aztec and the Maya women are not alike in appearance, and their artists note the fact. One questions whether the quite different national motives could not have made the difference mentioned through unconscious selection from two quite diverse ideals of perfection.

In this environment was on exhibition the whole range of woman's share in American culture. The great variety of surface, soil, and climate, for her physical, industrial, intellectual, and moral uplifting or degradation, had as its fruit a wide range of cultural results. In the best associations of conditions were the Aztec and Maya groups, and the worst products were dwellers in caves—types of lowest savagery. It is an inexhaustible field of research, a little world by itself. Some of the languages were widely spoken; others restricted to narrow boundaries. The same is true of the arts. From north to south, North America is a cumulative poem, in which the last verse contains all the rest and more besides.

The Food Question.

The very first question in culture is that of food. Where there was abundance of food, in sufficient variety, and of good quality, there was progress; but everywhere in the Isthmian portion the lack of good meat told on the stature and, it is feared, encouraged cannibalism.

Maize, beans, tomatoes, and peppers mixed with a variety of things, were the staple foods. Then there were some excellent fruits, among them the banana, which was cooked or eaten raw. The giant cactus bore a delicious edible fruit—*pitahaya;* they also ate the blossom and made bread from the seeds. Genius was stimulated by the thorny stem and covering to invent a gathering apparatus somewhat like the English apple picker.

The Otomi women in the west did little cultivation, consumed the grain before it ripened, and trusted to game—rabbits, deer, moles, and birds, also foxes, rats, snakes, and other reptiles—to help them out. They made a dish of ground corn cobs and *cacas* and baked it. About the Valley of Mexico flies' eggs were pounded, moulded into lumps and fried. They were esteemed a delicacy.

Photograph by C. B. Waite, Mexico.

MAKING TORTILLAS (MAIZE CAKES) IN MEXICO.

Other tribes cultivated the soil and lived almost wholly on artificial industries. They planted corn with digging sticks. They hunted bees, stopped the entrance of the log where the insects worked with clay, and carried the hive to their homes. After a short time they removed the clay, and the bees were domesticated.

Quite universal as food are the tortillas, or corn-cakes. The tough outer skin is removed by soaking the grains of maize for a night in weak lime-water. The product is then mashed or ground on a metate. From the paste the tortilla is formed by patting it into a thin cake and cooking it on a slab or in an earthen pan. The tortilla is eaten with boiled beans and a mixture

Photograph by C. B. Waite, Mexico.

A STREET BAKERY, MEXICO.

throughout our continent and survive among the Pueblo Indians) it is to the fostering care, forethought, and labour of countless generations of women, the 'Corn Maidens and Mothers,' that America owes the priceless legacy of a food plant which has already sustained untold millions of lives. While the ancient 'Daughters of the Earth' have given to their country a gift which will last for all time, the pyramids, temples, and cities reared by the 'Sons of Heaven' have fallen into ruin, and their complex organisation, government, and calendar now lie superseded under the dust of time." It would not be unreasonable to imagine that, in pre-Columbian times, Mexican women observed the maize plant beckoning to them, and plucked the little ears for food. They selected the very best each season for the gods, and at the proper time committed the grains to the earth with imposing prayers and ceremonies. The modern Burbanks were thus anticipated by centuries.

of chile and fat. The soaked corn is also roasted and made into gruel, in which *cacao* and sugar are mixed. *Tamales* are chopped meat, peppers, and onions, covered with corn paste, the whole enveloped in corn husks or plantain leaves, and boiled or baked.

The Importance of Maize.

The most far-reaching of woman's industries in Mexico are associated with maize. Mrs. Nuttall calls attention to its cultivation in the valley from remote antiquity. The name *Flaxcalla* means " bread," and its hieroglyphic symbol is two hands holding a tortilla, or maize cake. This plant has not been identified with any native grass, and the development must have been slow. It is interesting, says Mrs. Nuttall, " to reflect that (as clearly shown by ceremonial usages which existed

Primitive Intoxicants.

In this area, going southward, one encounters for the first time intoxicating beverages. Tobacco and a few other plants were smoked at the north. But fermentation and, some say, primitive distillation, appear in this environment. An intoxicating drink was from the fruit of the *nopal* or prickly pear (*opuntia*), which was first peeled and pressed. The juice was then passed through straw sieves and placed by a fire or in the sun, where it fermented.

Chicha is made from raw sugar-cane, mashed with a wooden mallet and passed through a press. *Pulque* is a well-known drink, made from the *Agave Americana.* When the plant is about to bloom the heart or stalk is cut out, leaving a cavity in the centre, which is covered with the outer leaves. Every day the cavity fills once or twice with the sap, which is taken out by sucking it into a long gourd and pouring it into a skin receptacle. The sap is mixed with some already fermented *pulque* and the process continued. The liquor is very intoxicating, and leaves its impress on the hardened faces of many women.

In Payne's "History of America" the invention of intoxicants is laid at the door of agriculture. "The use of corn, of all descriptions, for this purpose is of scarcely less antiquity than its general use as food; and from our knowledge of the tastes of savages it may be fairly inferred that the practice received a powerful stimulus from the discovery that infusions of corn, like drinks made from the juices of fruits and the sap of trees, acquire an intoxicating quality from fermentation.

Dress.

From the varied environment dress differs greatly. Children in Tehuantepec and thereabout wear no clothing. Women have modified their costume much under Spanish influence. In Tehuantepec it is a skirt of cotton or wool reaching to the ankles, often elaborately embroidered in various designs and colours; the ***huipil,*** a chemisette, with short sleeves, often adorned with lace and threads of gold and silk; and a white cotton head covering, drawn on like a sack and hanging down the back. In Tabasco the cotton petticoat, with a few yards of calico about the waist, or a sleeve frock, is the dress. Essentially these garments make up the clothing of southern Mexican women.

The women of Guatemala, Salvador, and Nicaragua, when at home, wear the waist

Photograph by C. B. Waite, Mexico.

A STREET BREAKFAST IN MEXICO.

cloth, generally blue checked, secured by a twisted knot. On going abroad they put on the *huipil,* a piece of white cotton, having a long slit in the middle for the head, and covering the breast and back as far as the waist. The women manufacture and dye all the clothing, and expend their best efforts upon their outer garments. They embroider or dye the neck and shoulders with tasteful colours and designs. These are distinct for each village, so that it may at once be seen to which tribe the wearer belongs. Indeed, on festive occasions the women are extravagantly fond of gaudy dress and flowers.

In southern Mexico, both sexes wear the hair long, parted in the middle, and hung in loose tresses over the shoulders, or looped up on the back of the head. On festive occasions they wear flowers in the hair and phosphorescent beetles. Feather tufts and skins of green birds are used as ornaments, as well as necklaces of gold nuggets, and amber beads. Formerly noses and ears were pierced for plugs of stone, wood, or amber, and rings of gold. The face was also painted and stained.

Photograph by C. B. Waite, Mexico

A LEMONADE STAND IN OAXACA, MEXICO.

In the southern Mexican States, earthquakes, as well as hot suns and most abundant materials, gave lessons in home building for women. A framework of branches in a double row was filled in with earth, or wattled cane-work was plastered with clay. There were no windows, and the roofs were thatched with palmetto. The interior was divided into compartments after the manner of the North-West coast houses. The wilder tribes dwelt in caves, the Tzendals, of Chiapas, painted their houses, and the Ahualulcos lived in communities in commodious houses of cane.

Tropical Houses.

The dwellings of the central Mexican wild tribes varied with climate and locality. In the lowlands they were sheds consisting of poles stuck in the ground, the spaces between woven with rushes and the roof thatched with palm leaves. In the highlands women had more substantial homes. Trunks of trees were tied together with creeping vines, the walls plastered with clay, the roof made of split slabs kept in place with stones. In treeless areas the houses were of sun-dried bricks or stones, and the interior walls hung with mats. The best of them were one storey high, and the humbler one would scarcely allow the mistress to stand erect in it. The entire home was one room, in which all the family lived. Furniture was lacking, the inmates were born, sat, slept, and at last died on the bare ground. A few stone slabs in the middle of the floor served for cooking range. In Vera Cruz there was a separate small hut for a kitchen.

The Chichimecs (barbarous hordes) lived in caves situated in precipitous valleys, while the Pames, a branch of them, contented themselves with the shade of the forest trees.

Modern Mitla, jewel of ancient architecture, is now a village chiefly of thatched houses on frames of poles and canes, obscured by clusters of trees and cactus fences. It is located at the lower limit of water supply in the dry season. In the wet season the flow extends into the lower valley; but in winter it barely suffices to supply the village with water for domestic purposes and for stock. The antiquities of Mitla are its great attraction, but it must not be overlooked that the guardians of the spring had a voice, as elsewhere, in choosing the site. The women were the practical exploiters of home sites, and consequently of temple sites, and it has already been mentioned that the mosaic patterns in the stone are to be seen in countless varieties in the textile productions.

House Furnishings.

The furniture of the humble dwelling was as forlorn as the structure itself, but the utensils were sufficient for woman's demands. The indispensable piece was the *metate*, an oblong volcanic stone about 12 by 18 inches, smooth on the upper surface and resting in a slanting position on three legs cut out of the same piece. Some of them were beautifully carved. With this was the *metlapilli*, or muller, and a large earthen pan, the *comalli*, in which to cook the tortillas. Their dishes and vessels were of calabash fruit, gourds, or pottery, some of which were tastefully decorated. A block of wood for stool or table, and palm leaf mats for beds, completed the household and kitchen furniture.

A Curious Bath.

For artificial heat the people of Queretaro, when basking in the sun does not yield sufficient warmth, scoop out a hole in the ground, burn in it branches and leaves of the *maguey*, and when the pit is sufficiently heated, lay themselves down in it and cover themselves with a mat or the loose earth. This scarcely allies itself with the ceremonial sweat-house, chiefly belonging to men. The *temazcalli*, or sweat-bath. was used in cases of severe illness. The bath-house stood close to a spring, and was built like a bake oven. When heated the fire was withdrawn, water thrown in, and the naked patient thrust in feet foremost on a mat. The breathing hole was about 18 inches square. When sufficiently steamed, the body was beaten with rushes. A cold water bath and brisk rubbing completed the operation.

Indian Weaving.

Weaving in its native simplicity furnished one of the best examples of the tropical Indian woman stepping into the domain of invention. The woman's muscles are at their best—fingers, hands, arms, back, lips, and mouth play their parts, assisted by bobbins, spindles, fly-wheels, stone and shell knives, yarn beams, dye pots, cloth beams, shuttles, batten swords, harness, tension, appliances, all of the most primitive sort. The woman's hands and mouth prepare the hair, wool, or agave fibre; the fingers twist the yarn or spin it with a simple spindle, of which the fly-wheels are pretty whorls of pottery ornamented. The distaff has hardly been born, the fibre being simply bunched together. The cotton warp is wrapped around two coarse sticks—by courtesy they may be called beams—at the proper distance for the garment, or utensil to be made, for cloth in the piece had not been invented when this loom came into existence. By a martingale, one beam is attached to a tree or any other convenient support, and by means of breeching or a breech strap the inner or cloth-beam is harnessed to the woman's body. This gives her perfect control over her tension, and makes the process of weaving rhythmic. The warp is nearly horizontal and the harness is exceedingly simple for shifting it. The woman lays a rod across the threads and wraps another thread about it in a spiral so as to pass between warps and enclose the under one each time. When the harness stick is lifted a shed is made by pulling the under warps to the top, the other shed results from the release of the cross-piece and letting the under warp drop into place. Each time a shed is made the batten sword is pushed between the two series and tilted on edge so as to allow the shuttle to pass through. As soon as the weft is passed and drawn taut, the tension apparatus (the woman's back) straightens up, the batten is laid flat and beats the weft home. The woman sits at her task or stands, and as her work is done she has it in her power to loosen the outer beam of her warp and keep her position, or she makes tucks in the finished piece at the cloth-beam.

Photograph by C. B. Waite, Mexico.

AT THE WELL.

In looking at a collection of these tropical textiles one is at once arrested at the sudden change from the fine basket-work of the United States to the ware of Central America and Mexico, both in materials and technique. In Jalisco the women wove the celebrated mantas and blankets, in other parts the cotton stuffs, on their hand looms. The designs were in stripes and dainty figures.

About Santa Cruz the fibres of the aloe, crushed on the *metate* and cleansed, are made into twine, nets, bags, and pelotas, used in rubbing down the body after the bath. Palm-leaf mats in different styles of weaving and qualities of texture enter largely into the industrial life.

Maya pottery may be traced by its Yucatec characters in the ceramic art of at least three of the United States on the Gulf coast. Earthenware obtained from the southern Maya ranks among the highest of its class in the world.

Photograph by C. B. Waite, Mexico.

FETCHING WATER.

Photograph by Pittier.

A KECCHI GIRL WITH WATER-VESSEL; SENAHU, GUATEMALA.

Pottery.

The art also flourished within the Aztec area. Holmes says that Teotihuacan furnished a greater variety of wares than any other district in America. A long period of occupation is represented, and vessels vary in treatment from the lowest limit of simplicity to the most elaborate phases of the native art. Dark plain ware, the simple red wares of the Aztecs, and fragments of vases beautiful in colour and design may be picked up in the same neighbourhood. The pottery, in its shapes and colours and embellishments, was the outlet of conceptions in technical processes, colour schemes, the use of the brush, detail and abbreviated symbolism and the imagery of religion.

The two areas of tropical North America differed in devices for transportation from natural causes. In its eastern portion there is such a repetition of insular South-Eastern Alaska that the stone collars of Porto Rico remind one of the Tlinkit regalia made of cedar bark. The large dug-out canoe was the vehicle of war and peace. The western side of the area was the land of the Cargadores, where the absence of safe and navigable waters made land travel necessary. Social conditions had advanced far enough to call for slavery, which in a way was woman's emancipation. The professional carrier had studied out the problem of load distribution over a human body to procure the greatest economy.

Indian Methods of Travel.

Transportation of the old kind was still on women's backs, and for them also was the trade of a local nature. The wider commerce and transportation were for men; but food materials and products, pottery, cordage from aloe and other fibre, woven fabrics, and ornamental work were its commodities, and they were woman's care.

Indian Trade.

Commerce had proceeded so far as to have standards of value. Indeed, a look at the finer work in basketry and embroidery in other areas shows the existence of shell and other money lower down the terraces of culture. Here woven garments, cacao beans, gold dust, and even human beings had fixed values. The most precious commodity of all, which hastened the progress of money standards, was woman. It did not enter into a man's mind on any other terms. Marriage was business. The things that women needed and used had often to be brought from afar. In the Arctic the soapstone of her lamp might travel a thousand miles, and in the tropic environment the same conditions obtained.

Indian Women as Artists.

The æsthetic activities of women found their expression in ornamental designs upon the products of their handiwork — weaving, pottery, gardening, and the making of garments. The possession of fine materials for textiles in their area gave them opportunities that they were not slow in grasping. The clay and calabash fruit opened the way to their freehand drawing and painting, while the weaving was their guide in mosaic designs. The result was the production of endless variety in the potter's art, and the manufacture of exquisite embroidery of vegetable and animal as well as geometric motives in their clothing and matting.

The author is indebted to Mrs. Zelia Nuttall for the following thoughts on ancient women's share in Mexican art: "They were undoubtedly very industrious, and it is to them that the development of the chief decorative arts is to be assigned. The women were the weavers and designers of the intricate patterns employed in the ceremonial *tilmatle* or blankets. Women are spoken of as skilled in painting these designs, and it may be reasonably inferred that female artists also painted the *Codices*. They were the potters, and painted the designs thereon. To this day native women artists decorate the lacquer ware made at Uruapan in Michoacan, a fact not generally known. I cannot divest myself of the thought that women designed the decorations on the ruins of Mitla. The effect is that of a sampler, and as women plaited the coloured *petates* or palm mats, the geometric designs of which seem copied in the stone panels, the suggestion of feminine agency seems to me to be very apparent."

To this very day skilful women produce world-famous laces and embroideries, and their fingers go on preserving the same old characteristic patterns; but masons no longer immortalise them in stone.

Woman and Indian Architecture.

Much has been written about the wonderful architecture and sculpture of this tropical North America. The Spaniards were accused of destroying a civilisation superior to their own. In fact, the Middle American culture epitomised all the stages of the continent along every line of artificiality. Women had their share in this, and it will be pleasing to inquire how. They were not stone-workers, but in many ways, while the German women of Cæsar's day were bringing food and cheer to their husbands, the Central American women were making it possible for the men to erect and adorn the wonderful temples and palaces of their land.

Men's labour culminated in architecture and sculpture. Content to dwell in tenements of reeds and mud. their most exalted efforts were given to the gods. In the fruits of their labours women shared also. With better foods the population increased, more food-stuffs were demanded than women could supply, and the industrial professions of men were organised. The love of decoration and embellishment took the place of drudgery in their minds. Little remains in the relics dug up to attest this, but their thoughts and imaginings survive until now. Out of men's minds the "pride of other days" has passed, but the thrill of art is still alive in the women.

Musical instruments of the tropical North Americans belonged to the rattle, drum, and whistle classes. The rattle, *ayacachtli*, might be of calabash, metal, noisy bodies hung together or notched sticks. There were membrane drums, *huehuetl*, and wooden drums, *teponaztli*. The former had a single head of skin, stretched by means of snares, and was played with the hands; the latter was of wood, often of immense size, having two parallel slits forming two tongues and often artistically carved. The tongues were beaten with sticks tipped with rubber balls. The whistles, which concern this narrative more directly, and the flageolets, were of pottery. They were modelled into all sorts of grotesque shapes, chiefly imitating animals, and painted. The art of making them at least was woman's, and much study has been given to the method of playing them, with the view of discovering what scale, if any, these Indians possessed.

Indian Music.

Photograph by C. B. Waite, Mexico.

INDIAN WOMAN WEAVING THE SERAPE IN MEXICO.

Sociology finds its lowest unit for women in kinship and those associations of the sexes that take the place of the family. It widens out to examine the infant civic life, with its varied industrial associations, and ends with the

Mother-right.

ceremonial and religious life. The largest social organisation was the tribe ; all notions of reading European political phraseology into tropical North America must be put aside. Bandelier states that the so-called Confederacy was only a partnership for war to increase the means of subsistence, and not for the extension of territory.

The existence and predominance of the kin system supposes the duty of marrying outside the clan. Bandelier says of the ancient Mexicans that they had advanced to descent in the male line and a nascent state of the modern family. But the kin feeling was so persistent that marriage was exacted for the purpose of increasing the

Photograph by C. B. Waite, Mexico.

MAKING THE MEXICAN DRAWN-WORK.

group. The youth who refused to take a wife was expelled from the kin. Through the establishment of descent in the male line, woman lost her hold on public life and became a chattel. But her duty to marry was also obligatory, and one who was not misshapen or "under vows" was an outcast if she refused. Having no other resource, the outcasts became slaves. Bandelier says that her position was little better than that of a costly animal, and protection was awarded her only as property—the kin was obliged to protect that for self-protection.

Tribal society was based upon kin, the initial or lowest expression of which was the mother-right—that is, the kin, or "lineage," as Spanish authors had it. A certain ancestress far back, and all her descendants through females, make up the kin and form the unit of social organisation. As yet there was no complete family, in which descendants of both males and females were recognised. Political society based on territory was also unknown at first, and so was the descent in the male line undeveloped. What was going on with varying rapidity, answering to the growth of population, the differentiation of trades, and the artificialisation of life, was the slow change to descent in the male line, called father-right. As this process went on at first, bearing the mother's name became a kind of fiction in custom.

The wife was nearly as badly off as the outcast ; any act of the man's that tended to increase the clan was condoned, while straying on her part was severely punished. In reading through the abundant literature collected by Bancroft and others,

Photograph by C. B. Waite, Mexico.

TEHUANTEPEC WOMEN IN NATIVE COSTUME.

it is surprising to find so little of romantic love in connection with the family life. In the Aztec kins the young girls were safeguarded, but in other tribes not, and romance had full sway. This had nothing to do with the cool business by which partners for life were chosen, and not by gallant youths and charming maidens, but by scheming fathers and mothers.

Position of Primitive Women.

Facts connected with marriage have been collected by Bancroft. It usually takes place at an early age, girls being seldom found single after fourteen or fifteen years. In some tribes, if the girl has not chosen a mate by this time, her parents or guardians select one for her. Trial marriages are allowed in some places. Among the Chichimecs the consent of the parents is necessary. The preliminary meetings are held by both sets of parents. The conclusions are made known to the young people, and, if the decision is favourable, the girl sends her husband presents, they consider themselves married, and friends give themselves up to feasting and dancing.

Marriage in Mexico.

A plurality of wives was found among the women of this area at the time of the Conquest, the first wife taking precedence. Among the wilder tribes, where one wife was the rule, it was not rarely that she was repudiated and another taken. Ethical standards in the family were not high, and this fact stood in the way of progress even more than hard conditions and poisoned atmosphere. Chivalry did not flourish. Women were under subjection to their husbands. Yet attention is called again to the fact that the kinship tribe, together with its adopted members, was the unit in the social struggle and the multiplication of its membership restrained all cruelty to mothers. Barrenness was a crime.

Photograph by C. B. Waite, Mexico.

MAKING CLAY BRASEROS, MEXICO.

When a babe was about to be born, the mother retired to a dark corner of the house, attended by an aged woman, who pretended to sing and call the infant from afar.

As soon as the child was born, the attendant covered her face with her hands and walked around the house once. The first object she saw on opening her eyes was chosen as the name of the child. Among the Otomi, north of the Mexican valley, the young mother was the victim of exacting and terrorising superstitions. Happy and unhappy omens met her at every step—a black dog, a singing bird, the phases of the moon. She was loaded with charms and amulets, and subjected to taboos. Actions were prescribed that were hurtful and often fatal.

How Children were Named.

When the child was a girl an old woman painted a flower over the heart, on the palm of the right hand a spindle was pictured, and on the left a bunch of wool.

The Coras named the child after one of its uncles or aunts. At the end of the first year there was a feast in honour of the babe, at which the father and mother and the sponsors were the honoured guests. Salt was for the first time placed in the infant's mouth. Another feast came at the cutting of the teeth, and the child received its first meal. This was a very important matter in the tropics. At the age of twelve the youth took the first drink of wine. Bandelier quotes fully the old authorities about Mexican birthdays. Shortly after the child's birth its mother, in the presence of the clan (*calpulli*) gave it a name through the midwife, which was generally the day of its birth. It had a superstitious import and was retained during helplessness. Several months later the medicine man of the kin

Photograph by C. B. Waite, Mexico.

MUSIC IN MEXICO.

Photograph by C. B. Waite, Mexico.

IN THE STREET, MEXICO.

conducted another "naming." These names were preserved, and if in manhood some noble deed were done in their service, the whole tribe gave the man a third name, which was his title.

The Aztecs.

On the eastern side of the environment was a curious state of affairs. The old-time Indians of the Antilles were called Arawaks, but the great family of Caribs—rovers from South America — had swept over the sea named after them, about killed off and adopted the men, but enslaved and often married the women. The latter, when the Spaniards found them, were speaking two languages—that of their conquerors and literally the mother tongue. Payne speaks of agricultural communities composed of women alone, deriving their continuity from periodical visits by men from other tribes. Columbus heard of such a community from an Indian who visited him on board the *Nina*, January 13th, 1493.

Aztec children of both sexes, says Bancroft, were carefully instructed by parents and the priests. In spite of the superstitions that flavoured their customs, care was taken to inspire the young with a love of truth, respect for elders, modesty, and a horror fo vice. In a most interesting series of Aztec paintings is to be seen how the children were brought up, the amount of food allowed them, the duty they had to per-

Photograph by Fittier.

KECCHI WOMAN AND CHILD, NEAR CAHABON, GUATEMALA.

form, and the punishments for neglect. For a girl, three small circles show her to be three years old; half an oval indicates that her meal ration was half a cake. During the fourth and fifth year the girl is shown a distaff by her mother, and she is instructed in its use—ration, a whole cake. In the sixth and seventh years the girl is spinning under the mother's eye—ration, a cake and a half, continuing so until her thirteenth year. The punishments are as follows—at eight, the instruments were being shown to her as warnings; at ten, girls were pricked in the hands and wrists with *maguey* thorns or beaten with sticks; at eleven, they were held over a pile of burning *chile;* at twelve, the naughty girl was obliged to rise in the night and sweep the house. Between thirteen and fifteen, girls ground corn, cooked, and practised weaving. Schools and seminaries for both sexes were a monopoly in the hands of the priests; but no women were allowed to enter the colleges. Bancroft says that large seminaries for girls were attached to the temples. They were presided over by matrons brought up in the institutions. The building was strictly guarded by old men. If a maiden left her apartment without a guard her feet were pricked with thorns. The girls went out together accompanied by their matrons, at which times they were not allowed to raise their eyes. It was their duty to sweep their precincts of the temple and to attend the sacred fire. They were taught religion, to make feather-work, to spin, and to weave mantles. Frequent bathing, household duties, humility, reverence, modesty, and respectful demeanour were commended, and their neglect punished.

Photograph by C. B. Waite, Mexico.

HOME WORK IN MEXICO.

Nieboer, in his studies of slavery, quoting Rochefort, observes that when a captive woman was taken as a wife, the children were free, the mother remaining a slave, and concludes that the other children of captive women and children taken as prisoners were slaves. The Maya had female slaves, and it is reasonable to suppose that the men were killed. In Mexico human sacrifices were offered in their bloody religion, men being the victims. This also left the woman alive for a fate similar to that mentioned above. In this connection it might be profitable to refer to the fact that the sexes were like races of men and species of animals. Those species and races that submitted to enslav[illegible] survived; those that would not had to die. The women of this area were prepared for slavery by their allotted industries.

A Mexican Tradition.

In later times, after the intricate Mexican government had been worked out, Bandelier finds curious survivals of the more ancient rule of woman. Among the officers of the tribe was *Tlacacllel*, who was also called *Cihuacohuatl*, the "Snake-woman." Mrs. Nuttall has a most interesting comment on this woman. Huitzilopochtli, in his wanderings, was accompanied by his sister, who was a great sorceress. She and her family were left on the road by reason of the animosity against her. In reply to some menaces from the war chiefs, she said: "I am Quilaztli, your sister, and of your tribe. Besides this name, I have four titles. The first is Cihuacohuatl, the Woman Serpent (or twin); the second is Quauh-cihuatl, the Eagle Woman; the third is Yao-cihuatl, the Warrior Woman; and the fourth Tzitzmicihuatl, the Woman of the Under-world." Mrs. Nuttall, quoting Chavero, thinks that this tradition refers to an important event in the history of the Aztec tribe. Here is a woman, termed the sister of Huitzilopochtli, who exerted high authority, and whose titles were the names of the highest female divinity. Quilatzi, a goddess—the same as Cihuacoatl—was the mother of all, also named Tonantzin, "our mother." In all historical records antedating the conquest, a man entitled Cihuacoatl is mentioned as the coadjutor of the Mexican ruler, having equal rank with Montezuma.

Photograph by C. B. Waite, Mexico

A MEXICAN INTERIOR.

The Popol-Vuh, the ancient records of the Quiché tribe of Guatemala, names the four wives of the four first men, and says: "These engendered mankind, the large and small tribes, and they were the stock of us, the Quiché tribe."

Enough has been said to show how the nucleus of social life in the tropical environment sprung from motherhood; but there is another feature of our theme. When the Mexicans conquered a tribe they usually exterminated the men or made them pay tribute. But the Tlatilulco tribe were degraded to the rank of women, their market closed, their council house abandoned, and their young men compelled to become common carriers for their captors.

but later on, and at the time of the Conquest, the bloody wars of Mexico had also reorganised the religion. Human sacrifices of diabolical character formed one of its chief

Photograph by C. B. Wait, Mexico.

GALTIPAN INDIAN MAIDEN WATER-CARRIER.

Religion.

In the torrid environment religion was still the personality of Nature. Her forces and phenomena were, to tropical Indians, not results, survivals of the fittest, products of selection, but each one was somebody at work. We say "man is the creature of his surroundings," but it is only a figure of speech; on the contrary, with all primitive peoples it is the one reality. We would say that the resources and powers about us are God's agencies as well as His handiwork; to them, the heavenly world is the counterpart of ours. In primitive times women held high rank among the celestial chiefs; features. The result, however, is still the same. The real potters, weavers, and painters on earth are represented and worshipped in the world above. Earth mothers are matched by sky mothers; or, since kin is more binding than laws, the sky sister is the peer of the Head Chief of the world above. In the sky above, as on the earth below, throughout tropical North America, the weaker sex was the preserver of forms, the binding and abiding link.

On the whole, in the old days the women of North America, like all others that dwelt on our planet, lived the natural life and the culture, or vocational, life. In both there were good and bad. As in the atmosphere there were for them the life-giving oxygen and the poisonous malaria, so in the culture life there were dreadful evils for them to perpetrate and suffer as well as elevating duties and pleasures. It may have been necessary here and there to mention their wrongs and sins, but the aim of these chapters has been to record the North American woman's share in those inventions which constituted the humanities. It has been the endeavour to show where they stood on the ladder of progress and how Nature has treated the sex.

As has been shown, the complete study of North American aboriginal women includes their biology and their rounds of duties. The latter embrace all the artificialities of life that come under the term of inventions in its widest acceptance. This forms one of the most fascinating chapters in human history, inasmuch as all the higher races were at one time in similar circumstances to the lower. The women who were the ancestors of the queens in every walk of modern society spoke with their lips, wrought with their hands, adored the beautiful, associated with men and with one another, explained Nature and communed with the spirit world, in the same delightful simplicity as those about whom it is here written.

Photograph by C. B. Waite, Mexico.

A MEXICAN WOMAN AT HOME.

FISHERWOMEN AND GIRLS OF NORTHERN JAPAN.

JAPAN

By CLIVE HOLLAND

Characteristics of the Race—The Ainu—Japanese Characteristics—Beauty in Japan—The Mental Qualities of the Japanese—Art and Dress in Japan—The *Kimono* and *Obi*—European Dress in Japan—The Children of Japan—Child Nurses—Household Duties—Feast Days and Holidays—Courtship—Japanese Marriage Customs—The Training of a Japanese Girl—Japanese Home Life—Divorce—Education—The Japanese Lady of Fashion—Women of the *Samurai*—The *Geisha* Girl—Work-women in Japan—Professions for Women in Japan—The Servant Question—Women Agricultural Workers—Happiness is with the Peasant Women—The Future of Japanese Women

JUST as the English race is an admixture of the characteristics of several peoples, so is the Japanese. Indeed, the similarity in the geographical position of the two countries would lead one almost to expect this. Both are "island kingdoms"; both are in close proximity to continents of wide extent, both are in a very similar latitude, and the shores of both are beneficently washed by tropical currents: ours by the Gulf Stream, and those of Japan by the waters of the Pacific.

Characteristics of the Race.

The analogy might be carried further as regards population and extent; but it is unnecessary.

Nippon, "the Land of the Rising Sun," though consisting of many thousands of small islands, is chiefly comprised of four large ones—Yezo, the northernmost; Hondo, the largest, and "Nippon" proper; Shikoku the smallest, and Kiūshiu the southernmost. These islands, forming a sickle-shaped group, are distant at their nearest point only some hundred miles from Korea. The innumerable Kurile Isles and those of the Loo-choo group also belong to the Mikado's Empire, as does the large island of Formosa, which was ceded by the Chinese after the war of 1895.

Japan is only separated from the continent of Asia by the narrow strait which divides it from Korea. It is in a measure connected with Kamschatka, and even with the North American continent to the north by chains of islands; whilst to the south it is similarly linked to the Malay Peninsula. By these channels Japan has in the past received racial influences which are traceable in her people of to-day.

Photograph by Karl Lewis, Yokohama.

A YOUNG WOMAN OF CENTRAL JAPAN.

The Ainu.

The original inhabitants of the greater part of Japan were probably akin to (if not actually) Ainu, of whom there survive at the present day but a comparatively small number in the Island of Yezo. But in far off ages they undoubtedly inhabited the main island or Nippon as far as the Hakoné Pass. Many authorities think it probable that their influence extended even further south.

The origin of the name Ainu is not for certain known. This strange people, in common with the inhabitants of the Kurile group of islands and the Japanese portion of Sakhalien, call themselves Yezo. By several authorities, as well as by the Japanese themselves, the word Ainu is believed to have been derived from *inu*, dog, and was given to them as an expression of contempt. Physically they are a sturdy and well-developed race, and, although many doubt whether these now docile and amiable people can be the remnants of the race which was once so troublesome and barbarous, it should be remembered that for centuries the strongest means were taken by the Japanese proper for their repression, and for driving them back whence they had come. The number of Ainu in the island of Yezo at the present time is variously computed at 15,000, or 16,000; this number is, however, gradually decreasing.

The Ainu women possess an abundance of hair, and most of the older ones are of a rather hard and masculine type of face. In all matters relating to civilisation they are most primitive. Their dwellings, ideas of family life, food, clothing, and implements are of an elementary character; and they are of much less cleanly habits than the Japanese. To wash their persons and clothing might be called an act of religion with the Japanese and an accident with the Ainu. This primitive and interesting race is treated separately in the succeeding article.

Japanese Characteristics.

As it is recognised to-day the Japanese race proper is a mixed race of considerably differing elements. And although the amalgamation of the various types of which it is composed has been going on for many hundreds of years, yet the variations which distinguish individuals can still be traced and recognised. In the north and chiefly amongst the labouring classes the face is broad, the nose flat, the eyes horizontal, and the cheek bones prominent; whilst the frame is robust and muscular rather than well-proportioned. In the south, on the other hand, and more amongst the ruling and upper middle classes than the lower, is often found a type of refined and even delicate appearance, possessing an oval face, a well-modelled and slightly Roman nose, the oblique eyes so generally associated with the idea of the Japanese woman, and a well-proportioned though slight figure. Both these types, which distinguish the women as well as the men (perhaps even more so), are found everywhere.

But it is in the regions in the vicinity of Kioto, and on the more western side of Nippon, that the prevalence of the more refined, and what may indeed be called more aristocratic, type is noticeable. Kaempfer, at the time of the establishment of the Dutch factories and trade with Japan, speaks of the women of Saga on the south side of the Inland Sea as being "more handsome than in any other Asiatic country." In the northern districts the inhabitants embody in a larger degree the elements of the coarser and more robust type. In them is undoubtedly to be traced the characteristics which have arisen from intermarriage and intercourse with the Ainu race, which once inhabited these regions and the ancient provinces of Dewa and Matsu.

TYPE OF MIDDLE-AGED WOMAN OF THE WORKING CLASS.

The duplex nature of the Japanese race of to-day is traceable to two important migrations from the neighbouring continent of Asia. Authorities incline to agree that the first of these, almost certainly came from Korea, the invaders effecting a landing on Nippon in the province of Izumo. The chief effects of this first migration from the mainland was the settlement in Japan of a stronger, more hardy, and more barbarous tribe of the Mongolian race, which has contributed during the centuries which have since elapsed the more robust and muscular traits to be found in the Japanese of to-day. Concerning the second invasion of an alien race there is less certainty. It seems likely, however, that (as in the first case) the easiest route through Korea and across the narrow intervening straits was taken, and that the settlement was first made upon the most southern island of Kiūshiu, the invaders afterwards penetrating to the province of Hiūga, where we find them first mentioned in Japanese history.

On the other hand this second invasion or migration may have arrived from the south through the large island of Formosa, and onward through the various and almost innumerable Loo-choo Islands, which form a chain-like connection with Kiūshiu. Indeed, this supposition would in some measure account for the Malay element which is stated by some authorities (and denied by others) to be discoverable amongst the population of the southern islands.

But whatever the route was, there is no doubt that the second immigrants were of the same race as the first, but probably of a more cultured tribe of the great Mongolian people.

From the very elaborate and painstaking measurements of two celebrated ethnologists, Dr. Baelz and Dr. Scheube, the average height of both Japanese and Ainu has been found to differ very little, the former stating that of the Japanese to be in the case of the males 5·02 feet, and ranging from 4·76 feet to 5·44 feet; females, 4·66 feet, and ranging from 4·46 feet to 4·92 feet, whilst Dr. Scheube's measurements of numerous Ainu has produced the following results: average height of males, 4·9 feet to 5·2 feet; of females, 4·8 feet to 5·0 feet.

THE TRUE JAPANESE TYPE.

The chief physical characteristics of the Japanese women of to-day are a rather accentuated flatness of the forehead; a small but frequently well-formed nose, with slightly raised nostrils; well-shaped ears; black eyes of below the average size, and slightly less oblique than those of the Chinese, eyebrows further apart than is usual with most other peoples; rather coarse, black hair; legs inclining to shortness, which somewhat spoils otherwise well-proportioned figures; and low stature. Their skin is less sallow than that of the Japanese men, and this is more especially the case with the women of the upper class, when their complexions are less exposed to the weather, and have been less affected by outdoor occupations. Many Japanese women and girls, indeed, possess skins scarcely more olive than those of Southern Europeans. One curious circumstance distinguishes the race—whilst the complexion of the face is olive, and sometimes even sallow or yellowish, the skin of the body is frequently even whiter than that of the average Englishwoman. This is not the case with the Chinese, who are "yellow" all over.

Beauty in Japan.

It is unnecessary to state that the Japanese ideal of feminine beauty differs very materially from our own. Some of the points in which it varies may, however, be of interest. An excellent summary of these, by one who has had the opportunity of studying the Japanese women of all classes more closely and intimately than most Europeans, states that "the ideal feminine face is long and narrow, with the forehead high, and narrow in the centre, but widening towards the sides. The hair should be jet or blue-black in colour, long, straight, and smooth; never curly. The eyes to be really beautiful to a Japanese must be long and narrow, slanting upward slightly at their outer corners; the eyebrows delicately pencilled, and placed high above the eyes. The most esteemed type of nose is aquiline, low at the bridge, and the outward curve commencing low down. The mouth must be small, whilst the lips are full and brightly coloured; the neck long and slender and with graceful curves. The complexion most esteemed is white, smooth, and with little colour in the cheeks. The fresh-coloured type of beauty found in many country and peasant girls is not at all admired by the better class Japanese. The figure must be slender, the waist long, and the hips narrow, so as to ensure the best effect of the national style of dress. The head and shoulders should be carried slightly forward, and the most graceful and womanly carriage is obtained by also bending the body slightly forward at the waist. The most elegant Japanese walk is quick, with short steps, and it is not considered correct to lift the foot clear of the ground, so that in the house there is always a *shoo-shoo* of the *tabi* on the floor, and out of doors the scuff of the *waraji* or straw sandals, or the ring of the *gheta* or clogs." A very clear idea of what the Japanese ideal of beauty is can easily be gathered from the women depicted upon the old colour prints of Kunisada, Hiroshige, Utagawa, Hokusai, Isai and others.

Japanese babies are positively horror-stricken at the first sight of light-haired, blue-eyed foreigners; and it is only after a considerable time that they can be induced to approach them. One of the most curious things about the effect wrought upon the mind of the alien who dwells amongst the Japanese for any length of time is the gradual change that takes place in his ideas regarding the standard of feminine beauty. It must be considered a victory for the gentle Japanese women that he almost invariably begins at last to regard their beauty as of the truest type.

Having dealt thus briefly with the chief physical characteristics of the Japanese race past and present, let us consider the mental qualities which differentiate them from other far Eastern peoples, and also in a measure from the race that has in the past impinged upon them.

It is often difficult correctly to infer mental characteristics or qualities from physical, and in the case of the Japanese an

Photograph by Karl Lewis, Yokohama.

A PEASANT GIRL IN HOLIDAY GARB,
Showing the *Kimono* and *Obi*.

inference of the mental based upon what one knows of the physical would be unusually erroneous.

The Mental Qualities of the Japanese

Compared either with the average Koreans, with whom they have been in the past intermingled, or even the Chinese, they appear physically at a disadvantage. For though possessed of considerable powers of endurance — which was wonderfully illustrated in the Russo-Japanese War—they are physically weak, with far less natural muscular development than the races to which we have referred, and with narrow chests. But mentally they hold pre-eminence over the other Mongolian races. Indeed, recent events have shown that intellectually the Japanese can claim to rank with the more advanced of European peoples. They are of a high standard of intelligence, quick-witted, eminently adaptable, progressive, and brave to an extent unequalled by any other race. Under the ancient feudal system of Japan the sense of personal honour, which does not as a rule distinguish the Asiatic races, was developed in both men and women until it became a passion and almost a religion, and led and still does lead to acts of devotion and self-effacement which to Western ideas are little less than astounding.

Though possessed of much originating power and enterprise the Japanese are known all over the world for their extraordinary imitative faculty, which surpasses even that of the Chinese. How remarkably this faculty is developed was shown very clearly many years ago in the early days of the introduction of machinery into Japan; when, not only was the first steamer made with perfectly complete engines entirely by the aid of a Dutch book upon shipbuilding, but much other machinery was constructed in the same way, and with no practical assistance or instruction from experts. These characteristics and mental qualities not only in a measure explain the rapid rise of the Japanese people to a place of prime importance amongst civilised nations, but also, now that the education of girls has received so great and satisfactory an impetus, the charm and intelligence of the women of modern Japan.

Art and Dress in Japan.

Art enters very largely into the life of the Japanese; into that of Japanese women more especially. It is the art instinct of the race which is seen in the national love of flowers, in the fact that all girls of the upper and middle classes are taught flower arrangement, and in the costume and elaborate *coiffures* of the women. The native dress of girls and women of the better classes ranks, not only amongst the most beautiful, but amongst the most truly artistic of the world. Beauty of colour and design of a high order is wedded to an artistic simplicity of form.

The Japanese women are fond of dress, but it is only with those of the *yoji* or courtesan class that there is usually anything approaching the meretricious or flamboyant. There is a saying which freely translated reads—"The richest garments are often those which are in closest accord with nature." Very often, indeed, is this the case with the dress of the Japanese women. Harmonising, though bright, and what might be called "quiet" colours are more prevalent than vivid or garish hues. The beauty of a *kimono* is often to be found rather in its delicate embroidery than in its vivid tints or mere richness of material, though the latter plays its due part in the garments worn by the wealthy and by women of the upper classes.

The *Kimono* and *Obi*.

The dress of Japanese women consists of a *hitoma* or under-garment, which all who can afford have of silk, generally of a bright colour. The other garments (varying in number according to the temperature and season) are the well-known *kimono;* loose-fitting, flowing, dressing-gown-like robes made of silk, crêpe, or more substantial cotton fabrics according to the social position and wealth of the wearer. The undermost are of light, and the outer one of dark colours, blues being the most popular. The *kimono* has no fastenings; it is merely folded over on the right side (never the left on a living person), and confined round the waist by a broad sash, about ten to twelve inches in width, known as the *obi*, generally made of wadded brocade, which is folded several times and tied behind in a broad flat bow. This sash is generally the most expensive item of a Japanese woman's attire. Some are of extremely rich fabrics, and beautifully embroidered. Fifty pounds is by no means an unheard-of sum for an *obi*, and many are handed down from generation to generation as heirlooms. The tying of the *obi* is an elaborate ceremony, and to tie one well is by no means so easy a matter as might be imagined.

Tabi, or digitated hose of white cotton, are worn in the house in place of shoes or *gheta*, which are always taken off before entering a temple or house, but out of doors the feet are protected by the *gheta*, secured to the feet by straps passing between the big and second toes, or *waraji*, sandals of straw, used chiefly when travelling, according to the time of year. Some of the *gheta* belonging to women of the upper classes are beautifully carved and lacquered; but the commoner clogs are generally made of elm-wood.

JAPANESE GIRLS OF THE WORKING CLASS.

Although European dress in the shape more particularly of bowler hats, trousers, and coats, amongst the men of the commercial as well as the upper classes, has somewhat displaced the old and more picturesque style, it is as yet only the women of the official and upper classes who have to any extent abandoned their national costume for European modes. That they should have done so must be matter for regret by all who possess a sense of the beautiful, appropriate, and artistic. Modern European fashions (seldom beautiful) appear singularly unlovely and out of place upon the women of Chrysanthemum Land; and one could almost wish that some law might be passed forbidding the abandonment of the picturesque and graceful native dress.

European Dress in Japan.

Perhaps the fact that the Japanese are a nation of artists, and that in the women is an inherent appreciation of the artistic, may save them from further adoption of Western forms of dress. Happily the corset has not yet supplanted the picturesque *obi* as a means of indicating the waist line, nor has the "Princess" robe replaced the more graceful *kimono*.

The Children of Japan.

We have dealt as fully as our space permits with the origin of the Japanese, and the special peculiarities of physique, character, environment and dress, which distinguishes them as a race. And now we come to the various types, and more intimate life of the women and girls of this favoured and beautiful land. The Japanese baby, let it be said, differs little save in racial type from the babies of other lands. But whether it be a girl or a boy baby it is generally a quaint and fascinating scrap of humanity; and worshipped by its parents and relations. The children of Japan, indeed, should be (as they appear to be) happy, for so much is done to secure their well-being and enjoyment. The girl baby is more warmly welcomed than amongst the Chinese and some other Eastern peoples, even though she may be considered of less importance than a boy.

Her arrival into the world is immediately notified to relatives and the more intimate of her parents' friends by special messenger, whilst, amongst families of the better class, grandparents and others closely related receive letters of formal announcement. As all who are thus made aware of the baby's arrival are expected to call as soon as possible "bearing gifts," both the mother and the baby have a fatiguing time during the early days of the latter's existence. The presents may be eatables—in the shape of eggs—toys, or pieces of silk, brocade, or other material for the baby's dress. All gifts are wrapped in white paper, written upon, and tied with a particular make of paper-string, red and white in colour.

A strange Japanese custom is that of reckoning the baby as already a year old on the day of its birth. And on the next following New Year's Day it is reckoned as being two. Thus a baby born during the month of December (even right at the end of it) will be two years old on January 1st. As a natural consequence of this strange custom one would not be much astonished to find that all birthdays were celebrated on January 1st. But this is not so. All boys celebrate their birthday on May 5th, and all girls on March 3rd, in each year.

On the seventh day baby is registered at the district registrar's and receives her name; generally that of some flower, tree or other beautiful natural object, such as Cherry Blossom, Plum, Gold, Pine, Sunshine, Iris, Chrysanthemum, Bamboo. Often on the seventh day after birth, or soon after, the Japanese mother begins to try experiments with baby's *coiffure*, shaving its little head till there is only a wisp of its jet black hair left on the back of its head just above the neck. As baby grows older the attempts at hair-dressing are more elaborate. Sometimes a "top-knot" is left; at others a rim of hair with a tonsure in the centre, the general effect of which style of hair-dressing resembles more than anything else a chimney-sweep's brush. Later on other more elaborate and artistic styles are tried. Children are very seldom given the name of any living member of the family, and

Photograph by Karl Lewis, Yokohama.

JAPANESE BABIES AND THEIR LITTLE NURSES.

JAPANESE WOMEN.
DRAWN BY C. PRAETORIUS.

Facing on page 496

In Japan to name a child after any particular individual is not considered complimentary. "A little more than three weeks later occurs the *miya mairi*, a ceremony which in a measure corresponds with that of christening in Western lands. The child is taken to the temple, dressed in the best clothes the parents can afford, made specially for the occasion, on which is emblazoned in several places the family crest. Taken to one of the Shinto temples the baby is placed under the protection of the patron deity of the temple, who is supposed forthwith to become the special guardian angel of the child through life. Offerings are, of course, made to the god and also to the priest, and when the blessing of the latter has been obtained the baby is taken home again, where an entertainment of one kind or the other is held."

A GEISHA DANCING.
Note the "Tabi" (Digitated Socks).

Japanese babies seldom appear to cry or be troublesome—although there is, let it at once be said, no physical deficiency to prevent them doing so. It is possible that they at least appear better-tempered from the healthy, open-air life—even in the larger cities—which they lead, although we have heard some authorities ascribe the Japanese child's good humour and greater gentleness than distinguishes Western children to less robust physique and a more moderate allowance of animal spirits.

The first few years of the little girl's life are uneventful enough. Less so, indeed, than those of the children of more Western nations. She is left far more alone, is less fussed over, and in consequence grows to early childhood with a much more placid outlook upon life in general than that of the modern English or American child.

Child-Nurses.

Very soon—in fact within a few weeks of their birth in the case of those belonging to people of the lower classes—Japanese babies are handed over to the care of elder sisters or brothers, or young girls who are engaged as nurses. And the quaint sight is seen throughout the length and breadth of the Mikado's Empire of young children of both sexes, some of whom are not more than six or seven years of age, staggering about with the latest arrival in their own or someone else's family tied with long strips of cloth to their backs. These little nurse-girl sisters are usually sunny-tempered, tender little souls who trudge about the streets with their animated baby burdens all the year round; for the Japanese baby is essentially a "fresh air" child. When it is hot the little nurse's parasol, of gay or delicate coloured paper as the taste of the owner may dictate, keeps the sun off the child's head, and in windy or cold weather her *haori* or overcoat or *kimono* is wrapped around the baby as well as herself. It is, of course, only the children of the poorer class who live in the streets, those of the middle class, though carried on the backs of their little sisters or of their nurses till they can walk, play in the gardens of their homes—few houses of any pretension but possess a garden plot—whilst the babies of the richest families are carried in the arms of their nurses, European fashion, or of late years are wheeled about in mail-carts and perambulators, some of which are like miniature *rikshaws*, and other old- or new-fashioned European types, according to the social position of the parents. Royal babies are held in the arms of some attendant from the moment of their birth till they are able to walk, and are seldom or never laid down on the floor or upon a bed.

From the first children are taught to sit with their knees bent under them, instead of with their legs stretched out in front. It is from this mode of sitting from early infancy that some authorities are inclined at least partially to attribute the low average stature of the race.* The legs (which are always abnormally short in the Japanese, both men and women) are through this custom prevented from growing to their normal proportions. The abnormal shortness of the lower part of the body is less noticeable amongst the women of the labouring classes, and least of all with peasants and the fisherfolk of the coast and Inland Sea, the reason being that they sit less and walk more than women of the upper or middle classes, who may in factories, etc., follow sedentary occupations. It seems more than probable that the introduction of European furniture, and the removal of the necessity and habit of sitting upon the floor, may in the course of a few generations materially alter the physique and proportions of the race.

The feet of Japanese girls, unlike those of their Chinese sisters, are not deformed in infancy by compressing bandages. They are sensibly clothed by soft digitated *tabi*, which not only permit them to run about freely on the matted floors of the houses, but are as hygienic as any foot covering can be. Very early in her existence, however, the Japanese baby girl has to learn to walk in the light straw sandals or *zori* worn out of doors in fine weather, and the *gheta*, or high clogs, worn in wet weather, or on rough country roads. These last, though seemingly awkward to walk in, are soon mastered, and one sees tiny tots of three or four running about quite comfortably in them. There is one good point *gheta* possess—they cannot, even when too small, in any way distort or hurt the foot.

The dress of the little girls is distinguishable from that of the boys from babyhood. A very young baby, whether boy or girl, wears gay colours, such as yellow, bright blue, green, and red, but as soon as it can run alone, or sooner, to the boy are relegated the soberer tints, whilst the girl continues to be adorned with the gayest of colours, which she only gives up on marriage.

The Training of a Japanese Girl.

From babyhood onward the life which comes to her proves a very bright and happy one as a general rule. It is, however, hedged around in all grades of society save the lowest with much etiquette and many rules of conduct. One thing she has early to learn is the fact that from her earliest years until she passes away to the land of shadows she is destined to be under the rule of someone or other of the opposite sex. She has also to realise that cheerful obedience, personal cleanliness, neatness and pleasant manners are expected of her, and that her happiness and ultimate position in life depend very largely upon her cultivating these virtues. In the past there was no calling of a public nature open to her, and even now there are comparatively few. As a consequence the average Japanese girl or woman finds her vocation in the care of her home, or, if of the peasant or farming class, then in her home and on the soil. Since the war, and the rapid acquisition by her nation of Western ideas, the field of woman's labour has become somewhat less restricted.

She is, therefore, as will be readily understood, dependent upon either her father or

* *See* recent "Medical Report." Also the work of Drs. Baelz and Scheube.

some other male relative, husband or son, and her greatest success and happiness are to be won not by scholarship, "higher education," or great mental capacity, but in the careful and early acquisition of charming manners, and the powers of self-effacement, obedience (taught by that famous work, "Onna Daigaku"), and self-control, which are expected of her. To women of more Western nations the perfect self-effacement of their Japanese sisters may appear both unnatural and irksome. The women of Japan do not find it so. Self-control with them, moreover, does not simply mean the disguising of outward and visible signs of disagreeable emotions such as jealousy, anger, grief, or disappointment; but it goes further and enables them to assume a pleasant smile, and an appearance of good humour and agreeable manners and politeness under the most distressing or trying conditions. This duty is taught to the girls from their earliest years, with a result that it becomes a second nature (not merely a deceptive mask), and makes them the most truly fascinating and, probably, happiest women in the world.

Japanese women and girls, almost without exception, are attractive, dignified and polite. Even little girls have charming manners; and whilst free from bashfulness they are equally so from pushful or forward ways. By those who know Japanese girl children, the statement that to "a truly childlike and fascinating simplicity is united a remarkable consideration for the feelings and wishes of others" will not be questioned.

The Japanese girl is, however, not truly known until one has lived in the family circle. It is only then that one has the opportunity of discovering and appreciating some of their most charming traits of character and upbringing. The true type is not that which usually comes under the immediate notice of the travelling European, the Cook's tourist, or those who merely come and go at the great seaports. Even the tea-house attendants, and native girls in the shops—more numerous now than even five years ago—and those who are seen in the streets and public parks and temple courtyards, give but a faint impression—well-mannered, dainty, and picturesque as most of them are—of the charm of the real Japanese young lady, or of the average home-keeping girl of the middle and upper middle classes. It is away from the stress of big cities, and of the rapid changes which are taking place in most of them, in the smaller country towns and villages which as yet the railway has left untouched, that one can most readily find the type of Japanese

A JAPANESE WOMAN OF THE WORKING CLASS AT HOME.

girl which years of careful training in the doctrines of Kaibara Ekken, the famous moralist and author of "Onna Daigaku," and many ages of the persistence of the feudal idea has produced.

Mrs. Hugh Fraser, who lived many years

A TEA-HOUSE ATTENDANT.

in Japan, where her husband was the British Minister at Tokio, sums up the distinguishing feature of the Japanese women very aptly and truthfully as follows: "In real womanliness, which I take to be a combination of sense with sweetness, valour with humility, the Japanese lady ranks with any woman in the world, and passes before most of them."

"Onna Daigaku," which has had in the past so much to do with the moulding of Japanese female character, contains some home truths which would, we fear, be unpalatable teaching to some at least of our insurgent Western sisters. Thus, "It is a girl's destiny on reaching maturity to go to a new home, and live in submission to her father-in-law, and it is incumbent even more upon her to receive with all reverence and meekness parental teaching, also to obey and reverence her husband."

The same book tells the Japanese girl, who may and often does receive the instruction from her aged grandfather, that a virtuous heart is more to be desired than a beautiful face. And, though it is difficult to imagine the invariably gentle and soft-voiced Japanese maiden or woman as capable of anything of the kind, it goes on to say that a "vicious woman's heart is never at rest; that she glares wildly around her, vents her anger on others, and her words are rough and her voice loud and vulgar." Then "Onna Daigaku" proceeds to assert that such women are desirous of setting themselves above their fellows, being envious, proud, prone to jeer at others, and to try and outdo their companions—indeed, to be "guilty of everything that a good woman should not be."

To the modern suffragette of Western clime the following injunction would, of course, be anathema. And yet this teaching has produced a type of the most charming, domesticated, and truly womanly and capable of women. "From her youth upwards a girl should learn to observe the line which separates her from men in physical, mental, and other attributes, and should not seek to be 'loud,' pushing, man-like, or coarse."

Several ancient customs regarding the demarcation of the sexes have, even in Japan, fallen nowadays into desuetude; but happily the barriers separating domestic and public life have been preserved almost intact. A very quaint provision—still obtaining in some country districts—was that which insisted upon women, when walking abroad at night, carrying with them lighted lanterns, and the not undesirable one which said that they should not speak with nor accost strangers. Regarding the women who do these undesirable things, "Onna Daigaku" goes on to say, "But alas! in our days the women of the lower classes, ignoring all rules of this nature, behave themselves disorderly, thus contaminating not only their own reputations, but also bringing reproach down upon the heads of their parents, instructors, and friends."

To Western minds the position of

Japanese women may seem a hard one, and it is possible that the Japanese girl sometimes has a yearning for greater freedom. But if she has she does not show it; and never having enjoyed the "forbidden fruit" she does not, in reality, keenly miss it. All along she has been taught to regard her future life from maidenhood onwards as one which must be modelled upon that which her mother and her grandmother before her led. And why not? No "advanced" thoughts or aspirations disturb the Japanese girl's head. She has never expected anything different.

Her life is to all intents and purposes bound up with and environed by the circumstances which arise out of the "three obediences," which are (1) obedience to her parents, (2) afterwards to her husband and his parents, (3) and, should she become a widow, then obedience to her eldest son, or in the absence of a son, then to the head of her husband's family.

Japanese Home Life.

Age always commands respect; but notwithstanding the formality which prevails in the domestic circle it does not lead to stiffness nor estrangement, but rather to a happy and united family life.

The grandfather and grandmother come first, then the father and mother, then the children in accordance with their respective ages. And thus they enter a room and are served at table. The girls of Chrysanthemum Land are indeed favoured by Providence. They are, when babies and young, the pets and playthings of their fathers, mothers, and elder brothers. And they are never addressed by any member of the family save their parents or grandparents except by the title and ceremonious courtesy due to their positions. The eldest daughter is to the servants of the household *O Jō Sama*, or honourable young lady; by her brothers and sisters she is called elder sister. Should she be one of the younger girls of the family she is known to all save her grandparents and parents by her name preceded by *O* and followed by *San* the equivalent of Miss. Thus *O Mume San* is

Photograph by Karl Lewis, Yokohama.

A MUSMÉ.

literally the Honourable Miss Plum, and *O Fuji San* the Honourable Miss Wistaria.

Although during the passage of a girl from babyhood to girlhood and womanhood her life in most instances is a happy one—made so by the love, care, and consideration of her relatives and friends—she is not permitted to grow up without the opportunities to acquire the knowledge which will fit her to meet the trials and perform the duties which will ultimately devolve upon her. She must, and does, generally learn all the details of household management —the washing, mending, and making of garments; the ordering of food, and care of children—which fall to the lot of the mistress of a house, as well as acquire a working knowledge of mathematics, history, geography, and other subjects, which of recent times has become more and more common.

A FISHER-GIRL OF THE COAST.

From the time when she emerges from childhood she has been trained to take her share in the household duties, and to entertain and minister to the comfort and enjoyment of guests. And she must wait upon the latter herself unless she be a member of one of the highest families. Thus is the guest in Japanese houses peculiarly honoured with an old-world and delicately unobtrusive courtesy which is as rare as it is charming. There may be numerous servants available, but it is the wife or daughter who attends with quaint ceremoniousness and charming politeness to his wants.

The Japanese house is simply furnished, guiltless of mirrors, grates, carpets, and the other oddments which make up that conglomerate thing, an English or American home. But there is, nevertheless, plenty to occupy the careful housewife, who generally superintends closely the work of the household, or does it herself according to her station in life. Beds have to be aired, and then rolled up and stowed away in the *fukuro dana* or cupboards in the walls, which strangers often take at first for doorways leading into other apartments. The rooms themselves, with their spotless matting, have to be swept. Flowers have to be arranged. There is, too, in addition to the preparation of the various meals, the *engawa*, or verandah, running round the house to be washed, and in some cases polished. The marketing, as is the case in France, is often done by the housewives themselves, even among the upper middle class, which entails a journey to the town, or much good-tempered bargaining with the itinerant sellers of fish, vegetables, and other comestibles who make a house-to-house visitation in the country or suburban district. Their goods are stored in buckets, boxes, baskets, or trays, according to their nature, which are slung by cords from a long "yoke" and pole carried on the shoulders—somewhat resembling that still sometimes seen in use by milkmen in the country districts of our England.

Household Duties in Japan.

Simple as regards make, the greater number of Japanese garments, especially those of the upper classes, are often so exquisitely embroidered as to become real works of art; but nevertheless there is plenty of plain needlework to occupy the ever industrious Japanese women and girls. Fashions do not change with them as with us, and in consequence the fashionable dressmaker has practically no existence; most garments are made by the girls themselves, or at least at home.

A cotton *kimono* may cost anything from 25 sen (sixpence) to two or three yen (four to six shillings); silk and brocade garments any sum from four or five to two hundred yen (eight or ten shillings to twenty pounds), sometimes three or four times the last-named sum.

The Japanese are a cleanly race, and garments are frequently washed. With the commoner folk new garments are seldom purchased so long as the old can be got to hang together, or are sufficiently good to be "turned." But on New Year's Day most Japanese manage to have at least some new article of clothing, thus in a measure copying their Western sisters, who do so at Whitsuntide. The Japanese washing day differs materially from that of most other countries in that, as a rule, neither hot water nor soap are used; as a substitute for ironing the cotton garments are merely hung out to dry on a bamboo pole after the clothes have been carefully pulled straight and smooth. Silken garments are almost invariably pulled to pieces before being washed, and after washing are pressed out, while wet, upon long planks, similar to European ironing boards, before being placed, generally leaning, against a fence or the side of the house to dry.

Most Japanese maidens are taught cookery as one of the things every girl must know ere she is fit to assume the cares and responsibilities of a house of her own. The cooking of rice in Japan is an elaborate art. So essential, indeed, is this considered—from the fact that rice forms so important an item of diet—that for a wife to be sent back to her parents for not knowing how to cook it properly is by no means an unknown occurrence. Of soups there are many, all the simpler of which every girl is expected to be able to prepare, and in addition many other of the (to the European) mysterious dishes that appear at Japanese meals of ceremony.

But it must not be supposed that the Japanese girl's life is made up entirely of duties, domestic and otherwise. There is

A COUNTRY WOMAN IN WINTER DRESS
On her way home from a shopping expedition in town.

much of joy in it, and it is by no means lacking in the simpler forms of pleasure which as yet suffice this ingenious, progressive, but simple-minded race. The Feast of the New Year, for instance,

Feast-Days and Holidays in Japan.

with its fun, sports, temporary laying aside of the more ceremonious usages, and the prevalence of games of different kinds in which fathers and mothers join—such as the *Hana* game, played with loops of string fitted over the heads of the players, coming round behind the ear and over the end of the nose, the object being to "make faces," so that the loop slips off up over the nose; the Japanese equivalent of "knuckle-bones," played with small bags filled with sand; and "bobbing" for cakes, fruit, or sweetmeats suspended by a string, the players kneeling near

A COUNTRY WOMAN AT WORK.

the elusive object with their heels held up behind them. It is no easy task to preserve one's balance and win the bobbing prize.

Then there is the most loved festival of the whole year—the Feast of Dolls—which commences on the third day of the third month, and lasts three days, during which not only many new dolls are purchased by the wealthy for their children—Emperor and Empress dolls, and Court ladies, *samurai* dolls, and common folk—but also the family dolls of their mothers and even grandmothers are brought out from the cupboards in which they have been so carefully stored away.

Then there are the almost indescribably beautiful flower festivals to give colour and variety to a Japanese maiden's life. And when she reaches to woman's estate she is the pure, charming, and amiable being who fascinates Westerners by reason not alone of these qualities, but also of the power of self-control and surpassing knowledge of what to do in all emergencies of social life.

It is only right to add, however, that with her emergence from girlhood into womanhood the happiest pages of life are often turned. By a strange perversity of fortune just as her mind opens, just as her outlook upon life seems about to broaden, and her thirst for knowledge increases and aspirations assail her, her sphere becomes suddenly more restricted. Checks and restraints are placed upon her, and the young girl, loved and petted at home, though withal wisely trained, who may be expected to have looked out upon the future of her life as something mysterious but beautiful, and with expectations of happiness and usefulness, too often in but a few brief years becomes a listless, disillusioned, and saddened woman.

Courtship in Japan.

As in most other countries, marriage means much to the gentler sex in Japan, and whether it be celebrated in the hut of a peasant or in the palace of a prince the ceremony is distinguished by refinement, beauty, and good taste. Even in the latter case it has little of the often extravagant pretentiousness of such ceremonies in more Western countries, and nothing of the brutality which often distinguishes those of semi-civilised people. Three points may be noted in relation to the marriage customs of Japan; (1) the similarity which exists between them and those of ancient Rome; (2) that whilst most other Eastern brides are attired and veiled in red—which is held to be the festive colour in the Orient—the Japanese women are veiled and robed in white; and (3) the refinement of all customs relative to marriage.

Whilst the art of wooing is much the same (with few exceptions) all the world over, flowers by a singularly appropriate circumstance may, and generally do, play an important part in the wooing of a Japanese maiden. In several districts of the country the lover will approach the home of the girl he loves at night and fasten a branch of *celastrus alatus*—a variety of the spindle tree—above the door, returning later to see what has happened to it. If it has been taken in or sprinkled with water to keep it alive his love is returned; if it is taken down, and thrown aside, or allowed to wither neglected, he knows that his suit is not looked upon with favour. Sometimes the lover will adopt a slightly bolder method by casting a spray of plum blossom into the maiden's *kaga* (carrying hammock) as she is entering it to go to a friend's wedding. If she fastens it in her *obi*, or girdle, she intimates that he finds favour in her eyes; if on the other hand his offering is cast away there is little or no hope of his suit prospering. But it must not be supposed that all marriages have so romantic a beginning, or that Japan is a land where the marriage of convenience is unknown. The Japanese are emotional, but they are practical also. They generally endeavour to make the best out of marriage from a material as well as a sentimental or spiritual point of view.

A male go-between almost always arranges the preliminaries and terms of a Japanese marriage, and it is he who takes the bridegroom-elect's betrothal gift to the bride-to-be. The acceptance of this complimentary gift is held to seal the contract, from which the bride or her relatives cannot in honour draw back. In most other Eastern countries the "matrimonial agent"—the Moorish or Egyptian *khatbch,* for example—is a woman, generally of the lower middle class, who through business relations or some other cause has access to the women of various households. The bridegroom's presents to the bride are always numerous—in costliness of course they vary according to his wealth and social position—and the prescribed gifts number three score, consisting of silk, silken girdles, sweetmeats, garments, wine, and other things. The barrels of wine are generally given by the bride to her father and mother. In addition to these many gifts, the bride of any position always receives from her future husband the white silk for her wedding gown, and a length of gold embroidery out of which is fashioned the wedding girdle—a custom which would with us be deemed a breach of etiquette, if not positively "improper."

Japanese Marriage Customs.

The wedding day is generally fixed by the "wise people" or soothsayers, and the Japanese bride and bridegroom soon discover that there are many unlucky or prohibited days. No ordinary Japanese maiden would for worlds consent to be married on any one of them. The bridegroom is expected to make his future father-in-law and mother-in-law the handsomest and most costly presents he can afford. Until the wedding day the bride makes her future husband no presents of any value, but on the day itself she sends symbolic, carefully chosen, gifts as costly as her means permit or station in life demands.

The actual wedding ceremony is somewhat long drawn out. But it seldom has any legal significance; and never (except in the case of converts to some type of the Christian faith) any religious meaning or character. It is not until sunset or twilight that the bride leaves her old home for the new. Then she enters her *kaga,* or carrying hammock, clad in white and wearing a veil of the same colour, and followed by gift-bearers, many or few according to circumstances. The most important of these latter is he who bears the bamboo, or lacquer, bucket of clams which every bride—with a handsome ceremonial dress—is expected to bring her husband, whatever else may be omitted. The gift of these un[illegible] shell-fish is made so that the bride and bridegroom may partake of clam broth together, which is believed to ensure tha[illegible] they will long dwell together in happiness; whilst the taking of such a gift to her husband is believed to ensure beautiful, as well as dutiful, children. The other numerous gifts (including usually a fine sword, a fan, two silken robes sewn together, and no fewer than seven pocket-books) which a bride of any position is expected to make her husband, are carried on trays by coolies.

When this procession arrives two fires or torches are found blazing on either side of the threshold, each tended by a man and a woman pounding rice. New matting leads up to the door, and as the bride, after alighting from her *kaga*, passes along it and enters her new home the rice from the pile at the left hand side of the portal is mixed with that on the right. And at the same moment that she crosses the threshold two great candles are tied together by their wicks by one of the bridegroom's near relatives, to symbolise the union of the souls and bodies of the contracting parties. Then follows a touching little ceremony. The joined wicks are lighted, allowed to burn for a short time, and then blown out, thus symbolising the wish that the bride and bridegroom may not only live in unity, but may, when the time comes, die together.

The bride's trousseau, which in the case of girls or women of high social position is almost as important and manifold as regards robes and under-robes—*gheta* and *tabi*, and *obis*—as that of a Western bride, is carried into the house. Then the various articles, after being taken out of their lacquer boxes and cane baskets, are tidily put away in the wall cupboards and other suitable places.

At the marriage feast which follows the dishes are, in the case of the well-to-do, almost innumerable. Much *sake* is consumed, or rather should one say, perhaps, many cups are drunk, but then they are scarcely larger than a good-sized thimble! The wine, which is hot and perfumed, is poured from beautiful little Satsuma kettles, to each of which are fastened three or more paper butterflies, so exquisitely and carefully painted that they often deceive the unwary into believing them to be real. These signify that the marriage shall be blessed with children not only well-favoured but highly endowed mentally. One kettle of the number—furnished with two spouts—is especially beautiful, and from this the bride and bridegroom drink in company, indicative of their intention to take the good or bad things of life together.

After the feast is done and the bride and bridegroom have changed their outer garments for the ceremonial attire which they have given to one another, the bride goes to the apartments of her husband's parents to pay them homage, after which both bride and bridegroom pay like homage to the ancestral tablets of each other. And with this ceremony, which is perhaps the nearest approach to anything of a religious nature that enters into the marriage rites of the Japanese, the long-drawn-out ordeal for the newly-married pair is practically at an end.

Contrary to Western customs the bride's apartments are not prepared for her reception by her future husband, his mother or his or her servants, but by the bride and bridegroom's own intimate feminine friends.

In the well-arranged and well-ordered Japanese home—and most are both—there is nothing ostentatious, nothing superfluous. There is room in the apartments for the Japanese woman to move. There is comparatively little furniture and but few ornaments, but what there is of both are the best that the owners can afford. From time to time the artistic and charming mistress may add a beautiful vase, a cabinet of lacquer work, a delicately painted screen, an exquisitely decorative *kakemono*; but she will never be worried by an accumulation of furniture for which there is little use.

Divorce in Japan.

Perhaps because there is no religious idea connected with the ceremony of marriage in Japan, divorce is astonishingly easy, though by no means so prevalent as many Western writers have stated and led European and American readers to suppose. Confucius himself gives the right to a divorce for the following seven reasons (there are not a few others):—(1) Disobedience of the wife to her mother-in-law, (2) drunkenness, (3) jealousy, (4) infectious disease, (5) thieving, (6) gossiping and mischief-making, (7) childlessness. It will not, therefore, be a matter for much surprise that the percentage of divorces is undesirably high, though not, some authorities state, higher than in France and America. Perhaps one might add that surprise might be felt that the number of permanent and happy marriages is not lower.

Education in Japan.

The Japanese woman is superstitious, and around this survival of bygone ages are many quaint and charming ideas and legends, but with that phase of her character there is no space to deal here.

Though it may be said that few Japanese women are deficient in that subtle element of charm which seems partly inherent to the women of the race, and partly to arise from her up-bringing, like the women of other nations there are many types.

It may be well first to consider the lives and types of the women of the towns before proceeding to a brief consideration of the women of the country villages, and the peasant class.

The systematic education of girls in Japan, as we regard education, is yet in a somewhat elementary stage. Each year sees an improvement; but it is only in comparatively recent times that public girls' schools have become at all numerous. The most famous of all these in the Mikado's Empire is undoubtedly the "School for Peeresses" in Tokio. This, established for the benefit of the daughters of noblemen by the Imperial Household under the patronage of the Empress Haru Ko, is situated in the centre of the city, and is built upon European lines. The schoolrooms are furnished much as they would be in England, and in the general conduct of its affairs it is very similar to a high class boarding-school for children of the upper and upper-middle classes in England.

There are at the present time nearly eight hundred pupils attending the school, of whom about twelve-and-a-half per cent. are children in the kindergarten. The teaching staff numbers about fifty, of whom two or three are Europeans. In this truly modern and in many ways magnificent institution not only are the usual subjects and foreign languages taught, but also all the ceremonial and traditional etiquette which it is necessary for every pupil to learn so that she may take her proper position in after life. But although the highest accomplishments are carefully taught, the simpler duties of plain sewing and cooking find places in the education of these high-born young ladies, many of whom become not only expert cooks, but also skilful embroiderers. To the girls who now attend this famous and interesting school much of the etiquette seems irksome and unnecessary, but all who have witnessed the charm and grace of manner which the old *régime* has produced in the women and girls of Japan will surely echo a wish that this may never be weakened or supplanted by the intrusion of more modern methods.

This School for Peeresses may be taken (except for the rank of its pupils and a few minor details) as fairly typical of the new order of schools, the number of which is being gradually multiplied, for the education of Japanese girlhood.

The Japanese Lady of Fashion.

The highest rank of Japanese women of the towns represented by the ladies of the Court, lead lives of comparative ease and luxury, but by no means of idleness. Although attended by many servants, and in receipt of a salary always sufficient for her reasonable needs—and, be it remarked, such is the Japanese horror of personal debt, seldom exceeded—a lady of the Court has a number of complicated duties to perform. The etiquette is extremely strict and intricate. To many of them, however, all these formalities are as second nature, for they have been brought up in the atmosphere of the Court, and have probably entered it when quite small girls. In a measure as regards charm, intellectual attainments, refinement, and beauty, the women of the nobility are only typical of the women of the upper middle classes.

TOKIO GEISHA.

Women of the Samurai.

The *samurai*, which was anciently the class coming midway between the nobles and those engaged in business, art, or agriculture, and was of a distinctly military type, have always been fearless and brave, and the women have in a large degree inherited these qualities. Japanese history and legend are full of the gallant and heroic deeds of men and women of this class. In many a story does the *samurai* woman, and even young girl, figure who infinitely preferred a death of horrible torture not only to personal dishonour, but even to dishonour brought about by the betrayal of a trust or of a master.

In ancient times the *samurai* women were taught fencing and drill, and wore uniform. Upon them often—gentle-mannered, truly feminine and delicately nurtured as they were—devolved the task of defending the castle which belonged to their fathers, husbands, brothers, or to which by ties of service they were attached. They seldom failed to perform their appointed task with skill, heroism, and valour, for in their veins—notwithstanding their gentle demeanour in ordinary life—ran the blood of generations of fighting ancestors.

This type of women still survives in modern Japan, although the necessity for the exhibition of martial gifts has passed away with the establishment of the reigning dynasty, the disappearance of internecine warfare, and freedom from invasion. But doubtless the spirit only sleeps, and should necessity arise the girls and women of modern Japan, descendants of the old *samurai* race, would prove equally effective "Amazons" as those of the past. Not a few women belonging to *samurai* families have of recent times risen to positions of importance in the Court. They are almost certain from their ancestry and up-bringing to be possessed of high intellectual character, steadfastness of purpose, and unswerving loyalty.

Perhaps no greater contrast could be presented to women of the *samurai* class than by the *geisha* of whom so much has been written in modern times. It is not easy to overstate the charm of these, but it is possible to over-exaggerate their importance in Japanese social life. And, although they do not loom so large in the eyes of the Japanese themselves as in those of foreigners, these little "butterfly," charming creatures add much to the colour of everyday existence, and an entertainment of any importance is scarcely regarded as either complete or successful without the music, dancing, and graceful attendance of the dainty little maidens who though often frail are nevertheless so delightful and pleasing.

The Geisha Girl.

Combining the entertainer with the waitress they are found at all tea-houses and restaurants of any standing. They are trained when young (having adopted, or been delegated to the profession, or leased out by their parents) in singing, dancing, and fascinating manners. In a word their education is almost solely in the art to please. In it manners stand higher than morals; and there is therefore little cause for wonder if they have no keen ethical sense. The *geisha* is not always inherently bad, but in her usual environment, mode of life, and the standard of morals (or lack of them) expected of her there is so much that is questionable, that it is not at all surprising if many cross the rubicon which divides respectability from the *demi-monde*. But so fascinating, witty, pretty, well-dressed and charming are they that quite a considerable number ultimately marry into good families, and there are at the present time many ex-*geisha* as the heads of upper middle-class households.

The Japanese dances in which the *geisha* excels are modest and graceful; and she is a past mistress in the supple and pantomimic swaying of her little body, and the skilful arrangement and management of her garments and draperies during the various movements of the dance. She, of course, knows nothing of waltzes, polkas, quadrilles, or the "kitchen" or other "Lancers," although the "cake walk," alas! has travelled over from America, and may be seen at the less high-class and reputable *geisha-ya*, or dance-houses, and resorts. The dances most favoured are those which depict some picture or incident, either of a dramatic or artistic character, such as the story of the plum or cherry trees from the time they were planted until the blossoms burst into flower to make the world beautiful; or some legend, or a dramatic or domestic event, or stirring warlike incident. Every movement of a *geisha* is perfection, arising from close and careful study; although such is the art, one is apt to imagine them spontaneous and even commonplace. The natural ease and grace has been acquired only by long months and even years of training.

For many years dancing had fallen so low in public estimation that the *geishas* were practically ostracised and relegated to public resorts of questionable character. But at length there came a revulsion in their favour, and they were permitted to re-enter (or at least entertain) good society. Nowadays the *geisha* forms an important adjunct in the social life of Japan; and a picturesque figure as she moves about in the dance to the rather unmelodious accompaniment of the orchestra consisting of *samisen*, *kota* and drum, with the wide and flowing sleeves of her *kimono* and gaily-coloured skirts swelling and contracting with each movement and graceful curve of her supple figure. She is, notwithstanding her rouged lips and powdered face and artful artlessness, a dainty and winsome figure, and generally not only a skilful dancer but a witty and well-informed conversationalist. And then, when their dancing is over, they become once more the charming attendants, waiting upon their employers and the guests, laughing and jesting, and using to the full all the arts of fascination in which they have been so carefully trained. If they have hearts (and doubtless they have) they do not wear them on their sleeves; but the *geisha*, come good fortune or bad, is always the same smiling, untroubled, and apparently carelessly happy creature which her education in self-control enables her to be.

The women of the lower class in the towns follow chiefly the occupations most closely identified with indoor and domestic work. In many of the smaller stores or shops, however, the wife and daughter of the proprietor assist him in the management and general conduct of the business. As in European towns these people mostly live "over the shop" or rather behind it, where there are generally well-kept and spotlessly clean apartments leading out into pretty garden plots.

Work-women of Japan.

Although of recent years a few factories, more nearly approaching in their general scheme those of Europe, have been started with their concomitants of noise and machinery, the factory girl in Japan is of a very different type to that of England. In place of the coarseness, which seems almost inseparable from the mode of life, one finds refinement; in place of gaudy, tawdry and unkempt raiment, brightness and neatness; and in place of dirt, which seems to be almost hereditary, cleanliness. Although girls—some of them seem little more than babies—and women are largely employed in the decoration of pottery in the eastern quarters of Kioto; at Obuke, near Kuwana, where the famous Ban-ko pottery, the invention of Nun-ami Ban-ko, is made; and at Seto and elsewhere they have not yet by the employment of machinery been turned into machines, and in all Japanese manufactures there yet enters that personal element which makes for efficiency, quality, and artistic merit.

HOTEL SERVANTS OF JAPAN.

Professions for Women in Japan.

Although as we have said the more domestic occupations of life are mostly followed by women, there are yet others in the larger towns and cities by which women and girls may earn a living for themselves and those dependent upon them. In hotels, for example, throughout the country women and girls find employment in large numbers. Waiters of the conventional type are happily unknown, and their places are taken by low-voiced, generally pretty, and always charming and daintily dressed girls. Not seldom, too, the owner or the manager is a woman. How vigilant as regards the comfort of their guests most lady hotel proprietors are travellers soon learn. Even if men or the husbands are seen about they usually appear to be carrying out the orders of the women. They are wise enough to know that as managers the latter are hard to excel, and that their guests will appreciate to the full "service by women." In Swiss hotels there is a tradition that the proprietors, waiters, and other people connected with them sleep only in winter. One wonders after an experience of a Japanese hotel when those responsible for its management, and the delicate and constant attendance on guests, take their rest.

The tea-houses both in the town and country also provide employment for numbers of girls and women, for at every convenient halting place on highways and byways the traveller finds a tea-house. There are hundreds of them scattered along the great Kaido which lies between Kyōtō and Tōkyo, and along the other main roads of Japan. It is true that sometimes it is but an elementary affair at which little more than tea and perhaps bread and eggs (and not always the last) can be obtained, but the tea-house proprietress and her little waiting-maids will always make the welcome go as far as possible towards a forgetting of the shortcomings of the fare available. In the larger tea-houses and restaurants no charge is made for either the tea or the sweetmeats offered, but the guest is expected to leave a small *chadai* or tip as a present. After anything approaching a stay at a restaurant or inn the *chadai* naturally amounts to an important sum (calculated usually at about the equivalent of sixpence per person per day), which has to be presented, wrapped in paper and inscribed "*O chadai*," or the "Honourable Tip," to the landlord. Both the giver and receiver are expected respectively to depreciate the *chadai* and the services rendered. The guest has given only a miserable recompense (but as much as he or she can afford) for all the extraordinary comfort and services enjoyed; whilst the recipient of the *chadai* has had his or her miserable house over-honoured by the guest, and has done absolutely nothing to deserve *chadai* at all!

A WORK-GIRL GRINDING COLOURS FOR CLOISONNÉ VASE-MAKERS.

After the formality of the gift the departing guest is speeded on the journey by loud shouts of grateful thanks. So perfect is the self-control of the tea-house attendant or proprietor of an inn that, however disappointed he or she may be at the amount received, not a suspicion of this is apparent in either face or manner. How different from the waiter of the West!

Women of the cities, too, although the tailoring is mostly in the hands of men, gain employment by taking in sewing in their own homes, and also by giving sewing lessons. Many, too, earn more or less precarious livings by giving instruction in etiquette, flower arrangement, music, painting, and in the complicated ceremonies incident to tea drinking, where the mere putting down, handing, or filling of a cup is a matter of the greatest consequence. The art of flower arrangement is, however, much in the hands of the men in its more elaborate ceremonial and mystical branches.

Amongst the other professions and businesses open to, and more especially suited to, women is that of the hair-dresser. They form not only a type but a class amongst Japanese womenkind. A specially skilful hair-dresser, or *kamiyui*, speedily gathers around her a large *clientèle*, and earns an income which is sufficient not alone for living but even for luxury.

JAPANESE LADY GARDENERS.
In the cultivation of flowers many women are employed.

Indeed, hair-dressing amongst the Japanese of the upper classes is such a science that perfection in the art deserves and obtains fair remuneration. Several hours' constant work is often needed for the proper building up of one lady's *coiffure*. Five hours or more may be spent over the most elaborate forms of hair-dressing. The most popular and skilful hair-dressers cannot obviously do all the work themselves, and this fact is the means of providing employment for numbers of girls and women assistants, who do the preliminary work of washing, pomading, and plaiting, leaving the finishing touches to the hair-dresser-in-chief.

One of the most charming professions followed by women in Japan is undoubtedly the manufacture of the exquisite artificial flowers. So beautiful, indeed, are some that the result is rather a paraphrase than an imitation. For festivals and other occasions, thousands and thousands of cherry-blossoms are fashioned by the skilful fingers of the flower-makers, and the bare trees are covered with blooms so exquisitely made and perfumed that only on the closest examination is it possible to discover they are not the work of Nature but of human hands.

Throughout the Japanese Empire domestic service is an occupation followed by many thousands of women and girls. To the newly-arrived foreigner and the casual tourist the relationship existing between the employer and employed is not at first easily understood. There is a freedom which is strangely puzzling, and an independence of judgment and action which strikes the Western mind as unusual. Although industrious, clean, and loyal, the Japanese servant only follows out orders if she can see the reason for them. And frequently when they do carry out orders it is in quite their own way. But there are nevertheless few more charming domestics than the Japanese girl, who possesses unflagging good humour, and is painstaking.

The Servant Question in Japan.

One quaint custom of the many connected with domestic service may be noted. It is for all the unoccupied servants as well as the members of the family to see the master off when he leaves in the morning, and welcome him back at night. A strange picture is formed, where there are numbers of servants kept, by the bowing line of domestics at the front door or along the verandah of the house when the master or the other members of the family leave it or return.

The women of the countryside play a very important part in the bread-winning occupations of the land. There is, indeed, little work performed by men in the rural parts of Japan which is not more or less shared by women. Industrious as the small farmers and cultivators of the soil undoubtedly are it is a keen struggle with most to make both ends meet, and it is recognised that the women and girls of the household must play their part in the battle of life, even in the more exhausting varieties of toil and labour on the land.

Women Agricultural Workers.

In the rice fields the women and men work side by side, the former with their *kimono* tucked up round their waists, and their lower limbs either bare or clad in blue cotton trousers, standing in the none too sweet-smelling mud in which the tender rice plants thrive, planting, transplanting, weeding, and tending the delicate green shoots from morn till eve. The rice fields, which are usually of comparatively small size, and seldom perfectly square (more often hexagonal, sexagonal, and pentagonal in shape), are little more than huge tanks of liquid mud retained by earth banks beaten hard, sun-

A FARM WOMAN SEPARATING THE RICE FROM THE STRAW.

baked and sloping. It is the women, too, who gather the winter's store of fire-wood, ultimately returning with loads, tied to a wooden framework on their backs or carried on their heads, which would be considered in Western lands as far too heavy for women to carry.

MODERN JAPAN.
A group of Red Cross Nurses.

In the harvesting of rice, the threshing and winnowing, and the subsequent grinding, women play an important part; as they also do in the silkworm industry. In the latter the care of the worms and cocoons, and the winding off of silk and weaving, is left almost entirely to the women and girls; so much so, indeed, that it would be little exaggeration to say that this industry, one of the most important in Japan, is practically worked by the women.

In the tea fields, too, and in general farming, and the cultivation of flowers for sale in the markets of the larger towns women also play an important part. Many of the women gardeners of Japan have won considerable fame quite outside the particular village or town where they happen to reside.

Three occupations, at least in rural Japan, may be termed ideal for the women who follow them; the silk industry; the cultivation and harvesting of tea; and the tending of the many exquisite flowers which make their native land the Garden of the East.

Happiness is with the Peasant Women in Japan.

It is amongst the peasant classes of Japan that women enjoy the fullest independence and freedom. Most, though leading a laborious existence and enjoying few comforts, lead lives of industry, and, within their limitations of intelligence, are respected by the men with whom they labour in common. The wealthy women and those of the upper middle-class when they marry lay aside their independence, and even though treated with kindness, affection, and consideration, become the superior servants of their husbands' households, and it is soon borne in upon them how much of what is best worth possessing they have resigned. With the peasant woman of all grades it is different. She has merely stepped from one position of toil in her father's household to a very similar one in that of her husband, often sharing his occupation, and entering fully into the interests of his life, which are outside the sphere of her own more domestic duties. It is in the peasant woman in consequence that one often finds the happiest nature, and the smiling face unmarked by lines of illusion, boredom, or sorrow as the years roll on and life's lessons and life's enigmas have been faced and solved.

The Future of Japanese Women.

It is difficult to forecast what the Japanese woman of the future may be. For generations yet to come she must be charming until she has unlearned or forgotten (if she ever does) all the sweet feminine graces handed down to her from her ancestors. But it is also safe to say that her natural intelligence will respond to the greater opportunities of expansion of mind and education both mental and physical, which the new order is slowly but surely establishing.

One can wish nothing better for the women of Japan than that they may, whilst gaining much from education and extended freedom, lose nothing of those softer graces and more tender refinements which have distinguished them in the past.

Photograph by T. Enami, Japan.

JAPANESE TAILORESSES AT WORK.

AINU WOMEN WEAVING.

They do not wear moustachios, but are curiously tattooed round their mouths.

THE AINU

By JESSIE ACKERMANN, F.R.S.G.S.

Tattooing Customs—Position of Ainu Women—The Woman's Part

IN common with Oriental races, an Ainu girl is the most unwelcome creature ever thrust into being. She is but another burden-bearer among a peculiar people, doomed to a life of hardship and toil.

Tattooing Customs. A curious custom of tattooing the lips of a girl in infancy has always obtained among them. No one seems to have any idea of either its origin or meaning. It is probably as ancient as foot-binding in China, and its purpose, beyond that of a tribal badge, is completely lost in the dim ages of the past.

When a girl is about two years old the mother begins the disfiguring and painful process of tattooing the lips, without which mark she could never hope to win a husband. The work, being very painful, is done a little at a time, and a period of two years is covered before it is completed, the result being a large diamond-shaped patch of dark blue completely surrounding the mouth and extending in points well towards the ears.

The concoction used is prepared by the mother, and is easily brewed in every home. Ash-bark is soaked for some days, and to

A GROUP OF AINU.

The women are distinguished by the curious tattoo marks round the mouth.

this is added the soot of burned birch-bark. A goodly portion is rubbed over the surface to be operated upon, and the wriggling, screaming girl is placed under the torture of a sharp instrument which pierces the skin and absorbs the colouring matter. The work is continued from time to time as the irritation ceases. As the child grows the blotch spreads until it becomes a most disfiguring feature to an otherwise not unpleasant face — a type wholly unlike any of the Far Eastern races.

In olden times it was the custom to continue the work of decoration after marriage by tattooing a band across the forehead, rings on the fingers, and many circles about the arms. These outward evidences of the married state may still be seen among the very old women, but the custom has largely passed away.

Position of Ainu Women.

There is a remarkably peculiar fascination about these frank-faced, guileless children of Nature, and although utterly degraded in the minds of the men, they are the "motive power" in all affairs.

In height they about average the women of Japan, although they are greatly superior in physical strength, and can endure no end of hardship—a lot to which they are born. They are most abject slaves to men. If a woman meets one upon the highway, she at once turns aside and covers her mouth with her hand that the air may not be polluted for a man by a woman's breath; the cloth head-gear is instantly removed, and, bowed in the attitude of humility, she stands until the man has fully passed.

When a woman marries she is not honoured by bearing the name of the man of her choice, but is designated by her maiden name, or as the wife of So-and-so. If widowed, she takes the name of her son, if she has one, which is usually the case. It is considered a great disgrace for a woman to remain childless, a fact which forms sufficient grounds for a man to refuse to live with his wife. In such a case it is supposed that the gods are punishing the woman for some of her evil deeds, and without trial by judge or jury she is declared an unfit companion for any man, there being no higher court than the will of her husband.

The Woman's Part.

Everything is most primitive. The manufacture of cloth is a household matter, and every married woman is expected to produce the family supply. After she has helped in the field, and the scanty supply has been gathered in, she hurries off to the woods to gather nuts and bark. The nuts are stored for winter supply, and the fibre of the bark is twisted into thread used both for weaving and sewing. Roots are gathered, and indigo grown for dyeing purposes. The chief pride and delight of every woman is to bedeck her husband in garments "fearfully and wonderfully made." Although quite grotesque when taken apart from the wearer, they well become his unique style. The background is usually a dull, almost dirty, blue; and upon this irregular designs wander at large over the entire surface. When a bear-feast—the great event of the year in each village—is to take place, the fond wife puts the finishing touch to the make-up of her husband, and if by any means she can secure a horse upon which he may go forth, she follows through the ankle-deep mud, often almost breathless in an attempt to keep up with the animal, that she may be at hand to render service.

As their religion is one of evil spirits, and these spirits demand constant sacrifice in the form of valueless offerings, the Ainu woman is most useful in preparing worship-sticks and placing them where they will ward off the wrath of the spirits or call down their favour. Shavings of pine sticks are placed in the east window, at the well, in fields, and beside the fire, that the man may enjoy freedom from the wrath of the spirits as well as bask in the sunshine of their favour. From childhood to old age the Ainu woman has but one mission—that of spending her life to minister to the comfort of man.

KOREA

By JESSIE ACKERMANN, F.R.S.G.S.

Class Difference—Girls' Work—Girls Have No Names—Korean Dress—A Land of Laziness—Woman and Religion—The High-class Girl—A Curious Hat—Position of Married Women

THE life of a Korean woman depends largely upon the special class into which she is born. The difference between the high and low class women is so wide that they almost belong to two worlds.

Class Difference.

The advent of a girl among the lower class is a matter of the least possible interest, scarcely beyond the annoying fact that the mother is not at her usual post of service and men's wants are less well supplied.

Of education the Korean girl requires none. Until quite recently, schools for girls among the common people—usually called " low class "—were considered wholly unnecessary—that is, if any consideration was given to the matter ; and even now, apart from the free instruction given at mission schools, this class is almost wholly neglected. Of necessity a girl must learn how to cook and to help in the tobacco field—for almost every house has a patch of " the weed," and women as well as men —yes, even children—are given to smoking. The use of tobacco, indeed, is common among all classes, but not, as in many places, for chewing.

Girls' Work.

If a girl's help is not required in the home, and the parents live in or near villages and cities, the girls at a very early age become burden bearers or vendors of flowers in the market-places. While young, they wear trousers and a short tunic, which enables them to move quickly about in search of work. With a bamboo rack fitted to the back and a skirt made of grass or reeds, they gather in the markets where women are out getting supplies for the day. It is surprising to see the weight these frail-looking girls fairly march off with in their eagerness to earn a cash or two.

Girls Have No Names.

Tradition and superstition have relegated the girl to a place where is she not considered even worthy of a name, and the luxury of any individual designation from other girls is not hers. She merely sustains a relation to the district from which she comes. She is simply " it " or " that " until married. Then her identity is completely lost in that of her husband. Her own people call her by the name of the district from which her husband comes, but when a boy is born to her she is called the mother of that boy.

Korean Dress.

The girl, in some manner, but at no stated time or experience, finds herself in a dress. It is a national costume, and would seem comfortable if properly adjusted. It consists of two pieces—a waist and skirt. The former is so abbreviated as to extend only to the armpits ; the thickly-gathered skirt is supposed to be on friendly relations with the waist, but usually it falls some six or eight inches short, and a dark girdle of " real skin " is the only belt in vogue among them. It often comes to pass among the lower class that a woman, having once put her dress on, removes it only when she sheds it in fragments, a scrap at a time.

Oppression among the officials is so great in the way of taxation that there is little inducement for men to work. They are content with a patch of tobacco for family use, and as the climate is mild, there is no suffering from that source. Women follow the lead of men in the matter of subdued energy, if, indeed, they ever possess any; and are given to spending whole days in the shade of the house quietly smoking the hours away in a dreamy fashion, from which even a knock-down squabble of the children fails fully to arouse them. The pipes have very long stems and tiny bowls, which hold hardly more than a thimble-full of tobacco; this is consumed in a whiff or two, and the pipe passes freely about from one to another.

A Land of Laziness.

Although woman seems to have no civil being, the men in a sense stand in awe of the fair sex. Perhaps it should be called a superstitious dread. Believing that religion is intended for women and children, a man's constant fear is that a woman will have more influence with the gods than he, and in a vexatious mood will avenge herself by calling down their wrath upon his defenceless head. These customs may be said, generally speaking, to prevail throughout the country, for they are usual among the masses.

Women and Religion.

KOREAN STREET CHILDREN.

The life of a high-class girl is superior in that she has better clothes, is surrounded by a larger degree of comfort, enjoys a limited amount of education, and cultivates such gifts as a taste for painting and needlework, which has at least the advantage of giving her mental occupation.

The High-Class Girl.

A newly-married couple form a most picturesque sight. The groom is clad in white, with only a coloured tunic. The acme of originality is reached in the hat, woven from the hair of his lamented ancestors on

A Curious Hat.

KOREAN BRIDE AND BRIDEGROOM.

his father's side. At the passing of each generation a lock of hair is woven into a braid, which is added to the hat, often of fantastic shape, but usually of ordinary pattern, with high crown and broad brim.

The bride appears in public places with him, and he seems in no way ashamed of her. The upper class women arrange matters of dress with great care, and when leaving the house, even in a closed conveyance, are always accompanied by one or more women attendants. Those who belong to the best families never venture from the house unless properly veiled, peeping out through a small opening to see their way.

Position of Married Women.

As the country is slow to move, even under the inspiration of rushing Japanese enterprise, it will be long before woman comes into her own in this land.

CHINA

By A. R. COLQUHOUN

Popular Misconceptions on the Position of Chinese Women—Women Coolies—Conditions of Women's Life in China—Legal Disabilities of Chinese Women—The Principle of Woman's Inferiority to Man—Reasons for Infanticide—Child Life—Betrothal Customs—How a Marriage is Arranged—Marriage Rules and Customs—Position of Wives in China—The Suicide Habit—Secondary Wives—Family Life—Women Workers—Seclusion of the Better-class Women—"Foot-binding"—Clothing—*Coiffures*—The Use of Rouge and Powder—The Chinese Ideal of Beauty—Literature and Woman—"Henpecked" Chines —Influence of Woman in China—Devotion to Parents—The Position of Widows—The Future of Chinese Women

Popular Misconceptions on the Position of Chinese Women.

IT is always difficult to give a fair idea of any people by describing them from the outside only, and therefore (as Chinese women do not at present rush into print with their feelings and experiences) one is at a disadvantage in attempting to draw a picture of a side of Chinese life with which it is only possible to be acquainted as a superficial observer.

It is easy enough to catalogue a Chinese woman's clothes, to describe her appearance and the customs to which she must conform, to explain her legal and social status and the duties she must fulfil. But, when we have done all this, we have merely the shell; of the living, breathing woman we hardly catch a glimpse. Writers who adopt this photographic method leave us with the impression that the Chinese woman is so hemmed in with restrictions that she scarcely has a personality, that she is so brought up by rule that she can hardly have a soul to call her own. Human nature, however, is the same all the world over, and there are reasons for believing that, although etiquette not only enforces the seclusion of the Chinese woman but forbids even the mention of a Chinese wife in society, yet women occupy, whether as mothers or wives, a position of great importance and considerable influence in the Middle Kingdom. In any case, a Chinese woman would hardly agree with the foreigner in his estimate of the indignity and helplessness of her position.

Women Coolies.

A new-comer to China will be struck at any of the Treaty ports with the crowd of active brown-faced coolie women—dressed, like their men folk, in black or blue cotton tunics and trousers, and only distinguishable by their head-dress—who are swarming about the streets and adjacent country, doing every kind of work. On the rivers of the South he will see these broad, sturdy creatures working the heavy boats, their babies strapped on their backs. If he journeys into the interior he will meet them in every village or market place buying and selling, doing field work, carrying weights, and generally taking a share in all rough work. At the same time he will note the almost complete absence from all public places of women of the better classes. These, he is told, are secluded, not with Mohammedan rigour (even when the Chinese profess Islam they are far from orthodox), but prohibited by public opinion from going abroad to be seen of men.

It is obvious that the greatest difference must exist, in every relation of life, between the woman who shares her husband's work and perhaps supports him, going abroad freely to do it, and her sister who lives in the seclusion of the woman's court, engaged in household work and endless embroidery, like European ladies of an earlier age.

Conditions of Women's Life in China.

an important part only as a mother. Marriage is the one honourable career for a Chinese girl, and when she marries she loses, absolutely and entirely, any identity she may have possessed and becomes part of her husband's family.

It is the aim of every Chinaman to have a male descendant to carry on those rites

Photograph by N. P. Edwards, Littlehampton.

CHINESE LADIES.

In generalising, therefore, about the women of China, one must keep clearly in mind the fact that there is almost as much difference in the lots of Chinese women of the upper and lower classes as between the Duchess of Sangazure and 'Liza of Lambeth—almost, but not quite, for through the lives of Chinese women of all classes runs a thread which gives them closer kinship than sex alone. Chinese society is not built up in the somewhat haphazard manner of our own. It is founded on strict lines and permeated with strong convictions. In it the family is the basis of everything, the individual is of no account, and in this scheme woman plays

of ancestral worship which he believes to be essential to the prosperity of his family, not only on earth but already in another sphere. A daughter cannot do this. As soon as she is marriageable, therefore, she passes into another family and can worship only at the ancestral shrines of her husband. The complete break between a girl and her parents, when she marries, can only be realised when we remember that, unlike her European sister who may still run to her mother for advice and guidance, she becomes the absolute property of her husband and is bound to render implicit obedience not merely to him but to his parents also. It follows, then, that a woman is in every way less free and less important than a man, and it is the blind, unquestioning acceptance of this doctrine in every rank of life which constitutes the main difference between the women of China and their European or American sisters.

Photograph by N. P. Edwards, Littlehampton.

CHINESE LADIES PLAYING CARDS AND DRINKING TEA.

Legal Disabilities of Chinese Women.

The legal status of the Chinese woman leaves much to be desired. No provision is made for daughters in the division of property, which is an additional reason for the anxiety of parents to get their girls married early. As a child the girl is subject entirely to her father, and among the poorest classes in certain districts it is not only possible but is condoned by public opinion that a father should sell his daughter. When she marries her husband has entire jurisdiction over her, and his parents, to whom he himself is subject as long as they live, have even more authority. But she is to a certain extent protected, especially among the upper classes, by public opinion and by custom.

A marriage can be dissolved by mutual consent or the man can divorce his wife for any of seven reasons (one of which is over-talkativeness). But he may not get rid of her thus unless her parents are still living (so that she has a home to go to), nor may he send her away if he, being poor at the time of the marriage, has since amassed riches. Also when the wife can prove that she has served his parents faithfully she may not be divorced. Apart from these slight safeguards, however, a married woman is without protection until she has a son, after which happy event she shines with reflected importance. In the case of ill-treatment by her husband or his people her own relations may remonstrate or interfere, but on the whole public opinion, as well as immemorial custom, is on the side of parents-in-law.

The fundamental principle underlying this whole question of relations between the sexes is that woman is inferior to man. Chinese philosophy attributes death and evil to *Yin*, the female principle in Nature, while life and prosperity come from *Yang*, the male principle. Very few Chinese probably stop to reason on the subject, for it appears to them to be a Law of Nature that women should occupy an entirely different position from men in the scheme of life, and the women themselves would not question the dispensation.

The Principle of Woman's Inferiority to Man.

From the practical point of view the entire submission of women and their lack of individual rights seem to the Chinese to secure that symmetry and continuity in the family which is his highest ideal. These generalisations are true in every class of life, and the effects of the entire subservience of women, whether they are high-born secluded ladies or women workers in the fields, vary only in degree.

Reasons for Infanticide.

The fact that a daughter is only a temporary resident in her father's home, and that any care bestowed on her will in the end only benefit her husband's family, makes the advent of a girl baby an affair of moderated rejoicing. Among the poorest families, especially in times of famine, the event is sometimes a calamity; and it is the thought of the future, in which it may be impossible to provide for the little girl's marriage, which leads so many parents to practise infanticide. It is quite impossible to get any reliable statistics as to the prevalence of this custom. Evidence is forthcoming that a great number of girl babies disappear without funeral rites, but a certain number are probably the victims of ignorance and immaturity, whose parents are unable or unwilling to incur the heavy expenses of a funeral.

Child Life.

There is no reason to suppose that the Chinese are callous to their offspring; indeed, they give every outward sign of tenderness while their children are in the baby stage. The little girl, therefore, though her father may not mention her with pride to his friends, is carried in his arms, fondled, and played with, and as soon as she can walk is dressed in clothes which are exactly like her mother's in miniature. On the great feast of the New Year she will be decked in garments of red and yellow, her little face painted, and her chubby wrists and ankles hung with beads. She will enjoy a certain amount of liberty while still a child, and will not be pestered with many attempts at education. At the age of seven or eight she will be separated from the boys, who then go to school. If she is the daughter of a well-to-do family she will learn to read and write and to do fine embroidery. But among the working-classes she will run about wild or help her mother in the house-work and (among the peasantry) in the fields, until she arrives at an age when her marriage must be thought of.

Betrothal Customs.

It is not etiquette, even in the poorest classes, that the future husband or his relations should see the prospective bride, and therefore the moment she is betrothed she is obliged to stay closely at home. To avoid a possible breach of propriety the custom is to choose a *fiancé* from another town or village. Both this and other marriage customs are sedulously upheld by the matchmakers or go-betweens, who arrange all Chinese marriages, and naturally do not desire to simplify matters and thus lose their opportunities for fees and perquisites.

The parents anxious to marry a son or daughter resort to one of these go-betweens, who at once looks round for a likely match. Sometimes the betrothal takes place in childhood, and it is very rarely that the engagement is broken, whatever happens. After betrothal the little liberty hitherto allowed to a Chinese girl is at once restricted, and she is forbidden to go abroad, where she might possibly be seen by some member of the family into which she is to marry. If Chinese etiquette were strictly observed no husband would ever see his bride's face until he had escorted her home, but human

A MARRIAGE PROCESSION IN CHINA.

Photograph by Afong, Hong Kong.

nature asserts itself, and, although love finds no part in the outward appearance of a Chinese marriage, and though the Chinese proverb says:

> "No whispering beneath the trees,
> Ere yet the knot be tied,"

romances are not unknown in which mutual attraction, stolen interviews, and clandestine love letters play a part. If these things did not sometimes happen in real life the romances, which are eagerly read by the youths and maidens of the Flowery Land, would lose all interest. It may be noted that, although Chinese opinion and philosophy are against educating a daughter, because it is merely "tilling another man's field," yet the heroine of romance is always highly educated and capable of making beautiful, impromptu verses.

How a Marriage is Arranged.

Marriage customs vary greatly in different parts of China, but there are some which are invariable, and the chief of these is the employment of the inevitable go-between who arranges every detail. This important intermediary settles the principal conditions before the heads of the two families actually meet, advises concerning the respective circumstances of the families, fully guarantees the honour on either side, and reports on the characters of the mothers-in-law. It is very common for horoscopes to be cast to ascertain if the heavenly portents are favourable.

When all the preliminaries have been settled the engagement is usually concluded by the exchange of red visiting cards of enormous size. The custom as to interchange of presents is one of the most varied of all.* In parts of Southern China the parents

* A Chinese proverb makes the custom as to dowries fairly plain, when it says that "the upper classes endow their daughters on marriage, the middle classes simply rear and marry them, while the lower classes make money by marrying them."

of a boy almost literally purchase a wife for him, and great are the chafferings of the go-betweens. The instinct of a Chinaman for a bargain will sometimes induce him to bid for what is obviously a this side of Chinese marriages presents great similarity to our own customs, and there is even a duplicate of our own *corvée* of presents expected from friends and relations, who are invited to the wedding.

Photograph by N. P. Edwards, Littlehampton.

CHINESE LADIES IN OUTDOOR COSTUME.

They are riding in the native "wheelbarrow" carriage.

damaged or inferior piece of goods, if he can get it "dirt cheap." On the contrary the expenses of the wedding often weigh very heavily on the bride's family, for they may have to provide her with a large outfit and even a dowry.

Among the educated classes, and especially the high officials, it is customary not only to provide a daughter with many pieces of furniture and bedding, but to spend a large sum on elaborate wedding festivities, while the bridegroom on his part must contribute pieces of silk and satin and jewelled hair-pins, ear- and finger-rings. On the whole,

Marriage Rites and Customs.

The feast is the main feature in every marriage. Among people who are too poor to give the wedding feast unaided it is customary for the guests to bring a contribution in food or money, which is regulated as to amount by etiquette, though, as a matter of fact, the "share" given is frequently smaller than what is promised or expected.

The essential part of the Chinese wedding ceremony is the arrival of the bride at her husband's home, when she is carried across the threshold over a charcoal brazier, or red-hot coulter. In modified forms this custom obtains everywhere, and is indeed found in the primitive marriage customs of all four continents. The journey to her new home is made by a Chinese bride in the red sedan-chair which she can only occupy once in her life. She is dressed in her best clothes, covered with a red silk veil, and then bundled into this close red chair. Brides have been suffocated, or (in bad weather) even frozen to death, during this bridal journey, so that the experience must be one which few girls would wish to repeat.

The bride has, perhaps, spent the days preceding her wedding in mourning and wailing with her female relations and friends, a form prescribed by etiquette rather than feeling. In any case, she will have a long ordeal to go through after she arrives at her new home, sitting side by side with her husband while relations and friends offer congratulations; it is a test of good breeding not to show the smallest sign of fatigue or emotion. When her brief day of importance and grandeur is over—and among the poorer people even the wedding garment is hired, and returned as soon as the bride arrives at her home—the Chinese wife settles down under the rule of her mother-in-law. Honeymoons are not *de rigueur* in any class of society, nor are endearments and caresses considered an essential feature of newly married life.

Position of Wives in China.

The Chinese bride does not, like the European one, expect to have "a good time" while she is young. She simply looks forward to the day when she herself will be a mother-in-law. The first few years of her marriage, before she has shaken down and become accustomed to her new and exacting relations, are the most trying of her whole life. The husband is her master. Her duty is to be merely "a shadow and an echo." Even the affection of her husband cannot protect her against his parents, and she may be scolded, punished, and beaten without hope of redress. Notwithstanding all this it seems probable that the rule of an elder woman is of great service in a home where the wife may still be a mere child in years and experience, and the habits of subordination and obedience in which girls are trained make their subservience less difficult than it appears.

To the question "Are marriages happy in China?" it is difficult to return a satisfactory answer, because the ideal of happiness is so different in East and West. From our point of view Chinese marriages seem mere business arrangements for continuing the race, accompanied by a subjection of one of the contracting parties which almost amounts to slavery. Viewed from the point of view of the Chinese, however, Western marriages seem equally infelicitous.

The Suicide Habit.

Certainly the Chinese race does increase and multiply, family scandals and divorce are comparatively unusual, and the one really abnormal circumstance is the prevalence of suicide among girls and young wives. The former sometimes band themselves together under a vow of celibacy, to which death is the accepted alternative. But this phenomenon, no doubt partly due to the tendency of girls of a certain age to hysteria, is less remarkable than the number of women who make away with themselves during the first few years of married life. This distressing fact is usually attributed to the unkindness of mothers-in-law rather than of husbands. Probably the irritation of the young wives' nerves, and their desire to "get even" with their tormentors who (to use the Chinese phrase) have made them "eat bitterness," have a good deal to account for it. To the Chinese there is no more subtle way of "paying out" one's enemy than by committing suicide on his premises. The lack of self-control usual among Chinese women, especially of the lower classes who have no training or education to help them, must be largely answerable for the suicidal tendency.

A frequent cause of married unhappiness is undoubtedly the custom of taking secondary wives, which is allowed all over China, but is deprecated on the score of wisdom

Photograph by N. P. Edwards, Littlehampton.

CHINESE GIRLS LEARNING TO WRITE AT A MISSION SCHOOL.

by most Chinese and condemned by their philosophy. It is naturally a habit restricted to those who can afford it, but is by no means invariable even among the wealthy. It is, of course, considered almost necessary should the first wife be childless or have no son.

Secondary Wives.

Family Life.

From the time the Chinese girl, herself almost a child, becomes the mother of a son she is a much more important person, but as long as her husband's parents live she will be subject to them, and in many cases will continue to reside with them. This patriarchal custom, whereby several sons and their wives and families may all be quartered under the parental roof, is by no means conducive to a peaceful and well-ordered home, nor are the family habits sociable. Wives and husbands do not eat together, nor, in the poorer classes, are there any set meals—rice and millet are boiled by the women and eaten by the men folks sitting outside in the sun, or squatting on the *k'ang*, and the women eat afterwards with the same lack of formality. Among the better-to-do the women eat in their own court, and the men in theirs, and any guests are entertained separately. But at the same time outside the house the wife can claim a certain amount of consideration. The man must harness the horse or donkey, arrange the cart and seat his wife in it, and he himself must walk alongside while she rides.

Perhaps it may be well here to give some idea of the structure of a Chinese home. Of course there is great variety, according to the social position and means of the owner, but an almost invariable feature of all Chinese houses, whether in town or village, is that they consist of a walled-in court, with one-storied rooms running along one or more sides, according to the size of the house. The outside of the court—the part bordering the street or other dwellings—is devoid of windows. A two-leaved door gives access to the enclosure, and the house opens upon the court only. In a better class home there is a series of these enclosed courts, to secure the separation of the sexes which Chinese etiquette demands.

Very few houses have more than one storey, and the domestic arrangements seem primitive for so highly civilised a people. In a cottage home the stove faces the door in the principal room, and the smoke and heat are forced by a system of flues under a sort of divan of bricks—the *k'ang*—which is the family bed, seat, and general receptacle for clothes, food, babies, or other goods which cannot be left on the mud floor.

The home of a wealthy Chinese is decorated with carving and gilding, silk hangings and snowy matting, and furnished with handsome porcelain, carved chairs, tables, and cabinets. The lady of the house has her wardrobes and chests full of beautiful silk and satin robes and boxes of jewellery. But she will sleep, not on a bed with sheets, but on a glorified *k'ang*, covered with cushions and quilts. She will eat at a low table, out of china bowls on lacquered trays, while she squats on the floor, and her domestic arrangements will be simplified by the comparative scarcity of furniture and belongings, and especially of knick-knacks, in her house. Nevertheless in a household where everything is made by hand—bedclothes, wearing apparel, even shoes—she will have plenty to do and will keep busy her little maids or slaves, many of whom are sold into domestic bondage by their parents.

Women Workers.

In Chinese shops one sees a great deal of fine embroidery done by men, but it is to a great extent women's work in the homes, and the beautiful shoes for "lily feet," the bands of sleeves and other decorations are made by the wearers themselves. It would be impossible to give an idea of the multifarious occupations in which poorer women are engaged. Every department of the tea industry is served by them, and babies go with their mothers to the factories, accompany them to market or to the fields, apparently none the worse for spending their little lives strapped to the back of the vigorous, hard-working women, whose every movement seems to jog the tiny heads till they threaten to fall off.

Seclusion of the Better-class Women.

We have already spoken of the boat-women in the South of China, who bring up their families in floating homes, and who seem to do the hard work while their men folk sit and watch them. To our ideas, however, even a life of hard labour is more tolerable, if spent in the open air and amid changing scenes, than the monotonous confinement which is the lot of the better-class women. Many of these never leave what we should call their "back-yards" save to go to the parks once a year on New Year's Day, or to pay a visit to their maternal home. In the absence of the husband no self-respecting woman should be seen in public, and the Chinese are never tired of quoting the modesty of the Lady Poh-ki, who when her house was on fire refused to escape. "When the chief of the household is abroad, no woman should leave the palace at night."

The home-visits and the New Year's picnic, when women of all ages and classes flock to the nearest park or open space with trees, are practically the only breaks in the monotony of their lives. The occasional return to the maternal roof is by no means always a success. The returning wife takes all her children with her, and may not be very warmly welcomed. Probably her brood quarrels violently with their cousins, the children of her brothers, and the sisters-in-law do not make things too pleasant for her, regarding her visit as an expense. Nevertheless, the visit to the "mother's people" is an institution and no self-respecting wife would omit it unless obliged. She probably feels that it helps to keep up her position in her husband's family by showing that she has "people of her own," and in this as in other matters the similarity between feminine character and customs in East and West is amusingly illustrated.

Such amusements as theatre-going are not possible to better-class Chinese women, but a wealthy man will sometimes engage a theatrical troupe to perform in his women's court, when all the friends of the lady will be invited. The poorer women are free to stand and gape at the rude shows which are given in open booths in the streets, or they can attend a more sophisticated form of amusement with their families by paying a few cash. On the whole, however, their lives are, like the lives of the women of the industrial and agricultural classes in other countries, devoid of those forms of intellectual or artistic enjoyment which are usually regarded as amusement. In one respect they are singularly unfortunate, for the consolations and pre-occupations of revealed religion, which mean so much to most women, are denied to the Chinese. They cannot get much satisfaction of a spiritual kind out of the philosophy which serves their husbands but which relegates them to such an inferior position.

"Foot-binding."

The clearest evidence of the opinion of the Chinese themselves as to the comparative happiness of the free coolie wife and the secluded middle-class one is found in the custom known as "foot-binding." No satisfactory history of this custom has ever been set forth, but it appears to be of considerable antiquity, and has resisted many attempts on the part of the rulers to put it down. No detailed description of the "lily feet" is necessary here, as the method of contraction is well known. It is sufficient to say that by a system of binding the feet and ankles tightly in extreme youth, the former are converted into little more than pegs. The toes are tucked under and frequently drop off, and the whole process is not only painful but even, at times, dangerous.

The girl thus crippled is incapable of any work which involves standing or walking, and this is exactly what is aimed at. To have a "lily-footed" daughter—that is one brought up to a life of comparative ease—is a mark of social distinction, and until quite recent times no girl could expect to marry into a family of good social position or to become the wife of one of the "literati"

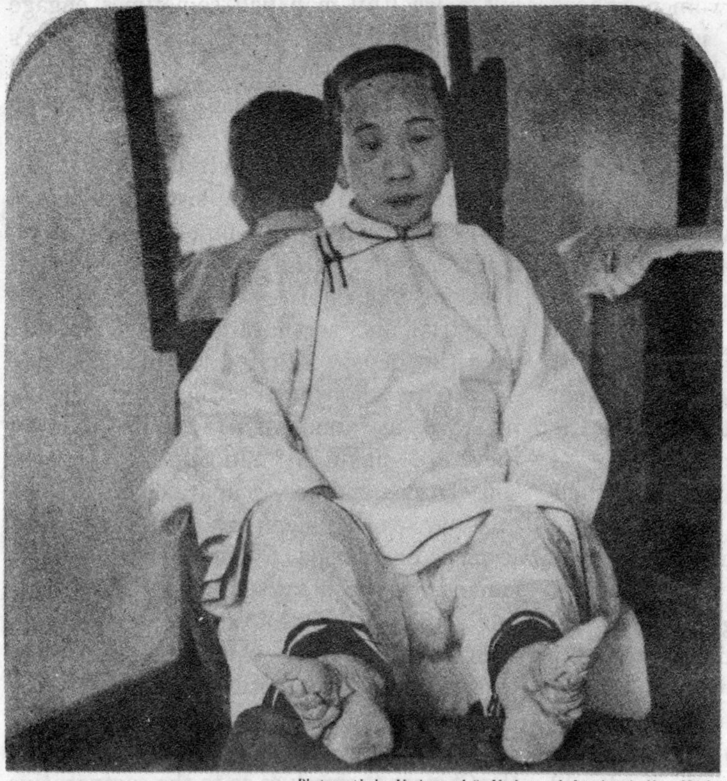

Photograph by Underwood & Underwood, London & New York.

A HIGH CASTE LADY'S DAINTY "LILY FEET."

Showing the deformation (the shoe is worn on the great toe only).

and even the material are rigidly prescribed by custom. The lady of the court must wear a round hat like her husband's; it must be lined with dark satin or cloth, and surmounted by a tassel of red silk. Only women of a certain rank are permitted to adorn it with a golden ornament. The coolie woman, at the other end of the social scale, has a hat of straw or bamboo like a mushroom. Sometimes it is merely a huge halo, and her hair sticks up through the hole in the middle.

The style of dress, with slight differences in such matters as the breadth of sleeves and length of coats, is the same everywhere, and for all classes. It consists of two essential

without possessing this trade mark of gentility. Even to-day, when the energetic campaign of foreigners against foot-binding has received strong official support, the custom has only been very partially discontinued in certain limited areas. The practice is the more curious because the ruling race has never conformed to the custom, and Manchu women, from the Dowager-Empress downwards, are large-footed.

Perhaps in no respect are the women of China more to be pitied by their sisters of the West than in the great matter of clothes. Not for them is that perennial source of amusement, the changing fashion. They cannot solace themselves in moments of *ennui* by purchasing a new bonnet. Should they happen, by chance, to belong to one of the two classes of women who alone wear headgear of any kind they cannot let their imaginations play round fresh "creations," for the form

Clothing.

garments—the trousers, tied round the ankles in the North and loose in the South, and the loose coat or tunic fastening on the left side. The better-class women usually wear also a petticoat, which is shaped like two aprons, one in front and one behind, and they have under-garments of fine white material and white woven socks over which they draw shoes of embroidered satin or cloth with thick white soles.

What a Chinese woman misses in variety of fashion she makes up by attention to detail, for all these garments (except in poor families) will be made of silk, satin, or cloth elaborately embroidered, and every garment is made by hand. Besides the work involved by the mere making of clothes for all members of the family there are shoes to be thought of. The "lily" shoes are almost always home-made, and beautifully embroidered. Then there are bed quilts and cushions, quilted coats for winter, curtains, and hangings—an endless task of needlework for the women of a family.

Children are dressed like miniature grown-ups as soon as their clothes become a matter of importance at all. On New Year's Day the streets are full of these quaint little people, whose gaudy dresses betoken loving care on the part of hundreds of proud mothers. When the weather grows cold (especially in Northern China where the winters are very severe) it is amusing to see the increase of bulk caused by putting one coat over another, till at last the children are like round bundles of clothes, and can hardly toddle. Among the poorer classes who cannot afford the satin fur-lined coat used by wealthy Chinamen, the winter clothes are made of wadded and quilted cotton and involve much work on the part of the family dressmaker and tailor.

Coiffures. One of the important features in a Chinese woman's toilet is her hair, and in every class above the humblest great attention and care are bestowed on the *coiffure.* The girl baby is shaved as soon as she is a month old, and only two funny little tufts are left at each side of her head. When she is a few years old her hair is allowed to grow and may be cut in a straight fringe across her forehead. A certain amount of change is observable in the fashion of doing the hair among the better class women, and at present it is taken away from the forehead and dressed in a chignon at the back of the head, but not on the nape of the neck as with us.

The Chinese pillow—a hollowed-out block of wood in which the nape of the neck rests—makes it possible to keep even an elaborate chignon in perfect order for a week, and it is only those to whom time and expense are no object who would have their hair dressed every day.

When the smoothly oiled loops have been symmetrically arranged they are secured with jewelled pins, and the head-dress is adorned with artificial flowers or jewels. In ranks of life where such adornments are unattainable there will usually be pins of shell or semi-precious stones, for a set of hair ornaments is part of the outfit for every bride, as are also earrings, which may

Photograph by Spooner, Strand.

A CHINESE WOMAN OF THE WEALTHY CLASS.

be of gold and pearls, of jade or of glass beads, according to the means of the bridegroom. A very usual hair ornament is a band of embroidery round the forehead ending behind the ears and sometimes having a row of pearls or a jewel in the centre—a style

A FOOCHOW LADY'S HEAD-DRESS.

which recalls that in vogue in Europe in the days of side curls.

A custom which seems more strange to us is that of letting the finger nails grow, and protecting them with metal sheaths. Only the wealthy and aristocratic can cultivate this habit, which renders the hand almost useless.

The Use of Rouge and Powder.

Although the apparent uniformity and prescribed monotony in the matter of dress argues, to our minds, a lack of vanity and interest in her personal adornment on the part of the Chinese woman, and although the relations between the sexes do not seem to admit of coquetry on her part, yet the prevalence of certain customs seem to argue that she is not so indifferent either as to her appearance or as to the opinion of the other sex as she appears. Of course we know that women dress for each other, and even adorn their hair with flowers and their sleeves with embroidery so as to outdo each other, but no woman rouges and powders to please her own sex. There is a Chinese proverb to the effect that "a good-looking woman requires no rouge to make her so," but the majority of Chinese women do not seem to have faith in their natural charms. Even among the poor artificially whitened faces and reddened lips and cheeks are frequently seen, and the eyebrows are carefully blackened to come up to the ideal of beauty which likens them to the silk-worm moth. The complexion of the Chinese belle is said to be "like congealed ointment," her lips "red like the dawn of day," her eyes limpid, her teeth like melon seeds, and her fingers like the blades of young grass, while her ungainly gait, as she totters along on "lily feet," is likened to the waving of willows.

The Chinese Ideal of Beauty.

This whole picture seems to point to an ideal of feminine beauty not so very far removed from our own—the slender fingers, limpid eyes, glossy eyebrows, and pale skin making up a picture by no means unpleasing. Naturally our own much admired blonde beauties were unthinkable to the Chinese poets, and indeed it is only by accustoming themselves to the sight of foreigners that they are able to accept blue eyes and fair hair as belonging to human beings. Chinese devils have blue eyes, just as the crude devil of Mediæval Europe had a cloven hoof and forked tail.

Beauty is, in fact, like morality, very much an affair of latitude and longitude, and the blue-eyed foreigner will not find much to admire in the average Chinese woman. The features seem coarse and heavy, while the Tartar strain is clearly visible in the North in the high cheek-bones, and small slanting eyes. The most that can be said for the crowds of coolie women and villagers whom one meets in one's walks abroad is that they have an air of sturdiness and good-humour, and their ruddy brown faces are far from unpleasing in consequence. Their more favoured sisters of the "lily feet" and their servants and slaves, who spend their time in the women's courts, are less healthy looking, and their broad faces and lack-lustre eyes are only redeemed by the picturesqueness and colour of their clothes and ornaments. The young girls have the comeliness of youth at the beginning of their married life, but before thirty they are old and wrinkled.

Literature and Woman.

Having gained some idea of the outward appearance of the Chinese woman, her home and habits, we must turn to Chinese literature for a more intimate view of her place in Chinese society. Theoretically she is simply the adjunct of her husband, the necessary second factor in the continuance of the race. Etiquette prescribes that there should be practically no social intercourse between the sexes, and Mencius laid it down that propriety required that men and women should not even touch each other in the ordinary acts of everyday life. An inquiring disciple asked him whether propriety made it improper to rescue a drowning sister-in-law, to which the philosopher was obliged to reply in the sense that propriety must give way to the ordinary instincts of humanity. Fortunately for their women this very commonsense view is the one which will recommend itself in nine cases out of ten to a Chinese man, and although he will endeavour to preserve the outward appearance of decorum his conduct in family life is not as devoid of human impulses as one is led to imagine.

In the important affair of marriage, which the Chinese affect to regard as a mere matter of business, there is abundant evidence of very human interest on the part of the young people. Mencius speaks severely of the youths and maidens who are not content to wait for the commands of parents and the arrangements of a go-between, but "make holes through walls in order to see each other secretly, or get over walls to follow each other," and we have already spoken of the Chinese romances in which true love plays no inconspicuous part. Even in cases where the marriage is arranged without consulting the young people there is evidence that, especially among the more educated and enlightened, care is taken to ensure a happy union.

Chinese good sense condemns a marriage in which the parties are of unequal social station, and at the same time Chinese proverbs inculcate the duty of seeking for virtue and excellence in a son or daughter-in-law rather than rich wedding presents or a large dowry. A whole group of proverbs and philosophic sayings—part of the classics which until recent times formed the only education of the Chinese—insist on the importance of the marriage relation and the wreck which an unhappy marriage can make of life, and a number of these wise sayings are concerned with the fact that it is wiser to marry goodness than beauty ; for instance "A good-looking woman in the house is the foe of all the others," and "Ugly wives and stupid maids are priceless treasures."

The number of these sayings (and some little observation of family life in China) leads one to believe that whatever the ideal of feminine beauty may be its effect on man is much the same in every clime. The possibility of taking a young and pretty concubine in addition to the wife provided by the parents is by no means forgotten, and many women are trained for such a position in the arts of pleasing and are better able to hold the affections of their masters than the legitimate wife. Under such competition it is not surprising to hear that "nine women out of ten are jealous," that "a wife's resentment is without end," and that "men are worn out and horses exhausted, people do not know east from west" when a Chinese wife has a grievance and lets herself go.

"Henpecked" Chinese.

The fact is that Chinese husbands, like those of other countries, value peace and quiet more than anything else in the home, and if the wife is blessed with a shrill, sharp tongue, and a temper to match, she can hold her own with him, and even with her mother-in-law. There are many Chinese jokes about the henpecked husband, and many stories illustrating the fact that a man may not always be master even in his own house. On one occasion a foreigner, who had been present at a meeting of Chinese gentlemen, was asked by one of them whether he feared the "hidden ones" of his inner chamber, *i.e.*, his women folk. "*He* does," they all said, chuckling and indicating the stern and stately looking Prefect who had been presiding, and who was visibly disconcerted at the allusion.

Apart from the power wielded by the termagant, however, there is no doubt that many women hold sway over their husbands by reason of their superior character and force of will. Except in rare cases this superiority is natural, and is not aided by

Photograph by Spooner, Strand.

A CANTONESE LADY.

education, but at the same time it is by no means uncommon. In one of the Chinese encyclopædias three hundred and seventy-six books out of sixteen hundred and twenty-eight are devoted to famous women, and eleven chapters deal with female knowledge and literary works, but except in the regions where foreign ideas are gaining ground few women have any real opportunities for enlarging their minds.

Influence of Woman in China.

CHINESE SINGING GIRLS.

It was native force of character and shrewdness which gave the Dowager-Empress her ascendancy, for though she was not a poor slave, as is sometimes asserted, but the daughter of a respectable family, she had no educational advantages in her youth. She is the second most famous woman ruler of China, the other being the Empress Wu, who in the seventh century was the consort of the emperor and ruled both him and his country. After his death she deposed his successor, and was sole ruler, her sway lasting some thirty-five years. The Empress Dowager is, of course, a Manchu, not a Chinese, but the extraordinary position to which she has attained shows that in the matter of the prerogatives of women the Chinese are no more consistent than they are in other ways.

Photograph by N. P. Edwards, Littlehampton.
WOMAN OF NORTH CHINA.
Showing the finger-nail protectors.

Chinese Devotion to Parents.

When a Chinese woman becomes a mother the traditions of filial piety secure to her more consideration than heretofore. A son or daughter must reverence their mother almost equally with their father. Chinese children are regarded as the chattels of their parents, and no duty or obligation can supersede that of filial obedience and care. While marriage is considered necessary for every adult there are cases, much commended in Chinese annals, of daughters who voluntarily gave up the idea of marriage in order to devote themselves to their parents. In the *Peking Gazette* it is by no means unusual to read recommendations that rewards or posthumous honours should be given to daughters who have distinguished themselves by devotion to their parents or by their virtue and industry. These instances of appreciation must be set against the prevalent view that to Chinese eyes a woman can never do more than is required of her by plain duty, and it is equally necessary to remember, in reading of the sale of wives and daughters and the low estimation of women generally among the poorest classes, that these people are inconceivably poor and ignorant judged by European standards, and must not be taken as representing the whole Chinese people.

There are many cases in history of mothers whose influence on their famous sons has been very great, and who are held in honour accordingly. The loss of a mother must be mourned for three years, during which time all public business must be abandoned. It will be remembered that when Li-Hung-Chang lost his mother he asked leave to retire and mourn for the prescribed time, but after a few months the Empress-Dowager had to send for him. Not to be able to mourn a parent is regarded as a great deprivation, for it is one of the firm beliefs of the Chinese that any dereliction in their family duty not only brings trouble on their ancestors but will reflect on their descendants.

The Chinese attitude towards widows is marked by considerable commonsense. A widow is spoken of as "a rudderless boat," and this is literally true under the conditions of Chinese society unless there are sons to support her. In some parts of China a form of suttee has been practised, even within recent times, but it is not countenanced by the authorities, nor is it prescribed by Chinese philosophical teaching. Re-marriage of widows is quite usual, and as there is less ceremony and less expense in taking a widow to wife they are not unpopular as brides. ' A widow's marriage," says a proverb, "should always be consummated immediately," otherwise she may change her mind—a privilege denied to girls.

The Position of Widows.

CANTONESE WEAVERS.

The life of a Chinese woman may seem intolerable to her European sister, but it is not without its compensations. For one thing, the period of middle and old age which is anticipated with dread, and staved off as long as possible by most Occidental women, who regard youth as the best of their possessions, presents fewer disadvantages to the Chinese. Rather she fears the first few years of her married life, and the period which must intervene before she gains the dignity and importance of being a mother and later a mother-in-law. By middle-age the worst of her troubles are over, and she has not the dread of a lonely old age, or the possibility of being supported by strangers or forced to go into the workhouse so long as her sons can work for her. Among well-to-do families, where there is no question of anxiety about daily bread, she will have the satisfaction, denied to many of our own women whose sons must seek fortunes abroad, of having her children with her and presiding over the nursery of her grandchildren.

The Future of Chinese Women.

There are, therefore, it must be owned, compensations in her lot for the lack of the "good time" in her girlhood which she does not expect or miss. At the same time it is undeniable that the traditionally low place occupied by women, their lack of legal protection, and the neglect of their education are blots on Chinese civilisation. It will be impossible to effect the social and administrative reforms upon which enlightened Chinese are now bent without some change for the better in these matters. One of the first steps must be in the direction of education, and schools are already being established throughout the country; while in the principal centres where foreign influence has prevailed a really good modern education is given to better class girls. The most enlightened Chinese opinion is also strongly in favour of monogamy as the best foundation for the family, and the position of an educated Chinese wife who is able to understand her husband's interests cannot fail to be a stronger one than is at present sanctioned by custom. In the great awakening of China that is taking place, there is no doubt that women must play their part, and it is to be hoped that, while the Chinese ideal of woman's mission and place in society will be widened and elevated, it will not lose its conception of the home as the best sphere and the care of the family as the greatest work for women.

Photograph by Underwood & Underwood, London & New York.

A WEALTHY MANCHU MAN AND WIFE IN FESTIVE DRESS, PEKING.

MANCHURIA, MONGOLIA, AND TIBET

By A. R. COLQUHOUN

The Merging of the Mongol and Manchu—The Freedom of the Steppe—The Buriats—The Nomadic Mongolians—Mongol Dress—Marriage among the Mongols—Position and Duties of Mongol Women —Women in Tibet—The Emancipated Women of Tibet and Polyandry—Dress and Ornaments in Tibet—Tibetan Marriage Customs

The Merging of the Mongol and Manchu.

OUTSIDE China proper, there are three great countries belonging to the Empire the women of which have naturally much in common with their Chinese sisters. All these countries have contributed something to Chinese ideas and customs, and all have, in return, been affected by the civilisation of the suzerain country. On the frontiers of China the people melt into each other imperceptibly, and even where the difference of race is clearly maintained the richer and more educated classes borrow their ideas from China. Some of these people were originally conquerors of the land which now dominates them. The Mongols, who at one time spread their conquests over half Europe as well as Asia, had a famous empire and court at Peking, while the Manchus conquered the Chinese capital in 1644, and have held the throne ever since. But although these conquests modified the Chinese type and introduced foreign customs—for instance the Manchu pig-tail—yet in the long run Manchu and Mongol have been the losers from the national point of view. The first still form a ruling caste and monopolise many of the high administrative posts in China, but their own beautiful country has been overrun, in return, by Chinese. In writing of Manchu and Mongol women, therefore, it is only necessary (especially with the latter) to remark those points in which the native customs and ideas still persist, and have not been altered by contact with the civilisation of China.

The Freedom of the Steppe.

Both Manchus and Mongols were originally Tartar tribes of kindred stock and pastoral habits. But, whereas the former inhabited a rich country of mountain and river, the latter were mostly dwellers on the vast Mongolian steppes. There are distinct differences between the customs of pastoral people and of those who, like the Chinese, are essentially agricultural or given to congregate in towns. A pastoral life, whether nomadic or settled, is always hard on women, and that in quite a different way from the hardships of a Chinese woman's position. The idea of seclusion for their women is not convenient to a people living largely on horseback and in tents, and so we find that, outside China proper, woman enjoys considerably more freedom, although it by no means follows that her position is better.

The Manchu women, retaining their natural liberty and never having adopted the "lily foot" custom which would have deprived them of it, go abroad freely and have an independence of carriage which marks them out from the Chinese. In Northern China and in Manchuria itself it is hardly possible to distinguish between Manchu and Chinese men, but the women are marked by their carriage, and by certain features in their

Photograph by N. P. Edwards, Littlehampton.

A MANCHU LADY AND CHINESE WOMAN.

by the sturdy character of the women and their comparative freedom from the etiquette of seclusion. There are, however, many semi-civilised or nearly savage tribes living in Manchuria, especially on the coasts and rivers of the north. Some of these display almost primitive forms of society, others retain traces of a civilisation differing in some points from that of the Mongolian races. Of the tribes which are closely akin to the steppe-dwelling Mongol, though found in northern Manchuria, the Buriats are the best known. They are a cattle-breeding tribe, very hardy, and very primitive, who retain their Tartar type and customs and their allegiance to the Tibetan hierarchy, which is the highest in the Mongol Buddhist world. The lives of their women is that of other tent-dwelling Mongols, and the emergence into anything approaching civilised life means the adoption of Chinese ideas.

dress and *coiffure.* We have already seen that the Manchu court ladies alone wear hats, and they have a peculiar style of head-dress, profusely decorated, with two bunches of artificial flowers over either ear. Their shoes, too, are distinctive. Being free from the "lily foot" convention they still wish to mark their aristocratic birth by some footgear that precludes much walking, and accordingly they have boots with thick white soles, narrower at the base than directly beneath the foot, sometimes six inches high, and so giving the wearer a most impressive height.

The Buriats.

In all civilised Manchu communities the domestic arrangements are similar to those in North China, and the legal and social position of the wife is much the same, though modified

The Nomadic Mongolians.

When we turn to Mongolia we find among the tribes which still maintain nomadic habits more distinctive forms of social customs and family life, but, as we have said already, the change is not necessarily for the better in the position of women. The Mongolian nomad of the steppes lives in a felt tent called by Europeans a "yourta," and his sole occupation is the care of his cattle. The tent is formed of a skeleton framework of wooden laths which is fastened to a round hoop at the top, and thus forms a rude chimney. The felt has a flap to open at one place, but, when the Mongol is inside, this is closed and all air and light he needs come through the chimney, which also allows escape for the smoke from the fire continually burning in the centre of the tent. Round this are spread felt or skins, or, in well-furnished tents, rugs, and carpets. The wife sleeps next the door on the thinnest rug or poorest skin. No one undresses to go to bed, but simply fastens up the outer coat. No one washes when he gets up, or eats breakfast. The wife is the first astir and prepares meal tea, a kind of gruel made with fat or butter. With this, and cheese, hunger is staved off during the day, and the one meal of the day is eaten just before settling down for the night. It consists of chunks of meat sawn off the joints which are kept dried or frozen in a sort of cage outside the tent. The chunks are boiled, and when sufficiently done are fished out with the fingers and eaten. Mutton is the favourite food, and, even after this primitive cooking, is sometimes very good.

When the Mongol lady wishes to wash she may fill her mouth with water and squirt it into her hands as she rubs them over her face.

Mongol Dress.

Her dress is like that of her men folk, except that he wears a belt and she does not, and consists chiefly of a long loose coat which is buttoned up or left open according to the temperature. Usually of a sombre colour, this garment may be of a bright red or yellow on festal occasions, and will furthermore be adorned with a perfect curtain of bright-coloured beads.

The one great vanity of the Mongol woman is her head-dress, which is most elaborate, and varies with her status as maid or wife, and with her family. The hair is frequently smeared with glue to keep it in order, and from it depends an array of silver ornaments, coins and beads. Even the poor possess some of these, and the rich are loaded with them. Some tribes wear a metal band round the head, with ornaments hanging down each side, and held in place by hooks in the ears, the weight being such that the lobe of the ear is often distended or split. Evidently the Mongol belle is quite as ready as her more sophisticated sisters to suffer in order to be beautiful. No description of her equipment would be complete without mention of the snuff-bottle—often a flat stone without much holding capacity and frequently empty, but carried nevertheless with dignity, in emulation of the sterner sex, and offered in politeness to all guests.

The marriage arrangements of the Mongols are more free than those of China, and give more scope to individual choice. The marriage customs, particularly as to present-giving, are not, however, substantially

Photograph by Underwood & Underwood, London & New York.

A GROUP OF MANCHU WOMEN, WITH TYPICAL HEAD-DRESS

different. The bride is endowed by her parents according to their means, and her dowry may vary from a *yourta*, with all its fittings and a herd of cattle, to a single sheep. The bridegroom presents gifts in return, and among people of

Marriage among the Mongols.

Photograph by N. P. Edwards, Littlehampton.

A TIBETAN BELLE IN A WHEAT-FIELD.

substance the wedding is an important affair, spreading over many days, and involving a huge amount of eating and drinking. A typical Mongol wedding retains distinct traces of the primitive manner of winning a wife, the bride being expected to weep and bewail, and being finally carried off with a show of force, after feigned resistance by her own people. As the Mongol rides more easily than he walks, a genuine bridal should resemble the exploit of young Lochinvar, and the bride is borne off on horseback, wailing piteously, though probably not more reluctant than brides of more sophisticated races.

Position and Duties of Mongol Women.

Once married, the Mongol bride becomes the household drudge. The Mongol can have but one lawful wife, but he can divorce her without much difficulty if he is not satisfied with her. Her only protection is the marriage settlement, as he is expected to refund part of what her parents gave unless he has flagrant cause for divorce. She can divorce him also, on the ground of ill-treatment or "lack of affection," but as she is bound to refund part of the nuptial presents made by him, which in all probability were seized by her family, she has very little chance of obtaining her freedom. The Mongols have proverbs similar to those in Russian: "Love your wife as your soul, and beat her like your fur." "It is my wife, my thing."

The debased form of Buddhism professed by the Mongols and interwoven with Shamanism or worship of devils does not provide the smallest moral protection for women. They are permitted to become nuns and serve in the lamasseries, but no sanctity appertains to this way of life. Even the exaggerated respect to parents which is the mother's protection in China is lacking in Mongolia.

Woman's work is all that is hardest and most monotonous. Their industry collects all the *argol* (dried dung) which serves as fuel; they herd the cattle and milk them; make the felt rugs from camel's hair; drive and ride bare-backed over the steppes, and do the same work as men in addition to their domestic duties. In the summer, while their women are so profitably employed, the Mongol men ride about visiting each other and drinking tea in each other's *yourtas*, exactly like fashionable, idle women! They organise pony and camel races, of which they are very fond, and in these the young girls take part, but with this exception they know little of amusement in our sense of the word. Whatever happiness they find in life must be the mere physical enjoyment of an outdoor existence while they

WOMAN OF LHASA, TIBET.
DRAWN BY NORMAN H. HARDY.

Facing on page 544

Photograph by Johnston & Hoffmann, Calcutta.

A GROUP OF TIBETAN BUDDHIST NUNS.

One of them holds a prayer-wheel, which she keeps in constant motion by a swinging movement of the wrist.

are still young and strong, but too soon the hardships of their lives cause them to contract diseases, and they become prematurely aged.

Woman in Tibet.

When we turn to Tibet, whose people are closely akin in race to the Mongols and Manchus, we find a domestic and social structure of a rather different character. Tibet borders India, and derived a great deal of her civilisation as well as her religion from Indian sources.

The influence of religion has been the paramount factor in this most priest-ridden state, for here, alone among the countries of the world, the supreme ruler is a spiritual and not a temporal monarch. Of course his position has long been modified by the suzerainty of China, and, recently, by European intervention, but the power and influence of the Dalai Lama are nevertheless far in excess of those enjoyed in the nineteenth century by any spiritual Pontiff.

It is therefore of peculiar interest to find that in this priest-ridden country women enjoy a freedom and independence only equalled, among Asiatic women, in Burma. They not only trade freely, carry on businesses, and take a full share of all commercial enterprises, but are allowed to manage them.

In religious life women play a most important part. One of the most sacred personages is the abbess of a nunnery, who is believed to be the reincarnation of one of the goddesses of the corrupt pseudo-Buddhist Pantheon of the Tibetans. She is treated with veneration by men and women alike.

The Emancipated Women of Tibet and Polyandry.

Women mix freely with men, receive them in their rooms, and join in their parties of pleasure, and even take part in their ceremonial dances, whereas in China such an idea would be entirely subversive not only of etiquette but of moral feeling. As for marriage customs, it is notorious that Tibet carries the emancipation of women so far as to permit polyandry—a woman may have more than one husband.

With regard to this extraordinary state of affairs, there has been as yet no sufficient enquiry, by those versed in sociology, as to the extent and origin of this custom. In one form it is known to have existed among European peoples at no very remote period, and this appears to be the form in which it is most usual in Tibet. The sons of one mother share a wife between them, the eldest brother retaining ultimate rights over her and all children being regarded as his. Among a very poor community living in patriarchal style such a custom was dictated by considerations of economy but, when we remember that woman's work is the property of her lord and master, this explanation does not seem quite sufficient, especially as cases of polyandry occur in Tibet, where the men are not brothers. A similar argument applies to the reason sometimes given of a desire to keep the family property together, which would only apply if the husbands were invariably members of the same family. In any case the custom is one which could only have obtained a foothold among a people whose male population has been emasculated, as have the Tibetans, by a form of religion calculated to deaden every virile impulse, and to turn men into lazy, indifferent lookers-on at life. Monasteries are full of men who enter them merely to escape responsibilities; and here, as in Burma, the result of masculine effeteness has been to foster more practical characteristics among the women.

Of course the Tibetans have to contend with Chinese ideas and philosophy, which affect the more educated of them, but in everyday life they manage to maintain their position. In some parts, where Chinese influence is strongest, polygamy is practised, and nowhere is monogamy usual.

Dress and Ornaments in Tibet.

Tibet has long been considered a land of mystery owing to the strict seclusion which it was the policy of China to enforce. Even to-day no really comprehensive modern account of her people exists, but the observations of those who visited the country when the British expedition penetrated to Lhassa seem to confirm the idea that domestic life is little changed since the days of the Abbé Huc. He describes a visit to Tibet in the middle of last century, and notes there European taste to render the precaution necessary, but *autre pays autre goûts*, and, if the care spent by the Tibetan woman on her personal adornment is any criterion, vanity is not the least of her failings.

Photograph by Johnston & Hoffmann, Calcutta.

A TIBETAN WOMAN OF THE UPPER CLASS.

Her jewellery is of silver set with turquoises and carnelians.

many curious features in the life of the people. At Lhassa, for instance, which is the centre of religious life and always full of pilgrims and priests, the women must wear clothes of a certain colour and must black their faces so that their comeliness may not disturb pious meditations. The appearance of Tibetan women, with their broad features, little twinkling eyes, and coarse black hair, does not seem to

Here, as in Mongolia, the head-dress is the focus of decorative skill. A lady of wealth and position in her festal dress has her hair elaborately plaited, and wreathed round her head, and wears across or round it a metal band from which ear-pieces hang down. A sort of head-piece or crown is strung all over with necklaces of precious stones and beads, till it looks like a halo, and some of the jewels are of real value, including rubies, emeralds, cats'-eyes, coral and turquoise as large as hens' eggs, pearl drops, amber and jade. Necklaces are slung over the breast, and all who can afford it wear robes (like the Mongol coats in shape) of silk, satin, or fine cloth elaborately embroidered. Needless to say, charms are frequently suspended round the necks, especially of children, and each woman carries in her breast the bowl of wood or metal which is the invariable companion of all Tibetans and forms their one eating utensil.

When the death of a Dalai Lama or any such untimely event plunges the Tibetan nation into mourning, it is chiefly observed by forbidding the women to wear their head-dresses or jewellery—a serious deprivation.

Photograph by N. P. Edwards, Littlehampton.

TIBETAN MOTHER AND HER SONS.

The boys are all destined to become monks.

It is interesting to find that a Tibetan woman, even when she loves finery, does not lose her practical spirit, for an account is given of one who, wearing a head-dress covered with pearls, which was estimated to be worth as much as £225, yet superintended personally an inn and restaurant, and, although the daughter of a noble family, did not think the work beneath her. Another

Tibetan wife, herself a native of Sikkim, complained that although her husbands' family (she was wife to two brothers) was rich, they all worked like ploughmen, and she particularly was the victim of a mother-in-law who thought she was made of iron.

Marriage ceremonies in Tibet are very much like those of China. Go-betweens are used in every class of life except the poorest, and the exchange of presents is a most important feature. Although there is no actual religious ceremony, it is customary for the lamas to offer prayers for the happiness of the union, which is not consummated until the third day after arrival at the bridegroom's house, when the bride changes her clothes for others provided by him, and enters into his family in earnest. Divorce laws are chiefly concerned with the amount of the dowry or marriage present to be refunded by the party desiring divorce. The murder of a wife is not a capital offence, and is punished merely by a fine and the payment of funeral expenses, like any other crime. In default of payment, however, the murderer may be thrown into jail.

Tibetan Marriage Customs.

Meagre as is our information concerning the more intimate existence of Tibetan women, it is plain that they play a great part in social and national life. With the spread of modern civilisation, which must inevitably filter into the country now that the barriers are thrown down, it is to be hoped that they will be the gainers, and that their energy and industry will be rewarded by an improvement in their legal position, and by the recognition of their right to education, which is the weapon they most need.

Photograph by Rischgitz, Bayswater.

TIBETAN PRAYER-WHEEL.

SIAM AND CAMBODIA

By W. W. SKEAT

Geographical Considerations—Mongolian Influence—Indian Influence—Problems in Race Fusion—General Position of Woman in Siam—Characteristics of the Siamese Woman—Woman's Work—A Boat-race for Women—The Dress of Siamese Women—Motherhood in Siam—He-Girls and She-Boys—"Is it a Boy or a Child, I wonder?"—A Girl's Progress—A Princess's Tonsure Ceremony—Royal Women and Women of Honour—Marriage Mysteries—Bizarre Forms of Burial—Methods of Mourning

Geographical Considerations.

SIAM is divided into two zones, approximately by the 17th parallel, the northern part consisting of a number of mountain ranges continuing the Shan-Tonkin system, but considerably lower, none reaching much above 8,000 feet. The southern zone includes vast tropical plains suitable for rice, and is comparatively free from mountains, which, however, crop up again in East Cambodia and Annam. In Cochin-China the country consists generally of low-lying country intersected by a network of streams, but on the western frontier of Siam a tongue of territory runs south along the mountain backbone till it reaches the Malay countries in the broader part of the peninsula. The ranges of the northern zone run north and south, or at the most north-east and south-west, and this, taken in conjunction with the direction of the two chief rivers of this region, the Menam, running north and south, and the Me-khong, running similarly for the greater part of its course, but thenceforward with an easterly bias, helps to explain the movements of the population.

As a further help to the appreciation of the position of woman in this part of Indo-China, we may picture that region as a melting-pot or crucible, in which various races have for many centuries been subjected to a process of gradual fusion, under influences derived mainly from countries lying within the Mongolian and the Indian spheres of influence.

Mongolian Influence.

The Mongolian influence is, of course, most strongly marked in that section of these races which, issuing from the frozen ranges of the north, overran the country here for the most part then possessed by the Cham, and spread out to the southward like the spokes of a fan. Of these races the most important are, firstly, the Thai or Siamese proper, who, linking the Shans on the west to the Laos on the east, extend under a great variety of local names from the frontier of Burma to Cambodia, and mix, under the name of Samsam, with Malays in the southern Chersonese; and secondly, the Annamese, somewhat sweepingly described, by a high authority, as "almost slavish copies of the Chinese," inhabiting the coast of Annam, the delta in Tonkin, and most of Cochin-China, with colonies in Cambodia, and forming an exceedingly dense population.

Indian Influence.

The Indian influence, on the other hand, is seen most strongly amongst the Cambodians or Khmers (once the most civilised race in Indo-China), and the Mon-Khmer-speaking tribes dwelling between the Mekhong and the Annamese seaboard, as well as in south-east Siam and north-west Cambodia. Besides these there are the Cham, who are apparently allied to the Malayan family, and are the existing representatives of a once powerful race, the founders of the empire of Champa, the first great kingdom of Indo-China, which included part of Central Siam, the whole of Annam and South Tonkin. There are also some Karens, as in Burma, under which latter heading they will shortly be described.

Problems in Race Fusion.

From the foregoing facts it is clear that this region, lying as it does half-way between the two parts of the world where population pressure is severest, India and China, presents some interesting problems in race fusion. Of the two warring influences here evident, the culture of Indian origin has proved incomparably the stronger, making important conquests even among the Thai (a race admittedly of Mongolian extraction), where its effects are shown, for instance, in the widespread observation of Hindu customs, the introduction of Buddhism, of Pali as the sacred language, and the use of the Siamese alphabet, adapted from a form of the rock-cut Pali.

Photograph by Isonaga, Bangkok.

SIAMESE WOMAN
Wearing the "Pannung" and Scarf.

The boundaries of civilisation and race do not, however, always coincide, and from a racial point of view the Mongolian influences appear to have long been gradually swamping the Indian populations, a tendency which is growing stronger as time goes on.

It should be noted that at Bangkok, where the total population was recently placed at 500,000, and indeed in most other towns of the country, the vast majority is of Mongolian origin, and this Chinese preponderance bids fair to carry all before it, thus yet more profoundly influencing the racial problem.

Owing to extreme pressure of space, it is unfortunately quite impossible to do more here than to touch lightly upon the most representative of these races, the dominant and still independent Thai race, who will be called in these pages Siamese.*

General Position of Woman in Siam.

Woman in Siam was formerly a mere chattel, and was sold at marriage by her father or brother. The birth of a girl brought no joy to her parents; she was endured as a more or less valuable speculation, that might bring its price (the "price of the mother's milk," as it is called) at some future period. The fact of her being a chattel explains why she was not allowed to perform the all-important sacrifices to the souls of the dead ancestors, that should be paid by the eldest-born; for a similar reason she was excluded from inheriting property. Under the old feudal *régime* the children of debtor slaves or captives became, if they belonged to the odd numbers, the property of the slaves' master, those of the even numbers belonged

* The facts concerning the up-country Thai have been translated from "Les Thai," in recent numbers of *Anthropos*. For the illustrations I have to thank my friend Mr. W. J. Evans, of the Siamese Legation, 23, Ashburn Place, and (for the Cambodian) M. A. Cabaton, one of the greatest living authorities on the language of "Champa."

to the father, if he were free, or to his master if he were a slave. The slavery, though of a mild kind, was general, and the gradual liberation of the country from this burden (by decree that all children born of slaves should henceforth be free) is one of the many important advances in the path of reform made by the present statesmanlike monarch, Chulalongkorn. Another Siamese institution was the division of the people into bands for military purposes; with regard to which it may be noted that women, though excluded from service, were nevertheless set down in the rolls of the nation. Though polygamy is established as the outward sign of wealth and magnificence, monogamy is general among the peasant population, with whom, although marriages are almost perhaps too easily dissolved, matrimonial fidelity is nevertheless the rule.

Photograph by Isonaga, Bangkok.

A SIAMESE FAMILY

Wearing "Pannungs" and Scarves. The anklets worn by the little ones over their boots should be noted.

To-day the Siamese woman is as free as her Burmese, if not quite as emancipated as her European, sister. She often works hard and is frequently the real bread-winner of the family, though she naturally lives when she can upon the exertions of her children, which she calls, in her own expressive phrase, "eating their strength." If judged by the highest standards it must be admitted that she is plain of feature, with lozenge-shaped face, yellow-brown skin, short blue-black hair, and till recent times, in accordance with old custom, artificially blackened teeth, a practice which, however, has now gone out of fashion. Yet she possesses a not inconsiderable power of fascination, and her business-like instincts are shown by her preferring a wealthy and indulgent Chinese husband to what is only too often her indolent and impecunious fellow-countryman. Though gentle and sweet-tempered, she is not incapable of boldness and enterprise; though inclined to be vain and devoted to jewels and finery, her general character remains simple, and makes an impression of naturalness that has a charm of its own. Her national costume is not in itself attractive, but, like the Malay woman, she has had the good sense and taste not to stoop to the vulgarities of European attire. Like the women of other races in a similar environment, she possesses considerable imitative faculty, a retentive memory, and a sensitive artistic impulse, which is shown, for instance, in the management of colour in her own dress and that of her children, to whom she is passionately attached.

Characteristics of the Siamese Woman.

But, as is often the case with people of her easy-going temperament, her surroundings are often untidy and even insanitary to the utmost degree. The work that falls to her share includes the lighter agricultural work, cooking, weaving, mat-making and basket-work, with embroidery as a change of occupation when her other duties permit.

Woman's Work.

Successful girls' schools have been established at Bangkok, upon the development of which the future of the sex in Siam will undoubtedly to a great extent depend.

The following amusing account of a boat-race in which women took part may be taken as showing the stage to which the emancipation of the sex has arrived in Siam. "A larger class of market boat, paddled by mixed crews of men and women, to the number of ten or twenty, gave capital sport. The women crews, with their cross sashes of yellow, green, or blue, not only looked but often proved the smartest. Their rate of stroke was from thirty-six to thirty-seven for the first half-minute, after which it varied — now a long, sweeping dozen to rest the tired muscles, then a spurt again, and finally they passed the line going splendidly and striking sixty-two to the minute, soaked, but laughing and ready to do it again."*

A Boat-Race for Women.

* Warrington Smyth, "Five Years in Siam," vol. i., p. 9.

There is probably no civilised city where the dress of a woman appears more like that of a man than at Bangkok, what with the cropping of the hair, and the form taken by the national lower garment (*pannung*), which is so arranged as to appear, especially at a distance, not unlike a pair of knickerbockers or bloomers.

The Dress of Siamese Women.

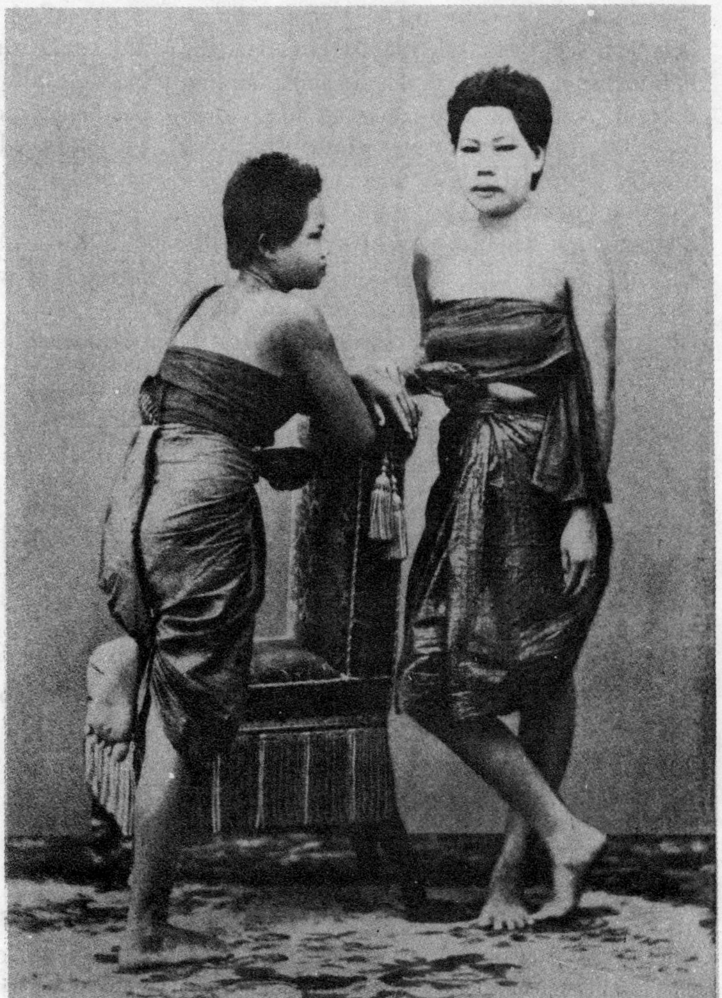

Photograph by Isonaga, Bangkok

A SIAMESE NOBLEMAN'S MAID-SERVANTS.

To this is added for "dress" purposes a bright-coloured scarf wound round the breasts; ladies substitute a white tunic, with a sash worn bandolier fashion, black stockings and shoes. Yet when the material of the *pannung* is of some brightly dyed shot silk, worn in combination with a gaily coloured silk scarf under the arms, the effect is not altogether as ungraceful as might be expected. A worse fault from an artistic point of view is the cropping of the hair, the ends of which are often made to stand straight upright, blacking-brush fashion, the effect of which is to murder that glory of womanhood. Up country, however, the Siamese women not unfrequently wear their hair rolled up and knotted at the back of the head. In some parts a compromise between the two styles is to be seen, the hair being cut short as usual, and standing upright, with the old-fashioned long locks over the ears. In former days they also greatly admired teeth blackened by the chewing of betel leaf, and the native dentists kept whole sets of black teeth ready to replace any that might be lost! Many charms (especially in the form of small silver tubes) are worn by women and girls alike, and the lower orders are often quaintly tattooed—*e.g.* with dragons or crosses, or, as Mr. Thompson points out, with scroll charms representing the seated Buddha.

Taking the country as a whole, the women of Siam are simple in their dress. Yet at the same time no people better understand the use of colour, the quality of material or rich embroideries, and a Siamese tonsure ceremony, wedding, or nautch in Bangkok is a veritable feast of rainbow-coloured silks, of brilliant jewellery and gorgeous gold-thread work. It is said that it was once the custom to have a complete set of seven differently coloured *pannungs* (one for each day of the week), but no such rule is now observed.

Motherhood in Siam.

The great problem of motherhood does not sit lightly upon the majority of Siamese women, for the mother is subjected to the terrible ordeal of exposure to fire which is found in many parts of Indo-China. We are told by a quaint old writer that they kept their women at child-birth before a continual great fire for a month, turning them sometimes on one side, and sometimes on the other. The smoke, which greatly incommoded them, passed slowly through an aperture in the roof. On their purification they returned thanks to the fire, and at the banquet which followed ate nothing which was not first offered to the fire. The old women who attend the mother at this period make three balls of rice and throw them in three lucky directions to propitiate the spirits, and the child, though it is called "Red" at birth, is forthwith smeared all over with yellow turmeric, a practice which is extended even to kittens and puppies! At birth the child is laid in a wicker basket, but is afterwards transferred to a peculiar cradle, suspended from the roof by cords, which is not rocked but swayed to and fro by hand.*

He-girls and She-boys—"Is it a Boy or a Child, I wonder?"

When a child is born, divination is used to see if it was born on a lucky or unlucky day, some days being destined for girls, others for boys. Of course, if the child has inadvertently, it may be, committed the terrible error of being born on the wrong day, up-country parents think they have to rectify the mistake at once. A girl born on a wrong day is given names which signify, for instance, the "little she male-child," or the "little she-boy"; if a boy, the child is called the "little young he-girl." This choice of a name is a matter of life and death to the child itself. Indeed, we even read in old writers of the name of the king being concealed for fear that any enchantment should be made on it.

A Girl's Progress.

As soon as the child is big enough to work it begins, if in the country districts, by scaring away birds from the rice, or fishing for small fish or frogs, and gradually learns the use of the simpler agricultural implements. A young girl learns to pound rice in the big mortar, to work the rice-mill, to take care of chickens and pigs, and help her mother in the housework. Up to the age of five she is not troubled by clothes, but at six years old she is given a species of large

* Young, "Kingdom of the Yellow Robe," pp. 49, 50.

Photograph by Isonaga, Bangkok.

A SIAMESE WOMAN WITH UNCUT HAIR.

skirt, which she rolls up round her waist and fastens tightly with a wide sash. In the towns she wears a *panung* and jacket and sometimes a scarf. She is not taught to read or write until she is twelve or fifteen years of age, though she learns a few songs, usually love-songs, to sing in competition with other young people at the feasts. She also takes up weaving or silkworm keeping (in bamboo baskets, purposely ranged in subdivisions) and spins the silk on a country spinning-wheel.

The cutting off of the girl's top-knot, at the age of eleven to thirteen, is the greatest pageant of her life next to her wedding, and is ushered in by a really splendid and gorgeous spectacle. In the procession at the tonsure of a princess, a number of high officials, in long white muslin robes and conical white "steeple" hats, are followed by "girls dressed in cloth of gold, holding golden lotus-flowers," the young princesses coming next "in cloth of gold, carried on a heavy gilt throne," and followed by women from all parts of the country.* The actual ceremony in such a case is performed by the king. The poorest classes have their children tonsured gratuitously at the expense of the Government during the remarkable "swinging" festival † at the harvest ceremonies.

A Princess's Tonsure Ceremony.

According to De la Loubère, in the latter part of the seventeenth century, to possess

* McCarthy, "Surveying and Exploring in Siam," pp. 19, 20.

† Young, p. 80.

Photograph by Isonaga, Bangkok.

A SIAMESE LADY.

a number of wives was in Siam merely a necessary mark of magnificence, and the daughters of his subjects, taken by the king, could be redeemed for a money payment, so that many were taken merely for the sake of extortion.

Royal Women and Women of Honour.

The queen had her own elephants and barges and officers, but never went abroad except in a closely curtained chair, etiquette requiring that if any of the people could not avoid her, they should turn their backs to her by prostrating themselves till she had passed.

Photograph by Isonaga, Bangkok.

A SIAMESE LADY IN FULL DRESS.

Besides this she had her own store-houses and treasury, and she engaged in foreign trade, a privilege of which she was very tenacious.

The real officers of the King of Siam's chamber were women, who alone had privilege of entry. They made his bed and dressed his meat, clothed him and waited on him at table, but none but himself touched his head when he was being attired, nor put anything over his head. The only exceptions to this rule were the royal officials in charge of his wardrobe, which was not in the care of women. The master of the wardrobe was a prince of the royal blood of Cambodia, from which the king claimed to be descended. He alone was allowed to touch the king's "bonnet," though even he was never allowed to place it on his royal master's head.

The women of the palace never stirred out but with the king, except by express order. In former times the queen was, as in Egypt, both the king's wife and sister. The king's other wives rendered obedience to the queen as to their sovereign, and were subject to her jurisdiction, but of course, if the king had any favourites, he took steps to protect them. Daughters did not succeed to the crown, since they were hardly looked upon as free.

A perennial leap-year is the result of the Champa custom, according to which it is the rule for the intending wife to ask her future husband's hand in marriage. Among the Siamese it is arranged by an intermediary on more ordinary lines. In the capital the old customs are being continually modified, but a strange feature of the rite in the up-country districts is the offering of tubes of fermented fish mixed with pounded rice, sometimes exceeding a hundred in number, with presents of betel leaf and chewing bark, cotton stuffs, and silk. A buffalo and pigs are slaughtered for the feast and the young girls deluge the youths with syringes filled with a "corrosive and stinking liquid," to which the latter have to submit without retaliation, their retreat being barred by thorny stems, and from which they can only escape by paying ransom in kind, sometimes as much as a buffalo or a bar of silver or so many tubes of fermented fish. On the other hand, the bride-price for a chief's daughter (called the "price of the mother's milk") may be as much as ten to twelve bars of silver, but the ordinary

Marriage Mysteries.

price is three to five bars and three big brass pots. A jar of wine, two eggs, and a chicken are set on brass plates between the bride and bridegroom. A sorcerer offers the right egg to the bridegroom on his left and the left one to the bride as a symbol of union; the same is done with the legs of the chicken. The wine is then drunk through two crossed pipes, while the priest utters good wishes. The bridegroom is introduced to the family spirit, and a feast follows. The bride, on reaching her husband's house, waits at the foot of the house-ladder, which she ascends simultaneously with her husband. Three days later they visit the girl's parents and bid adieu to the family spirit. Among the very poor the man sometimes binds himself to serve his parents-in-law till their death.

There is also a form of elopement recognised and regulated by custom. The girl deposits a ten-cent piece given her by her lover at night in the basket used for cooking the rice, and then elopes with her lover to his own house, on crossing the threshold of which she is considered an actual bride, and, unless she is pursued and recaptured before this happens, her parents lose the right of taking her home again. Of course, this custom often leads to trouble.

Divorce is allowed. If at the husband's instance, he loses the bride-money and his presents; if at the wife's, she pays double. Adultery was formerly punished by lashing the woman and her accomplice together on a raft, which was allowed to drift with the current; nowadays the culprits are allowed "to pay the price of their heads," the man's life being fixed at twelve bars of silver, the woman's at six. Polygamy is in full vogue among the rich. A curious fact is that a great man does not choose his own legitimate wife; his choice belongs to his people, an experiment in practical socialism which does not always work happily!

Bizarre Forms of Burial.

At death the body is laid in a coffin and a wake is kept, some priests or *talapoins* chanting in the Pali language and pretending, amongst other things, to show the soul of the deceased the road to heaven. The pile, which is composed of fragrant wood,

Photograph from A. Cabaton.

A CAMBODIAN LADY AND HER HUSBAND—THE GOVERNOR OF A PROVINCE.

such as sandal wood and eagle wood, is surrounded by representations of houses, movables, and domestic or wild animals. The honour done to the deceased at a funeral consists in the height of the scaffolding on which the coffin rests.

The body is never consumed, but the remains, deposited in the coffin (which should be lidless) are laid under a pagoda. In former times those that had no pagoda kept the half-burnt remains and presented an idol to an existing pagoda. A revolting practice of eating a small portion of the unburnt flesh, to obtain invulnerability, is ascribed to the more superstitious.* The very poor bury their dead or expose them on a scaffolding, where vultures and crows devour them. In epidemics they bury the bodies and dig them up again and burn them some years after, when it is thought that all danger of infection has passed. Criminals, still-born infants, women who die in childbirth, suicides, and those who meet death through some extraordinary disaster—*e.g.* by a thunderbolt—are deprived of funeral honours. At one of the pagodas in Bangkok a large flock of vultures is, or was until recently, kept, to which were thrown the bodies of criminals and paupers.

In the provinces of Lower Siam, where methods of funeral antecedent to the practice of cremation were till recently prevalent, the Phram buried their dead in a sitting posture in an upright box, and the corpse was sometimes exposed, either in a rectangular box supported by high uprights, or in a huge cigar-shaped wrapper fixed between trees at about eight feet from the ground, so that the grim jest formerly current in the Bangkok clubs that in some parts of the jungles of the peninsula it was necessary to beware of corpses falling from the branches of the trees upon the unwary traveller was at the most an exaggeration!

* "Lotusland," p. 144.

Methods of Mourning.

While mourning for a mother, "dog's flesh, lampreys and frogs" in the up-country districts are forbidden as food, these being the very dishes which a mother foregoes from the time of the birth of her first child till death. No parents wear mourning for their children; children mourn for their father fifteen months, but for their mother three years, because they say the mother has more trouble in bringing up the children than the father. Late though it comes, this posthumous reparation is the least that is her due, for thus, when her life is closed, the Siamese mother receives some measure of the recognition which should have been hers in her lifetime, she is more honoured in mourning than any other member of the family.

Photograph from J. McCarthy. By courtesy of the R.G.S.

WOMEN FROM MUANG SAWN.

Photograph by Watts and Skeen, Rangoon.

BURMESE WOMEN MAKING CIGARETTES.

Smoking is indulged in from childhood by both sexes. The Burmese "cigarette" is as large as an ordinary cheroot.

BURMA

By R. GRANT BROWN, I.C.S.

"Her cheek is more beautiful than the dawn, her eyes are deeper than the river pools; when she loosens her hair upon her shoulders, it is as night coming over the hills."

—*Burmese Love-song, in "The Soul of a People."*

Burmese Childhood—Demeanour of Girls—Education—Religion in its Relation to Woman—Duties of Burmese Girls—Burmese Propriety—Marriage—Domestic Morals—Elopements—A Parent's Vengeance—Women and Crime in Burma—Position of Burmese Women—Rights of Married Women—An Ugly Feature—Women as Traders—The Great Market at Mandalay—Dress—The Use of Cosmetics—Jewellery—Smoking—The Charm of Burmese Women—Other Races in Burma—The Shans—The Karens—The Chins—The Kachins

Burmese Childhood.

IF the chief business of a maiden's life is to charm and captivate those around her, the Burmese girl begins her business career early. Watch her, at the age of three, toiling bravely up the steps of the great Rangoon pagoda. Her tiny hand is grasped high above her head in her mother's slender fingers, and a shapely little naked foot is planted firmly on the cold smooth stone before the next stride is taken; a big stride for her, though the step is only an inch or two high, for a tight petticoat of many-hued silk encumbers her chubby legs. When the two reach the topmost step, the mother buys some wax tapers from a girl at a stall, and passes on to one of the shrines. Here she kneels devoutly and bows her head, clasping her hands, with the tapers between the tips of the fingers; then she turns to her little one, and, putting her soft hands together, teaches her to do likewise. It would be hard indeed to find a prettier picture.

Demeanour of Girls.

No archbishop at a State ceremony could be more solemn or dignified than this little girl at the pagoda. But Burmese children, and for that matter Burmese grown-ups, are not naturally serious, like their neighbours of India and China. They are taught, however, to suppress their feelings, whether of grief or mirth, and to the bubbling gaiety which is her nature the Burmese maiden adds from her earliest years a dignity of movement, a demureness of manner, which are no less characteristic. It is thought unseemly for her to smile in public so as to let her teeth appear, and to a European it is amusing to watch the demeanour of a well-trained girl accompanying her mother on an official call. Nothing will induce her to part her lips, however much the corners of her mouth may twitch. Sometimes, indeed, the river bursts its banks. Then the laughter is infectious, and I have known a whole school set laughing at nothing by a dot of five shaking with merriment behind her slate, and peeping now and again with bright, humorous eyes at the English inspector. His efforts to be stern were a sorry failure, and he soon joined in with the rest. But a visit to the pagoda is a different matter. The child has hardly ceased to toddle when her carriage becomes erect and dignified, though losing none of the grace and suppleness which are manifest when she is playing with other children at the water's edge, unrestrained by clothes or by the necessity of adapting her demeanour to a solemn occasion.

Education.

A good many girls, even in the Burmese king's time, learnt to read and write. The accomplishment is a useful one for those who wish to send and receive love-letters, and what girl does not? It is poor fun using a scribe. But, as girls are excluded from the monastery schools, they do not share with their brothers the benefit of a universal system of free education, and special arrangements have to be made for them. It is true that there are convents of nuns, who undertake the teaching of little girls, but they are very few. The census returns show six in every hundred of the female population of all ages as able to read and write, while the proportion of males is forty-nine. But their capacity for mental arithmetic must needs be considerable, seeing that nearly all the petty trade of the country is carried on by women. I have seen a little girl, who could not have been more than eight years old, sitting by herself at a stall on which quite twenty different kinds of goods were displayed. She had to remember the price of each one, and to calculate the amounts due in payment without any assistance from her elders.

Religion in its Relation to Woman.

Apart from her visits to the pagodas, religious ceremony plays little part in a girl's life. Whereas every boy must, if only for a few hours, put away his gay clothes, shave his head, and become a monk, no such obligation is incumbent on the girls. Comparatively few become nuns. There are 5,000 nuns in Burma, and 75,000 monks. Why this is so I have never been able to understand. A cynic would perhaps compare the unlovely appearance of the Burmese *mèthila*, and her shaven head and dirty white clothing, with the becoming dress of a nun of Europe, and point to this difference as a reason; but he cannot be taken seriously. The women are certainly not less inclined to devotion than the men. At the pagodas and shrines, and on the platforms where the monks read the Law, there are few but women and old men to be seen.

Duties of Burmese Girls.

While her brother is at the monastery school the little girl makes herself useful at home. She minds the baby, learns to cook and to weave, accompanies her mother to market, and perhaps even does the marketing herself. In the country she may tend the cattle, or help in the fields. As soon as she is strong enough she is taught to fetch water for the house, balancing a round pot on her head; and this is a pleasant duty, for it is at the well or the riverside that the village girls meet for gossip and their daily bath, and exchange chaff with the young men. Loosening her *tamein* from her waist, she refastens it under her armpits and divests herself of her jacket, the *tamein* serving as a bathing-dress. Her ablutions finished, she washes any spare garments she may have brought with her, and perhaps changes her *tamein*, slipping a dry one over the other, which is allowed to drop. Towels are dispensed with, and having filled her water-pot she makes her way home, her wet skin glistening in the sun.

Photograph by Watts and Skeen, Rangoon.

A BURMESE TOILETTE.

She is now approaching the marriageable age, and her parents watch her with anxiety. The young men treat her with respect —not, perhaps, in their language, for delicacy of language is not a strong point with the Burmese, and I have heard a little girl of seven use words to an intrusive dog that, translated into English, might make a coal-heaver blush — but none other than a favoured suitor would dare touch her hand, and for even him to do so in public would be esteemed an insult.

Burmese Propriety.

The strictness of Burmese notions of propriety in this respect surprise a stranger, and a good-natured Scotch captain of a river steamer who patted a young girl on the head was considerably taken aback at the storm of indignation which he aroused among the passengers. But a little consideration will show that it is necessary for the public morals. The clothing of Burmese women is very light and thin, and the *tamein* (which, in its old-fashioned form, is only a square of silk, exposing the thigh at every stride) is merely tucked in round the waist. On the other hand the utmost freedom of social intercourse with men is permitted, and it is easy to see that no approach to horse-play can be allowed if decency is to be maintained. Accordingly we find sentences of great severity inflicted by Burman magistrates for what seem to us very trivial offences. Six months' imprisonment seems a heavy punishment for upsetting a girl backwards while sitting in a merry group round the fire. An equally severe sentence was passed on a young man who, having been permitted to escort a damsel to her home, kissed her cheek (or rather smelt it, for smelling is the Burmese method of expressing affection). Perhaps the most unreasonable to our ideas was one of three months on an old man who had seen his servant-girl eavesdropping while he was talking secrets with his wife, and had pursued her when she ran away and seized her wrist. All these sentences were reduced on appeal to a European judge, but it is doubtful whether the first two would not be endorsed by Burmese public opinion.

This strict propriety of behaviour between the sexes seems to contrast strangely with the looseness of the marriage tie. The fact that it is often difficult to say at what precise point a couple are married does not appear improper in a Burman's eyes. No ceremony is

Marriage.

Divorce, for which mutual consent is sufficient, is also a simple matter, but is often more formal, as a division of property may be necessary.

This somewhat casual way of entering on the marriage contract is often thought to

Photograph by Watts and Skeen, Rangoon.

A BURMESE MILL.

This primitive mill is worked with the foot by the woman on the right of the photograph.

necessary. All that is needed is that the couple should live together. If the lover proves faithless, and the girl becomes a mother, he is regarded as a husband who has deserted her; and I have known of a case where the man, after an interval, actually claimed restitution of conjugal rights, though the two had only met clandestinely. It is usual, however, for the bridegroom, or someone on his behalf, formally to demand the girl's hand from her parents; and the old people meet together and invite a few friends, whom they regale, if they follow the old custom, with pickled tea. If they can afford to pay a company of actors, and give an open-air play in front of the bride's house, so much the better.

imply a laxity in morals which by no means exists. There is probably no country in the world where married women are given so much freedom and are yet so faithful to their husbands. Under the Indian Penal Code, which was framed for a society where the wife is kept in confinement and is regarded as, in a manner, the property of her husband, adultery is a criminal offence, and the enactment is in force in Burma, where the conditions in this respect resemble those of our own country. I have known of many prosecutions for adultery in Burma, but never one in which the wife was of pure Burmese race. Even in their conduct before marriage, I doubt whether Burmese girls

Domestic Morals.

Photograph by Watts and Skeen, Rangoon.

A BURMESE BULLOCK CARRIAGE.

are as unchaste as is commonly supposed. Those who err are, indeed, more leniently treated by their sisters than in Europe, but that is another matter.

Elopements.

Usually the girl is allowed to choose her own lover, but when her choice is not approved by her parents, disastrous consequences sometimes follow. Many a tragedy must lie hidden behind the police returns which tell of young girls hanging or drowning themselves for love. More often there is an elopement, and the police are asked to uphold the parents' authority. If the girl is proved to be under sixteen, the young man is probably sent to jail, for the law does not permit him to take her from her natural guardians without their consent. Usually she is older, and then various devices are resorted to by the angry parents to revenge themselves on the couple who have defied their authority. The simplest is a false statement as to the girl's age, which leads to the arrest of the lover and the return of the girl to her parents; after which the statement is retracted, and the lad released. Strange as it may seem, the girl is often persuaded, when once she has fallen again under her mother's influence, to make cruelly false charges against her lover, who is accused of using force or threats to gain her. A mere boy is thus too often kept for days in the cage at the police-station, while the case is being prepared for the magistrate. In court the witnesses retract all the statements made to the police, or go through a weary recital of false evidence which ends in an acquittal.

A Parent's Vengeance.

In 1903 several persons were punished by the courts in a town in Lower Burma for making false charges of this kind, and the mother of a girl who had defied her authority devised new means of wreaking her vengeance on the lover. The young couple were happily married, and living in the same quarter. The mother put a long knife into the hands of another of her daughters, aged eleven, and sent her, ostensibly to cut a certain kind of grass, to a field where the bridegroom's little sister, aged eight, was tending cattle. What instructions she gave her can only be guessed, but during a friendly conversation the elder girl suddenly stabbed the younger in the abdomen. Happily the child was wearing a *tamein* which was much too large for her, and was rolled up at her waist to prevent her from tripping over it. The knife passed through eight folds of the stuff before it reached the body, and inflicted only a slight wound. The youthful criminal was arrested and tried for attempt at murder. She stood in the dock, erect and defiant, and denied all knowledge of her act, though she admitted that a knife had been given to her by her mother to cut grass. Nothing could be proved against the mother, but it could hardly be doubted that the foul deed was inspired by her, and the magistrate was greatly puzzled to know what to do with the little girl, as there are no girls' reformatories in Burma. Eventually she was sentenced to three months' imprisonment.

Women and Crime in Burma.

Happily such a crime is rare in Burma; nor are false charges, except of the particular kind I have mentioned, common. And be it noticed that even in this case the knife was chosen as the weapon of revenge. In India it would have been poison, and it is greatly to the credit of the Burmese people that I have never heard of a poisoning case in which a Burman was accused. And crime is rare among the women of Burma. The English jails at the end of 1905 contained thirty-two women for every hundred men; the jails in Burma contained only three women to a hundred men. Even these were, some of them, scapegoats for their husbands. When a woman insists that illicit spirit belongs, not to her husband, but to her, the magistrate has no course but to convict her.

It has often been said that the women do most of the hard work of the country. But this is not because they are the slaves of their husbands, as among savage warlike races On the contrary, they occupy a position of independence and responsibility, and it is precisely this sense of responsibility, added to maternal love for their offspring, that makes them work hard when the husband fails to do his share. The disregard of the value of money, which has brought on the Burman more abuse and more compliments than any other of his qualities, is not always to be found in his wife, who, as she grows older, is apt to become as hard and grasping as she is practical and self-reliant.

Position of Burmese Women.

A recent writer on Burma has commented on the beautiful character of the old men, which is reflected in their faces. They have had an easy time in the battle of life The thin, pursed lips of the grandams show where the brunt of it has fallen.

Photograph by Watts and Skeen, Rangoon.

A SHAN WOMAN AND HER HUSBAND.

The Shans live in the mountainous district of Burma.

The doctrines of Buddhism, which are Indian in their origin, teach that every man is a potential Buddha, while a woman, though she may attain Nirvana in the next existence, cannot become a Buddha without first existing on earth as a man. In every-

Photograph by Watts and Skeen, Rangoon.

BURMESE WOMEN POUNDING RICE.

day life, too, she is in some respects made to feel her inferiority. She ought not to walk about upstairs when there is a man below, though this rule is frequently neglected. She may not bathe in water from the same jar as her lord, and at public feasts the women must wait till the men have eaten, though in the house the members of the family eat together. No Burman will touch a woman's *tamein* with his hands when it has once been worn, unless it is his mother's or grandmother's.

Rights of Married Women.

On the other hand, not only do sons and daughters inherit equally from their parents, but a married woman has an absolute right to dispose as she pleases of property acquired or inherited by her either before or after marriage. She is usually a partner in her husband's business, and as such has just as much right to sign for the firm as he; but she may have a business of her own, with the proceeds of which he cannot interfere. Even in matters in which she has no part, she is usually consulted before an important step is taken; and it may be guessed, when her acquisitive propensities are considered, that her influence is not always for the best when her husband is an official. In writing to a Burman it is common to add his wife's name on the cover, and it does not very much matter whether the husband's name or the wife's comes first. The fact that a man has taken a second wife does not in itself give his first wife a legal right to divorce him, though polygamy is not looked upon with favour; and a certain amount of outward submissiveness is expected in the woman; but in other respects the wife has the same right of divorce as her husband, and usually takes half the joint property. In the Kyaukpyu district of Arakan there is a singular custom by which a wife may turn a lazy husband out of doors on paying him a fixed sum (I think thirty-two rupees) if he neglects to work for the support of the family, and this act has all the effect of a formal divorce.

This freedom of woman is, I think, a natural result of the Burmese political genius, which is intensely individualist and, in a sense, democratic. Feudalism and the *patria potestas* are equally unknown. Even the children enjoy a larger measure of liberty than in most countries. So the Burmese law, while speaking of woman as an inferior animal, gives the wife the management of her own property, which we have learnt to do only in the last few years.

An Ugly Feature.

A very ugly feature in Burmese life is the use of abusive language. In this unpleasant accomplishment the man is no match for his gentle companion. Bad language is not often employed in ordinary conversation, even by the lowest of the people, and its use is not treated lightly as among the lower classes in Europe. It is a weapon to be held in reserve for important occasions, when it is unsheathed and wielded with terrific effect. If a wife abuses her husband he would probably be held justified in divorcing her. For abuse of a neighbour a Burmese magistrate will always, if he is allowed, inflict a very heavy fine, if not imprisonment. It is strange to see a woman, by no means a vixen in ordinary life, going out to battle with another who has offended her. Standing in the middle of the street before her enemy's house, she will scream uncomplimentary epithets at the top of her voice until vanquished

Photograph by Watts and Skeen, Rangoon.

BURMESE GIRL HUSKING PADDY.

by force or a greater flow of language from the other side, and will return home with what seems to us the singular notion that she has somehow vindicated the justice of her cause and brought disgrace on her adversary. Sometimes the combatants proceed to blows. A slipper is invariably the weapon used, for the object is to shame rather than to hurt the enemy, and to touch her head with one's shoe is perhaps the greatest insult that can be conceived.

I fear that this picture, though true, may create a false impression in the mind of English readers, if they are not warned that in ordinary life the Burmese woman, even of the poorer class, is by no means ungentle, so that it would be difficult to believe her capable of such behaviour as I have described. Nor must it be thought that the scene is a common one. It is depicted because it is characteristic and remarkable. An explanation of these outbursts, as of the occasional outbursts of bloodthirstiness and cruelty on the part of the men, may perhaps be found in the fact that the Burman, though entitled to a high place in the scale of racial types, has not yet lost all his savage instincts, as have the races in which civilisation has become second nature.

Women as Traders.

The trade of the country, in so far as it is carried on by the natives, is nearly all in the hands of the women. There are a few shops in the houses and the very poor expose their goods on road-side stalls at night; but most of the business is done at the market in the centre of the town, a delightful institution which greatly adds to the interest of the country and the joy of its inhabitants. The building is usually owned by the municipality and yields large profits, which often far exceed the amount raised by the rates. Here is to be bought every kind of thing that the town yields, and here the Burmese maiden is in her element. Never was there a better invention for combining business with pleasure; the business of money-making, and the business of love—the pleasures of admiring and being admired. The market is a marriage-mart, and a school for manners; an effective advertisement, and an unequalled convenience to the buyer. It is not surprising that many families which could well afford to do without this source of profit have a stall in the bazaar. How dull the girls would be without it!

The Great Market at Mandalay.

The great Zegyo market at Mandalay covers an area of twelve acres. There are endless rows of fish and grain, vegetables and fruit, hardware and lacquer, old silver and modern gewgaws. But it is the stalls where piece-goods are sold that most attract those who have not come solely on business; not the cotton goods, for behind these appear too often the brown wooden legs of the native of India, whose strident voice for ever calls attention to his wares; but the silk stalls, where bright eyes and rounded forms, in a rainbow-tinted setting, lure the passer-by, if not to his destruction, at all events into spending more money than his economical wife would approve. And the European, if he is wise, will send a Burman to buy for him, for his attempts at bargaining will only raise peals of laughter, and will probably be unsuccessful.

Dress.

The European artist in woman's dress seems to aim at exaggerating the natural curves of the body; hence such devices as corsets, and, formerly, bustles and crinolines. The Burman's notions of beauty are quite different. His ideal seems to be that of a sapling, straight and lissom, and the dress is arranged accordingly. The bosom is compressed by a tight inner bodice, and its outlines, with those of the waist, are concealed by a loose jacket, a kind of sleeved cape, which just reaches to the hips and forms almost a straight line with them. The width of the hips is also minimised by the single tight garment which encircles them. It is hardly surprising that European ladies who pride themselves on their figures do not look particularly well in Burmese dress.

The Use of Cosmetics. The favourite cosmetic is thanakka, the scented bark of a tree, which is ground down on a stone with the aid of water. Visitors to Burma are perhaps unaware how much the Burmese woman owes to this cosmetic. When plastered on thickly, as it often is on the faces of children or women of the lowest class, its effect is decidedly unpleasant; but when skilfully used on a suitable skin it produces a kind of bloom which is very becoming. This effect cannot be obtained on a fair skin, and the prettiness of the Mandalay girls has been attributed (by a Lower Burman) to the darkness of their complexion, which is warm tinted, but differs from the black tinge of most Indians as the tan of a sunburnt Swede from the swarthy pallor of the Spaniard.

Jewellery. Jewellery plays an important part in the adornment of the person for those who can afford it. Its use is by no means universal, for though a Burmese lady's jewellery takes the place of her banking account (and her husband's), she will have pure gold and real stones, or nothing. Silver ornaments are regarded as only fit for children, and even eighteen-carat gold is despised. Cylinders of coloured glass or other cheap material are indeed worn in the ears by the poorer girls, but these are only meant to keep the holes open for more precious ornaments, which are easily borrowed for great occasions.

Photograph by Watts & Skeen, Rangoon.

BURMESE WOMEN WEAVING: KAREN STYLE.

Smoking. The smoking habit is nearly universal with both sexes. Even young children take to it, and a naked urchin may sometimes be seen swaggering with an English pipe in his mouth. The national smoke is a kind of monster cigarette, sometimes as much as a cubit in length and two inches thick, and never smaller than an ordinary cheroot. The stalks of the tobacco-plant are cut up, pounded in a mortar, soused with tamarind-juice, dried in the sun, roasted, and mixed with tobacco-leaf. In some parts of Burma the wood of the *on-hnè* tree is used as a substitute for tobacco-stalks. The mixture is wrapped in betel, maize, or other leaves, and the ends tied up, no paste being used. A visitor is always offered a smoke and a chew of betel, and it is considered polite to light the cheroot in one's own mouth before passing it to one's guest.

Most travellers agree in enlarging on the fascination of the Burmese women, and in rejecting her claim to be considered beautiful. It is difficult to say wherein the fascination lies; it is easier to point out that she usually has a snub nose, high cheek-bones, and too wide a face for European taste. Artists seem to find her difficult to portray, and so far as I know none but Mr. Middleton * has attained any measure of success. It is not her face that attracts, but rather the general effect of a graceful carriage, slow rhythmical movements, and supple limbs; a slender figure well displayed by a tight-drawn skirt of rich silk; spotless white jacket, and bright-hued kerchief; pleasant face and laughing eyes; and a mass of glossy black hair, in which a flower or two is daintily set. Her voice, though sometimes hard, is more often musical, and the Burmese language when prettily spoken is as melodious as any.

The Charm of Burmese Women.

* *See* the reproductions from his pictures in "The Silken East." These have succeeded in conveying to the reader at home some idea of the feast of colour which is so characteristic of Burma, as Mr. Hall's admirable "Soul of a People" has given him a glimpse of the inner life of the Burmese.

Photograph by Watts & Skeen, Rangoon.

A KAREN GIRL IN BURMESE COSTUME.

Other Races in Burma.

There are other races inhabiting Burma besides the Burmese, but their numbers are comparatively small, and their civilisation far less advanced. Out of a total of ten and a-half millions in the province seven and a-half speak Burmese, and of the remainder about a million live in the Shan States to the east, outside Burma proper. The Karens, who are scattered about the delta and along the South-East frontier, number about three-quarters of a million, and the Chins, inhabiting the hills which separate the Irrawaddy valley from Arakan and Eastern Bengal on the west, about 200,000. Far in the north are the Kachins. They number in the more settled tracts about 67,000, but most of them live in country only partly administered, or in the no-man's-land towards the sources of the Irrawaddy.

The Shans.

The Shans, who are closely allied in race and language to the Siamese, are fairer than the Burmans, and rosy cheeks are to be seen in the mountainous regions which they inhabit. The women when they enter Burma are easily recognised by their wearing a turban, which among the Burmese is the privilege of the male sex. No jacket is usually worn, but

Photograph by Watts & Skeen, Rangoon.

A "YEIN PEVE" IN BURMA.

A native dance performed by women. The "dance" consists entirely of rhythmical movements of the body.

the *tamein*, which is sewn up as in Lower Burma, is fastened over the bosom. The people are described by Sir George Scott, who knows them best, as quiet, mild, and good-humoured.

Photograph by Watts & Skeen, Rangoon.

KAREN WOMEN.
Showing the Native Dress and Ornaments.

The Karens.

The Karens also are lighter in complexion than the Burmans. They are a shy, retiring race, living in isolated houses in the depths of the forest, or eking out a scanty subsistence in the hills. They are spirit-worshippers rather than Buddhists, and many have adopted Christianity and with it a degree of civilisation which enables them to hold up their heads among the Burmese, who once oppressed them and still treat them with contempt. Burmese dress is adopted at the same time, and a Karen girl is then often distinguishable from her Burmese sister as much by her greater prettiness as by a certain lack of finish in her toilet. In their natural state the women of most tribes wear a smock with a low neck cut to a point, often ornamented with beads or embroidery. Ropes of beads or seeds are hung in profusion round the neck and waist of the Red Karen women, and lacquered rings surround their legs in such numbers that they are described by Sir George Scott as walking like a pair of compasses, and sitting with their legs stretched out in front of them, a very ungraceful and improper attitude in a Burman's eyes. The Zalun women carry leg-rings of solid brass, five or six inches in diameter, and others wear coils of brass on legs and arms. Even more remarkable are the brass collars worn by the Padaung women. Five of these, each as thick as the little finger, are welded on a little girl's neck, which is stretched to a grotesque height as she grows by the gradual insertion of more and more rings. Similar rings are worn on the legs and arms, so that some women carry as much as eighty pounds of brass. The lobes of the ears are distended by cylinders, often of enormous size. Personal cleanliness is unknown to those who have not adopted Burmese customs, and is one of the last habits to be acquired. In a delta village I once asked the father of a Karen boy of ten when his son was last washed. "When he fell into the mud." "When was that?" "Oh, he was about four then."

Most of the tribes have a curious system of marriage regulations, only cousins, or members of certain villages or groups, being allowed to intermarry.

The Chins.

If the Karens are dirty in their habits, the filth of the Chins—"stinking Chins," the Burmese call one tribe of them — is unspeakable. The Chins are on a far lower plane of civilisation than the Shans and Karens. They are, in fact, savages, and are described by Messrs. Carey and Tuck as all liars and thieves, cruel and cowardly, without respect for age, and debauchees from childhood. But they have a great reverence for birth, and in this they differ from the races surrounding them. Their mistrust of one another and feebleness of mind have made them less formidable than they would otherwise have been, but they were nevertheless once the balance due on account of his grandmother. The sole garment of the women is usually a strip of cotton cloth, so short that, to make the most of it before strangers, it is

Photograph by Watts & Skeen, Rangoon.

A GROUP OF KACHINS.

These people live in the North of Burma.

terror of the dwellers in the plains along their borders. The women are little better than slaves. They are priced according to their capacity for work or their pedigree, and sold to the highest bidder. Sometimes the bridegroom is allowed to pay the price in instalments, and it is said to be by no means rare to find a man fighting for the hung below the hips, and looks in imminent danger of falling off. Marriage is celebrated by a drunken orgy, in which the low-born and even the slaves become for the moment the equals of the chiefs, and all crimes are condoned.

A contrast to this gloomy picture of savagery is to be found in the Taungthas

("Sons of the Mountain"), who are clean in their persons and comparatively civilised in their habits. They speak a Chin dialect, but repudiate all connection with any of the tribes, and represent themselves as sprung from the sacred mountain of Pôppa, on the other side of the Irrawaddy river. The men wear Burmese dress, but the women have a pretty and distinctive costume of their own; it consists of a loose skirt, which gives free play to the limbs, adorned with a wide belt of cowries or silver filigree work, and a long strip of cotton, which is wound round the body from the shoulders downwards, and is of different pattern and colour according as the girl is below the age at which she is considered marriageable, or is ready for a husband, or is mated. The villages lie along the foot of the hills among the Burmese population, but intermarriage is strictly forbidden. Few of the Taungthas have embraced Buddhism, and even they give themselves up once a year to a drunken orgy, in which all morals are cast aside.

Photograph by Watts & Skeen, Rangoon.

KACHIN MAN AND WOMAN.

One of the hill tribes has a curious custom of tattooing the faces of its women so as to make them perfectly black, the black of a polished fire-grate. The Burmese say that a King of Burma once fell in love with a beautiful Chin girl, and ordered her to be brought to his palace. Her relations could not refuse, but to make her distasteful they tattooed her face black. Thereupon the king in his anger commanded that all the women of the tribe should have their faces blackened for all time.

The Kachins.

The Kachins of the north, like the Chins, show much diversity of type. The face is usually Mongolian and unattractive, but the nose is sometimes aquiline, and the features regular. They are primitive in their habits, but are on the whole a finer race than the Chins. Among the ruling classes the business aspect of the marriage ceremony is concealed by the bridegroom going through a form of abduction; with the common people free intercourse is allowed before marriage. The girl selects her husband after a stay, in turn, with any likely young men, at a hut on the outskirts of the village, has enabled her to judge between their attractions. If there is a child the man has to marry or pay a fine. Marriage between persons of the same surname is forbidden; so is marriage with a father's sister's daughter, though with a mother's brother's daughter it is expected. Though polygamy is not usual, a man is bound to marry the widow of his elder brother, whether he has a wife or not, unless he can get a younger brother to relieve him of the duty.

KUKI COOLIES: THE FIGURE ON THE LEFT IS A WOMAN.

The kilt and upper garment worn by the women are generally of dark blue cotton cloth.

THE KUKIS AND NAGAS OF THE NORTH CACHAR HILLS, ASSAM

By MRS. FRANK WILDE

A People without Records—The Kukis—Distorted Ears of the Kuki—Women Coolies—Simplicity of Kuki Women—Religion—Curious Wedding Customs—The Work of the Kuki Women—A Lover's Ordeal—Kuki Funeral Customs—Kuki Dances—The Nagas—Bachelor Huts—Village Feuds—Naga Costumes—Naga Views of Marriage—Naga Dances—A Primitive People—Why Naga Children are Buried in the House

THE hilly and mountainous district that separates the two valleys of the Brahmaputra and Surma rivers in the province of Assam, on the North-Eastern frontier of India, offers to the student an interesting field for ethnological research. This hilly region is but a tangled mass of rolling uplands covered with dense jungles, sparsely inhabited by many primitive tribes. Very little is known of the history of these people, for, having no written language, they possess no records. The accepted idea is that in past centuries the tribes living on the Chinese and Burmese borders were oppressed and driven into the hills by more powerful tribes, the oppressors, in their turn attacked by others,

A People without Records.

were forced to retreat southwards and westwards into the vast stretch of jungle-covered hills that for a time at least offered a safe refuge. In course of time the result was the formation of several tribal groups of Indo-Chinese or Tibeto-Burman origin. Owing probably to the inaccessibility of these hills, the groups, though living comparatively near each other, have survived as separate units, each with its own language, manners and customs, the hills they inhabit being distinguished by their tribal names; thus we have the Khassi Hills, Garo Hills, Naga Hills, Mikir Hills, etc.

It was my fortunate privilege some years ago to accompany my husband on survey and location work through the hill section of the Assam-Bengal Railway.*

The Kukis.

There were no roads, no food supplies; the railway survey parties were dependent on the hill tribes for the labour necessary to "blaze the trail" through the dense forest, to transport the baggage and stores, and to build the "bashas" or grass huts that in Assam generally take the place of tents for camping purposes. On our section this labour was supplied by Kukis and Nagas.

In the illustration on page 575 is a group of three Kukis, two men and a woman. The ordinary costume for a woman is a narrow kilt of dark blue cotton cloth reaching from waist to knee; a second cloth is wrapped tightly round the upper part of the body under the arms, and is kept in place by one end being tucked in under the other across the breast. The cotton is grown in the village clearings and the cloth is woven by the women in a primitive hand loom. Indigo is the predominating colour, but saffron and madder are occasionally used.

Gaudy colours have always exerted an irresistible fascination on primitive people. One evening we received the visit of two women arrayed in gorgeous *saris** of bright red, ornamented in one case with a design of £5 Bank of England notes, and in the other with a series of black and white chessboards! The wearers were evidently very proud and conscious of their finery! We wondered how these cheap Manchester goods ever came to find a place in the scant trousseau of a Kuki belle, and discovered that twice a year the men folk go down to the plains for a supply of salt. They take with them from their villages lac, chillies, cotton, etc., and by the sale of these articles obtain, not only sufficient salt for six months, but an extra rupee or two to spend on one of these hideous products of Manchester enterprise that so charm the vanity of their womenkind.

Distorted Ears of the Kuki.

Numerous bead necklaces adorned with silver rupees, eight and four anna bits, are worn by the women, as well as bracelets, armlets, and anklets of brass. Curious silver earrings are worn both by men and women. A hole is pierced in the lobe of the ear and a small piece of bamboo inserted, this is soon replaced by a larger, or, I should say, a thicker piece of bamboo, and the process is repeated until the hole can be stretched so as to allow the insertion of a silver ring, the diameter of an ordinary serviette ring! The ear will sometimes not stand the strain and splits under the process. I have read that a torn or split ear is a sign of the displeasure of the gods. A silver tube is worn through the upper part of the ear, and is useful as a holder for the brightly coloured flowers with which these children of the forest love to adorn themselves. Coloured paper took their fancy, and we found that the roseate hue of a certain London newspaper made the possession of that journal the object of keen competition; as a novelty in the way of ear ornament, a roll or twisted slip of the paper in question had a decided success.

It cannot be said that the Kuki women

* The A.B.R., begun in 1892 and opened for traffic by the Viceroy, Lord Curzon, in 1903, starts from Chittagong on the Bay of Bengal, and on its way north to Dibrugarh, on the North-Eastern frontier of Assam, cuts through the heart of the North Cachar hills, and then sends out a branch line to Gauhati on the Brahmaputra.

* A *sari* is a muslin drapery some six yards long by one yard wide, worn by the ordinary coolie woman in India, The cheap *saris* are all made in Manchester for export only, and the colours and designs are of the crudest.

have any claim to beauty, the younger ones have bright dark eyes, and that is about all that can be said in their favour. Though their skins are of a darker shade than the tribes more nearly allied to the yellow race, the high cheek-bones and flat noses betray Mongolian descent. The hair is generally drawn back tightly from the forehead and twisted in a knot fastened with bamboo or brass pins.

Women Coolies.

The Kuki huts of grass and bamboo are, as may be seen from the illustration on this page, built on a raised platform some three or four feet from the ground; the platform extends beyond the main entrance, thus forming a sort of roofless verandah.

As few Englishwomen had been in the district before, I knew that the advent of a white woman was bound to cause a certain interest, but I was not prepared for, and certainly hardly flattered by, the sensation I created at the first meeting with Kukis of my own sex. A few days after our arrival in the hills, while marching along a narrow track in a belt of bamboo jungle, we came across a party of Kuki coolies, among whom were three women, one a very ancient dame, who became my first acquaintance among the Kukis, and two younger companions. Already accustomed to the semi-nudity of the men, the sight of three squat figures in scant but modest costumes of dark blue cotton cloth immediately arrested my attention. At the first glimpse of me, however, they uttered a startled cry and plunged into the bamboo thicket, where they remained till we had passed!

Simplicity of Kuki Women.

Soon after we had settled in our jungle home, a Kuki village was built near our headquarters, and this old lady frequently came to see me. Needless to say, our intercourse was carried on chiefly by pantomime, sometimes with a Hindu overseer as interpreter. Many of our possessions seemed wonderful to these simple people, and their simplicity taught me many a lesson. On one occasion, while camping out on survey, a party of Kuki women arrived in camp with a load of rations. Depositing the bags of rice at the store shed, they drew near to where I was seated outside the "basha," and, while chatting gaily together, they watched my every movement. Presently, I rose and went to the filter for a glass of water; a

NAGA WOMEN CARRYING WATER IN BAMBOO "CHUNGAS."

chorus of laughter and excited exclamations startled me. I looked round to see what had happened and found that I was the unconscious cause of their amusement! It seemed to their primitive minds extremely comical that, by a turn of the wrist, I could get water out of a stone jar. I persuaded them to come up and inspect the filter, and then showed them an automatic weighing scale; the movements of the indicator were followed with intense interest, especially when they themselves placed the articles in the scale. Great amusement was caused when I brought out a looking-glass, evidently the first that some of them had seen. In turn each girl came up shyly and gave a swift glance amid the laughter of her companions. The experiment produced various effects; some uttered a little shriek of astonishment, others looked stolidly at the glass as though they neither saw nor understood; one young girl, certainly not beautiful, gave a cry of horror, and hiding her face hastily rejoined her friends. An old man who happened to be passing was called up, and, to the great delight of the girls, solemnly proceeded to apostrophise his own reflection, and when, receiving no answer, he hurriedly glanced behind the

HUT OF THE CHIEF, OR HEAD MAN, OF THE KACHCHA-NAGA VILLAGE OF KUILONG IN THE NORTH CACHAR HILLS.

The large basket suspended from the projecting roof is used for measuring grain.

chair on which I had placed the glass, his puzzled expression proved quite as comical to the women as to me.

Three years later, on our return to the jungles from a trip home to England, we took back with us some mechanical toys, and amongst others a doll with articulated limbs, and with eyes that would open and shut. This doll was a never failing source of wonder and curiosity. Old and young, men and women, would come up to the bungalow and ask to see the "child" as they called it. It was nearly the size of a small baby, and it was quite pathetic to watch a withered old hag take the doll into her skinny arms, dandle it, croon to it, as if it were indeed a live child. The eyes of boys as well as girls would shine with pleasure if allowed to handle the pretty toy, its fair hair, blue eyes, pink cheeks, arousing in turn their wonder and admiration.

Religion.

The religion of most of these hill tribes is a form of animism. They believe in two or three principal gods and a host of others; each stream, rock, tree, has its own presiding spirit. There are no temples, and the only outward worship seems to be the sacrifices offered by the priests to appease the anger of the gods should an epidemic occur, or to propitiate their favour at rice planting time. The daily visit to the temple, the attendance at the many religious ceremonies and festivals that form so important a part in the existence of the women of India and Burmah, have no counterpart in the simple lives of these hill folk.

Wedding and funeral ceremonies bring some variety into their lives, however, and

NAGA WOMEN FROM THE PATKOI HILLS, ASSAM.

These women were employed in carrying rations for the staff engaged in a survey of these hills several years ago. It was with difficulty that they were persuaded to pose for the photograph, and only one negative was secured.

vary in detail in different villages. When a man wants to marry a girl, he offers a present to her parents, and if they agree to the match he is bound to serve his future father-in-law for five years, three before, and two after the marriage—not till then is he at liberty to build a separate hut, and to start life on his own account. At the wedding ceremony the bride and bridegroom sit side by side on the ground; the priest, standing over them, holds a fowl by the neck and slowly strangles it—from the contortions that the bird's body goes through during this painful process the priest judges whether or not the marriage will be a happy one. A glass of rice-beer is handed to the husband, who drinks half and gives the rest to his wife. The priest then cuts off the wings of the fowl, and placing the right one on the man's head, and the left on the woman's, completes the ceremony. Great freedom is allowed in the intercourse between the sexes before marriage, but after marriage a Kuki wife is rarely false to her husband.

Curious Wedding Customs.

To the Kuki woman falls a large share of the work of a village community. She gathers wood, spins, weaves, and toils in the village "jhooms" or clearings, where are grown sufficient food crops for the year. A large number of women were employed on the railway for clearing the undergrowth, carrying in loads of grass for thatching and in transporting baggage; indeed, as porters they did well, for notwithstanding the rough, steep path, a 60 lbs. bag of rice was a very usual load. The loads are carried on the back, attached to the ends of a broad band of plaited cane that passes over the forehead; the strain thus falls on the muscles at the back of the neck.

The Work of Kuki Women.

The late C. A. Soppitt, subdivisional officer in the North Cachar Hills, relates a curious ordeal to which the suitor of a Rajah's daughter is subjected, an ordeal that must mean much excitement among the women folk as it falls to them to test the courage and perseverance of the young man. A leg of pork is hung up inside a house and all the women of the village are assembled, each armed with a strip of cloth to the end of which is fastened a bag of stones. These women, of all ages, place themselves round or near the house, so that anyone entering the house would be bound to pass by them. The young suitor is bidden to seize the leg of pork and to carry it out of the village; on a given signal, he makes a dash for the house, the women striking him with their slings as he rushes past. Should he succeed in seizing the pork, he has yet to get clear of the village with his booty, while chased and struck at by the women; should he drop the meat, he is jeered at by the mocking crowd, and told that he had better return whence he came as he is not good enough for their Rajah's daughter. Should he succeed in getting clear of the village, his companions, who are waiting, take possession of the girl and remove her without further trouble.

A Lover's Ordeal.

Most of the Kuki tribes bury their dead, though some dispose of the bodies by cremation. Domestic animals are sacrificed at the funeral feasts, and the heads of the victims are placed on poles round the grave; the ghosts of these animals are supposed to accompany the deceased into the next world, where they may be of use. After death, good and bad alike are believed to go to a "village of the dead." There seems to be a general belief in re-incarnation and that, after a certain number of years, the dead return to earth in the body of a new-born child. It is not so very long ago that slaves and prisoners of war were sacrificed at the funeral feasts.

Kuki Funeral Customs.

Dancing is the chief amusement of the Kukis, and is indulged in separately by the sexes, the men's dances being more energetic and more varied than those of the women. The latter content themselves with slowly moving round in a circle with a shuffling step, their eyes demurely fixed on the ground, the arms, which are held close to the sides, are occasion-

Kuki Dances.

ally stiffly raised to the height of the shoulders with the palms of the hands outwards, and as stiffly dropped again. The whole performance is gone through without a smile. On each occasion that we witnessed a dance, time was kept by the men clapping their hands and striking the ground with bamboos, the resulting " thud " varying in tone according to the diameter and length of the bamboos.

A PRIMITIVE LOOM.

The cotton kilts and blankets worn by the hill tribes of Assam are all woven by the women folk in this primitive hand-loom. The cotton is grown in the village plantation, and the cloth is coloured with vegetable dyes.

The Nagas.

Far more interesting than the Kukis, however, are the Nagas. The Nagas are divided into many tribes, each tribe speaking a different dialect, and these dialects vary so much that the inhabitants of villages in adjoining valleys are often unable to understand one another. Fifty years ago the Nagas were savage head hunters; this was specially the case with the Angami Nagas. The girls of this tribe would not marry a man unless he had heads to show as proof of his courage. Having slain an enemy, a warrior may wear a kilt decorated with cowrie shells. Collars are also worn, ornamented with cowries, tufts of goats' hair dyed red, and locks of hair from the heads of persons killed. Some tribes wear a curious wooden tail decorated with hard white seeds and goats' hair. I have in my possession a Naga tail to which are attached long locks of human hair which must represent the spoil from many a scalp. Helpless women and children are often the chief victims.

Among the Angamis blood feuds are frequent and deadly. But little provocation starts a feud, and it is stated that owing to their facility for taking offence, the Nagas are generally courteous and polite so as to avoid all occasion for quarrel.

Naga villages are built on inaccessible hills, or along a steep spur; their huts differ entirely from those of other hill tribes. They have high gable ends and the roof slopes down and back till it nearly touches the ground; the eaves also almost touch the ground, as shown in the illustration on page 578. The hut is divided into three compartments; the large one in the centre is used as a sleeping or living-room, the small division in front serves as a grain store, and here the women pound the rice for making the rice-beer which is the favourite drink of the Nagas. It is made and stored in the small compartment at the back of the living-room.

Bachelor Huts.

Nearly all Naga villages have a large hut which serves as a club and sleeping apartment for the bachelors, and not a few have a similar hut for the unmarried girls, which is presided over by a widow or elderly female; in other villages, the girls sleep together by threes or fours. Each hut has a platform jutting out over the hillside and commanding a view of the surrounding country; this was necessary in former days when the villages were so constantly raided by warlike neighbours. The young women spend the day on this platform, preparing the cotton yarn for weaving; the primitive hand looms are tied to the house posts, the girls sit on the ground and swiftly throw the shuttle backwards and forwards (*see* p. 581).

Village Feuds.

The villages are divided into wards called khels; each khel is a distinctive unit, and is ruled by a headman. Should one khel be attacked by another khel the members of adjoining khels will calmly look on and never attempt to interfere or even to defend the women and children. In one of the Government reports a Naga, giving an account of a village fight, stated that one man, five women and twenty children were killed. He described the killing of the children as rare sport, like the killing of chickens.

Naga Costumes.

The dress of the Naga and Kuki women is very similar, but the lower garment of the former is extremely ornamental on festive occasions. The general design is a series of dark blue triangular patterns on a white ground. On the lower border various patterns are worked in with dark blue, madder, crimson, or saffron, coloured wool or cotton, each pattern separated with tiny tassels of rice straw dyed a brilliant yellow. It is not what could be called a graceful dress, for there is neither fold nor curve; it is, however, distinctly original and effective.

The women of some of the tribes living in the more remote hills wear circles of cane round their waist and strips of cane wound round the legs below the knees. The illustration on page 579 is from a photograph taken by the late R. A. Way, Esq., Chief Engineer in charge of a survey expedition in the Patkoi Hills. These women were employed in carrying rations. It was with great difficulty that they were persuaded to allow themselves to be photographed. The nose ornaments are not worn by the Nagas of the North Cachar Hills.

Naga Views of Marriage.

The Naga girls wear their hair cut short, but after marriage it is allowed to grow long; the girls wear necklaces of beads and shells, bracelets and anklets of brass, sometimes of silver. On marriage these are discarded. A married woman no longer joins in the dances; for her the serious business of life has begun, such as helping her husband in the village "jhoom," gathering firewood and carrying water. The latter task is no light one, for the water supply is frequently 300 to 500 feet down the hill side, and the water is carried up a steep path in sections of thick bamboos called "chungas" (*see* p. 577). One wonders why, with so little inducement to marry, the Naga girls give up the freedom they enjoy as maidens; for in most tribes there is no restriction placed on the intercourse between the sexes before marriage. The ceremony of marriage, however, confers a certain position and certain rights of inheritance which are, apparently, quite as much appreciated by those in a lower stage of civilisation as by ourselves. But though entire freedom is allowed before marriage, a Naga wife, like the Kuki, is seldom false to her husband; in former days, any breach of the marriage vow was punished by death, but now the guilty couple are both turned out of the village.

The marriage customs are simple. If a couple fancy each other, the man goes to the woman's parents, and if they are willing he pays a price for his intended bride; should they marry without the consent of the parents, no money is paid, or, if any, only a nominal sum.

A widow inherits all her husband's property on the condition she does not re-marry, and at her husband's death she is called upon to state whether or not she intends to do so! Should she retain the property and afterwards re-marry, the case is arranged among the relatives, but formerly she was put to death by her husband's relatives.

Naga Dances.

Dancing is also the chief amusement of the Nagas, though among some tribes on certain festivals the young folk of both sexes join in a game resembling our "tug-of-war," jungle creepers being used for a rope. The young men allow the girls to pull them over at first, but eventually win; the girls are then bound to serve them with drinks.

If the dance of the Kuki women is dull and uninteresting, on the other hand that of the Naga girls is varied and lively (*see* p. 584). We first saw it under somewhat picturesque circumstances. For the sake of a holiday, we had taken a short trip into the hills, and were camped for a night near a Kachcha-Naga village. The villagers turned out to give us a nautch. The night was dark and cloudy, but bonfires and torches soon threw a circle of flickering light into the camp clearing. The dancers stood facing each other in two rows, and, with the exception of a young man at the head of each row, were all girls, the music being supplied by the male non-dancers who kept up a weird chant in a minor key. Very quaint the girls looked in their pretty variegated kilts and dark blue upper garments, their numerous bead necklaces and brass bracelets jingling as the wearers moved through the various figures of the dance. The girls clapped their hands, and moved their feet with a light, springy step in time to the rather monotonous song of the men; sometimes, with a supple, graceful movement of the wrists, the hands, held about the height of the shoulders, were turned alternately inwards and outwards. The whole scene, lit up by the fitful glow of the torches, was picturesque in the extreme.

A Primitive People.

Shortly afterwards a party of men and women from this same village came to visit us in our jungle home, wearing for the occasion all their finery and the men carrying spears ornamented with dyed goats' hair, so skilfully arranged and cut as to give the spear-shaft the appearance of being covered with rich red plush. Presenting me with a small basket of rice, some bananas and a couple of eggs, the head man announced in broken Hindustani that they had travelled three days to see the bungalow, rumours of its wonders having reached them a few days previously. I think that of all they saw the piano impressed them most; they were invited to touch the keys; one of them, being bold enough to do so, was so much pleased with the result that, beginning at the bass, he struck each note in succession, the exclamations of his companions growing more emphatic as the treble notes were reached. Everything in the bungalow interested them, a peep into the bedroom and the sight of a dozen pairs of boots and shoes in my husband's dressing-room led to much animated discussion amongst themselves. The sewing-machine was a mystery and its results viewed in awed silence; a repeating clock had greater success, for they could see and watch the striking lever.

I have already mentioned that things which appear to us simple and ordinary are, to these primitive minds, wonderful and extraordinary. On the occasion of a nautch given by some Naga villagers, one of the girls could not keep her upper garment in place and there was a good deal of giggling at her expense. The nautch over, I called up the girl, and showing her a large safety pin, I pinned together the ends of the cloth across her breast. She kept her eyes fixed on my face, then, putting up her hand and finding she could not loosen the garment, she glared at me with dread and fear written on every feature, evidently under the impression that I had laid a spell on her.

Seeing my mistake, I hastily took out the pin and showed her on my own dress how to use it. Somewhat mollified by the demonstration, she reluctantly accepted the pin, while her companions, who had watched the scene with interest, eagerly held out their hands for a similar gift.

The religious ideas of the Nagas resemble those of the Kukis. Most of the tribes bury their dead, and in the funeral ceremonies a woman's basket and weaving sticks are placed over the grave. The dead are buried either in the village street or outside the village bounds. In some tribes the corpse of a child or young girl is buried in the earthen floor of the house, and a pathetic reason for this custom was given to a Government official by a Naga who had just lost a young daughter: "She might be frightened if left out alone, with nothing but the sky above her at night."

Why Naga Children are Buried in the House.

A NAGA DANCE.

Dancing is the favourite amusement of the Nagas. Girls are the principal performers, though the dance is generally led by two or three young men who carry in their hands one of the ornamental tail feathers of the hornbill.

Photograph by S. Narayan, School of Art, Bombay.

HILL WOMEN SPINNING COTTON.

The girl on the left has a bunch of cotton in her hand.

NORTH INDIA

By F. E. F.

"The Land of the Bharatas"—The Origin of "India"—A Land of Contrasts—Caste—The Hill Tribes—Curious Marriage Customs—All Hindu Women Work—Woman's Part in Religion—Life Behind the *Purdah*—A Hindu Wedding—The Marriage Horoscope—Hindu Music—Hindu Dancing—Jungle Dances—Other Dances—Child Marriage—The Rani of Sikkim—Marwari Ladies—The Parsees—The Buddhist States—Practice of Magic—The Smoke Charm—Amulets—A Spell of Evil—Witchcraft—The Mohammedans—Attractiveness of Children

INDIA is, comparatively speaking, a name of modern invention. It is intended to comprehend the vast extent of country ruled by the British Government. In ancient times the basins of the Ganges and the Indus were known as the Bharatvarsa—the land of the Bharatas. It is still the classical name for India in Sanskrit literature. The Bharatas were a noble race of warriors who came from the north. They were attracted by the smiling valleys that lay on the southern slopes of the Himalayas. In course of time they were succeeded by other races that poured in by way of Baluchistan and the mountain passes on the north. They were Dravidian, Aryan, Scythian, Mongolian, Persian (Parsees) and Mohammedan (Arabs, Turks and Afghans). They brought with them their language and their customs, but very few women. Wives were sought among the conquered, and the children born of them felt themselves to be natives of the country allied by blood to the conquered. The invader pushed the previous occupants of the land southward, and thus the confines were periodically extended far beyond the limits of the district known as the Bharatvarsa.

"The Land of the Bharatas."

The Origin of "India."

The Indus, with its mighty volume of water flowing towards the sea in smooth, silent reaches, was an impressive sight to the strangers. They came from the plateaux and the mountains. In their hill fastnesses a river was a noisy torrent that might be bridged with jungle-rope, or forded in its shallows. The Indus was unlike anything that they had ever seen inland, and they took it for an arm of the sea. They named it Sindhus, after the ocean. In the mouth of the Greek it became Indos, and later the country was known as India, the land of the Indus. It embraced provinces and kingdoms that were far beyond the valley of the Indus, until in the present day, under British rule, it includes an enormous area stretching from the confines of Persia, Russia, and China to Cape Comorin.

Photograph by Johnston & Hoffmann, Calcutta.

A BHUTIA WOMAN, MONGOLIAN TYPE.

A Land of Contrasts.

India has thus become the home of many nations and many tongues—of many forms of religion and many degrees of civilisation. On the one hand there are people who are justly proud of a civilisation older than that of the nation by which they are governed; on the other, there are tribes living in the forests who are as savage and uncivilised as the Polynesians.

In its geographical features the North of India presents every variety of form and climate. There is the plateau where the blizzard rages in winter, and the land is iron-bound in frost; the arid plain, waterless and sun-scorched; the snow-capped mountain, inaccessible to the hardiest mountaineer; the smiling valley, a veritable paradise to ease-loving humanity; the poisonous swamp and the dense forest, the home of the wild beast and deadly snake. Most extensive of all are the broad level tracts of fertile land, which yield two crops a year to the industrious agriculturist. In such a country there was room for a long succession of invaders without the extermination of the weak. Descendants of the different types are still to be found throughout the breadth of the land. They have adapted themselves to the climate and to the nature of the country in which they have settled, and consider themselves in every respect the inheritors of the land.

Caste.

Although of varied origin the Hindus possess a characteristic which is common throughout India. This is caste. It links the people even whilst it divides them; draws them together whilst it keeps them apart. How caste arose is unknown. It is defined as "a collection of families or groups of families bearing a common name, which usually denotes or is associated with a specific occupation." The divisions and sub-divisions are literally innumerable. In the census of 1901 it was shown that there were two thousand three hundred and seventy-eight main castes and forty-three races or nationalities.

The Hindus themselves have a legend which they make an article of faith. It is related in the *Institutes of Manu* and runs thus: The Supreme Soul, which "contains all created beings and is inconceivable," by means of a thought produced a golden egg. In this egg the God himself was born, the progenitor of the whole world. From his mouth proceeded the Brahmin, the priestly caste; from his arms the Kshattriya, the warrior; from his thighs sprang the Vaisya, the agriculturist and trader; and from his feet the Sudra, or serving caste.

Every caste, high or low, claims descent from one or other of these four great divisions. In spite of the difference in race they jealously preserve the fiction of a common divine ancestor; and in that belief lies the bond that gathers them into one great system, making them one people of one country. At the same time it disunites them to the extent of precluding the possibility of uniting in a common defence of their country; and it militates equally against the formation of a paternal government that will administer justice for the benefit of the general community, and for the good of posterity. India is ruled by a foreign power, the people themselves say, not so much by the strength of the sword as by their own disunion under the system of caste.

Another bond that, like caste, links the Hindus into a concrete mass is their religion. It branches out into polytheism, giving rise to many sects and a great diversity of ritual. However diverse may be the ceremonies and numerous the sects, the religion is based upon an original and simple pantheistic doctrine, which is set forth in Sanskrit, the sacred language of a sacred literature.

Castes are not confined to any particular locality. Brahmins, for instance, may be found in all parts of India. In a village there are representatives of at least a dozen castes, each occupied with his particular trade or calling, each observing the rules of his caste with scrupulous care.

In the hill tracts, however, the home of the most primitive races of India, the people are divided into tribes. On the slopes of the Himalayas they are of a Mongolian type; and though some of them have shown a tendency to merge into castes, they retain many of their savage customs; this is especially the case with their marriage ceremonies.

The Hill Tribes.

The women of all the tribes wear uncouth jewellery. Their necklaces are formed of carved wooden beads, carnelians, and fragments of turquoise.

The girls are wedded by capture, purchase and the servitude of the bridegroom. Crooke says of the Birhors of Chota Nagpur:

Curious Marriage Customs.

"When the marriage is arranged, the father tells his daughter to show her lover how fleet she is. She runs off to the jungle, and after a short interval he starts in pursuit. The ceremony is over when the youth's shout, announcing that he has succeeded in catching the girl, is heard. . . . Another rude form of marriage union is that found among the forest tribes, where the youths and the girls of the village are kept in special halls, free communication between the sexes being tolerated, and permanent cohabitation ranking as marriage. Among tribes of this class there is no infant-marriage, and the bride has the right of choosing her mate."

In Kashmir the bridegroom serves his father-in-law for seven years before he is allowed to have his bride. It sometimes happens that he is cheated of his reward, and the hand of the lady is bestowed upon another man.

All Hindu women, whether they belong to castes or to tribes, have to work unless they are wealthy. In addition to their duties in the kitchen a great number give assistance to their husbands in their various trades. Others labour in the fields and look after the cattle. Or they may spin and weave whilst the men of the family are occupied with their trade. They are clever at basket and mat making, and in dyeing cotton cloth. In agricultural districts they gather opium and cotton; and they help to plant

All Hindu Women Work.

out the grain, harvesting it, cleaning and husking it ready for the market. Wherever woman is at work her tongue goes, and the merry laugh is heard. Gossip and scandal, love tales and tragic histories serve to pass the time and make the monotonous hours fly.

Woman's Part in Religion.

Although the Hindu woman is intensely interested in all matters of religion, she is not allowed to take any active part in public worship at the temples; but it is she who prompts the pilgrimage and who puts together the offering. It is she who relates the legendary histories of the sacred books to the children. In these days, when many Indian women of the larger towns are educated, they are able to read the *Puranas* to the younger and less well-informed girls. The wonderful stories of the deeds of the gods have a strange fascination for them, and they will sit for hours to listen, storing up the tales in their memories that they may pass them on in course of time to the succeeding generation.

Whether she is of high caste or low, it is part of the duty of the woman to see that the rules of her caste are kept by the various members of the family. If the rules have been broken she informs the *guru*—the religious adviser and domestic chaplain of the family—of the fact, on his periodical visit. He orders the necessary ceremonies for restitution, naming the sum of money that must be paid; and the woman sees that his directions are carried out. If there has been illness, he perhaps prescribes a pilgrimage with an offering at the temple in some large town. If children are desired he suggests that vows should be made as well as the pilgrimage.

Photograph by Johnston & Hoffmann, Calcutta.

A WOMAN OF NEPAL, OF MONGOLIAN TYPE.

The jewellery is silver, gold, and glass beads. The large beads are of carved wood.

Life Behind the *Purdah*.

The high caste Hindus of the north of India who are wealthy keep their women behind the *purdah*. The ladies are called *purdashin*. This seclusion has the same effect as the *gosha* system of the Mohammedans. It narrows their lives down to a little world that is confined within the four walls of a house. The windows are jealously screened with Venetian shutters or with pierced marble. The building is often enclosed within high walls that shut out the view. The only green thing visible is the palm-tree that grows in a corner of the yard; the rest is brick wall and blue sky. In such a life the monotony would be deadening were it not for such events as the visit of the *guru*, the birth of a child, the ceremonies of a wedding or the less joyful rites of a funeral.

A Hindu Wedding.

The event that gives the greatest pleasure is undoubtedly the wedding. Marriage is the most important occurrence in the life of a Hindu man or woman. It is the fulfilment of the sacred duty enjoined by their religion to raise children. Large sums of money are spent upon it, and it is talked of from the very birth of the child. The young couple

Photograph by Johnston & Hoffmann, Calcutta.

BHUTIAS FROM NEPAL.

Some of the *dandy wallahs* of Simla are drawn from this class. They make good servants in spite of their cut-throat appearance. The woman has adorned her hair with flowers.

on their wedding day are reminded of the reason of their union by the bridegroom's sister, who pretends to close the door of the bridal chamber against them. They entreat her to open it, which she only consents to do after she has extracted a promise that they will give their child in marriage to her child. The throwing of rice or wheat after the pair is an Oriental custom that has its foundation in the belief that it will ensure fertility.

The Marriage Horoscope.

Before any contract can be concluded the horoscopes of the boy and the girl have to be consulted. The horoscope is cast at the child's birth by a professional astrologer. A number of these men are undoubtedly rogues, but some have made predictions that have been strangely fulfilled. Europeans have listened seriously to their prophecies and been impressed. In the case of Mr. Hodges, James Forbes relates that one of these men predicted that he would be Governor of Bombay when there seemed no prospect of such a thing coming to pass. The prophecy was fulfilled. No marriage, whether among the high castes or the low, will be carried out unless the stars are favourable. Many a desirable union is prevented because the astrologer declares that it will be unlucky. On the other hand, many marriages have been promoted between men and women who were manifestly unsuited, merely because the astrologer had decided that their horoscopes were favourable. The result has been unhappiness.

In the big towns almanacs are published on purpose for the use of the astrologer. In casting a horoscope the time of the child's birth must be ascertained, as well as the day of the month ; and it is important that it should be exact. Each moment makes a difference in the position of the stars, just as each moment makes a difference in the position of an express engine upon the railroad. At the critical instant when it is dashing past it deals death to every creature that is on its track. An instant later and the creature may pass with perfect safety over the iron rails. The time of the birth is often taken by the father himself, who will entrust it to no one else. He stands where he can see either the window or door of the room, and the midwife makes a signal by waving a handkerchief as the child enters the world.

The astrologer is ready at hand to cast the horoscope. In it he professes to set down all the events of the child's life. He describes its enjoyments and its griefs, its gains and losses, accidents and diseases, when it will be married, and how many children will be born to it ; how many will grow up, and whether they will bring honour or shame to the parent. For a certain period perhaps there will be a bad star shedding an evil influence on its life. This will be followed by a good star bringing wealth and happiness.

The prediction of the future often has a baneful effect upon the individual. It encourages fatalism and apathy under trouble and tends to deaden the spirit. Hours that should be happy are poisoned by the dread of coming evil. In sickness the influence of the horoscope is absolutely pernicious, for it retards recovery and sometimes hastens death. The very dread of the predicted calamity brings it about. Nothing shakes the belief of the Hindu in his soothsayer. If by chance the prophecies prove false, the astrologer saves his reputation by declaring that a wrong moment was given for the hour of birth.

A Hindu father of good caste once awaited eagerly the birth of his child. The astrologer who had promised him the much-desired son had been summoned, and together they watched for the signal from the lying-in chamber that was to announce the event. There was a flutter of muslin at the window, and a messenger came running to say that it was a fine healthy boy. The happy father bade the astrologer begin his work. The horoscope was cast, but, horror of horrors ! it predicted that the newly-born child was to cause his father's death in a short time.

The man brooded over the terrible prophecy. His own horoscope had also foreshadowed the same calamity. He was young and prosperous, and had no desire to die in the midst of his prosperity. Creeping into the room where his wife lay, he stole the child from her arms and carried it out into the darkness of the night. There in the yard he strangled it, hoping to avert his evil destiny. The midwife missed the baby and hurried out, suspecting that some mischief was designed. She caught the man in the act of killing it. He was given up to justice and paid the penalty of his crime, thus fulfilling by his own action the prediction of the astrologer.

When consulting the horoscope for marriage, the soothsayer has to say, in addition to prophesying good and evil, whether the girl belonged in a former incarnation to a lower caste. If he declares that she occupied an inferior position, the marriage is broken off.

Means of evading the promised bad luck are sometimes proposed by the astrologer. For a certain sum of money he undertakes to point out a course of action by which the gods may be induced to smile on the unlucky ones, and to use his own exertions to remove their misfortunes. He prescribes a pilgrimage to some distant temple, with offerings and promises of further presents to the shrine if the requests be granted. The Hindu is not always complaisant under bad fortune. If the magician has undertaken to propitiate the gods himself and he is unsuccessful, the patience of the afflicted man is exhausted. He gathers together some of the strongest and most influential men of the village, and relates his wrongs, describing with great bitterness how the wise man has promised to avert evil and has failed. Under his leadership they go to his house, seize him and beat him severely, knocking out his front teeth. When once a soothsayer has lost his teeth, virtue leaves him, and his profession is gone. He has no power to read the stars, to prophesy, to command the attention of the gods or to bend the demons to his will.

Having settled on an auspicious day with the help of the astrologer, a Hindu marriage proceeds according to the rites usual with the caste. Although the ceremonies vary, they have certain features that are common to all in the rites that are performed to keep away bad fortune and to ensure fertility. Another class of ceremonies provides for the admission of the bride into her husband's family. The pair partake of food, and the forehead of the bride is marked with vermilion. "This is a survival," says Crooke, "of the original blood-covenant entered into by the pair. Thus the Haris of Bengal

Photograph by N. P. Edwards, Littlehampton.

HILL PEOPLE OF THE PUNJAB.

draw a little blood with a thorn from the fingers of the bride and bridegroom, and each is smeared with the other's blood. Lastly, they march round the sacred fire which consecrates the union."

Photograph by Johnston & Hoffmann, Calcutta.

A BENGALI SINGER AND DANCER.

Her eyebrows are painted; her complexion is "wheaten." The tiny bells on her head-ornament tinkle as she dances.

Hindu Music.

There is much feasting and wearing of new clothes and jewellery, which the women, whether shut up in the zenana or allowed their liberty, greatly enjoy. Another pleasure connected with the wedding throughout India is the presence of the dancing girl and her musicians. As the Hindu finds the astrologer indispensable, so he considers the accompaniment of music equally necessary at every function. No ceremony, joyful or sorrowful, can proceed without it. Marriages, funerals, religious festivals, must all have their drums and cymbals and their stringed instruments.

To European ears Hindu music sounds discordant and barbaric. It contains quarter tones which delight the Hindu but make no appeal to the European. Strangely enough, the Hindu claims superiority for his music, saying that it is far in advance of that of any other nation. Emotion can be better expressed through the quarter tones than through the half tones. To some people it may represent the many voices of nature, the songs of the birds, the deep tones of the mountain torrent, the patter of the rain, the cadences of the wind sighing through the trees, sounds that are discordant, but which yet produce a whole that represents the harmony of nature.

Undoubtedly Indian music —whether it be the crude drumming of the tom-tom, which is not without its rhythm, or the wailing of the pipes, or moaning of the strings — moves the Oriental strongly. Like the Greek music played before the great Alexander it excites every emotion in turn. When the voice of the dancing girl is raised in sensual song, and her limbs quiver with voluptuous movement, the audience is placed in strong sympathy with the couple who are on the point of culminating the most important event of their lives.

Hindu Dancing.

The dance performed is not of the nature of an agile springing step such as is shown on the European stage. It is a swaying motion that recalls the movement of a graceful palm bending to the breeze in the sunlight, every leaf instinct with vitality, and swinging in rhythm to the sighing of the wind. As the music rises and falls, the nautch girl sways her body, lifting her arms, extending her hands and treading on her heels, that, like the base of the palm, seem rooted to the ground, in spite of the slight locomotion that must of course take place in the nautch.

The Hindu women do not consider it respectable to dance themselves, although they have no objection to looking on; nor are they permitted to sing. They are content to leave such accomplishments to the nautch girls whose profession it is, added to another calling that is not respectable in the eyes of a European. In former days, when the English first held their dances and moved through the figures of the quadrille, the native gentlemen who were honoured with invitations could not understand the meaning of it. They imagined that it was done to amuse the lookers-on. It is told by an old historian that on one occasion, at a ball at Lucknow, the Nawab was present. He watched the evolutions for some time with curiosity and interest. Thinking that the dancers were performing solely for his benefit, he cried out, "That will do; let them stop."

Photograph by Johnston & Hoffmann, Calcutta.

A HINDU NAUTCH GIRL WITH HER MUSICIANS.

Her *saree* is of muslin heavily brocaded with gold.

Of quite another character is the dancing of some of the jungle tribes. These performances are of a religious nature. They are executed at the sowing of the seed and the harvesting of the crops in the belief that the earth will be gratified, and will yield her fruits. The women of the tribe take part in them without any loss of prestige. With the Kols of Chota Nagpur the women stand in a row with their arms about each other's shoulders. They begin with a gentle inclination of the head, advancing and retreating before a similar line of men. As in the devil dances of South India, they gradually work themselves up into a state of excitement, encouraged by the sound of the tom-tom to still greater exertions. Now

Jungle Dances.

and then the swaying body of the dancer bends, and the hand touches the earth. This is to remind Mother Earth that the dance is being performed in her honour, and to invoke her blessing.

Photograph by Johnston & Hoffmann, Calcutta.

THE RANI OF SIKKIM.

Her head-dress is composed chiefly of pearls. Her ear-rings are of turquoise. The necklaces are of carnelian, turquoise, gold and glass beads. Her dress is of the richest brocade.

Other Dances.

With the Santals the dance is different. A certain number of men place themselves on a raised stage. From this point of vantage they act as masters of the ceremonies. The women range themselves in lines radiating from the stage. They hold each other by the waistband. Their breasts are bare, and their hair adorned with flowers or bunches of tussore silk fibre. Musicians playing on drums, pipes, and flutes face them and lead the dance. The music that they make on their rude instruments seems to madden the dancers, and it incites them to all kinds of extravagance. The musicians throw themselves into grotesque positions, and the women follow their example. The peacock feathers that they stick in their hair give them a wild, crazy appearance, suggestive of nothing less than lunacy.

The Bhils have a similar dance, which in its figures is even wilder and more eccentric. Men as well as women take part in it, throwing themselves on the ground and rolling over in their ecstasy. Probably the performers are all more or less under the influence of intoxicating liquor which, added to the excitement of the dance, renders them practically mad for the time.

The Khattaks (Pathans) have a war dance, as also have the Kaffirs of the Hindu-kush mountains, in which swords are used. In every dance there is an abandonment to emotion that produces frenzy in the dancers, and it is frequently communicated to the audience. The use of *datura* and of concoctions made from hemp helps on the excitement until, as in the south of India, the dance degenerates into an unlicensed orgy.

Child Marriage.

The triumph of a Hindu woman's married life is the birth of a son, be she a high caste Brahman or a member of one of the least civilised of the aboriginal tribes. It is the fulfilment of all things, and it places her in the highest and most honourable position possible to attain in the household. In the North the family system has a firm hold upon the people. The zenana, whether *purdashin* or otherwise, is always under the rule of one woman whose word is law. She may be a mother or a grandmother, or a great-aunt. Her office is to perform the domestic religious ceremonies, to make the daily offering to the household deity, to chant the hymn, and to light the little lamp before the domestic shrine. She is autocratic to her finger tips, and governs the destinies of a horde of relations. Although she may have suffered herself in the matter of child-marriage, she does not spare the rising generation. Through her instigation the tender half-grown maid, perhaps her own daughter or grand-daughter, is united to the middle-aged man and handed over to him before she is ripe for motherhood. By her orders the unfortunate child-widow is stripped of her jewels, shaved, and degraded to the position of a slave in the house.

Efforts are being made to mitigate these two evils, but the conservatism of the women of India obstructs reform. The men are more ready to alter their time-honoured institutions, and to break the unwritten laws of their caste than their wives; but the dread of being outcast and degraded causes them to hold back even when they know that reform would be for the good of the community. Early marriage with early motherhood tends to weaken the race and shorten life. The fatalism inherent in the Oriental helps to produce the apathy with which these questions have been regarded for so many ages. In their minds the responsibility lies with the Creator, and not with themselves. God made the fingers of the hand of different lengths. Is it, they ask, our duty to cut them to a uniform length? It is by the will of God that women become wives, mothers, and widows. Shall we try to alter the decree of the Deity, and change a widow into a wife? These are some of the deeply-rooted sentiments of the domestic hearth in the hut as well as in the palace.

The Rani of Sikkim.

The Rani of Sikkim—a small state lying on the southern slopes of the Himalayas between Nepal and Bhutan—has the appearance (*see* p. 594) of being a child of ten or eleven. The little figure is loaded with rich brocade and masses of jewels. There is no sign in those placid features that she is discontented with her lot or that she has any thought of a different life. The same contentment may be seen on the face of the Hindu lady shown on p. 596. She has the greatly admired wheaten complexion, an olive tint that is common in the south of Europe. Her hazel-brown eyes, distinct in colour from the black eyes of her duenna attendant, are darkened on the lower lids to heighten their beauty. Her lips are reddened, and her skin, from seclusion and the use of cosmetic oils, is as smooth and soft as satin; her face is without a wrinkle. The skill of the artist was not needed on the negative of the photograph to erase the marks of age. To English eyes she is inclined to *embonpoint;* but this adds to her attractiveness in the opinion of native gentlemen. Her jewels, like those of the Rani, are of pearl, and gems set in gold of the finest workmanship; and in her hand she holds a few flowers. The vase upon the table is such as she might possess in her own house; but it would be put to another use and would contain drinking water. Her clothing smells of attar of rose, and her hair of sandal-wood oil. The dark line upon the lips suggests the lately chewed betel, of which the duenna sees that a supply is always at hand for her cherished mistress. Pride in her charge is shown on every line in the handsome face of the older woman. Although a servant she is probably connected with the family, the daughter or grand-daughter of a dark-complexioned slave by some ancestor of the house.

Marwari Ladies.

Of a different type altogether are the Marwari ladies (*see* pp. 597-8). The Marwari is a merchant and money-lender, known also as a *Bunnia*. He is a dealer in corn, in which commodity he makes "corners." The jewels worn by the women indicate the lucrativeness of his trade. There are *Bunnias* all over India, and the trade is not confined to one caste. By religion the Marwaris who come from Marwar and Guzerat are Jains. The Jains of the present day venerate the cow, employ Brahmans in their religious rites and worship at Hindu temples. In some of its features Jainism bears a resemblance to Buddhism, but it rejects the doctrine of Nirvana. The preservation of life in every form is an article of the faith. It has led to the establishment of animal hospitals called *Pinjrapoles*. The unfortunate creatures that find an asylum in these institutions would be happier dead. They are ill-fed and ill-cared for. If a Hindu woman marries a Jain she is allowed to retain her religion, and perform her domestic rites.

Photograph by S. Narayan, School of Art, Bombay.

A HINDU LADY WITH HER ATTENDANT.

Her jewellery is of pearl and gold and precious stones. She is *purdashin*, and of high caste. Her duenna attendant carries a brass jewel case.

The Parsees.

Foremost in culture and civilisation stands the Parsee lady. In primitive days the Iranian wife held a position that was not inferior to that of her husband. In these times she comes nearest among Orientals to the European wife and mother. She is not secluded, but may be seen driving and walking abroad like an Englishwoman. She conducts herself with a quiet, serious dignity, indicating the fact that she is enjoying an inherited liberty, and not a recent emancipation. Although the Parsees have selected Bombay as their headquarters, they are to be found as merchants and traders in all the large towns of Northern India. Wherever they settle themselves they are a prosperous, unassuming, and law-abiding people. The man marries late in life, and the woman is permitted to attain her full growth and maturity before she leaves her parents' house and takes upon herself the duties of motherhood. The advantage is seen in the fine figures of the ladies. The influence of Western civilisation is shown in their dress—which is Europeanised—and also in their occupations. They pay visits to England

and the Continent, and are intelligently interested in most of the topics of the day that attract the attention of their Western sisters. They worship fire as the emblem of the Deity. It will be seen from the photograph on p. 600 that they do not disfigure their nostrils with jewels nor overload themselves with a barbaric display of gold. Their taste is fastidious and dainty; like the Mohammedans, they love pearls and the finest workmanship in the precious metals.

The Buddhist States.

In the far north of British India lie the border states of Bhutan, Sikkim, Nepaul, and Kashmir, where Buddhism still lingers. In former days it extended all over India; but in the present time its adherents within the limits of the Indian empire are chiefly to be found in the frontier states and Burmah. It had its origin in Northern India. Its apostle, Gautama, lived in the sixth century B.C. He was called Buddha, the Enlightened One. His life and teachings have been described by Sir Edwin Arnold in his inimitable "Light of Asia." The story is full of romance, and the articles of faith as Sir Edwin recounts them were pure and simple. Their purity and simplicity did not last long. In succeeding ages the followers became degenerate by contact with idolatry. Tantric beliefs were introduced, and the religion became debased.

Tantrism or Saktism is Hinduism arrived at its last and worst stage of mediæval development, says Monier Williams. It is the worship of the female element, which worship Oman declares to be greatly on the increase among Hindus throughout India. With it is combined the practice of magic, white and black. The rites and ceremonies are of the most degraded form; and in the case of black magic they are loathsome and repulsive. Saktism has been described as an effort to accomplish the extinction of desire. Most religions endeavour to gain this end by the mortification of the body and the consequent subjection of the passions. Saktism professes to attain it by the gratification of the passions. It is a seductive creed to the Oriental, whose standard of morality is never high, and whose power of self-control and self-denial is not great. The art of black and white magic is set forth in the Hindu books of the Tantras. They contain *mantras* (formulas) for producing evil and for averting it. By their

Photograph by S. Narayan, School of Art, Bombay.

A MARWARI LADY, WIFE OF A RICH *BUNNIA* (MONEY-LENDER).

She is loaded with jewellery. The gold cylinders on her necklace contain amulets and charms to keep away disease.

repetition with certain rites the magician professes to be able to engender every emotion and produce every condition of life to which the human being is subject.

Photograph by S. Narayan, School of Art, Bombay.

A MARWARI HUSBAND AND WIFE.

He is a grain merchant, probably a Jain by religion. Her jewels are of gold set with rubies, emeralds, and pearls. The ornaments on her toes are of silver.

Practice of Magic.

The practice of magic is not confined to the Hindus and Buddhists. It has taken firm hold of the Mohammedans, who inherited it from their Arab ancestors. Every tribe lies under its thrall; and it is the woman who finds it most attractive. For her the occult has an extraordinary fascination. She consults the magician on every occasion, and for every complaint or misfortune. She employs him to weave spells that she may obtain an influence over her husband or other members of the family; that she may cause personal hurt in the shape of blindness, deafness, and disease to those who offend her; that the property of her more prosperous neighbour may be destroyed. Most common of all is the demand for love-potions, to be administered to lover or husband.

In the case of illness the women have more faith in the wizard than in the apothecary. He is summoned and he arrives at night, when work in the fields is over. If he has a great reputation for sorcery he is welcomed with beat of tom-tom and music; at all costs he must be propitiated. He brings a gong and a bundle of palm-leaves on which he has inscribed spells by the aid of a style. The whole village is awake and assembled to see as much as possible of the ceremonies. The lamps flicker in the soft night breeze of the tropics, children tremble with vague fear, and the women's eyes sparkle. The great man advances with slow steps to the house of the afflicted individual, and makes an imposing entry into the sick-room.

The Hindu is not as advanced in the black art as the Mohammedan magician, whose practices closely resemble those of the wizard in the Arabian Nights tales. The magic of the Mohammedan has caught something from the Hindu rites, but its basis is Arabic. The Hindu calls on the names of Kali and the lesser deities. The Mohammedan invokes the help of genii and the four archangels— Michael, Jibrael, Israel, and Israfel. Belief in genii (or jins, as they are better known) is general thoughout the whole of India. With the Hindu the jin (or *raksha* as he terms it) is the departed spirit of a bad man haunting a certain district, and working mischief to humanity if it is not propitiated. The jin of the

Mohammedan is a supernatural being, who is nine-tenths spirit and one-tenth flesh.

These beings are divided into two classes, the jins or genii who are disposed to act kindly towards mankind, and the demons who, under the direction of Shaitan (Satan), work evil. The assistance of the archangels and jins is invoked against the work of the devil. Shaitan shows his malevolence by sending demons to plague poor mortal man. They are the cause of bad dreams, palsy, hysteria, madness, fevers, and unreasonable fears—nerves, as they would be called in Europe. According to the magician, charms and incantations are the only means by which these maladies may be conquered.

Magic squares and circles enter largely into the composition of charms and spells. They are written on palm-leaves with a style or upon paper with some medium; or they are drawn in sand. If required for the protection of a building they are inscribed in chalk or charcoal on the walls or doors. In the case of disease the charm is written in ink, milk, melted butter, or even blood, upon a plate. The writing is washed off with water which the patient drinks. Or a magic square or circle is drawn upon the floor, and the patient's bed is placed over it. A favourite way of administering a charm is by fumigating the patient with the paper or palm-leaf on which a charm has been written. Smoke charms are used for fevers, neuralgia, and other ailments that are serious, or merely cases of hysteria or nerves arising from a disordered digestion. The simple forms are tried at first; but should the case prove obstinate, the magician, with a more elaborate ceremony, prepares another form on a larger scale, for which the patient has to pay a longer price.

A Mohammedan charm would contain the names of the four archangels, together with the names of four jins. Space is left for the invocation or exorcism which would run somewhat thus:—"Abdul Kadir! and Abdul Khuman! Kings of the jins! Whatever possesses this person bring it now to us to destroy and annihilate! Demon! fairy! or jin! come this instant and be burned to ashes! Oollaqun! the son of Moollaqun! Nimrod! Israel! O! Israfel! O! O! O! Yemmah! yemmah!" The word "yemmah" is equivalent to the "high cockalorum jig" of the amateur drawing-room conjurer in England. The invocations are written in any language that the magician chooses to adopt. With the Mohammedans it is Hindustani or Arabic. The Hindus use the language of the district;

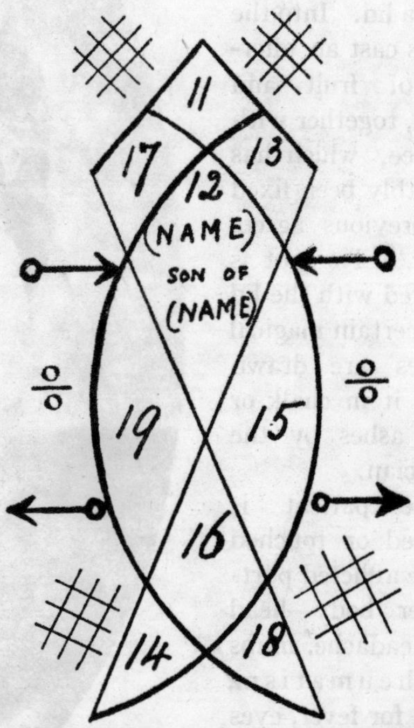

HINDU SMOKE CHARM TO CURE DISEASE.

The charm must be written on paper that has been in contact with the patient; and then it should be burned under the nostrils so that he inhales the fumes.

Sanskrit is occasionally employed, but for this the wizard requires more education than is usually the lot of the village practitioner.

The Smoke Charm.

The smoke charm is performed with a rite that varies at the discretion of the magician. He is visiting, let us say, the wife of a rich merchant, where he may expect a substantial fee. Having arrived in all the pomp and glory of tom-toms and torches at eight o'clock in the evening, he prepares to give at least a three hours' *séance*. He begins by overhauling his subject, feeling her skin and limbs, and examining her tongue and eyes. Far from being annoyed and disturbed, the patient enters thoroughly into the proceedings with a faith that is pathetic. A magic figure is drawn on the floor and she is placed upon it. The eager awe-stricken women bring, in obedience to the wizard's demands, a new earthen pot with a lid. Into the pot is cast an offering of fruit and grain, together with the fee, which has probably been fixed by previous agreement. The pot is covered with the lid and certain magical figures are drawn upon it in chalk or grey ashes by the magician.

The patient is stroked or touched in the afflicted parts of her body—head for headache, limbs for rheumatism, chest for fever, eyes or ears for failing sight or hearing—with the piece of paper on which the charm is to be written. The magician places himself in front of the patient, and writes the charm with solemn mutterings and portentous deliberation, which produces a profound impression on the assembly. The charm is completed with turns and flourishes, the ornamental figures depending on the wealth of the client. It is rolled or folded into a spill and bound with cotton thread.

The lamp is next prepared. Three kinds of oil are required, ghee, gingilly, and castor or linseed oil. They are mixed in a small earthenware lamp, which is placed in the centre of the lid of the earthen pot. A cotton wick is twisted, and with a hocus-pocus ritual the lamp is lighted. The flame is held under the nostrils of the patient, and the charm burned. All eyes watch for the signs which the magician interprets; ears are bent to catch the words that fall from the sick woman's lips. If she recovers the renown of the wizard spreads abroad through all the villages of the district. If she should die, it is because the fee was not large enough, and the spell consequently not strong enough to avert the catastrophe.

Photograph by S. Narayan, School of Art, Bombay.

A PARSEE LADY IN THE USUAL COSTUME.

The hair is drawn back and closely covered.

Besides being employed to cure the sick, smoke charms are also used where houses are supposed to be haunted by mischievous sprites that throw stones on the roof, and cause the crockery to slip from the fingers of the women when they are cooking. When the demon has been exorcised, a charm is put up in the house to prevent its return and to keep off the evil eye.

Amulets.

The magician finds a ready sale for amulets among the women, who not only wear them themselves, but take care to fasten them on the arm or round the neck of brother, husband, or son when he takes a journey. They are supposed to preserve the traveller from danger by land and sea. Magic squares are chiefly used for these. The square is written on paper which is enclosed with a claw or whiskers of a tiger, the feathers of a particular

WOMAN OF EASTERN INDIA.
Drawn by Norman H. Hardy.

Facing on page 600

bird, a tuft of hair or the bone of some creature. The whole is sewn in a covering of silk to be worn on the person night and day. With the rich the amulet is often encased in a golden cylinder or tiny silver casket, or the spell is engraved on a bangle or the gem of a ring. Charms are greatly in request for the purposes of revenge or some other passion. There are forms of magic to produce enmity between two friends, to inspire love, friendship, hate, fear, or even to compass the death of an enemy. Lest any ambitious amateur should attempt to practise a little magic on his own account and turn a penny by the preparation of charms, spells, and amulets, he is warned by the professional magician that the slightest error, omission or even careless slip in the repetition of the *mantras*, will not only render the spell ineffective, but will also bring about his own destruction. His creed is that while the demons are ready to serve mankind if properly approached, nothing angers them more than incompetent administration of the ritual by which they are propitiated.

A Spell of Evil.

Evil to an adversary is wrought by making an image of wax or clay, and by thrusting pins into it. The fruit of a lime will also serve for the purpose if the proper *mantras* are said. It must be buried near the dwelling of the person threatened.

A labourer on a tea-garden appeared before the planter one morning with a very long face. He was trembling in every limb and seemed to be really ill. The master inquired what ailed him. He replied that he was bewitched. An enemy on the estate had a grudge against him. He had made an image of clay, pierced it in the breast with nails and buried it. Already the spell was working. At night he could not sleep for the sharp pains that he felt in his heart and liver.

"Do you know where the figure is buried?" asked the planter.

"Close to my house, sir. The man who wishes me evil came in the night and made a hole at the very threshold of my door. Every time I go out or return home I have to step over the buried image and a fresh pain seizes me."

"If you know where it is, why don't you dig it up and throw it away?"

"Ah, bah! I dare not meddle with magic. The image would rise up and kill me on the spot."

The planter was a practical man. Labour was scarce, and he had no wish to lose a useful coolie. He walked straight to the man's house and was shown the spot where

Photograph by S. Narayan, School of Art, Bombay.

A PARSEE LADY IN THE REFORMED COSTUME.

Her hair is combed up and partially uncovered. She is of the Iranian type.

the thing was supposed to be buried. Taking out a knife that he carried in his pocket, he opened it and began to turn over the soil. It was soft and had the appearance of having been lately disturbed. In a few minutes he

Photograph by Johnston & Hoffmann, Calcutta.

A LEPCHA WOMAN.

Her necklace is of wooden and gold beads. The chain ornament is silver set with a turquoise. Her nose-rings and ear-rings are of gold.

came upon a small roughly-made figure of sun-baked clay. Its body was a perfect pincushion of pins and nails and thorns. He filled up the hole, and stamped it down with every expression of contempt, which was not lost upon the silent members of the family who were watching the master. Placing the image in his pocket, he said to the man :

" Now go to your work. You will feel no more pains as long as this image remains with me. I shall take out every pin and thorn and keep it safe in my strong-box as carefully as if it were a jewel."

The coolie recovered his health, confident that he was safe as long as the image was secure in his master's keeping. He remained on the estate for some years, a useful labourer in the tea-garden.

Witchcraft.

Witchcraft is at the root of many repulsive crimes. A woman was charged with the murder of the child belonging to her neighbour. The deed was brought home to her without any difficulty, and she did not deny it. She had been told by a wizard that if she bathed in the blood of a child she would bear a child herself. She actually carried out the horrible suggestion.

The Mohammedans.

The Mohammedan is to be found in most of the large towns of Northern India. The greatest numbers are in the Punjab, Kashmir, Oudh, and Eastern Bengal. They have greatly increased during the last twenty years in Bengal. In former days the Mohammedan was remarkable for his conservatism. His education was confined to the reading of the Koran, which he was taught to repeat constantly as a meritorious act. In these days of competition and public appointments he is no longer content with the old routine. He desires to qualify for Government employment like his neighbour, the Hindu, and has made a steady advance in educational matters which has been a distinct gain for the community.

It is to his advantage that he is not hampered by caste rules. There are no restrictions in the matter of food, and he eats meat as well as grain and vegetables. The re-marriage of widows is permitted, and he is no advocate of the child-wife. The girls are allowed to attain their full growth before they become mothers. The result is that his family is larger, and the children are stronger and longer-lived. He prefers to dwell in cities where life is less rough and presents fewer hardships than in the villages ; famine and drought press less heavily in the towns.

On one point he retains his conservatism—the seclusion of his women. It is not the master of the house so much as the mistress who insists upon it. The breaking of *gosha* is a dire disgrace. It is only the very poor Mohammedan woman who cannot keep her *gosha,* and she veils her face as much as possible when she goes abroad.

Photograph by Johnston & Hoffmann, Calcutta.

A COOLIE WOMAN ON A TEA GARDEN, DARJILING.

Her anklet and bracelets are silver ; her ear-rings gold ; her necklace is of glass beads with two large gold beads. The ring is a carbuncle set in gold.

It is impossible to obtain photographs of the *gosha* ladies either in India or in Kashmir. The pictures that are sold as representations of Mohammedans are mostly taken of dancing girls or of women of no reputation. In the absence of reliable photographs it is difficult to say whether the Kashmir women possess the beauty which historians claim for them. However, Mohammedan children are not *gosha*, and in many of their oval faces may be seen the promise of future loveliness.

Attractiveness of Children.

The children of the East, whether Hindu or Mohammedan, are very attractive. There are no nurseries in India; the little ones are always with the grown-up members of the family. The consequence is that they become precocious, and in many respects unchildlike. In speaking before them their elders exercise no reserve whatever, and there is none of that innocence which is the charm of the English child. They are early taught to observe the rules of their caste or tribe, and they learn to work almost as soon as they can walk and talk. The little girls cook and clean the grain, look after the cattle and the fowls, spin, weave, and assist their parents in the fields. They manage to find time to play games among themselves, and they have a great affection for dolls. It is shared by the older members of the family, who are not above taking part in their games. One of the most popular is the marriage of the dolls. Each rite is performed in all its details with dolls to represent the different persons engaged. The innocence of the child is sadly missing in these games, which, with the assistance of the elders, are coarse and indecent. In justice to the child and its guardians, it must be said that it is only in the opinion of the European that its games are open to such a charge. According to Oriental teaching, there is nothing to be ashamed of in matters that are perfectly natural.

Photograph by Bourne & Shepherd.

THE BURNING GHAT, CALCUTTA.

Showing the method of disposing of the dead.

WOMEN SHOPPING IN A BAZAAR WHERE ALL CASTES MEET.

SOUTH INDIA

By F. E. PENNY

Variety of Race—Conquered but not Absorbed—Race Characteristics Retained—The Mohammedans—Moslem Superstitions—Position of Indian Women under Islam—Submissive Mohammedan Women—Moslem Marriages—Story of a Blind Bride—Life of a Mohammedan Wife—Dress of a Mohammedan Woman—Religion and Divorce—Hindus of the South—Hindu Castes—The Brahmins—The Sudras—Hindu Women have no place in Religious Ceremonies—Domestic Position of Hindu Women—Not "Respectable" to Sing—Hindu Prayers and Offerings—Hindu Marriages—The Hindu Equivalent to the Wedding-ring—Hindu Polygamy—Pariah Liberty—Nautch Girls—The Todas—Polyandry in South India—Legendary Origin of Polyandry—Curious Custom as to Dress—Nomadic Tribes—The Hindu Ideal of Woman—The "Touches of Nature" that make the World of Women Akin—A Hindu Non-Talking Match: Man *v.* Wife

THE vast extent of territory known as India is united under one Government. This unity under one name and one Government does not mean one people. In race, language, and religion, as well as in form of feature and complexion, the natives of India vary to the same degree as the races of Europe. The fair Kaffir, or Kashmiri, is as unlike the dark Dravidian Tamil, as the Laplander is unlike the Neapolitan.

Variety of Race.

The races of Europe have been segregated under separate Governments, and the line of demarcation between them can be drawn territorially. The races of India have never succeeded in segregating themselves in like manner. Until British rule was established, India had always been the scene of invasion, of the subjugation of one race by another. The aboriginal was overcome by the Dravidian. In turn the Dravidian was conquered by the Aryan; and in course of time the Aryan had to submit to the Semitic race.

The vastness of the country prevented the extinction or absorption of the defeated nation. The aborigines, the only savage people of India, sought an asylum in the impenetrable recesses of the hills and forests, where they may still be found under the name of hill-tribes. The Dravidians exist in the South, classed collectively under the name of Hindus with their Aryan conquerors. The Semitic Moslems formed colonies in every district that was accessible, and are to be seen in every large town. No definite line was drawn by the invader to confine the conquered to any particular part. Each advancing horde pressed southward, spreading like water in a thousand runnels over the newly acquired land.

Conquered but not Absorbed.

Though ages have passed since the earlier invasions, the races of South India have not lost their characteristics. The hill-tribes retain their nature worship, the Dravidian Hindus their demonolatry, the Aryan Hindus their philosophical heathenism, and the Moslems their Islamism. Wherever the weaker nation may have been driven by the superior force of arms or by the cataclysms of nature, it carried with it the religion and the social customs of its ancestors. The Mohammedan, whether a subject of the Nizam, a merchant in Mysore, or a tailor in the city of Madras, is a follower of the Prophet on the broad outlines laid down by the Koran. The devil-worshipper appeals to his devil with sacrifices of blood, whether he lives in Tuticorin or is an inhabitant of Cuddapah. The devotee of Vishnu or Siva worships at the temple of his god, and practises the same caste rules, whether he is a Brahmin of Trichinopoly, or a Namburi of the West Coast.

Race Characteristics Retained.

Invasions with the cruel oppression of the weak by the strong have ceased. The races exist side by side in peace under the British rule, which has proved to be the only rule in the East sufficiently powerful to protect the weak, and to give strength to the pinions of Peace.

In a survey of the women of South India there must, therefore, be included Mohammedans, Hindus, and hill-tribes.

The Mohammedans, like other conquerors, came from the North. They were led by Aurungzebe, who appointed Viceroys over the different provinces and districts that he subdued. For a time these men performed their part faithfully, but as the power of the Great Mogul declined, they shook off their allegiance and ruled as independent princes. They pushed their arms to every quarter of the Peninsula, leaving colonies of Moslems in every Hindu town, and occasionally forcing their religion upon the conquered with great cruelty. Thousands of Hindus—Dravidian as well as Aryan—were obliged to submit to compulsory circumcision. The result is shown in the dark-skinned followers of the Prophet to be found in the present day in some of the cities of the South, such as the Lubbays of Trichinopoly. The racial characteristics of these dark people are markedly Aryan or Dravidian, and there is nothing Semitic about them whatever, except their religion. In the same towns and districts may be found Mohammedans of Arabian origin, the descendants of the colonists under Aurungzebe's rule. They are fair of complexion, and hold their darker co-religionists in contempt. It is the inbred contempt of the superior for the inferior, of the conqueror for the conquered.

The Mohammedans.

The religion forced upon the unwilling Hindus was accepted in its entirety as a necessity, and not from conviction. It veneered but did not displace their deeply-rooted heathenism. Many idolatrous customs are practised, such as would not be tolerated by the Semitic true believer. The creed of Islam admits the existence of Genii (Jins) and Fairies (Peris); but in addition to these the Mohammedans of the South believe in ghosts, devils, malicious spirits that haunt trees and rocks, even in the Hindu goddesses, Durga and Kali,

Moslem Superstitions.

whom they propitiate in times of sickness with sacrifices of blood. If conscience speaks at all, they silence it with the oft repeated verse from the Koran, "Allah is forgiving."

Position of Indian Women under Islam.

Woman's position in Mohammedanism is little better than that of an animal. It is worse than that occupied by the women of ancient Greece. In religion she finds no place at all. She was regarded by the Greeks as a means to an end, namely the perpetuation of the race. The Greeks had three reasons for marriage, and none of them indicated any esteem or respect for the sex. Their reasons were—(1) Deference to the gods, for it was incumbent on everyone to leave behind him those who should continue to discharge his religious observances. (2) Obligation to the State, since by generating descendants, its continuance was ensured. (3) A regard for their own race and lineage; it was necessary to leave heirs to discharge the duties of the departed.

The Hindus believe that, in addition to the important duty of child-bearing and the care of the house, the woman has yet another duty, which lies in the daily religious ceremonies performed in the privacy of her home. Some assert that the future happiness of her husband depends upon their due observance.

With the Mohammedan, the woman has but one end, namely to minister to the pleasure of her husband; and, if God wills, to bear him children. She is man's creature, his chattel, to be jealously guarded for his individual use, and for no other purpose.

Photograph by Nicholas & Co., Madras.

DRAVIDIAN NAMBURI BRAHMAN LADY OF THE WEST COAST IN FULL DRESS.

Her ornaments are of gold, and form the only covering she is allowed to wear above the waist in public.

For that she was created, and having fulfilled her destiny on earth, she passes away like an animal without any definite place or reward in the future.

So deeply imbued is the mind of the Mohammedan with this belief, that once, when a man was condemned to death for the murder of one of his wives in Bangalore, his co-religionists exclaimed :—

"What monstrous thing is this? Is one to be hung for the mere killing of a woman? As well might the Sirkar hang a man for the killing of a sheep!"

At the death of Queen Victoria a Mohammedan of good position remarked in all seriousness to an English gentleman:—

"Now, sir, I suppose you need no longer take off your hat to ladies, since you have only observed the fashion in honour of our Queen-Empress."

Photograph by A. W. A. Platé & Co., Colombo.

DRAVIDIAN HINDU OF THE SUDRA CASTE (ONE OF THE LOWER DIVISIONS).

Her *saree* is of unbleached cotton and her ornaments of silver, except a necklace of gold beads.

The Mohammedan woman, after many centuries of submission, thoroughly believes in the justice of her position. She accepts her rules of *gosha*, the state of being hidden, as she accepts the complexion and the features with which she is born. The horizon of her vision is narrowed down to the blank walls that hem in the courtyard of her house, and her eyes are focussed upon the interior of that house. If they wander at all it is only to gaze at the unfathomable blue sky, at the dazzling sun that shines down into the courtyard defiant of all *gosha* rules, or at the green depths of the palm tree that spreads its fronds overhead. Her mental vision is equally limited, and her mind is centred upon the drama of life enacted within those confining walls. Birth, marriage, sickness, and death are the great events that mark the days. Quarrels, jealousies, occasional visits, dress, jewellery, occupy her mind in the intervals.

Submissive Mohammedan Women.

The *gosha* of a woman is her god. Every action has to be considered from that point of view. Only if she is very poor can she disregard it. With some sects the rule is relaxed when old age has deprived her of every attraction. Even then the toothless old hag from force of habit will shrink from public gaze as though she were endowed with transcendental beauty, and every gazer were an ardent admirer.

The breaking of *gosha* is not only a disgrace but it serves as a sufficient excuse for divorce. The wife of a rich Mohammedan in the South lost her temper with one of her servants and caused her to be beaten with unusual severity. The woman threatened to revenge herself by bringing an action for assault. The husband heard of it and was very angry. He said to his wife:—

"You have done foolishly to put yourself in the power of this woman. If you are obliged to appear in court and break your *gosha*, I shall certainly divorce you."

Photograph by A. W. A. Platé & Co., Colombo.

ARYAN HINDU OF THE SUDRA CASTE.

accountant or clerk in a merchant's office, with his mother, sister, wife and children. Their *sarees* are of coloured cotton. Their ornaments in their ears and noses are of gold, and the necklaces are gold beads. The bangles are of glass and brass, and the anklets of silver.

It is a breach of *gosha* to be photographed so that a strange man may be able to look upon the presentment of the face that should be veiled. For this reason it is extremely difficult to obtain a picture for publication of a Mohammedan lady of good birth and position.

Moslem Marriages.

The most important event in the harem is marriage. The prophet allowed his followers four wives, a privilege that is not claimed by all Moslems. As a rule the first marriage takes place when the man is eighteen and the girl fourteen. It is frequently brought about through the good offices of an old woman, who combines the calling of matchmaking with that of pedlar and gossip. She is eagerly welcomed in the harem, professedly to sell her wares, but she finds it profitable to carry messages and suggest alliances which often result in the opening of negotiations between two families.

After the proposal and its acceptance, there are many matters to be settled before the ceremony can be performed. Seers and astrologers are consulted, and the horoscopes of the pair are cast. Enquiries have to be instituted respecting pedigree, connections, and sectarian customs. Visits are exchanged between the two families, each visit being the occasion of some ceremony. The rites are purely social, and have no religious significance. There is much feasting; dancing-girls are invited to sing and dance; and fun of all sorts, not always of a refined character, goes on. The festivities last as many days as the parents may choose. In the case of the rich it may be months. With the poor it is limited to three days or even less.

The actual contract is purely civil, and is performed by the Kazi, who is a magistrate. The marriage arranged by the bridegroom's mother is called the *Shahdi*. There are certain ceremonies in which she takes part, and as a rule they are never repeated. The *Shahdi* is the most important of all the marriages, and gives precedence to the wife who has been thus honoured. Any marriage contracted after the *Shahdi* is called *Nikah* or *Moorta*. The former is permanent as a rule, although it need not necessarily be so. A woman may be "*nikahed*" for one night only if the man chooses. He usually adopts the *Moorta* for temporary unions, especially if the woman is a slave. The facility afforded for making temporary marriages is for the purpose of preventing the birth of illegitimate children; and to give the offspring of such unions a legal claim upon the father. The *Nikah* and the *Moorta* may both be performed without any accompanying ceremonies. A declaration before proper witnesses of the man's intention, and the woman's consent—in the former case there should be the bestowal of a gift—is all that is necessary.

Story of a Blind Bride.

The bridegroom is not supposed to look upon the face of the bride until the civil contract is concluded. Sometimes the veil is not removed until he actually leads her into the nuptial chamber. A man was once assured that his bride was young and beautiful. The description given by all those who had seen her was the same, her skin was fair, her features regular, and her figure perfect. Nothing doubting, he entered the bridal chamber, and as the door closed behind him, he eagerly tore aside the veil. His bride was all that had been promised—young, beautiful, of fair complexion and perfect figure. Suddenly she put out her hands and groped before her. He started back in horror, his eyes fastened on hers. She was blind. The Oriental shrinks with an unconquerable aversion—bred of animal instinct—from anything that is maimed. The disappointed bridegroom turned from his bride and fled. Nor could he be induced by the prayers and entreaties of her people to approach her as her husband. As soon as he could, he divorced her and sent her back to her father's house.

The marriage, with all its festivities, over, the Mohammedan woman, who is not obliged to break her *gosha* to earn her living, has no other excitement to look forward to but the birth of her children. Her husband cannot be a companion in any sense of the word. Some of his time is spent in business, some in pleasures taken abroad among his own sex. The rest is divided between his wives, whom he visits in regular rotation, living with each in turn for a few days. On her marriage a wife is given two handmaids, to whom she may temporarily marry her husband, if she chooses. Should she have no children, they perhaps provide them for her. By nature and by religion polygamous, she thinks no harm of sharing her husband with other women. Yet jealousy is never far from the harem, and often the wife's whole life is embittered by it.

Life of a Mohammedan Wife.

Occasionally she is allowed to leave the house in a closely covered carriage or bullock-coach.

Dress of a Mohammedan Woman.

The Moslem lady of the South wears fine white muslin garments embroidered with gold. The little children of both sexes are dressed in drawers of cotton, silk, or satin. The drawers are also worn by the lady, but in the South they are covered with full skirts that come to the ankle. Over the skirt is worn a loose jacket reaching to the knees. When a lady goes out in the closed cart or carriage she envelops herself in a muslin cloth, the end of which is thrown over her head and forms a veil.

Like all Eastern women, Mohammedans love jewellery. Pearls are highly prized, and it is the desire of every lady of the harem to possess a rope of pearls with the ends ornamented with tassels of the same. This should be long enough for the tassels to brush the instep of her foot when the rope is thrown round her neck.

Religion and Divorce.

Although woman has no place assigned to her by the Prophet in religion, she is not necessarily irreligious. Like her husband, she repeats verses from the Koran, calling upon Allah to protect her and praising his prophet Mohammed. She has no definite hope of Heaven, and does not trouble herself about Gehenna. Her mind is totally absorbed in the present, which is never free from the terrors of divorce. The making of marriage is easy, but the unmaking is easier still. A man need give no other reason for proceeding to extremities than dislike or caprice. He separates himself from his wife for three months. At the end of that time he takes her into the four corners of the room, that is to say, to the four points of the compass, and declares before witnesses that he repudiates her. The repudiation may be registered by the Kazi, but the divorce is considered complete without it; the unfortunate woman returns in dire disgrace to her own family, where life is made a burden to her.

Hindus of the South.

The Moslem imprisons the softer sex within the harem. In the North the Hindu confines the ladies of his family to the zenana. This rigid seclusion is not practised in the South. The Hindu ladies observe a certain amount of retirement, and shrink from publicity; but they are not disgraced should the eye of man fall upon them. The wife of the late Maharajah of Mysore, and the late Princess of Tanjore did not go abroad unveiled or receive visits from gentlemen; but both ladies were willing to be present at social functions, behind a semi-transparent *purdah*. The light behind the curtain was shaded so that their forms were not distinguishable. Their vision through the curtain was unimpeded. They could see all that was transpiring in the Durbah Hall. The Princess of Tanjore was a Mahratta by birth. The Mysore Maharani was a Hindu of the Deccan.

Hindu Castes.

The Mohammedans are divided into sects, and trades or occupations. They have distinctions of birth, and are careful to preserve the pedigree; but they have no caste. The Hindus, on the other hand, are divided, subdivided, and divided again into innumerable castes. The ancient classification gave four groups, the Brahmin or priestly caste, the Kshattriya or soldier caste, the Vaisya or merchant caste, and the Sudra or serving caste. Outside these came the Pariahs or outcasts, many of whom were slaves. In the present day there are in Southern India Brahmins, Sudras, and Pariahs.

The Brahmins.

Some of the Brahmins of the South are Hindus of Aryan extraction; some are Dravidians. The "twice-born" of the North look down upon their fellow caste-men of the Madras Presidency on account of the Dravidian blood, and are inclined to deny them their rights. The Brahminism is of too ancient date to be disproved, however, and the claim to be numbered with the "twice-born" is reluctantly conceded. The caste is divided into several sects, which are distinguished by a difference in the caste marks and by religious rites and opinions that vary. Though they all claim to be Brahmins they do not intermarry or mix socially. It must not be supposed that the term "priestly caste" implies that every man born within the circle arrogates to himself the sacerdotal office. The "twice-born" are to be found in Government offices, in the service of merchants, in military employment, and in the pursuit of other honourable occupations. There are villages in the South composed entirely of Brahmins. The settlements are called *Agrahara,* which means "grant of land." Some Brahmins are rich and well educated. Their refinement and intelligence command respect and consideration from all foreigners. On the other hand, some are beggars who have no education, and whose mode of living is more in keeping with a savage race than with the descendants of an ancient civilisation.

The Sudras.

In the absence of the Kshattriya and the Vaisya, the higher divisions of the Sudra caste rank next to the Brahmin. Under this group come more than half the inhabitants of South India. Its subdivisions are literally innumerable, and they have never been tabulated in the rank of precedence. There is often great pride shown by the different members of the castes, who claim a higher place in the scale for their caste than they can establish historically. The Sudras and even the Pariahs model their rules and many of their domestic ceremonies upon the practices of the Brahmins, and they accept the sacred Vedas as their Bible.

Hindu Women have no place in Religious Ceremonies.

It has been said that "Hinduism is caste and caste is Hinduism." The whole life of the Hindu is steeped in religion from the time he is conceived to the hour of his burning or burial. He is compelled to be the subject of innumerable ceremonies, some of which would be considered degrading and possibly disgusting by the refined Englishman. The most rigid supporters of these ceremonies are the women of the family. Woman is held by the Hindu to be in complete subjection to the man. Though of Brahmin birth and the mother of Brahmin sons, it is never allowed that she can be twice-born. She cannot participate in any of her husband's religious exercises, his prayers or his sacrifices. She may urge their performance and incite him to make the pilgrimages. When the great festivals occur at the temples, she may accompany her husband and sons, arrange and carry the offerings, cook the food in the rest-house, and generally superintend the expedition. But if she wants to prefer a request and make an offering on her own account, she usually does it by stealth at night.

The excitement of attending the temple festivals forms a pleasant break in the monotony of her life. The gathering is attended by some of the features of a fair, with stalls of merchandise and shows. The idol is carried through the streets in gaudy procession, with the beating of drums and blowing of horns. It is a grand sight in the eyes of the women and children, and compensates for their exclusion from participation in the other rites.

In the privacy of her own house woman has an important part to play. It is she alone who can perform the domestic

Photograph by A. W. A. Platé & Co., Colombo.

ARYAN HINDU OF THE SUDRA CASTE (ONE OF THE HIGHER DIVISIONS).

Her *saree* and jacket are of fine cotton. She wears three necklaces of gold, and her bangles and the bosses in her hair are also gold. Her jewels are probably worth at least a hundred pounds.

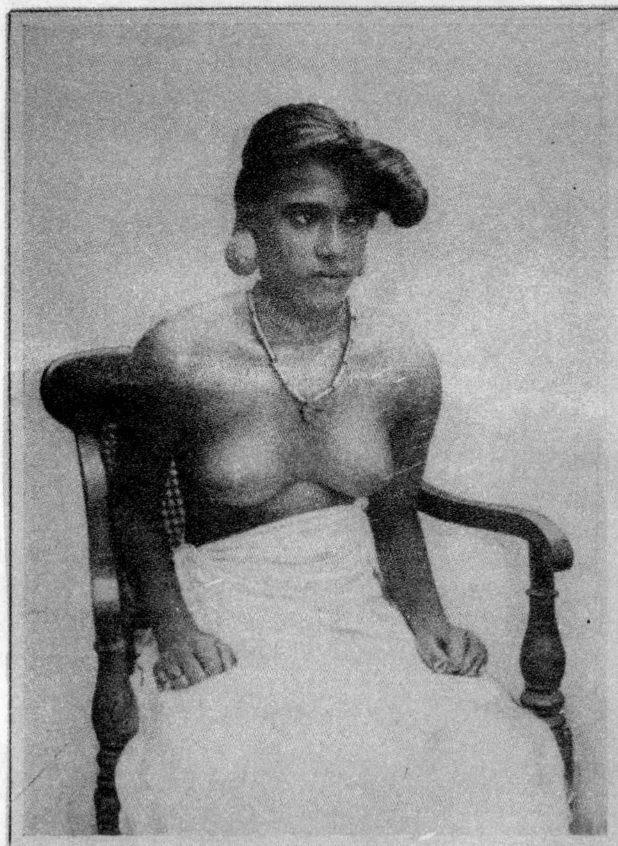

Photograph by Nicholas & Co., Madras.

DRAVIDIAN HINDU: A NAIR LADY.

Her *saree* is of fine white muslin bordered with gold. By custom she is compelled to uncover to the waist when in a public place.

ceremonies connected with the cooking vessels. It is she who says the daily prayer, and hymn, to the deity. In all domestic ritual she is to the fore, and the men have to take subordinate positions. So well is her supremacy in the home acknowledged, that it has been made the subject of a proverb, which says that "a man is a lion abroad, but a jackal in his own house."

Domestic Position of Hindu Women.

In the morning she is the first to rise. Before the sun is up she is busy at her ablutions. The last act in the making of her toilet is to imprint the little round red mark upon her forehead, or to trace the particular lines that indicate the god she worships. It will be seen in several of the photographs; it is always a sign that the Hindu woman is "dressed." The Namburi lady of the West Coast (p. 607) makes the horizontal lines. Some castes draw a perpendicular line from the hair to the top of the nose, level with the eyebrows.

Having finished her toilet, the Hindu wife cleans and sweeps out that part of the house where the sweeper who is of low caste may not enter. She rinses out the drinking vessels and cooking-pots, and begins her preparations for cooking the midday meal for the family. It is the first big meal of the day; the coffee and rice cakes, taken in the early morning, are not regarded as a meal.

Whilst she busies herself at her household duties, she chants a hymn in a low tone, addressed to Krishna or Siva. On no account may she *sing* it, as it is not considered respectable for women to sing. The following are three verses from a hymn translated from the Telugu in constant use among housewives:—

Not "Respectable" to Sing.

"Awake! Awake! Krishna divine,
Awake to save thine own.
Thou lord of all! Thou perfect one!
Grant us thy heavenly boon. Awake! Awake!

"Awake! Awake! Both old and young
Their sorrows to remove
Have sought thy presence now.
Oh grant them every good. Awake! Awake!

"Awake! Awake! I wait to bring
Sweet jasmine flowers to wave,
Thyself rouse quickly, Mahdava!
Shrihari! Come and save! Awake! Awake!"

When the curry and rice are ready, she serves her husband with his dinner before she eats herself; and she also makes her daily *pujah* to the household image of brass or copper before satisfying her hunger. The image is kept in a box or upon a niche in the wall, and is taken

Hindu Prayers and Offerings.

out each time for the ritual. A little oil lamp is lighted, and she repeats some simple prayers with clasped hands and bowings of the head. Offerings of fruit, sweetmeat, or betel are presented, and the image is sprinkled with sandal paste and coloured rice. A bit of camphor is ignited and waved before it. The ceremony is of short duration. At its conclusion she walks three times round the image and prostrates herself. As she begins her *pujah*, she rings a bell or strikes a gong to assemble the rest of the women and children of the family.

At night, when the household lamp is lighted, the housewife does *pujah* to the flame with the repetition of a verse which is translated as follows :—

> "The flame of this lamp is the supreme God.
> The flame of this lamp is the abode of the Supreme.
> By this flame sin is destroyed.
> Oh! thou light of the evening! We praise thee."

She repeats the name of her god before beginning to eat her dinner. It is her form of grace before meat.

Every mother is careful to teach her children how to put their hands together in prayer, and how to make the proper prostration, in which the ground is touched by the two feet, the two knees, the two hands, the forehead and the breast. From her they learn by frequent repetitions the stories of the Hindu deities, told in the sacred books. Many women worship the tulsi plant (*Ocymum sanctum*), a small aromatic weed sacred to Vishnu. It belongs to the basil tribe. In most of the domestic ceremonies it is employed, and it may usually be found growing in the courtyard of the Brahmin's house, ready for any emergency. The snake is also worshipped by women; they perform *pujah* to an image of a snake or to a real cobra living in some hole near the house.

Hindu Marriages.

Marriage with the Hindu woman comes early in her life. The higher the caste the younger the bride. The Pariahs and some of the lower castes are content to allow their daughters to wait until they are fully grown. The higher castes believe that their re-birth in a future life is imperilled by neglecting to marry their children before they attain maturity. The law has been brought to bear upon this subject, and of late years there have been fewer child-marriages. The betrothal ceremonies are still performed at a very early period, and create virgin widows as in former days; but there is a fixed age

Photograph by A. W. A. Platé & Co., Colombo.

ARYAN HINDU OF HIGH CASTE.

She wears a silk gold-embroidered *saree* and a satin jacket. All her ornaments are of gold. Her nose-rings are rubies and emeralds set in gold with pearl drop.

for consummation for Mohammedan and Hindu alike.

The marriage rites vary in detail with the different castes. The dowering of the bride and the tying on of the *Thali* are common to all. The dower is generally in the form of jewels and clothes, unless the parents' property consists of cattle or sheep or pigs. Then it is given in the form of animals.

BRIDE AND BRIDEGROOM OF ONE OF THE LOWER DIVISIONS OF THE SUDRA CASTE.
The wreaths are of jasmine blossom to which the *Thali* has been attached.

The Hindu Equivalent to the Wedding Ring.

The marriage badge is called the *Thali*. It corresponds with the wedding-ring of the European. If possible, it is made of gold, even if the people are very poor. It is in the form of a circular or oval pendant, on which figures are engraved or worked in relief. In Christian marriages among converts the use of the *Thali* has been retained. The heathen symbols, which are sometimes actually indecent, are replaced by others suitable to Christianity. At the ceremony it is attached to a wreath of flowers, and the bridegroom throws the garland about the neck of his bride, saying: "With this *Thali* I thee wed." In the heathen ceremony the bridegroom's sister or some other relative fastens the *Thali* about the bride's neck.

After the ceremony it is removed from the wreath and suspended upon a cord or necklace made of gold or glass beads, according to the means of the bridegroom. It is worn constantly, and is the very last ornament with which a Hindu woman will part, no matter what her caste may be.

During the great famine of 1877 a Brahmin woman who had lost her husband was reduced to poverty. She was left with three children, and her property was sold to provide food for the household. First the bullocks and cows went, then her personal ornaments were sold. Finally there was only the *Thali* left. This she disposed of, and with the proceeds she bought some poison. She mixed the poison with the food, which she prepared for what she believed was their last meal, for she had no money left to purchase any more. After partaking of their supper they were all ill and the baby died. She and the two elder children recovered, and she was brought before the magistrate. The tale of her distress was learned, and the woman was relieved in the famine camp. She showed no gratitude, for she would have preferred death by the poison to the breaking of her caste rules through accepting the food prepared in the camp kitchen.

Hindu Polygamy.

The Hindu, with whom polygamy is instinctive as it is with the Mohammedan, is allowed to have more than one wife. He has not the same dislike to illegitimacy for his children as the Moslem, and does not marry so frequently. If his first wife prove childless, he probably marries a second at the suggestion of his mother, or perhaps of the wife herself. His happiness in a future life is in jeopardy if he leaves no son to perform his funeral rites. Fidelity to one woman on the part of the husband is neither expected nor demanded. Under cover of religion certain unions are made without a shadow of dishonour. Union with a dancing girl, for instance, either at the temple during the festivals, or in the zenana, during her visit to the family, is an honour in the eyes of the Hindu who is not influenced by European thought. Monogamy and the spirit of monogamy is foreign to his nature. An Englishwoman would be roused to wrath at the thought of sharing her husband with another woman. The Oriental, whether Hindu or Mohammedan, on the contrary, accepts the position placidly.

A princess in the South was to be married to a man of royal lineage of the North. He came down with his retinue, bringing his first wife and her two children to witness the ceremony. The latter was asked if she was pleased with the marriage her husband was making. She replied unhesitatingly in the affirmative, saying that the bride, who was but fourteen, was like a sister to her. As long as the young wife remains subservient to the elder woman, and makes no attempt to obtain any undue influence over her husband, peace probably reigns in the zenana

Photograph by Nicholas & Co., Madras.

DRAVIDIAN HINDUS: NAIR SERVANTS.

and there is no jealousy. If, on the other hand, the young wife grows arrogant and proud owing to the birth of a son that is denied to the elder wife, there will be hatred and jealousy, and perhaps crime.

There is a story told of a wife who shared her husband with a slave. The slave bore him a son. In the pride and joy of motherhood she exulted over the wife. Indignant at the impertinence of one of such low birth, her mistress fettered the woman with heavy chains to her bedstead, and compelled her to stand for hours, an object of derision to the whole zenana.

Although the affections of the man may

wander, and nothing is thought of his infidelity, the desire of the woman must ever be towards her lawful spouse. With his neglect and the bad example he sets she sometimes proves frail. If discovered, her fate is terrible. The inviolate privacy of the harem and the zenana covers not only many cruel wrongs, but also hides tragedies that never see the light.

A DRAVIDIAN PARIAH GIRL PREPARED TO RECEIVE GUESTS.

Pariah Liberty.

The women of the lower castes and of the Pariahs have more liberty than those belonging to the higher castes, especially where there is poverty. They work hard and lead a simple, primitive life. The man cannot afford to keep more than one wife; and the pair spend their days in labour, he in the fields or at his trade, and she at her cooking and housework, perhaps assisting her husband in his occupation at busy times. The woman plucking tea on the hills comes from one of the villages in the plains. It is possible that the season has been bad, and that she and her husband are glad to find employment for a while on a tea estate. She wears no jacket under her *saree*, which is of strong, coarse, unbleached material. Her *Thali* is suspended from the necklace of gold beads. What wealth her husband has accumulated is invested in the jewellery which adorns her person. When a little money has been saved, a gold bead is added to the string, or a silver bangle to the wrist. The necklace of small glass beads is assumed simply from vanity; she knows by instinct that their colour, blue or red, is becoming to her complexion, which is almost black. The beads are like the gay ribbons that ornament the hat of an English maid. The only break in the life of the tea-plucker is a marriage or a death, which both bring feasts in their train lasting two or three days; or the periodical *pujah* at the village temple, where some demon spirit is propitiated with a sacrifice of blood. The women look on with unconcern for the sufferings of the creature—a buffalo, goat, or cock—as it falls before the decapitating stroke of the sword and its gory head is presented to the image.

Nautch-girls.

To every Hindu temple of importance is attached a certain number of women and girls called *Dasis*. *Dasi* means servant. They are better known, perhaps, under the name of Nautch-girls, as it is from their ranks that the dancing girls are drawn. The calling of the *Dasi* is generally acknowledged to be one of infamy in the eyes of Europeans, although no disgrace whatever is attached to it in the eyes of the Hindus.

Some of the more advanced of the Hindu gentlemen in the South of India are showing signs of disapproval of the exhibition of Nautch-girls at social entertainments, and would relegate them to their duties of ministering daily in the ritual of the temple.

From early childhood the *Dasi* is brought up at the temple, where she is to serve, even though her parents may be living in the neighbourhood. She is taught to read and write, to sing and to dance. As a child she is married to a tree or to the image of the god; hence the *Dasis* are sometimes spoken of as the wives of the deity. At an age when she should be entering her husband's house as a happy young wife, she becomes the mistress of a man who is rich enough to entertain her in his zenana, and present an offering of some value to the temple to which she belongs. After a few months she returns to the temple to minister to the pleasure of the worshippers. Her earnings go to its revenues in return for the education and support she has received. There is no shame attached to her calling, and her office is sanctioned by her religion.

A *Dasi* takes part in the daily *pujah* of the temple. She has to sing and dance before the idol, whilst it is being washed, anointed and garlanded. Her songs are often coarse and obscene, considered in the light of European opinion, though she sees neither coarseness nor obscenity in them; and her poses in dancing are calculated to rouse the worst passions in the Oriental, who does not fail to comprehend their meaning. She is bidden to every wedding and entertained at the houses of the rich. She is at the service of every worshipper at the temple who can afford the necessary gifts. Men and women still continue to give their daughters, often the eldest of the family, to be enrolled in the band of *Dasis* at the temple which they frequent. The three girls in the group on p. 620 are adorned ready for their dance at some festivity, social or religious. They wear the richest of silk drapery and jewels of great value, all of which belong to the temple, and are kept by the authorities for the use of the *Dasis*. Occasionally a *Dasi* has jewels of her own, the personal gifts of men whom she has captivated; but *Dasis* are not encouraged to become women of property and founders of families. If they should have children, the girls become

ARYAN HINDU: NAUTCH-GIRL.
Her jewellery is of gold, set with valuable gems.

Nautch-girls, and the boys servers in some capacity or other in the temple. The administration of the large revenues of the temples finds occupation for many people who have nothing to do with the ritual.

Although a Hindu wife sees no shame in the profession of the *Dasi*, and will even go so far as to give her own daughter to be trained as one, there must be an instinctive knowledge that the life is dishonourable. It is shown in her care not to imitate the manner and bearing of the Nautch-girl.

She is careful never to sing or to dance. To do so would be a sign of immodesty which would scandalise the neighbours and disgrace her family. It took some time to persuade the wives and daughters of India that education was not equally immodest and unbecoming, for the simple reason that *Dasis* were the only women who received instruction in reading and writing. Gradually the more enlightened Hindus have been brought to see no reason why education should be the special prerogative of the Nautch-girl.

ARYAN HINDUS: NAUTCH GIRLS
Dressed for a festival.

The Todas.

The aboriginal tribes of South India form but a fraction of the population. The most interesting are the Todas of the Nilgiri Mountains. Theirs is a kind of nature-worship wherein a shrine or image is not necessary. A sacrifice is offered to the ruling spirits, who are supposed to govern the elements. The object of the *pujah* is the same as that which animates the Dravidian in his demonolatry, namely propitiation and the desire to turn aside the evil that may be wrought by a stronger power than themselves. The Todas sacrifice a buffalo by clubbing it to death in a cruel manner. The Khonds, an aboriginal tribe upon the hills of Ganjam, believe that the earth will not yield her fruits unless their local deities are satiated with blood. In former days they sacrificed a human being, whom they had stolen as a child from a village in the plains. He was fed and nourished upon the best that they could offer him, and when he reached man's estate they fastened him to a stake and killed him. His body was cut up into innumerable little pieces, which the worshippers took away and buried in their fields. The English Government put down the *Meriah* sacrifice, as it was called, and the people have to content themselves with killing pigs and goats.

The Todas have no record of the kind against them. They have been content with a buffalo as their offering. They are a peaceable tribe, who live in huts and subsist by means of their cattle. They lead an idle life, but no one can accuse them of luxury. They allow the Budagas, a caste of Canarese Hindus, to cultivate the land, and they receive rent in kind from the industrious agriculturists, in consideration of the privilege of tilling the ground unmolested.

The Toda woman wears her hair in long ringlets. Her ornaments are of silver, and her necklaces are strings of bright-coloured beads. She has a weakness for turquoises, real or imitation, threaded as beads. Her dress is of coarse cotton material, and she often wraps herself in a rough woollen blanket, which throws off the tropical downpour and protects her from the chilly blasts that blow across the mountains.

Polyandry in South India.

A marked and peculiar feature of the hill-tribes on the Nilgiris is the practice among them of polyandry. The women are permitted to choose and to have more than one husband. Polyandry also exists on the West Coast among the people of Cochin and Travancore. The castes who practise it are the Nairs, the Tyars, and the Namburis. It has been suggested that the custom belonged to the aborigines; and that it arose from the necessity of sending a certain number of the tribesmen out with the herds. It was impossible to leave the women unprotected. They were therefore married to two or three men, who took it in turn to attend the herds, and to stay at home. With such an arrangement there naturally arose a difficulty over the succession to property. It was solved by making the inheritance descend through the female line. The bridegroom, instead of bringing his wife into his ancestral home, enters her family, and takes some buffaloes with him.

Legendary Origin of Polyandry.

The people of the West Coast who practise polyandry are more civilised than the hill-tribes. It is difficult to account for the custom with them, as there was no apparent reason for the men to absent themselves as there was with the Todas. They have a legend which says that the origin of the female succession was founded upon the noble conduct of a patriotic woman who was thus rewarded. The story is as follows :

A certain king learned that his kingdom was threatened by a great catastrophe, which was to overwhelm the ruler as well as the ruled. He sent his prime minister to the temple of Kali to inquire of the goddess if it was true, and if there was no way of averting the evil. The goddess replied that the prophecy was correct—a great calamity overshadowed the land. There was only one means of escape, and that was by offering a sacrifice to herself. A mother must be found who would kill her own son in the temple with her own hand. The minister returned to his house and begged his wife to make the necessary sacrifice, to slay one human being so that thousands might be saved. She indignantly refused, saying that she had but one son, and could not spare him. He then went to his sister and represented the matter to her, praying her to make the sacrifice for the sake of her fellow-creatures. She consented without a moment's hesitation. Taking her child from his bed she carried him then and there to the temple and slew him. Kali instantly restored the boy to life, declaring that the impending evil was averted by her action, and that the king and his country were saved. When the monarch heard the story of her devotion, and how she was ready to lose her son so that many lives might be saved, he decreed that as a reward the succession to property for the future should descend through the female line.

Although polyandry is permitted it does not follow that it is largely practised, nor is the woman depraved by the liberty given to her. As a rule she is satisfied to have but one husband, and it is only when he leaves her that she marries again. Many of the Nairs and Tyars are very fair of skin. It is supposed that this fairness was derived from European blood. The liberty of choice was exercised in the old days in favour of the Dutch, Portuguese, and Englishmen, who settled on the West Coast, and the result has been beneficial to the race.

Curious Custom as to Dress.

There is a strange custom still preserved amongst the women. Its origin, like that of polyandry, is shrouded in mystery. The supposition is that it was imposed upon their Dravidian ancestors by the conquerors. Women are not allowed to clothe themselves in public above the waist. It would seem that the order should be reversed, but it is not so. Within her house the woman of the West Coast may envelop her figure up to her neck. When she is abroad the *saree* must be dropped to the waist, as is represented in the photographs. If by chance she is covered, and sees a stranger of the same or higher caste approaching, she is obliged by long-established rule to remove the drapery until he has passed. To Europeans just arrived in the country the action is highly embarrassing. Some Nair ladies of education and refinement have lately made a protest against it as being contrary to all laws of civilisation. They went to a certain temple with their husbands and sons to worship, wearing jackets. The Adigari, or chief official of the temple, objected to their presence clothed in that manner. A complaint was laid before the Rajah, who issued an order that all women coming to the temple should remove their jackets before entering. An appeal against the order was made by the gentlemen belonging to the families of the offenders. The Rajah, however, declined to oppose the expressed wish of the Adigari.

Photograph by A. T. W. Penn, Ootacamund.

TODAS OF THE NILGIRI MOUNTAINS.

The most important Hill-tribe of the South.

Nomadic Tribes.

In addition to the Mohammedans, Hindus, and hill-tribes, there are a few nomadic people who wander through different districts, not confining themselves to one Presidency. The tribe most frequently seen is the Lumbadee or Brinjara. They are of Gipsy origin. Where they came from is not precisely known. They were the carriers of grain in the old days. The Duke of Wellington, as Colonel Wellesley, made use of them in the wars with the Mysoreans and Mahrattas to transport food and ammunition. They never failed him, and were faithful to their trust. They are, however, inveterate thieves where their word is not given, and the women are ugly and uncivilised.

The Hindu Ideal of Woman.

The Hindu ideal of beauty differs from the English ideal. A beautiful woman, according to one of their classical writers, should be plump to stoutness. Her eyes should be black upon milk-white; her eyebrows arched and meeting over the nose. Her fingers should be long and slender, the lips full and curved, the chin small and the cheeks rounded. "Her forehead, adorned by beautiful curls, resembles a piece of the moon," says the quaint old poet of the eleventh century.

Although beauty is the first consideration, mental qualities are not without their value. The Hindu makes four divisions of women. The first contains the most excellent, who combine physical beauty with intellect. The second embraces the talented. The third is composed of those who have no beauty nor talent but are worthy. The fourth includes the clumsy, the stupid, the ill-tempered, those in short who have nothing to recommend them.

Woman's greatest quality is devotion and obedience to her husband. Without a husband life should be a blank and not worth living. There are innumerable tales told of the devotion of good wives, the best known being the story of Sita, the wedded Elaine of Hindu legend. It was this devotion which is said to be the foundation of *sutti*, the burning of the widow upon her husband's funeral pile, a custom put down by the English Government. Life without her husband was thought to be intolerable to every right-minded widow. Her existence in the house of her brother-in-law was devoid of pleasure and honour, but it was not so miserable that a painful death by burning was preferable. Devotion to her husband—not escape from misery—prompted the deed. The evidence that exists tends to show that latterly *sutti* was not always a voluntary sacrifice made in cold blood, but it was done under great hysterical excitement probably induced by the administration of drugs.

The "Touches of Nature" that Make the World of Women Akin.

Oriental women have many traits of character that are common to their sex over the whole world from highest to lowest, from richest to poorest, from the most ignorant to the latest product of education. They all love dress, and are influenced by a natural desire to attract. They delight in flowers, a love which they share with their Western sisters. They do not cut the blooms for the decoration of the house as is the custom with the European, nor grow them for the beautification of the garden. But the blossoms are nipped off without stalks, and are strung into garlands upon threads of cotton or fibre. Bunches of jasmine flowers pulled from the calyx and rolled into a ball are thrust into the strands of the chignon. The bride and bridegroom, shewn on p. 616, are loaded with wreaths, and the bride in addition has a headdress made of white blossom. Nautch-girls wear something of the same kind. The Mohammedan bridegroom tosses flowers to his unseen bride behind the curtain. The Hindu husband, who may not speak to his young wife except with the permission of his mother, throws a wreath into her lap on his return from his daily occupation. This little attention sends a warm thrill through her heart, but she must not give a sign that it has influenced her. Flowers form the gift when ordinary social visits are paid—it is impolite to come into a house with empty hands. Flowers delight the living and flowers cover the dead as they are carried out to their last resting-place.

Photograph by A. T. W. Penn, Ootacamund.

TODA WOMAN OF THE NILGIRI MOUNTAINS.

All Indian women love jewellery. If they cannot afford to buy gold, silver, copper or brass, they content themselves with glass in the form of beads and bangles. When their husbands are absent they lay aside their ornaments and put on an old *saree;* they use no flowers for their hair, and refrain from cosmetics, especially from

Photograph by Nicholas & Co., Madras.

DRAVIDIAN GIRL OF THE CHERIMI DIVISION OF THE WEST COAST.

the yellow saffron, which is supposed to heighten the tone of their complexion—just as pearl powder is supposed to improve the complexion of the European—and to render their charms irresistible. Their personal adornment has but one object, the attraction of the opposite sex. If dress and jewellery fail they have recourse to the wise woman, who supplies them with love-philtres, which they administer to their unconscious husbands in the hope of finding favour in their eyes.

The women of India have a weakness which they share with their sex throughout the universe. They are great chatterboxes. The men have acquired a habit of uttering grunts at intervals whilst the women take fresh breath and continue their harangues. At the end of much talk perhaps the only reply will be the ejaculation of the single exclamation, "Pah," uttered in a contemptuous tone. It does not silence her, and she begins *da capo*.

A Hindu Non-Talking Match: Man *v.* Wife.

There is a story told which has its parallel in an old English song. A Brahmin chatting with his wife one evening declared that all women were talkers. She replied that they were no worse than some men.

"Let us see which of us two will speak first. A betel-leaf shall be the reward for the winner," was his reply.

They slept, and when they awoke the next morning, remembering the wager, they both preserved a strict silence. In vain their friends and relatives questioned and entreated. Not a syllable escaped the lips of either. Alarm filled the hearts of all, and it was feared that some enemy had cast a spell of dumbness upon them. A magician was sent for. He pronounced it to be a bad case of demoniacal possession. To cast out such a wicked and powerful devil would be extremely difficult and cost much money. The relatives, sooner than have two members of the family so grievously afflicted, agreed to pay the sum. Whilst the magician was making preparations for his exorcism, a friend quietly heated a bar of iron. When it was red hot he applied it to the sole of the husband's foot. He winced but did not utter a sound. The iron was then applied to the foot of the wife, who at once screamed out :—

"Appah! appah!" ("Enough! enough!")

"You have lost the wager. Give me the betel-leaf," cried the husband triumphantly. "Did I not say truly that women were incorrigible chatterboxes?"

DRAVIDIAN HINDUS: OFFSPRING OF THE LOWER DIVISIONS OF THE SUDRA CASTE.

Three styles of dress for girls are here shown. The second child from the left, seated on the floor, has a short jacket and skirt: the older girls have long jackets and skirts, and those who are no longer children wear the short jacket, skirt, and *saree*.

CEYLON

By E. A. CRAWFORD

Where Men Wear Combs and Petticoats—Women Not Secluded—Races—Veddahs—Tamils—Moors —Burghers—Sinhalese—Marriage Customs—Weddings—Coco-nut Palm—Cookery—Children—Toilet—Dress—Sinhalese Grace—Jewellery—The Betel Habit—Education—Lace and Basket Industries

Where Men Wear Combs and Petticoats.

MOST travellers east of Suez in these globe-trotting days touch some time or other at Colombo, and are more or less familiar with the brown faces, regular features, and deftly coiled long hair of the crowds thronging its quays and streets. Perhaps many also have shared the mistake of the English lady who wondered why so many more women than men walked abroad in this Oriental city. She soon discovered that the round tortoiseshell comb, to us reminiscent of little girls of mid-Victorian period, is reserved exclusively for male persons, and that the adornment of long hair and petticoats is shared by men with the gentler sex. So of the seeming feminine crowd, maybe, all are males.

Women Not Secluded.

Not that the Sinhalese women are secluded in the manner of many Orientals. There is, in fact, no *purdah*, or veiling, in Ceylon except among the Mohammedan Moor men and the very few Malays, who are likewise Mohammedan in religion. Thus the women and girls of the lower classes may be seen singly or in groups, passing amid the busy hum of the streets, going to market, to and from coir and plumbago mills, selling fruit and vegetables, or plying their household occupations in the open verandahs of their houses. Those who can afford it drive out in carriages to go shopping, or to give their children an airing, the commonest vehicle for this purpose being the bullock-hackery, a light two-wheeled cart protected by an awning from the sun's rays.

In spite, however, of this comparative freedom, a well brought-up Sinhalese girl does not appear much in public between twelve and twenty—by the latter age she is usually married—and then only accompanied by a duenna. After she is married she has her home interests, and very many ladies seldom venture outside their own "compounds," not because they are kept there by force, but because they find no particular attraction in going out.

Races.

The mixture of races in the population of Ceylon is a matter of general knowledge. There is a sharp dividing line in type, dress, customs, and religion between Sinhalese and Tamils, Moors and Burghers (Eurasians of Dutch descent), and their daily contact does not really merge them. These are the principal races inhabiting Ceylon, but there is also a sprinkling of others as dissimilar, Malays, Afghans, and Parsees. There are, however, so few women among these that they need scarcely be taken into account as inhabitants of Lanka, though the little band of Parsee ladies is conspicuous for intelligence and superior education, not to speak of graceful appearance.

Mention must be made of the Veddahs, aborigines of Ceylon, who, isolated in the forests of the interior, have remained for ages untouched by civilisation and the rise and fall of empires. This diminutive people, peaceable among themselves and also towards strangers, subsist on wild fruits and honey and the spoil of their bows and arrows. Nomadic in their habits, they dwell now in caves, now in trees or rude huts of leaves. They speak a dialect of their own, not understood of their Sinhalese or Tamil neighbours, and they are held in extraordinary veneration by the former. Their dress consists of aprons of leaves thickly strung together; they are strictly monogamous, and their women are remarkable for conjugal fidelity and devotion to their children. The Veddahs are rapidly dying out, and their identity will soon be lost among the neighbouring Sinhalese and Tamils, as from time to time they become domesticated and settle in villages.

Veddahs.

The Sinhalese population greatly preponderates, except in the north and east of Ceylon, conquered and colonised centuries ago by Tamils of Southern India.

Tamils.

The immigrant Tamils, especially on the up-country tea estates and south and west of Ceylon, are of the coolie caste, so that few Tamil ladies are usually met with. There are, however, some who in good looks, charm of manner, and education, need not fear comparison with their European sisters. Their dress is rich and effective, and they are loaded with costly ornaments in their ears, round the neck, in their hair, and across the forehead, and also round their arms, wrists, and slim ankles. The toes, too, are decorated with rings, and the wing of the nostril is pierced to receive a jewel.

Amongst the population of immigrant Tamils who cultivate tea and other products in the hill-country of Ceylon, large numbers of women and children of the coolie caste are employed chiefly to pluck the leaf and care for the bushes. One sees them dotted over the steep hillsides during the sunny hours, each with a large but light basket strapped to the back. The mothers arrive on the field with their babes across their hips, and, leaving them to slumber or kick about, innocent of garments, under the shade of a tea bush near, proceed to fill their baskets with the glossy leaves.

Photograph by Skeen & Co., Colombo.

A TAMIL LADY.

The Tamil mother brings her elder children to help in the plucking, and all day the family is out of doors, happy in the fragrant sunshine. It is an existence that may well be envied by struggling workers in murky cities. Perfect air, congenial labour, and freedom from care, on five shillings a week for a paterfamilias!

Ceylon is a kind of El Dorado to the dense population of the southern part of the Madras Presidency, whence the coolies (or labourers) arrive in crowds, often miserably emaciated. They soon fatten in prosperous Ceylon, and invariably return to their "coast," as they call the continent of India, in better circumstances, and not seldom purchase the coveted bit of land which is the summit of their ambition.

The women of that mysterious Mohammedan race called the Moors of Ceylon are, like their co-religionists all over the East, kept in strict seclusion. The *purdah* falls for the little girl when she is eight or ten years of age, her chances of education are at an end, and she practically goes no more out-of-doors, except, maybe, in a closely shuttered carriage. Thenceforward her life is quite uneventful till her marriage day, when, amid endless ceremonial and prolonged feasting on the part of the male members of the household, the girl-bride, tottering under the weight of all the family jewels, is borne, half insensible with drugs, to her husband's house. There she spends her days in much the same monotony as before, unless she has children to occupy time and thoughts. If the mother of a son, she will have attained the pinnacle of consequence in her small world, but only for the few brief years of infancy can she fondle and direct him. She can enter scarcely at all into his life as a youth, and he is afterwards beyond the sphere of her influence.

Moors.

When, in course of time, he, too, brings home his bride, the mother then enters upon her kingdom, and takes care that her daughter-in-law's character should not be spoiled by injudicious petting.

The long days in the harem are sadly lacking in rational occupation, even the feminine solace of needlework and embroidery being absent as a rule.

Photograph by Skeen & Co., Colombo.

TAMIL COOLIE WOMAN ON A TEA ESTATE.

Moor women have a considerable share of good looks for the most part, but the Moslem admiration for plumpness induces unwieldiness of figure when they are scarcely out of their first youth. As young children they are decidedly attractive, being comely in limb and feature.

Moor men are an industrious and law-abiding community; the appearance of their women in the law courts is almost unheard of. Such a case did, however, occur several years ago in the Southern Province of Ceylon, when a Moor woman stood her trial for murder, but the victim was a Sinhalese woman, and the motive undoubtedly jealousy.

Burghers.

The "Burghers" of Ceylon are mainly descendants of Dutch and Portuguese settlers who, during the time of their respective occupation of the island, mingled freely with the native population. With them are often reckoned all those who have an admixture of European blood, in whatever proportion. But the Burghers proper are proud of the name, and, indeed, they are in most respects superior to the Eurasians of India. They are intelligent and enterprising, and while their men have been specially distinguished for long past in the departments of law and medicine, and are the backbone of the clerical service, their women are not behindhand in cultivation, and may boast of attainment both in arts and letters. Many of them are admirable as school teachers, quick and sympathetic as well as industrious, and others devote themselves to music or painting with great measure of success. The Dutch language has ceased to be spoken among the Burghers for more than a generation, although the Dutch were the immediate predecessors of the British.

Photograph by Skeen & Co., Colombo.

SINHALESE FRUIT-SELLER OF COLOMBO.

Portuguese, on the other hand, in a debased form, still survives among the lowest class of mechanics of mixed race; while the family names of the purest-blooded Sinhalese in the Low Country are many of them familiar Portuguese cognomens, such as Pereira, Dias, Fonseka, and De Silva. So deeply did the Portuguese impress their language on Ceylon, as well as, in large measure, their religion and customs—at least in the case of the lower castes.

Sinhalese.

The Sinhalese, or "Lion" race, are an interesting people; proud, capable, and artistic, but with a full measure of Oriental indolence, accentuated by the passiveness accompanying, though not inculcated by, Buddhism.

The Sinhalese are now practically monogamous, so that the status of women is good—in fact, best among Oriental nations, excepting the Burmese. Polyandry used to prevail, mostly in the form of one wife between two brothers. It is still practised to a small extent in the Kandyan districts, though gradually dying out under Government discountenance.

Marriage Customs.

Family affection is strong among the Sinhalese, favoured by the dignified position of women under the marriage laws.

Marriage is of two kinds:—(1) *Diga*, (2) *Bina*.

In a *diga* marriage the husband takes the wife to live with him. In a *bina* marriage the husband goes to live in the wife's house, and is dependent on her or her relations. His case is not without its anxieties, however, as the wife may turn him out of doors at her good will and pleasure.

A *bina* marriage, where the woman is of superior position to her husband, gives her the right to hold and dispose of her own property in absolute freedom. This was so centuries before the "Married Women's Property Act" was passed in England, to the relief of oppressed wives! Such responsibility, as in the case of Burmese women pre-eminently, has developed quite marked business capacity in more than one *Kumari-Hamy*, or Kandyan lady of title.

The Sinhalese girl is not married very young, but she changes her state as a rule before she has left her teens. Child-marriage is happily not practised.

Weddings.

Sinhalese nuptials are shorn of a good deal of the elaborate ceremonial which formerly prevailed, when every detail was referred to an auspicious day or hour, and go-betweens and astrologers played an important part that is now filled by the prosaic registrar. Still, the rite of tying together the thumbs of the bride and bridegroom's right hands with a silken thread and pouring water thereon while verses from the sacred books are chanted, is still performed in Buddhist households.

The Buddhist priest, as a celibate monk, takes no part in the wedding ritual.

The wedding takes place amid much rejoicing. The house, even among the poorest, is hung with white cloths lent for the occasion by the local *dhoby*, and tom-tom beaters fill the air with their thumping. A characteristic feature is the adornment, within and without the house, consisting of arches of *ola* or fresh young coco-nut leaves. This form of artistic decoration, in which the Sinhalese excel, they delight to display lavishly on every festive occasion.

Coco-nut Palm.

The coco-nut palm is indeed a pillar of the state in Ceylon; its products being put to every imaginable use, it is indispensable in the daily life of the people. It affords food for man and beast, drink (in the form of arrack and the mild *kurumba* or coco-nut milk), bedding, furniture, building material, house utensils, fishing and boat tackle, carpeting, harness, and is even cosmetic and hair-restorer!

The Sinhalese women's long and abundant hair, as well as the unshorn tresses of their lords and masters, are kept in order by using the oil from this wonderful palm tree, which merits all that has been said or sung in its honour.

Under its wholesome shade the breeze circulates freely, and houses, wells, temples, the women pounding rice and the children playing by them, are protected from the sun's glare.

Cookery.

The women use the oil in all kinds of cookery, and to such an extent are their cakes and sweetmeats permeated with its flavour that it is no wonder if they do not recommend themselves to European taste. The Ceylon housewife is expert in making preserves of pumpkins and other fruits of the country. Lime pickle is also a favourite condiment, with chutneys of various composition, and *sambals*, a sort of *hors d'œuvre* more or less hot with chillies and other fiery ingredients, appreciated as accompaniments of curries. The early morning coffee is taken with *arpa*—a kind of flat pancake consisting of rice-flour and coco-nut—and plantains complete the meal.

Children.

Ceylon is the Paradise of children. They are surrounded with kindness, and cruelty to the little ones is rare indeed, unless a disciplinarian should count those cruel who err on the side of indulgence. They have all sorts of toys to beguile them, and kite-flying is a favourite diversion.

Toilet.

A Sinhalese mother fondles her baby by sniffing instead of kissing it. She bathes it daily, as she does herself, by pouring water over it in liberal potfuls. By every village well each evening is the ceremony of bathing carried on by family groups. A Sinhalese husband is not averse to his wife's ducking him in the picturesque fashion above described, while the neighbours look on and chew betel over a friendly chat. The open-air toilet includes the cleaning of teeth and washing of the outer garment, while the under one serves as a bathing-gown — straight pieces of drapery both.

Dress.

The *comboy*, or outer skirt worn alike by men and women, consists of four or five yards of cotton material tightly swathed round the hips and fixed by cunningly folding in the ends and tucking them into the waist independent of buttons or tapes. The Kandyan women pass one end of this drapery gracefully across the shoulder, but in the Low Country it is kept below the short, close-fitting muslin jacket universally worn.

In remoter Kandyan districts the jacket is discarded. The handsome but low-caste—or rather out-caste—Rodiya women go bare as to their comely shoulders, or drape a silk handkerchief across the bosom.

Sinhalese Grace.

Sinhalese women walk with ease and dignity, as Orientals are wont, and from the bluest-blooded Kandyan to the little plumbago girl coming out of the Colombo mills of an evening, sable-polished as an English kitchen-grate, they all can boast "fine little hands and fine little feet." Good features, too, are not rare, and glossy, well-kempt hair, sleek necks, and neat dress make the women pleasant to look upon. Indeed, here and there among the high castes, may be met a nobility of countenance and intelligence which combine to form an almost statuesque beauty. Perhaps an artistic effect is partly due to the absence of head- and foot-gear. A Sinhalese woman loses most of her charm when she covers her simply coiled hair with a befeathered hat European-wise, and squeezes her natural and prehensile toes into a pointed and high-heeled shoe.

Jewellery.

Though Ratnapura, the gem city, is in the very heart of Ceylon, and rubies, sapphires, cat's-eyes, and other precious stones are offered for sale by every *tamby* or hawker, yet a profusion of jewels is not so much a feature of Sinhalese as of Tamil dress. A wealthy lady, however, will show, in addition to the invariable necklace and filigree hairpin, diamond buttons, perhaps, in her dainty muslin jacket of snowy whiteness, and a bracelet or two, chain, or small earrings. But never does she display a nose-ring or forehead ornament such as Tamil ladies wear, nor a weight of metal pulling down and disfiguring the lobe of the ear. Kandyan dames, on the other hand, in their national dress are loaded with heavy gold, or gilt, chains and massive bracelets, that look as inconvenient to wear as manacles. The hair, too, is parted "Madonna-wise on either side the head," rather than brushed back from the forehead without division, the style in the

Photograph by Skeen & Co., Colombo.

SINHALESE VILLAGE GIRL.

Low Country, and most becoming to the shape of their heads.

The habit of chewing betel-leaf, rolled up with a slice of areca-nut and a dab of slaked

Photograph by Skeen & Co., Colombo.

KANDYAN SINHALESE LADY.

lime in a paste, is as common with the women as the men. The areca-nut is credited with whitening and preserving the teeth, but it gives to the mouth an unpleasing and gory appearance, due to the red colour the nut assumes when masticated. The custom gives occasion for the curiously shaped and chased betel boxes of silver which are so much sought after as curios.

The Betel Habit.

Girls' schools are well attended in Ceylon, there being no *purdah* (except among the Moors) to put practical difficulties in the way of education. Troops of happy girls file into the village schools all over the country, while in the larger towns—Colombo, Kandy, and Galle—there are various training institutions for their benefit, the largest of which are missionary foundations. In these all ordinary subjects are well taught, and the girls pass satisfactorily such tests as the University Local Examinations. Even in such a purely European art as modern music, they acquire a creditable skill, and many show talent in drawing and painting. In fact, they are teachable and docile and quick to assimilate ideas, but for the most part they are lacking in initiative, and, after school-days, are too prone to succumb to the influence of an enervating climate.

Education.

The girls are very apt at needlework, and take great pleasure in artistic embroidery. A large amount of pillow-lace is made in Ceylon, chiefly in the Southern Province, where many of the inhabitants, even the men, may be seen making it. Some quite fine specimens of the art are produced in the girls' schools, but it is mostly inferior makes that find a sale among the passengers on board the steamers that touch at Colombo.

Lace and Basket Industries.

The making of pretty coloured baskets is another interesting occupation of Sinhalese women. The baskets are finely plaited from variously dyed fibres, and are made oblong like boxes with lids to fit on neatly. These are sold in nests of different sizes, and are popular among visitors to the island. The designs on the baskets are good of their kind, and almost infinite in variety. This is among the few arts of Ceylon that have not decayed through Western civilisation and its all-invading machinery, which, seeming to achieve a more complete mastery over material, too often ends by weakening that most perfect machine, the human hand, and stultifying the minds of the workers.

We cannot march backwards, but alas! for the ancient art, dead or dying in Ceylon, as elsewhere.

BALCONY OF PERSIAN HOUSE. *Photograph by E. C. Sykes.*

PERSIA

By ELLA C. SYKES.

Birth Customs—Persian Infancy—To Ward Off the "Evil Eye"—A Child, a Doctor, and a "Demon"—Persian Girlhood—Household Arrangements in Persia—A Girl's Education in Womanly Duties—The Bath as a Club for Women—Persian Women and Religion—Women's Dress—How Marriages are Arranged—Betrothal Ceremonies—Marriage Rites—The Position of Married Women—A Magic Well for Women—Woman from a Persian's Point of View—Wifely Submission—Polygamy Unfashionable—Visiting—Persian Party Etiquette—Feminine Amenities—Persian Dances—Music—Superstitions—Unlucky Days—Charity as Insurance—The Significance of Sneezing—"The Healing Art"—How Women Attain to Paradise

IT may be of interest if I try to give some account of a Persian woman's life from babyhood to old age.

Birth Customs.

When a son is born to a well-to-do Persian he gives a feast to his friends, and there is much rejoicing over the happy event, but if a little daughter makes her appearance there is usually only disappointment, and practically no notice is taken of the small arrival.

Before the birth of a child, two cradles, one of common material, and the other gaily bedizened, stand in the prospective mother's room, while two little suits of clothes, the exact replica of those worn by adults, are in readiness. One suit is only of cotton, while the other is of silk, or satin, usually handsomely embroidered. The cradle and clothes of rich material are for the baby if it happens to be a boy, while the cheap ones are to be used if it be "only a girl."

When the child is born it is held on the left hand of the nurse, and water sprinkled over it, after which it is dressed in one of the suits, then swaddled and bound fast to a square pillow, only its head and hands being left free, and thus it will pass the first weeks of its existence, being occasionally dosed with opium if fretful or sleepless.

Persian Infancy.

The mother and nurse do their best to ward off the "evil eye" from their charge. Blue is the favourite colour for this purpose, and the swathing bands are fastened on the child's breast with a powerful charm. This is a sheep's eye brought from Mecca, when the great holocaust of these animals takes place, and into it is stuck a turquoise; while a camel charm consisting of a small rag and wool counterfeit of the "ship of the desert" is supposed to be efficacious in a minor degree.

To Ward Off the "Evil Eye."

Another plan is to dress the child of rich parents in very shabby clothes, lest anyone admiring it, and omitting to add the saving word "Mashallah" (God is great) to their remarks, should bring disaster upon it.

Photograph by H. R. Sykes.

PERSIAN WOMEN OUT OF DOORS.

Most illnesses are put down to the "evil eye," and one poor baby suffering from water on the brain was pronounced by a Persian doctor to be in the grasp of a demon. His prescription was as follows: The parents were to lay the child in a newly-dug grave and leave it there during the night. In the morning it would either be cured or the evil spirit would have made away with it. The advice was duly followed, and the parents found the baby next morning fast asleep in its novel cradle, but, strange to say, neither better nor worse for its cure!

A Child, a Doctor, and a "Demon."

Photograph by Sevruguine.

PERSIAN LADIES INDOORS.

Persian Girlhood.

The father of a Persian girl will in all probability ignore her, unless he happen to be the proud possessor of sons, in which case he may not object to a daughter, and may even play with her in the seclusion of the "Anderoon" or women's apartments. The little thing begins to grow up with her brothers, and is given some perfunctory schooling with them until she is eight, after which, save in the higher classes, her education ceases, at least in a literary direction. A Persian woman who can read and write is looked upon as a kind of wonder. At eight years of age she is separated more or less from her playfellows, and to understand how this is I must give some description of a Persian house.

Household Arrangements in Persia.

It is always built round courtyards, into which the doors and windows open, and is enclosed with high walls over which it is impossible to see, while a heavy door on the street admits the visitor into the "biroon" or outer apartments. These are only used by the men, and are badly furnished, opening on to an ill-kept court in which is a tank of water. Here the master of the house spends his days, transacts his business, sees his friends, and is entertained by his servants with the gossip of the bazaar. The brothers of our small girl bear him company, being handed over to the care of men-servants, and instructed by a priest to read the Koran in Arabic—without an idea of its meaning—and to write. But their sister may not come into this part of the house. A dark passage with a door at the end leads to the "anderoon," and here everything is far nicer than in the "biroon."

The rooms look on to a courtyard gay with flowers, and are furnished with carpets, soft divans, enormous silk-covered cushions, and usually some inferior European lamps, pictures, and knicknacks. This sounds pleasant, but it must be remembered that very little of the outside world penetrates into the "anderoon." No man, save the husband and his wife's male relatives, may enter it, and a Persian's most intimate friend would never ask after his wife or children, except by the vague term of "*khana*" or "the house." It is difficult for Europeans to understand the boredom and dulness of such secluded lives.

A Girl's Education in Womanly Duties.

Here, then, our little girl is taught to sew and embroider, to make sweetmeats and sherbet, and she seldom leaves the house except to go with her mother to the public baths, or perhaps to picnics with her in some garden during the heat of the summer, being carried there by a servant on a donkey, while her mother sits astride on a horse, which is led by one of the retainers.

The Bath as a Club for Women.

The Persian bath is practically the club of the women. Here they meet their friends and spend the day in the steamy hot atmosphere eating their lunch and indulging in any quantity of gossip. They are very particular to bring handsome cushions on which to repose, and elegant cases in which to carry their toilet requisites, as they have usually all too few opportunities of social intercourse. Before bathing a lady sits on a huge brass tray, and is covered from head to foot with fuller's earth, after which she descends into a large tank of hot water. A cold plunge in an adjoining room finishes the bath proper, and she is then rubbed dry and massaged. Her hair is dyed with henna and indigo, giving it a black hue, glossy as a raven's wing; her eyes and eyebrows are decorated with antimony, and her finger-tips and nails painted with henna, the brilliant red giving a curiously unpleasant impression to Europeans fresh to the East.

As water is an expensive commodity in Persia, it is renewed in the bath only at intervals, varying with the price paid by its customers. It can therefore readily be understood that it is by no means a sanitary institution. In fact, a low-class bath, seldom cleaned out, is a perfect hot-bed for the dissemination of disease.

Persian Women and Religion.

Friday, the equivalent of our Sunday, is the day on which all the men repair to the bath, for they must wash and be shaved before going to the Mosque. But as Mohammed hardly allowed that women had souls, and it is said that only the entreaties of his favourite wife Ayesha persuaded him to concede to the specially virtuous an inferior Paradise, it is not surprising that a Persian lady seldom visits the House of Prayer. If she goes, the only accommodation provided for her is an enclosure screened off from the rest of the building by a closely-barred lattice through which she can get glimpses of the proceedings while remaining unseen herself.

Women's Dress.

Indoors the ladies wear loose-sleeved jackets of gauze or velvet, and have short, much - stiffened - out trousers which do not reach to the knees, the toilette being finished off with coarse white stockings or socks. A square of stiff white muslin is bound round the head, a corner hanging down to hide the hair, which is either worn loose or in long plaits. This ungraceful costume was the result of Shah Nasr-ed-Din's inordinate admiration of the dress of the Parisian ballet-girls, but has not descended to the lower classes, who wear tight trousers to the ankles.

Photograph by H. R. Sykes.

WOMEN OF NEH WEAVING.

Out of doors all women of position are concealed from head to foot in a shapeless black "chadar," their faces are covered with a white silk veil, with only a strip of lace-work before the eyes, while purple or green trousers ending in stockings complete the costume. As they shuffle along in heelless slippers they are unrecognisable, and it would be very "bad form" for a Persian to salute his wife or mother did he happen to know that she was some particular waddling bundle of clothes. If any man dare to lift a woman's veil the penalty by Mohammedan law is death.

When a girl reaches the early marriageable age of Persia, her parents begin to look out for a husband for her, her own inclinations being hardly ever taken into account. I have heard of Persian brides of only twelve years, but, fortunately, fifteen or sixteen years is considered a more suitable age at which to wed.

How Marriages are Arranged.

When it is remembered that the girl may never show her face to any man save relatives, it will be understood that there is no social intercourse between the sexes, and that naturally things must be arranged for her. There is much marrying between cousins in Persia, but often the betrothals are planned by a professional go-between, who is treated with great respect by the mothers of marriageable sons or daughters, as she can make or mar a match.

When a *fiancé* has been found for a girl, the young man's mother and female relatives pay a visit of ceremony to inspect her. It may happen that her servants have pointed out her proposed husband to her when they have escorted her to the bazaar, muffled up in her disguising outdoor costume. If she has taken a dislike to his appearance, and is a girl of spirit, she will hand the tea, cakes, and water-pipe to her would-be mother-in-law with such an ill grace that the negotiations will be brought to an abrupt close. On the other hand, she may be eager for the novelty of marriage, and in this case all goes smoothly, and she and her mother will be asked to drink tea at the home of her future husband. The young man is not supposed to see his bride's face until the day of the public betrothal, but of course he will do his best to catch a glimpse of her features when she visits his house, his mother having hidden him away on some balcony for the purpose.

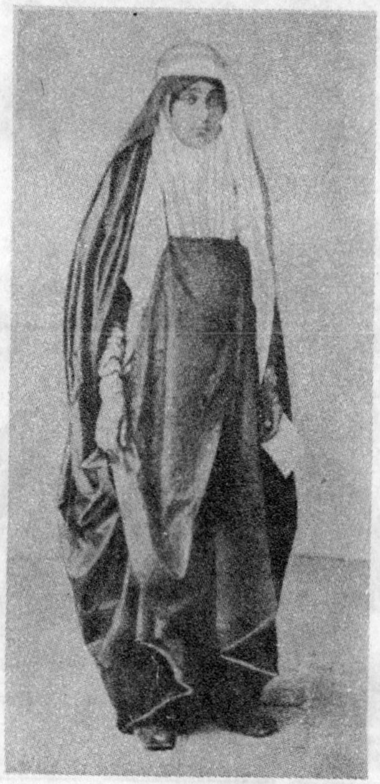

Photograph by Sevraguine.

PERSIAN LADY IN OUTDOOR COSTUME.

The formal betrothal by the priest is a solemn ceremony, and if the man dislikes the much-powdered and berouged face of his bride, he can now draw back, but only by paying to the parents half the sum that he would have received with his wife, and a man behaving in this way is socially disgraced. At the betrothal a lighted candle, the Koran, and a mirror, together with a tray on which are tapers, perfumes, dried seeds and dates, are placed close to the girl, and a green covering thrown over her. She may not speak to anyone. A lighted lamp is then put beneath a large brass bowl turned upside down, and on this latter a saddle and pillow are placed. The girl sits on this pile, which proceeding is supposed to symbolise the mastery of her future husband over her.

Betrothal Ceremonies.

The same green covering used at this ceremony also conceals her later on during the marriage ceremony, and when wedded she is given a piece of gold for luck, and carries bread and salt into her husband's house to ensure plenty, kissing the hearthstone of her old home as she leaves it

Marriage Rites.

The marriage is a grand affair. Persians often go deeply into debt on these occasions, as they feast their friends, the priests, and the beggars, on a large scale, and entertain them with musicians and buffoons.

It seems a matter of chance whether the young wife has a happy existence or the reverse, as so much depends on the character of her husband. Though there are laws for the benefit of the women in such cases as divorce, yet, owing to their seclusion, the husband is practically the sole judge to whom a wife can appeal, and it can easily be understood how hard it is for her to obtain justice unless she has influential relatives. In fact she is looked upon as a chattel, and her husband guards her more from jealousy than from affection.

The Position of Married Women.

She can be divorced with little trouble, and as the Prophet permitted his followers to have four legal wives she can at any time have a second inmate of the house thrust upon her, whom her husband may prefer to her. This is almost certain to be the case if the children born to her are daughters and not sons, and the misery and jealousy that ensue may be better imagined than described. One lady of my acquaintance suffered in this way, and, though she was the chief wife and the mother of his son, yet her husband put the new-comer, a woman of inferior social position, before my poor friend, and made much of her son by another husband.

Near the city of Kerman a small spring trickles out of the side of a high cliff, and popular superstition ascribes its origin to a blow from the hand of Ali. Women anxious to become mothers throng to this spot, drink the water and hang candles and rags on the bushes growing near in order to attract the notice of the saint. There are similar places of resort elsewhere throughout the country. Even if a woman becomes a mother of sons, she must suffer terribly from the ever-present fear of losing them. A family of fifteen or sixteen is not uncommon, but seldom more than six or eight survive the dangers of infancy.

A Magic Well for Women.

Photograph by Sevraguine.

HOW PERSIAN WOMEN KEEP WARM IN WINTER.

From early youth a Persian is taught by the priests to pay no attention to the counsel of a woman, indeed he is admonished to act in every way contrary to the advice of that inferior being. He also believes that women have practically no souls, and that he will never meet those whom he has known on earth. When he attains to the material Paradise of the Mussulman, *he* will be tended by fair "houris," who sing entrancingly as he sits beside the "River of Milk," or stretches his hand towards the delicious foods with which the boughs of a certain wondrous tree are laden. *She*, on the contrary, may be writhing in hell, as the Prophet told his followers

Woman from a Persian's Point of View.

that when he was permitted a glimpse of the Infernal Regions the vast majority of the victims there were women! Only by constant effort, and by the making of pilgrimages, can a woman be admitted into the Paradise reserved for her sex, which is a very inferior place of residence to that which her male relatives will inhabit, with apparently but little trouble on their part.

Wifely Submission.

There is certainly a great deal of wifely submission in Persia, and only once did I hear of a "hen-pecked" man. On one occasion when I was calling on a lady whose husband was present, the latter asked me whether I thought his wife pretty, much in the way that he would have discussed the points of a horse or a dog. I noticed how ill at ease the poor woman became, and he actually remarked on this to me, declaring with pride that if they were at table together she would tremble in every limb and be hardly able to touch food, so greatly was she in awe of her lord and master! After this experience I was not surprised that nearly every native lady I met advised me earnestly not to wed a Persian, assuring me that they made very bad husbands. This was quite a spontaneous warning on their part, because I was most careful never to compare their restricted lives with my free one, fearing to stir up discontent for which I could find no remedy.

I heard of one pathetic case of a woman of good position. She had been accidentally shot through the cheek by her own child, and went for treatment to the hospital kept by the English missionaries. In spite of all their care and skill she was terribly disfigured and when she was pronounced cured her husband came to see her as she was leaving the hospital. "Lift up your veil, woman, and let me look at you," he roughly commanded, and the shrinking woman timidly obeyed him. As soon as he set eyes on her marred face he turned on his heel abruptly and left her without a single word, and the poor wife understood without any further explanation that his action meant that he had divorced her, and had cast her and her son forth from his house. She was nearly heartbroken, not only because of his cruelty, but also because she, formerly a mistress, would now be compelled to earn her livelihood as a servant. No redress was possible in her case, and she had to work for hire to support herself and her child.

Polygamy Unfashionable.

Though I have said that Persians are allowed four legal wives by Mohammedan law, yet they do not avail themselves largely of the permission, and the country is gradually becoming monogamous. Persians themselves say that it is unfashionable and provincial to have more than one wife, but I believe that it is the poverty of the country which is chiefly answerable for this change in Mohammedan custom. The wives of a rich man have each their own establishment, but a poor man cannot afford this, and if he has two wives under the same roof the quarrelling and intrigue, that almost inevitably ensue in such cases, end not infrequently by one rival removing the other by means of poison, while the husband himself may fall a victim to the jealousy he has stirred up. The Persian sayings, "It is easier to live with two tigresses than with two wives," and "Two mistresses cannot be at peace in one house," point very clearly to the disadvantages of polygamy, and indeed the more thoughtful Persians are beginning to be dissatisfied about the status of their womenkind. I remember one man exclaiming in a burst of indignation, during a discussion with me on the subject: "It is all the fault of our cursed religion, which binds us in chains as well as our poor women!"

This is not the place to write about Mohammedanism, but it always seem to me to be one of the most petrifying of religions, holding its followers in a grip that admits of no progress or expansion. Indeed, how can a nation go forward in civilisation if the mothers of the race are kept in slavery and ignorance?

Of course I do not mean to say that the

PERSIAN WOMAN.
DRAWN BY C. PRAETORIUS.

Facing on page 640

life of a Persian woman has no bright touches. There is a good deal of sociability among the well-to-do, who are fond of having their friends to stay with them; in fact an acquaintance told me that by the skilful use of lucky and unlucky days a lady could inflict visitors upon her husband, who is obliged

Visiting.

Photograph by H. R. Sykes.

NOMAD WOMEN OF SOUTH PERSIA.

to make himself scarce on these occasions, for longer periods than he liked. For example, those who were in a house on Saturday must stay there on the Sunday night, while any who arrived on the Tuesday or the Thursday were forced to spend the Wednesday or the Friday under the same roof, as an earlier move would bring ill-luck to all concerned.

Persian women frequently give parties, and on these occasions wear their best dresses and jewellery, a man being looked upon as a good husband according to his capacity of providing finery for his wife. There is an elaborate etiquette observed at these parties, each lady exchanging the most polite salutations with her hostess, who advances to meet her just the distance which her rank demands.

Persian Party Etiquette.

"Your place has long been empty," "May your shadow never grow less," "May your nose be fat," are a few of such greetings, and then the guest takes a place on the carpet of honour. She will, however, alertly make way, and kneel upon a spot further removed from the giver of the entertainment, should a lady of superior position make her appearance, while any poor child-bride is usually treated with scant ceremony.

Tea, sweetmeats, and the inevitable water-pipe are handed round by servants. The tea is served in small glasses without milk, but so many lumps of sugar are put into

PERSIAN COUNTRY-WOMEN. *Photograph by H. R. Sykes.*

the drink of a favoured guest that a little island of sweetness stands up out of the thick, syrupy mixture. Almond paste, sugar pulled into threads fine as silk, toffee and candy are among the eatables, while the passing of the *kalian* or water-pipe is fraught with much tedious ceremony.

Feminine Amenities.

At Tehran, the capital of Persia, a lady will pay a large sum at the European shops for a piece of brocade, and will wear it ostentatiously in order to excite the envy of her guests. Retribution may, however, overtake her, for one of her visitors will perhaps buy more of the same material, and have it made up for her slave-girl. She will then invite all her acquaintances, and tea and the water-pipe will be handed round by the servant dressed in the rich silk in which the quondam hostess is probably arrayed, and later on the same girl will dance before the assembled guests, to the intense mortification of the one and the keen amusement of all the others!

The dancing at these entertainments is unlike anything to which English people are accustomed. The performers posture and come forward with bent legs, progressing by pushing their feet from side to side in most ungraceful fashion. I have also seen women stand and bend backwards until their heads touched the ground, and then slowly raise themselves, becoming scarlet in the face from their extraordinary exertions.

Persian Dancers.

Attempts are occasionally made to copy Western dances, and I was told that a woman, whose dance seemed to me to be a series of painful hops and jerks, was imitating a European waltz to the immense delight of all the spectators.

Music.

The Persian dancing is accompanied by singing and playing. The former, to my uninitiated ears, often sounded more like howls and yells than music, but after a time I got to enjoy some of the weird melodies pitched in minor keys, though I never appreciated the monotonous thudding of the tom-toms.

The women also play on a kind of guitar and a melon-shaped instrument, the strings of which they scrape with a bow, while I have come across a species of zither which emits curious sounds when struck with wooden sticks like spoons.

All Persian women are terribly superstitious, and firmly believe in ghouls, demons, jinns, and *afrits*. The ghouls are supposed to haunt lonely places, ruins and graveyards, luring unsuspecting travellers from the right road in order to devour them, while the *divs* or demons appear to be most active at night. No Persian will sleep alone for fear of these evil spirits, nor will she eat anything which has been cooked on the previous day, saying that a demon may have looked at it during the hours of darkness, and converted it into poison.

Superstitions.

The jinns and *afrits* are less powerful, but, as they can turn themselves into animals at will, no Persian will kill a dog or cat, lest, being forcibly ousted from their dwelling-places, the angry spirits may injure those who have evicted them. At Kerman a snake must never be killed on a Monday, the penalty for such an act being the death of a person in the house nearest to the reptile. Swallows, however, bring prosperity and are encouraged to build in the houses, but owls are unlucky, as are also cocks which crow at any hour other than the "lucky" ones of nine o'clock, noon, and midnight.

All women believe firmly in dreams, the taking of lots, days of bad and good fortune, lucky faces, charms, witchcraft, and so on, and nothing serious is undertaken without finding out from an astrologer whether the omens are propitious.

There are certain unlucky days, all Wednesdays being placed in this category, as the Day of Judgment is supposed to be destined to occur on that date, while the thirteenth of the month Saffar is peculiarly ill-omened.

Unlucky Days.

All Persians leave their houses on this day, and spend the hours between sunrise and sunset in the open air, in order to avert the disasters that might overtake them did they stay indoors: they are also most careful to refrain from quarrelling during this time from the same cause. A woman considers that a day will be fortunate, or the reverse, according to whose face she has looked upon the first thing after waking. The "lucky" face can only be known by experience, but it is a terrible thing for a

Photograph by H. R. Sykes.

PERSIAN NOMAD WOMEN ENGAGED IN CARPET-MAKING.

Persian to be credited with its opposite. On seeing the new moon for the first time it is wise to glance at a "fortunate" face, and the gaze of the Shah, who has the Royal prerogative of seeing any woman in his kingdom unveiled, is supposed to bring luck to those upon whom it falls.

Charity as Insurance.

All Persian women give money to beggars when they set out on a journey, as such charity will avert every accident; and their servants will show their mistresses mirrors, offer them water on which floats a flower, or burn certain herbs in order to ensure safety on the road.

The Significance of *Sneezing*.

It is most unlucky to sneeze *once* when starting on a journey, and the women will stare at the sun in order to induce a second or third sneeze, and, if unsuccessful, will repeat a certain invocation to Allah; however, they have not much faith in this latter remedy, and will usually give up the expedition for that day. Curiously enough they believe, on the other hand, that if they are wishing for anything very earnestly, and someone happens to sneeze, their desire is sure to be granted.

"The Healing Art."

Medicine in Persia is more or less a question of charms. Illnesses are divided into "hot" and "cold"; a "hot" disease like a fever being probably treated by immersing the patient in ice-cold water. A pearl ground up, or scrapings from the Mecca sheep's eye, to which I have alluded, act as powerful restoratives to those at the point of death, while a burn may be smeared with soot taken from the bottom of the cooking-vessels, the patient also drinking pomegranate-water.

When a Persian woman is advanced in years she often thinks of that inferior Paradise to which she can so hardly attain, and she will sell her valuables and persuade her husband to let her go on a pilgrimage. If possible Mecca or Kerbela will be her goal, though, if lack of means put these shrines out of her reach—Mecca in particular requires a long purse—she will perforce renounce the coveted titles of *Haji* and *Kerbelai*, and be content with that of *Mashtadi*, the title gained by those who visit the famous shrine of Imam Reza at Meshed.

How Women Attain to Paradise.

The journey is a serious affair for a woman, who travels in the jolting *kajaveh* or pannier strapped on to a mule, in which she must sit in a very cramped position, unless she can afford the expensive *takht-i-ravan* or litter. Her outer garment is a black shroud in which she is covered from head to foot with the exception of a strip of lace-work over the eyes, and, however hot the weather may be, she must not bare her face, while she has no better hotel than the miserable Persian "caravanserai." Her bedroom is merely a recess, innocent of door or window, opening out of the courtyard, and here she must pass the nights in close proximity to the camels and mules, probably kept awake by the conversation of the muleteers lying outside, and half-stifled by the heavy felt which her servant has fastened across the entrance to her cell.

When the goal of her journey is reached, after many weary days if not weeks of travel, she will probably settle down for a year, visiting the Mosque daily, and presenting offerings of gold and jewellery to the shrine. She will pay a priest to recite portions of the Koran to her, and will spend much of her time chatting with friends from her native city who meet her in the screened-off part of the Mosque.

She does not trouble about the husband and children left at home, for she has never seen much of the one, and the others are safe in the care of a faithful slave. As for the house, she has never been its real mistress, as her husband has managed the servants and paid for everything; therefore it will go on just as well without as with her.

If she dies at Meshed, she will probably be buried in a tomb already occupied, as the graveyards round the shrine are overcrowded, but her soul is secure of going straight to Paradise. If, however, she survives all the hardships of her pilgrimage, and returns to die at home, her corpse may perhaps form part of that terrible caravan of coffins which are sent from all parts of Persia to be interred near the sacred Mosque of Koom.

Photograph by H. R. Sykes.

MULETEERS IN A CARAVANSERAI (PERSIAN HOTEL).

TURKESTAN

By ANNETTE M. B. MEAKIN

The Russians in Asia—The Sarts—Sart Household Arrangements—The Sart Oven—The Water Supply—Sart Head-dresses—Feminine Artifices—Sart Dress—Sart Nose-rings—Marriage Ceremonies and Laws—Sart Baths—The National Dish—Sart Children—Women's Industries—The Kirgiz Nomads—The Tekke Turkomans—Turkoman Jewellery—A Turkoman Wedding—Birth Customs

MISS ANNETTE M. B. MEAKIN IN SART DRESS.

ALTHOUGH Russia had commercial relations with Central Asia as far back as the twelfth century, it was not until 1867 that Russian troops made their way from Siberia to Tashkent and took possession of the province which is now known as Russian Turkestan. Seventeen years later Transcaspia also came under Russian rule, and now all the stretch of territory from Andijan on the borders of the Pamirs to the eastern shore of the Caspian is ruled by one Governor-General, whose position is similar to that of our Indian Viceroy. It has been predicted that before many years have passed there will be a railway passing through Turkestan to Kashmir, and that at the railway station at Merv we shall one day hear the porter shouting, "Change here for Kandahar!"

The Russians in Asia.

Russian Turkestan is peopled partly by a sedentary people called Sarts, and partly by nomads. The chief Sart towns are Tashkent, Samarkand, Kokand, Margelan, Andijan, Namangan, Chyust, and Bokhara.

The Sarts.

The Sarts are descended partly from an Indo-Germanic race, the earliest inhabitants of Turkestan, and partly from the mixture of other races that has taken place there during the last two thousand years. Persian slave-mothers have left to the Bokharan and Samarkand women a heritage of Persian beauty, but in most of the towns Mongol and Chinese features have been handed down from Uzbeg and Chinese parents, and Sart women have, as a rule, high cheek-bones and flat noses, with somewhat slanting eyes.

It is from their Uzbeg ancestors that the Sarts got their language—Turki; and it is from the Uzbegs that the reigning Amirs of Khiva and Bokhara are descended. The people of Bokhara who can trace their descent from Persians call themselves Tajiks.

The Sarts are Mohammedans; they adhere more strictly to their religion than any people of Islam; they accept the *sunna*, or traditions, and the four Caliphs, as well as the Koran, and their women are kept in stricter seclusion than any women in the world.

No respectable Sart woman is ever actually seen out-of-doors, for when she does venture forth she is wrapped in a sombre grey garment, and her face is completely hidden by a black horse-hair veil. But there is plenty of colour in the streets from the flame-patterned robes of the men, who look like brilliant butterflies in the sunshine.

The women of every Sart home have their separate apartment, opening into a

Photograph by Miss A. M. B. Meakin.

A SART FAMILY OF KOKAND.

separate courtyard. No windows look into the street, but the rooms are open to the courtyard on one and sometimes on two sides, so there is plenty of light and air.

Sart Household Arrangements.

When I visited at a native house the master would meet me in the men's courtyard, and conduct me through a low doorway to the ladies' quarters. From fear of earthquake the houses are all built upon the ground floor only. The reception room of a Sart lady is also her living room and her bedroom, and it invariably contains a gorgeously-painted metal-bound trunk, in which her jewellery is carefully stowed away, except on high days and holidays, At one end of the room there is always a high pile of neatly-folded pillows and quilts, which are spread out on the floor at night time to serve as beds.

Across one corner of the room there is usually a pole or a cord, on which rich women hang their clothes, but which serves as a larder among the poor. One wall is always covered with little niches in which teapots and other household articles are kept.

The Sart Oven.

A native oven is like a huge round flower-pot made of clay, with a round opening in its side. It is bought in the bazaar, and has only to be built into the mud wall and plastered over with mud. When bread is to be made a fire is lit inside and allowed to burn itself out ; after the ashes have been taken out the oven is ready. I watched the women clap their flat cakes of bread on to the inner wall of this strange-looking oven, and they stuck to its hot walls till fully cooked.

The Water Supply.

A stream of muddy water runs through every courtyard, and the children stoop down and drink from it, although the water looks horribly dirty ; this is the only available water for cooking or drinking, and dreadful diseases result.

It is a rule that Mohammedans must wash face and hands five times a day, and a sink for the purpose is concealed beneath

Photograph by Miss A. M. B. Meakin.

SART WOMAN OF THE MIDDLE CLASS IN THE COURTYARD OF HER HOME.

one of the mats upon the floor. Ladies of rank perform all their ablutions at home, but ordinary people go to the public baths.

Sart Head-dresses.

Elderly ladies swathe their heads in turbans of transparent muslin, the long ends of which are brought round over the shoulders like a shawl. Unmarried girls wear no head covering in the house, their straight black hair is parted in the middle and hangs down their shoulders in plaits. Black silk plaits are added to the natural hair, and these terminate at the ankle in a tassel of coloured glass beads. On one girl's head I counted fifty-five plaits of her own hair. The hair of Sart women is very thick and very luxuriant; it is never cut, and only brushed once a week. A Sart merely puts her hand through her hair for her morning toilet, but she washes it regularly every Thursday. The hair is washed in boiled sour milk, and combed while wet. Rich women wash the milk out of their hair with warm water, but poor ones leave it in, and a strange odour is in their case very noticeable.

Photograph by Miss A. M. B. Meakin.

THE MAYOR OF SAMARKAND WITH HIS WIFE AND CHILDREN.

Feminine Artifices.

Sart girls have beautiful teeth, and they attribute this to the fact that they eat very little meat. After every meal a finger is dipped into water and the teeth are rubbed with it. After twenty-five they begin to lose their teeth, and, to hide the gaps thus caused, the remaining teeth are often painted black, as in Northern Japan. A herb is used to blacken the eyelashes, and the eyebrows are also painted, and joined together by a black line over the nose. The finger-nails and the palms of the hands are stained with henna, as in Morocco.

On her marriage day a Sart girl must have an artificial flush upon her cheeks, but otherwise the cheeks are not painted among ladies of rank.

As a rule, I found the faces of Sart women very broad and their noses flat and wide at the nostril, the chin was usually pointed, while the ears were large and inclined to stick out. This type is a blend between the Mongol and the Persian, and it is from the latter that they have their long curling eyelashes and their fresh, clear complexions. The Tajik women of Bokhara and Samarkand have small oval faces and dark Persian eyes.

Sart Dress.

All Sart ladies wear trousers, and over these their high boots are drawn; stockings are unknown. The sole of the boot is of soft leather, and there are no heels. Goloshes are worn over the boots out of doors. There is a special kind of boot for riding; it is worn by both men and women: its long heel tapers away till it is the size of a thimble.

Indoors the ladies wear many-coloured silken tunics over long silken robes, or loose jackets with wide sleeves.

The ladies of Bokhara wear a stiff band of coloured silk over the forehead, but the usual thing is a silk handkerchief tied over an embroidered skull-cap. The cotton tunic and trousers worn under the silk robe are retained at night.

Photograph by Miss A. M. B. Meakin.

SART SCHOOLMISTRESS WITH HER PUPILS.

A dozen strings of coral are often worn round the neck, and heavy silver earrings, and amulets decorated with turquoises, are very common; both are hooked into the hair above the ears. I saw a pailful of nose-rings for sale in the Tashkent bazaar, and watched a girl buy one and fit it on to her nostril, just as we would fit a *pince-nez*. I do not believe the ears or nostrils are ever bored.

Sart Nose-rings.

At Sart weddings there is no religious ceremony except the drawing up of a settlement, but there is often much preliminary dispute as to the price that is to be paid to the bride on her wedding day, and sometimes the marriage is greatly delayed on account of the dowry. In such cases the husband may visit his wife after the betrothal, but the parents must not see him come, or recognise him until the wedding day A man is not supposed to see his wife's father till his first child is born.

Marriage Ceremonies and Laws.

Mohammedan law allows four wives, but rich *mullahs* often have five. A man may change his wives as often as he likes, but a woman may only have one husband at a time. The first wife keeps house, and the other wives must obey her. On the death of the first wife the favourite wife takes her place.

When a man has his property scattered in several places, he generally has a wife in each, and in this way there is a house for each wife to keep.

Sart women sometimes dread prosperity for their husbands, because that generally means more wives. I have heard of cases where their jealousy has led them to poison their husbands with aconite.

Nothing will induce a Sart bride to lift her eyes when she is introduced to a visitor, for pretended shyness is considered good form. All through the feasting and her wedding she sits alone in a darkened room, while hired dancing girls, dressed in brilliant silk tunics, sit upon mattresses in the courtyard and sing and play with

Photograph by Miss A. M. B. Meakin.

WOMEN OF THE POOREST CLASS AT HOME, SAMARKAND.

tambourines, or twirl themselves round and round in wild dances, and catch in their mouths the coins that are thrown to them.

Sart Baths.

A native bath is an interesting place to visit: it is a perfect Babel. The only light comes from an opening in the roof, and as soon as our eyes have got accustomed to the dim light we begin to distinguish a writhing mass of women and children busy putting on or taking off their clothes. The bath is below the level of the floor, and steps lead down to it. Up and down these steps there passes an incessant crowd of naked figures. Mothers carrying their babies emerge with steaming skin, little children carrying smaller ones on their backs toil up the steps on all fours. I saw one child, about five, carrying its baby brother on its back. I followed them down the slippery steps, and entered the bath. The inclined marble floor was heated from beneath, and children who found it too hot for their little feet screamed and clung to their mother in fear. The mothers scolded loudly, and the uproar was indescribable. A still hotter room lay beyond, and here the excitement was even greater. Old hags, with only a bathing towel round their withered limbs, dashed water over their victims; while here and there a bather poured water over herself from a copper vessel with a spout. The noise and the heat soon drove us back to the dressing-room, where we found, squatted on the ground, an old woman, with three saucers on her lap containing red, white, and black powders, with which the cheeks, lips, eyebrows, and foreheads of the bathers were to be anointed. Another woman was selling pinches of powdered soap to the new-comers, while a third mounted guard over the clothes to see that none were stolen.

The National Dish.

All the cooking in a Sart household is done by the elder women, the husband's mother or the oldest wife. The national dish is *pilau*. A great copper stewpan is placed on a clay stove in the courtyard, and filled with purified mutton fat, which, when thoroughly heated, looks like boiling oil. The same lot of oil is used again and again, the scum being carefully removed on each occasion. Small bits of mutton are dropped into the boiling fat, then a lot of carrots cut into strips are added (they are bought thus sliced in the bazaar). After a little time rice is added, and a cover put on, so that the steam may be retained. The rice is stirred at intervals, and dried raisins and a few condiments are added to give a flavour.

Pilau is eaten with the fingers, but hands and lips are washed before and after every meal. Rich men generally dine before their women folk, who wait on them and have their own meals later.

Sart Children.

Sart cradles are long and narrow, and suspended from a rod over which a shawl is hung like a tent. Embroidered caps are placed upon the babies' heads when they are little more than a month old, and as the little things are left to lie for hours together upon a hard cotton quilt, the backs of their heads are flattened in consequence. Sart women often have very large families; to have sixteen children is not at all unusual, but a number of them die from lack of proper care, which is not surprising when we remember that girls are married even before they reach their teens, and have no idea how to treat their little ones when they come.

Women's Industries.

Silk weaving is one of the principal industries of Turkestan, and women and girls hatch silkworms' eggs in the folds of their dresses to make a little pocket-money: they often keep fowls for the same purpose.

Little children of well-to-do families are sent to day schools kept by women—they sit on the ground with their legs tucked under them, and learn to repeat passages from the Koran. As soon as a pupil has mastered a couple of lines its parents send the schoolmistress a present—a fowl, a log of wood for the fire, or an article of clothing.

All Sart houses are constantly in need of repairs, for they are built of nothing but mud and water, and every time it rains some of the mud liquefies. The sun-baked bricks of mud are covered with a smooth coating of the same, and this is constantly falling away. A woman can easily mend a crack in the wall of her house by filling it with mud from the street. In wet weather the streets are deep in mud, and the high native carts are very serviceable for getting through it, and also for crossing streams and rivers.

Sart women are not good at plain sewing, but their embroidery is extremely beautiful. Kokand work is especially prized, and fetches a high price all over Central Asia. Embroidery is the only kind of work a Sart woman may do on a Friday. The thimble is worn on the third finger.

The Sarts never let their women engage in agricultural work, but many women of the poorer classes go with the children to the cotton fields and help to pick the pods. While they are at this work their horse-hair veils are tucked up under their cloaks, but on the approach of a stranger they are hastily drawn again over their faces. Poor women whose veils and cloaks are gone to rags will sometimes borrow these articles from a neighbour when they have to go out into the street. Old women who are too infirm for active housework are set to pick the cotton from the pods and spread it out ready to be sewn into quilts. The winter robes of both men and women are quilted with cotton, and this gives them a somewhat bulky appearance.

The Kirgiz Nomads.

The nomadic Kirgiz, who settle in camps outside the towns in winter, and wander in the mountains and the steppes in summer, are also followers of Islam, but they are far less fanatical than the Sarts. Their women are given much more freedom, and they do not mind showing their faces. All the hard work in a Kirgiz household is done by the women; they put up the *yurtas* or tents, and they make the felt with which they are covered. Hard work makes these women very strong, and they look like sturdy men when they come riding straddle-back to the Sart bazaars.

Between Bokhara and the Caspian Sea there stretches the wide and sandy steppe of Transcaspia, which is inhabited by another race of nomads—the Tekke Turkomans.

Photograph by Miss A. M. B. Meakin.

A RICH FAMILY OF KOKAND.

The Tekke Turkomans.

These people live in felt-covered *kibitkas*, or round tents; a rich man generally has a tent for himself and one for each wife. The interior of a Turkoman *kibitka* is hung with native carpets and saddlebags, which give it a very warm and cosy appearance; these carpets are made by Turkoman women during the summer months, and often fetch a very high price.

Turkoman women may go where they like; they are unveiled, and mix freely with the other sex from their earliest years. They are not beautiful, unless descended from Persian slaves, and the purer their blood the flatter their noses and the higher their cheekbones.

Every Turkoman woman who can afford it wears masses of heavy silver jewellery studded with agates, while the very poor content themselves with imitations of the real thing. Their most striking ornament is a heavy silver breastplate; their caps are thickly covered with heavy silver buttons

Turkoman Jewellery.

Photograph by Miss A. M. B. Meakin.

WOMEN AND CHILDREN IN AN *ARBÃ* OR NATIVE CART.

sewn on; their feet are always bare, even when the ground is white with snow.

I saw some solid silver bracelets for sale in the bazaar, and on lifting one of them was much impressed by its extraordinary weight. On a woman's arm it would have reached from the wrist to the elbow. As for the necklaces, they looked like collars made to suit the necks of large dogs.

The solid silver jewellery that the men buy for their brides represents their capital: they consider it the safest investment. When there is a wedding, every available scrap of jewellery is displayed. On her right hand every woman sports a heavy silver thumb ring, and her hair is weighed down with amulets.

The following description of a wedding at which I was present is taken from my book on Russian Turkestan: "There was feasting in all the *kibitkas* at the same time; from where I sat I could see bowls of steaming *pilau* being carried past. The bride and her young lady friends had had theirs an hour earlier. Six carts were drawn up outside their tent. It is only quite recently that the Russian cart has taken the place of the Turkoman camel at these festivals. At a given signal the girls rushed out of their *kibitka* and hopped on to the carts like so many kittens, laughing merrily all the time. The drivers, who were already seated, now smacked their whips, and the six horses started off at a gallop. Another cart drove up to

A Turkoman Wedding.

Photograph by Miss A. M. B. Meakin.

A TURKOMAN FAMILY.

take the bride. We saw the mother step forward to receive the price that had been paid for her. Three women then rushed into the *kibitka*, and soon reappeared, carrying what looked like a large silk-covered bolster, suitable for a double-bed. They bundled it into the cart in a horizontal position. That was the bride! Two women jumped in beside her and off she went, but a shout from the men soon stopped the cart. I now heard that, as only half the money had been paid, she could not proceed. Then a man from the crowd stepped up to the mother, and put a silver coin into her hand. She looked at it, and, being apparently satisfied, let the cart go on."

That bride had to return to her parents after twenty days, for her full price had not then been paid.

The Turkomans have a tradition that a mother must await the birth of her child standing, and nothing will induce an expectant mother to lie down; her women friends stand round her and give her their support. A new-born child has its face immediately washed with a mixture of oil, mud, and native soap.

Birth Customs.

The Turkomans are splendid riders, and essentially a war-like race, and when the Russians conquered Merv in 1884 there was a hard and bloody struggle. But now the Tsar can count the Turkomans among his most faithful subjects.

Photograph by Lady Ramsay.

MOHAMMEDAN PEASANT WOMEN.

ASIA MINOR

By LADY RAMSAY

A Land of Varying Climates—Diverse Races—A Land of Beautiful Women—Mohammedan Dress—The Dirty and Ugly Jewess—Beauty Destroyed by Hardship—Progress of Education among Mohammedans—Christian and Jewish Schools—Mohammedan Woman as the "Handy Man"—"Seclusion" of Women—Religious Duties of Mohammedan Women—Truth about the Harem—Mohammedan Marriage and Divorce—Turkish Household Arrangements—Domestic Slavery—Jewish and Christian Households—Birth Customs—Mourning and Funeral Customs

ASIA MINOR, or Anatolia, or Rum, the most western part of the continent of Asia, is a great peninsula stretching towards Europe between the Black Sea and the Mediterranean; its western shores are bounded by the Ægean Sea, the Straits of the Dardanelles, the Sea of Marmora, and, finally, by the narrow strait of the Bosphorus, where the two continents are nearly within a stone's throw of each other. Its climate varies from the almost tropical summer of the southern coast, sheltered from the northern winds by the lofty range of Mount Taurus, to the intensely cold winters of the high table-lands of the interior and the mountainous districts of the north.

A Land of Varying Climates.

There is no country in the world of similar extent where greater diversity of race prevails. The limits of this article permit only a passing glance at its history, which is one of constant change and vicissitude, of conquest and reconquest by different invaders, with periods of repose, more or less brief, between. It has now been for more than four centuries under the dominion of the Ottoman or Osmanli Turks, who derive their name from the founder of the dynasty. The people are the descendants partly of the foreign conquerors, partly of more peaceable invaders pressing in from all directions, and partly of the races who inhabited the country before the time when history begins. They are classified politically according to their religion—Mohammedans, Christians, and Jews—and it will be convenient to consider the women of the country under these heads. Absolute freedom of religion is guaranteed by the Government to all the various sects, although Christians and Jews labour under certain disadvantages from which the "Faithful" are exempt. Many of these disadvantages, however, such as the compulsory wearing of a distinguishing dress by both men and women, are being gradually eliminated, and during the last forty or fifty years many changes for the better have taken place.

Diverse Races.

Besides the Osmanli, the Mohammedans include Circassians, Georgians, Kurds, Tartars, Turkomans, Yuruks, etc. The Christians are the various sects of Armenians and of Greeks, the Roman Catholics, and a few adherents of other sects. The Armenians naturally predominate in the east, and the Greeks in the west; but there are communities of both in towns of any importance throughout the country. The Jews are found in all the towns, but in greatest numbers in those of the coast.

Both the Christian and Mohammedan women of the wealthier class are often remarkable for their beauty, especially in Smyrna and on the shores of the Bosphorus. Whether dark or fair, tall or short, nearly all have fine eyes and eyelashes, delicately pencilled eyebrows, and soft, clear complexions. The Osmanli women show greater variety of type on account of their mixture of race, and are, on the whole, more elegant and graceful. The domestic duties of both allow them to devote plenty of time to the agreeable cares of the toilet and the enhancement of their charms, and they are adepts in the concoction and use of cosmetics and hair-dyes. The bath is an important function, especially with the Mohammedan ladies, and even when indulged in daily occupies several hours; while if used at longer intervals the whole or the greater part of a day may be given to it.

A Land of Beautiful Women.

Mohammedan ladies have not yet adopted European fashions in their outdoor dress as they have indoors. The hat to them is still anathema. The veil retains its place and power. But the shapeless *ferigee*—a sort of full double skirt drawn round the waist, the under half reaching to the feet, the upper turned up over the head—has been modified into a fashionably cut skirt and a dainty cape covering the head and pinned at the waist behind, the material being usually a rich brocade of some dark colour or combination of colours. A small square of stiff, but fine, black buckram is worn as a veil, and is attached to a small wire frame which fits lightly over the elegant *coiffure* under the edge of the cape, and can be raised at will. When the cape and veil are removed there is nothing in the dress to distinguish the wearer from other well-dressed ladies. This sedate costume is worn when shopping or visiting in the town. At picnics and other open-air parties, in which Turkish women of all classes—and, indeed, Oriental women generally—delight, it gives place to a long coat, not unlike a dressing-gown, of silk or alpaca or other light material, and of pale colour—blue, pink, grey, green, or white. The stiff black veil is replaced by one of transparent white muslin, which, worn over the head, enhances rather than conceals the effect of the elaborately dressed hair with its jewelled combs and pins, and by no means conceals the charming face of the wearer.

Mohammedan Dress.

Photograph by Lady Ramsay.

TURKISH GIRL WASHING AT A WAYSIDE FOUNTAIN.

Judged by the same standard as the Mohammedan and Christian women, the native Jewish women have small pretension to good looks, even when young; but the national costume worn by those of the lower order in Smyrna might make even a beauty look plain. Besides the usual Turkish trousers, it consists of as many voluminous coats of different material and colour (and generally dirty) as can possibly be put on at one time. The head-dress of the married women is a solid-looking bag of black silk or cloth, which entirely conceals what hair they have and hangs down the back, and is surmounted by a ridiculous little cap that looks like a caricature of a Scotch "Glengarry." The old women are pitiful hags, and the custom of leaving exposed their brown and skinny bosoms adds the finishing touch to their gruesome aspect. The Jews are, in fact, the most abject and degraded race in Asia Minor, and both men and women look so. At the same time, Jewish women have, among their own people, a higher status comparatively than Christian women have among theirs.

The Dirty and Ugly Jewess.

In certain districts the appearance of the people shows that, though separated now by difference of religion, they were of the same race originally, and all will show the same standard of beauty—or the reverse. Among the rich or well-to-do in the towns and villages of the interior beauty is by no means uncommon, although the pretty face is too often accompanied by an ungainly figure, and strange incongruities of costume, the result of injudicious mingling of East and West, meet the eye. Among the Circassians and the Kurds the women are often extremely handsome. But the countrywomen of other races, whether nomad or peasant, are so weather-beaten and sun-burned, and generally live a life of such hardship and privation, that such beauty as they may possess in their earlier years soon disappears.

Beauty Destroyed by Hardship.

Education has in recent years made considerable advance, although it is still in a very backward condition generally. Mohammedan schools for girls as well as boys have been established widely, but the education is only of an elementary kind. Wealthy Mohammedans send their sons to Europe, but in the case of daughters this is impossible. Many, however, have the advantage of resident foreign governesses, and speak, read, and write one or more European languages, and are acquainted to some extent with European literature. Considering their circumstances, the number of Osmanli women who have produced literary works is by no means insignificant. One of these is a graduate of the American Women's College at Scutari. For the translation of an English book, "The Mother in the Home," into Turkish, while she was still a young girl in her teens, the Sultan bestowed upon her a royal decoration. Halide Hanum, as she is named, was thus the first woman of any nationality to receive such a mark of distinction; and his Imperial Majesty Abdul Hamid may claim the honour of being the first monarch to bestow such a reward upon a woman.

Progress of Education among Mohammedans.

Christian and Jewish schools are also increasing in number, and among the Christians, at least, education is intensely desired. As Turkish is the language of the country, in many districts, though not invariably, it was until a comparatively recent time the only language known or used by both Armenians and Greeks. Nowadays, however, the younger generation of both peoples are learning their native language, and among the women as well as the men—perhaps more among the women—a national spirit is developing. The work of the American missionaries (whose aim is to enlighten rather than convert), though nominally confined to the Armenians, is greatly responsible for the revival of education throughout the country. Its ultimate effect can hardly yet be foretold.

Christian and Jewish Schools.

While the custom of marrying foreign slaves has made the Osmanli of the western seaboard a mixture of several races, the peoples of the interior, whether immigrant, like the Circassians and others, or native to the soil, retain their purity of blood and their characteristic traits unmixed by marriage. The Circassians and the "refugees" from the Crimea and the Balkan States are active and industrious, and the men take their full share of the work, and their villages and farms always look better than those of the native Mohammedan peasant. Among the latter it is the woman who does the greater part of the work—the man has practically no share in it worth mentioning. She spins both wool and cotton by means of a simple distaff and spindle; she weaves the carpets and the material for clothing her family or for making tents and sacks. She grinds the corn and milks the flocks and prepares the *yahoort*—a thick curd—which, with the paper-like bread that she bakes, forms the chief article of diet. She assists in the ploughing, and does most of the reaping and threshing. She sometimes helps to build the houses of mud bricks, sun-dried, the commonest building material in Asia Minor. In treeless districts, where dried cattle-dung is the only fuel, it is her business to gather it from the ground, roll it to a ball between her hands, and throw it upon the walls of the house, where it adheres till it is dry, when she collects and piles it in stacks for use. Villages where this fuel is used certainly have the advantage of tidiness; for, as no manure is used by the Turks in cultivation, and is only taken from byres and stables to be thrown on the nearest available spot, the other villages gradually develop into veritable dunghills. But when one has once drunk tea made with water boiled by its means, one longs for the untidy village and a wood fire.

Mohammedan Woman as the "Handyman."

Photograph by Lady Ramsay.

TURKISH PEASANT WOMEN.

Among these peoples the "seclusion" of women is by no means universal: many of the native races (for example, Turkomans and Yuruks) do not practise it; neither do Circassians and Kurds, and women and men associate freely. Of course, the women cover their heads, but as a protection from the sun and weather; the face remains unveiled. There are, however, many districts in which even the poorest peasant women are closely veiled, though their clothing be but rags and their feet bare. If a stranger meets them on the road they draw their veils closer, turn their backs on him, and cower down by the roadside till he has passed. In the towns of the interior, where the Mohammedan element predominates, both Christian and Jewish

"Seclusion" of Women.

women often adopt the custom of veiling in public as a protection from possible molestation. The condition of both Greek and Armenian women in agricultural districts differs little from that of Mohammedan women. There are, of course, varying degrees of prosperity and poverty; but

Photograph by Lady Ramsay.

WOMEN IN THE HAREM OF A DERVISH SHEIKH.

The wife holds a bouquet. The mother is the dark figure on the left.

one and all suffer under the life-crushing system of taxation practised by the government.

Religious Duties of Mohammedan Women.

The Mohammedan religion does not, as is sometimes supposed, deny to women either the possession of a soul or a share in the joys of paradise. Women make pilgrimages to the holy places and observe fasts as strictly as men, and they are expected to make the requisite number of ablutions and prayers daily. Prayers for the dead include both sexes. Forgiveness and reward in the after life are promised by the Koran to all good women as well as men. "Enter ye into paradise, ye and your wives, happy," says one verse, and there are many similar passages. Although women are not expected to go regularly to mosque, their presence there is not forbidden, and there are usually galleries for their accommodation. Also women, like men, are believed to be attended through life by two spirits, one good, the other evil, urging them to do right or wrong. All children are taught to recite the Koran, and when they know it by heart girls as well as boys receive the title of "Hafiz."

Truth about the Harem.

To the Western mind the prominent features of Mohammedanism—frequently the only ones—are the seclusion of women and the practice of polygamy. The harem is pictured as a prison where the several wives of a more or less tyrannical husband pine behind latticed windows, if not iron bars, tremblingly awaiting the pleasure of their lord and master. The reality is not quite so bad, for although the Mohammedan woman is "secluded" from intercourse with men, except her own husband and near relatives, her personal liberty is not so restricted as might be supposed. The wife is as much mistress of her own house as most married women; she comes and goes as she likes, asking leave of no one; and she has absolute control of her personal property, including her slaves. As monogamy is the rule and polygamy the exception, her husband is usually hers alone, and if the first reason of this be an economical one—polygamy being always a more or less expensive luxury—there is certainly very often the other and equally old-fashioned one—mutual affection and esteem. Among educated Mohammedans also there is the all-powerful factor of public opinion against it. Polygamy is not "good form."

Mohammedanism did not institute polygamy, but, on the contrary, restricted its unlimited practice, and laid down laws as to the relations of men and women which enormously improved the position of the latter, giving them, whether free women or slave women, certain legal rights, both for themselves and their children. A man cannot sell a slave who has become the mother of his child. Whether he marries her or not (which, however, he commonly does), she and her child remain in his house, and the child is considered legitimate and has the same rights as the other children.

Mohammedan Marriage and Divorce.

Marriage is a purely civil act, and the wife's rights are secured to her by a properly attested contract, by which the husband binds himself to maintain her according to his rank and means, and, in case of divorce, not only to deliver up to her all her personal property, but also to settle on her a certain sum of money for maintenance, the amount being fixed at the time of marriage. The act of divorce is a simple one. Without assigning reasons, the man has only to say three times in the presence of witnesses, "I divorce you," and the thing is done. The conditions of the marriage contract, however, have a restraining effect on the practice of divorce as they have on that of polygamy. Except in the case of an heiress, the Mohammedan bride seldom has any dowry beyond the provision of clothing and household furniture, etc., made by her parents at the time of her marriage; but each wife must have her separate establishment, though it be but a couple of rooms and a single slave.

Polygamy is allowed by the Jews, but only when the first wife has no children or no son. It is not practised by the educated classes, who, when childless, frequently adopt children. Divorce is as easy with the Jews as with the Turks; but the same obstacles are placed in its way by the marriage contract.

Early marriage is the universal rule. Girls of whatever nationality generally marry in their teens—sometimes when they have barely reached that period. The parents or guardians arrange the match,

Photograph by Lady Ramsay.

GREEKS OF THE INTERIOR OF ASIA MINOR.

the girl at least having little or no say in the matter—though there are exceptions to this rule. The actual rite of marriage varies in character among the different races, but in every case the ceremonies and festivities cost a considerable amount of money, and occupy at least a week, and the etiquette and formalities peculiar to each nationality are strictly observed. Space does not allow of a detailed description of them. The Jewish marriage ritual is long and complicated, and both the Armenians and the Greeks have an elaborate religious ceremony. Both Christians and Jews provide a dowry for their daughters. The trousseau in each case consists, like that of the Turkish bride, of personal clothing, bedding, carpets, pots and pans, and other household gear.

Turkish Household Arrangements.

The house of the wealthy or well-to-do Turk consists of two parts, the *haremlik*, sacred to the women, into which no strange man may enter, and the *selamlik*, for men only, in which the owner receives and entertains his friends. These two parts have separate entrances, or they may even be entirely separate buildings. The *haremlik* is always more or less spacious, the *selamlik* may be of any size from a whole house to a single room. Where there is facility of intercourse with Europe many innovations in furniture, as in dress and customs, have been introduced; but in the typical house the furniture is very simple. The floors are covered with rugs and carpets. In each room the divan, or sofa, is a fixture, and extends along one or more sides of the room. It has a stiff mattress, and is covered with rugs and supplied with cushions varying in hardness and covered with brocade or satin or calico, as the case may be. The rooms are spacious and airy, and the windows, of which there are as many as possible, are draped with pretty curtains, and, except when they look into the private garden, are shuttered half-way up on the outside with fine lattice-work. Open cupboards in the walls, which are often lined with ornamental woodwork instead of plaster, contain candlesticks, coffee services, etc., and there is generally a large press at one end of the room in which piles of bedding are kept, ready to be spread at night on the floor as required. There is probably a fireplace with wide hearth but no grate. In cold weather *mangals* are used. These are braziers of copper or brass, of elegant shape and often of enormous size, filled with glowing charcoal. Some lamps, a mirror, one or more clocks, a few chairs and inlaid coffee-tables, complete the furnishing. Any room may be used as a bedroom. Several mattresses, stuffed with cotton-wool, are piled one above the other on the floor, and a sheet of home-spun silk or muslin spread over them. Some stiff pillows, in embroidered, lace-trimmed slips, are placed at one end, and at the other a folded quilt, or quilts, of brocaded silk or embroidered satin, and the bed is ready. Clothing, jewellery, and other treasures are kept in chests and boxes in the private apartment of the owner. The kitchen and store-room accommodation are ample, and food for guests in the *selamlik* is usually prepared by the women.

The harem includes all the females of the household and (incidentally) the children, and as the family system is patriarchal, the household may be large. Besides unmarried daughters there may be one or more daughters-in-law, and perhaps other relatives, with a greater or smaller number of slaves. The wife—or, should there be more than one, the chief wife—of the master is supreme head of the harem, although each wife and each son's wife must have her own private domain. A mother, however, if her husband be dead, retains her position as head in the harem of her son. Her rule may be kindly or the reverse, but she is invariably treated with the greatest respect. Neither her grown-up sons and daughters nor her daughters-in-law may sit in her presence without leave. At the same time the warmest affection between mothers and children—especially sons—is the rule, not the exception.

Domestic Slavery.

The system of domestic slavery must, apparently, always be co-existent with the seclusion of women. No other way is known of providing the service necessary in the households of the wealthy and the well-to-do. The free Mohammedan woman cannot enter the service of strangers, as no man is permitted to see her face unless he be a near relative. The slave, as the property of her master or mistress, occupies a different position. Theoretically, slavery has been abolished for some time, and there is now no public slave market. But the traffic goes on as extensively as ever. The white slaves are mostly Circassians, Georgians, and Kurds, races all famous for the beauty of the women; and the conditions of slavery are such that parents are willing to sell their children and even anxious to do so, while the children are often equally willing to be sold. They are treated with great kindness and never overworked. They are fed and clothed in the same manner as their owners, and share in their pleasures and amusements. A man suffers no degradation in marrying a slave, and attractive girls generally make good marriages—arranged by their mistresses—and marriage is still the goal of the women of Asia Minor. Marriage with a slave has also economy to recommend it, as it does not entail the expensive festivities that marriage with a free woman does, of which the bridegroom has to pay a substantial share. Slave-girls are nearly always bought young and trained and educated in the houses of their owners. A man has no personal rights whatsoever over the slaves of his wife. Many black slaves are imported. The women usually perform the more menial household duties, and the males supply the eunuchs of the wealthier classes, the only male servants allowed to enter a harem. Considering social conditions, mulattos are rare in Asia Minor.

Jewish and Christian Households.

The houses and household arrangements of Christians and Jews in the inland towns and country are so similar to those of Mohammedans of the same class that in a brief sketch such as this detailed description is uncalled for. In those remote districts the patriarchal system is still more or less strictly the rule among Christians as among Mohammedans and Jews. In Smyrna, by far the most important town of western Asia Minor, and wherever modern ideas have penetrated it is now practically abandoned by them. The deepest respect for parents is still manifested, however, and the widowed mother still keeps the place of honour in the house of her son.

By Mohammedan, Christian, and Jew alike childlessness is regarded as a dire misfortune. The birth of a child, whether

Photograph by N. P. Edwards, Littlehampton.

A BETHLEHEM BEAUTY.

boy or girl, is a happy event and celebrated with festivities and rejoicing. Boys, as a rule, are preferred; but among the peoples who supply the slave-market the girl-child receives the warmest welcome. A short time ago I happened to be spending a couple of nights with a tribe of nomadic Kurds. In the course of conversation a Greek servant of ours remarked that the Greeks preferred sons to daughters. The Kurdish chief answered with a laugh, "We prefer girls. I can get £70 for a girl."

Birth Customs.

Special ceremonies, differing somewhat according to nationality, are connected with the birth of a child. The most important matter in every case is to guard against the power of the evil spirits which on such occasions are specially prone to mischief its arms and legs are straightened, and it is then firmly swathed in a long bandage which covers everything but its head. A tiny cap is added, ornamented with blue beads and amulets to protect it from the evil powers. In some places warm ashes

ARMENIAN WOMEN.
A "Sociable" at the American Mission House, Tarsus.

towards both mother and child. The baby must not be openly admired, or if it is the speaker must immediately spit, or pretend to spit, upon it, or use some other unpleasant gesture, to avert the power of the "evil eye." But some slighting remark is safer and gives no offence to the mother or other relatives, who quite appreciate the reason for it. Infant mortality is enormous, which is not surprising where ignorance and superstition rule. Among the Turks it is not compensated, as among most of the other peoples, by a correspondingly high birth-rate. The custom of swaddling is universal. The baby is washed, a tiny shirt and wadded jacket are put on, it is laid on a little quilt, are spread on the quilt on which the child is laid, occasionally with disastrous results. When I was living at Konia a case came under my notice. The new-born baby of an Armenian woman wailed so unceasingly for a day and a night that the friends and relations were convinced that, in spite of all precautions, an evil spirit had succeeded in taking possession of it. The mother's employer (a European lady) insisted on the swaddling bands being undone, and a burn, two or three inches in extent and penetrating to the bone, was found on its hip. Of course, it died.

The Mohammedan baby receives its name at once, without special ceremony. Boys are not circumcised till they are seven years old.

The Jewish birth customs and ceremonies are the same as are observed by that people elsewhere, and the Jew baby-boy is circumcised on the eighth day. The Christian baby is christened on the first Sunday after its birth. The ceremony takes place in church under the charge of sponsors accompanied by a crowd of friends, and the child is undressed and immersed in the font and immediately confirmed by being anointed with holy oil. After the christening the baby must not be taken out for forty days for fear of the evil spirits. It is then taken to church for another religious ceremony. During these forty days the child of more enlightened people is undressed daily, and it is in any case supposed to be washed once a week; but in Konia, for example, it is common among even well-to-do Armenians to swaddle it in such a manner that it is considered unnecessary even to undress it during the whole period. Some mothers do not even lift it from the cradle to suckle it, but kneel down beside it for that purpose.

Mourning and Funeral Customs.

The custom of weeping and wailing aloud, beating the breast and tearing the hair, on the death of friend or relative is universal, and so also is the practice of burying the dead within a few hours after death. Among the different peoples the ceremonial is practically the same for women as for men. Mohammedan burial rites are simple. The body is gently but carefully washed and enveloped mummy-wise in linen or calico, and borne to the grave, covered by some beautiful garment or cloth, on a stretcher or in a rough shallow coffin, from which it is lifted to be placed in the grave. It is carried first to the mosque, where part of the funeral service takes place, there being a special prayer in the case of women, and thence to the burying-ground, where the service is finished. It is believed that the soul does not leave the body at the moment of death, but hovers near and will resent any roughness or indignity put upon it; and after interment it still lingers for a time to answer "the Questioners," two spirits who, when the body is laid in the grave, demand an account of its life while on earth, and when the mourners quit the spot the *imam*, or priest, remains for a little to assist the dead in answering. There is no further ceremony at the grave, but forty days later money and food are distributed to the poor, and, after a second interval of the same length, a second distribution is made and a service held in the mosque. The grave is not deep, but the soil is piled high above it and built into the form of a sarcophagus. The headstone of a man is shaped like a small column with a turban carved on the top; that of a woman is flat and somewhat pointed, and generally ornamented with some symbol, such as a flower, or with a verse or a text from the Koran. As soon as the funeral is over all signs of grief are suppressed, and the relatives resume—outwardly, at least—their ordinary aspect, and thenceforth the dead is left undisturbed. In the warmer parts of the country the cemetery, with its beautiful cypress trees, is a favourite place of resort on holidays.

The Greek funeral customs are practically the same in Asia Minor as in Greece, though in all popular ceremonial details vary in different localities. The funeral ceremonies of the Armenians resemble in some respects those of both Greeks and Mohammedans. Their ceremonies and feasts are elaborate. Like the Mohammedans, they hold that the soul lingers near the body for a time. They have certain days devoted to services for the dead in general. Also, like the Mohammedans, they leave the dead undisturbed, and do not, like the Greeks, take up the bones after three years, wash them in wine, and consign them to a charnel-house or to another tomb.

Jewish burial customs are the same as those practised by the Jews everywhere.

TURKEY AND GREECE

By LUCY M. J. GARNETT

Racial Groups—Polygamy—Position of Mohammedan Women—Relations of Mother and Son—The *Haremlik*—Slaves and Slavery—Recreations of Turkish Women—Western Influences—Education—Albanian Women—The Nomads—Christian Races—Provincial Life—Peasant Life

Racial Groups.

AMONG the women of Turkey and Greece may be found representatives of no fewer than thirteen different races. Limitations of space render it impossible to describe the women of all these various races in the order of their historical antiquity, and it may here be advisable to group them according to the creed they severally profess. The Mohammedan women include, in addition to members of the ruling race, Albanians, Kurds, Circassians, Tartars, Turkomans, and Yuruks.

Polygamy.

Although the law of Islam allows a man to marry four wives and to be the owner of an unlimited number of slaves, as a matter of fact, at the present day, among the working classes one wife is the rule, and among the wealthy more than one the exception. For, in addition to the various other considerations which make a plurality of wives undesirable, there exists also the grave question of expense. A second wife means an extra suite of apartments, an extra slave or train of slaves, according to her rank, as each lady must have her own special attendants, and an extra allowance of pin-money. There is, besides, no superabundance of women in the country, notwithstanding the influx of female slaves.

Position of Mohammedan Women.

The legal position of a free Mohammedan woman compares favourably with that of her Christian neighbours. As a daughter, she is entitled on her father's death to inherit his property in common with her brothers in a proportion determined by law, according to the number of inheritors. As a wife, she has uncontrolled possession and disposal both of the wealth which was hers before marriage and of any subsequent inheritance. No doctrine of "coverture" exists for her; she can sue or be sued independently of her husband, and may plead her own cause in the courts without the intervention of counsel. A husband, on his side, is bound to support his wife and her slaves according to his wealth and rank, and to furnish her with a suitable habitation. And though great facilities may appear to be given to a man in the matter of divorce, wives are, on the other hand, safeguarded from a too arbitrary exercise of this privilege by legal enactments which, in practice, largely modify this facility. One of these is the *nekyah*, the settlement upon the wife at the betrothal of a considerable sum of money to be paid to her in the event of dismissal from her husband's roof, without the payment of which no divorce can take effect.

Relations of Mother and Son.

In a Mohammedan household, the husband's mother occupies the most honourable position. Osmanli women are perhaps the most indulgent mothers to be found anywhere, especially to their sons, who naturally in early youth take advantage of their devotion. Arrived, however, at years of discretion, her foretime tyrant becomes

TURKISH WOMAN.

A TURKISH LADY.

his mother's devoted slave. Debarred from all social intercourse with women not closely connected with him by ties of blood, a man's mother and sisters are his only female friends, and to this fact is probably due the strong affection which subsists between mother and son, brother and sister.

The Haremlik.

A Turkish dwelling, however humble, is invariably divided into *haremlik* and *selamlik.* The latter, in an average house, consists of a couple of rooms on the ground floor, in which the master transacts official business and exercises general hospitality. The *haremlik,* which has its separate entrance, courtyard, and garden, constitutes the *sanctum sanctorum* of the women, the place secure from all intrusion, into which not even the master may enter should a pair of overshoes at the door of its reception room announce that his wife has a visitor.

Slaves and Slavery.

Inseparable from the harem system is the institution of domestic slavery: the law of Islam forbids a free woman to appear unveiled before any man not a close blood relation. Slavery, however, as now practised in Turkey, is in direct contravention of the same law, which only recognises as legitimate property non-Moslems who have fallen into the power of the True Believers during war; for the majority of the slaves now brought into the country are drawn from the Circassian race who profess the creed of Islam. Although the Porte, in deference to European opinion, has abolished the public slave market, so indispensable are female slaves in the social system of the Turks that the result has merely been to make the private trade in this human merchandise much more general than formerly. Ladies of high rank often carry on this traffic, purchasing children born chiefly in the tents of the nomad Circassians, and bringing them up in their own households. Under Islam slaves are protected by many humane laws; they are, on the whole, treated quite paternally, often set free and adopted by childless owners; and, not being looked upon as a class apart, they marry free men, and their origin is lost sight of. Speaking generally, indeed, female slaves in Turkey have little of which to complain, and their duties are by no means arduous. Be they housemaids, laundrymaids, nursemaids, or personal attendants on their mistresses, they have ample leisure for daydreams of the future, when they too may be *hanums* with slaves to wait upon them — dreams which have every chance of fulfilment in the case of those endowed with personal charms. For the good fortune of such is assured from the outset, as many Turks prefer to marry women who have been brought up as slaves.

Marriage with a free maiden is an expensive matter in any rank of life, owing to the lavish outlay in gifts and entertainments made obligatory by custom on such occasions. All Turks marry young, and consequently, if a father cannot afford to take a wife for his son in his own class, he purchases a slave who has been brought up with that end in view in some great lady's harem, and no expense is incurred beyond the purchase money. There is, too, the consideration that a slave, having no position of her own, is submissive and obedient to her lord, and has no interfering relations. Should a slave bear a child to her master, she cannot be resold, but has the right to bring up her offspring in its father's house. It is also considered legitimate, and inherits equally with the child of a free wife. In all probability the father will set his child's mother free and marry her, and thus bestow upon her the status of a free-born woman. Whatever the faults or failings of a slave, she may not be sent adrift into the world: her owner is responsible for her maintenance. If not married under the above circumstances, she may, at the end of seven years' servitude in one family, claim her freedom, when a husband will probably be found for her and a trousseau supplied.

Recreations of Turkish Women.

Paying calls, attending wedding, birth, and other family ceremonies, promenading and driving, form the chief amusements of women of all ranks; and going to the public baths is made an occasion of great festivity and ceremony. Osmanli women are also passionately fond of country excursions, and the number of charming resorts within easy reach of every considerable town, as well as of the capital, added to a magnificent climate, offer every facility for the indulgence of this taste. Curiously carved and gilded springless carts, drawn by a pair of oxen decorated with multi-coloured tassels and fringes, are the favourite mode of conveyance for these picnics; and it is almost impossible to visit any of the favourite rural resorts in the vicinity of Constantinople without finding there one or more groups of Turkish women and children "taking their *kaif*."

The average Turkish matron, however, by no means spends all her time in these diversions, and in "eating sweets and playing with her jewels," as is often assumed. She is, on the contrary, very domesticated, and her days are, as a rule,

TURKISH WOMAN IN THE CEMETERY OF EYOUT, CONSTANTINOPLE.

The pointed stones mark the graves of women.

quite as profitably occupied as those of her sisters in Western Europe.

Domestic pursuits are, however, nowadays being more and more abandoned by the younger generation of fashionable *hanums* in the capital, who, emulating the pursuits of the foreign ladies with whom they are now often brought into contact, manifest a preference for the acquisition of European languages and accomplishments. Wealthy families accordingly now engage foreign governesses for their daughters, and the native language and literature are usually neglected in favour of French, English, and German, piano-playing, drawing, and painting. Whether this fashion of Western education—for in the majority of cases it is probably little more—will have any result beyond rendering irksome the restraints imposed by Moslem religion and custom, which no woman can with impunity disregard, time only can show. There certainly exists among a certain section of the upper classes a growing desire for the emancipation of women, and for their better education. This desire must, however, become much more general than it at present is, and must be favoured, instead of repressed, by the Commander of the Faithful before such a social revolution can be initiated.

A KURDISH GIRL.

Western Influences.

Education.

As Turkish culture has now entirely lost the distinctive character it possessed in the palmy days of the Empire, and become a mere imitation of that of the West, methods of education have naturally followed suit, and the schools and colleges of the modern era are organised more or less on European models. For girls of the middle classes there have been established in the capital and the larger provincial cities good day schools. In the smaller towns, however, the instruction given is, generally speaking, but elementary, and the attendance in proportion to the population is lamentably small.

Albanian Women.

The social status and daily life of the townswomen of Albania differs but slightly from that of their Turkish sisters. In the remoter country districts, however, they enjoy a considerable degree of freedom, and lead outdoor lives of healthy industry, wearing no veils while pasturing their flocks on the hills, or fetching water from the village fountain.

The highlands of Asiatic Turkey are peopled by a great variety of nomadic tribes belonging to different races—Circassians and Kurds, Yuruks, Tartars, and Turkomans, all of whom are, at least nominally, Mohammedans.

The Nomads.

TURKISH GIPSY WOMEN.

Their conversion to Islam is, however, for the most part of but recent date, and they retain many of the customs, beliefs, and religious rites of their pagan forefathers. Within present limits it is not possible to describe more than one of these races, and the Yuruks may be chosen as illustrating, to a certain extent, the rest of these nomads. The Yuruks are extremely polygamous, the number of their wives frequently exceeding the limits fixed by the Prophet; a man of average wealth has at least seven. While to a Turk a plurality of wives is an expensive luxury to a Yuruk it is a necessity of existence as he requires a certain number of "hands" to enable him to pursue his calling of flock-master, camel-breeder, etc.; and as he cannot hire such hands, he obtains them by marrying their owners. Each wife has, however, her separate tent and her special occupation. The care of the flocks will be apportioned to two or three, each tending a certain number of the broad-tailed Karamanian sheep; a fourth looks after the camels, a fifth collects fuel and draws water for the joint family, a sixth will make the butter and cheese, while the seventh weaves on a primitive loom the brightly hued rugs, camel's-hair cloth, and other fabrics for clothing and tent furniture. Nearly every woman has a large family, but infant mortality is great owing to the rude lives led by these nomads.

Christian Races.

The Christians of Turkey belong to five different nationalities—Greek, Wallachian, Bulgarian, Servian, and Armenian. The Greeks of Turkey, though far in advance of their neighbours in point of education and general enlightenment, are still in many respects behind those of free Hellas, who rank very high educationally among the nations of Europe. For while instruction is, in the little kingdom, compulsory, no such authority exists in Turkey, and any initiative that Greek communities may take in that direction is prompted by the lively patriotism and love of learning usually evinced by this race. But though ever ready to make sacrifices for the education of their sons, it is only within the last half century that even elementary schools for Greek girls have become at all general in Turkey. At the present day, however, in all the large centres of Greek population, the primary and secondary system of education provided is the same as that followed in the Greek kingdom, and is found sufficient for existing social and intellectual needs. Teachers for these various schools are supplied from the training colleges established first in Athens and subsequently in the Ottoman capital.

Social life among the wealthy class in the large towns is very similar to that of Greeks of the same position in the Greek kingdom and in Europe generally; and the Bulgarian and Armenian ladies of the same standing, though less highly cultured perhaps, are not as a rule deficient in manners and attainments. Education is, in fact, becoming more general year by year, and the political rivalry between the Macedonian nationalities, Greek, Bulgarian, Servian, and Wallachian, has, during the past quarter of a century, proved a powerful incentive to intellectual progress; while among the Armenians aspirations towards national independence have had the same favourable result.

Provincial Life.

Women of the middle and lower classes of all nationalities lead, in the provincial towns, somewhat secluded lives, as it is considered an impropriety for girls and young women to be seen much out of doors, and their lives are passed, for the most part, in a dull enough routine of household duties, enlivened only by occasional attendance at church and invitations to weddings and christenings, with, it may be, on feast days a walk on the public promenade *en famille*. Occupation in shops is not open to girls, nor, unless compelled by sheer necessity, will they become domestic servants, who are drawn chiefly from the peasant class and from the islands of the Ægean. The majority of girls occupy themselves with needlework, lace-making, and other home industries; and it is only in the silk and cotton growing districts of Asia Minor that they are employed in factories.

Peasant Life.

Peasant life differs little in Greece and Turkey save that there is greater security for life and property in the former country. In Macedonia the Greeks seldom occupy the same villages with the peasants of other races. Their women, though not employed in field work to such an extent as are their Bulgarian sisters, take an active part in much of the labour connected with the farm and vineyard, and their household duties are many. To the Greek peasant girl is also committed the care of her father's flock of sheep and goats, which she leads every day to the pasturage, and secures at night in the *stania*, or sheepfold. The *voskopoúla*, or shepherdess, is one of the most prominent figures in rural folksong, and many a charming idyll has been composed in her honour. Little time is, however, at her disposal for sylvan dallying, for, in addition to milking and cheese and butter making, it falls also to her share to bleach, dye, and spin the wool of the flocks, and to weave this, as well as the produce of the flax and cotton fields, into stuffs for clothing the family, or for sale in the market of the nearest town. It is pleasant to watch the graceful motions and picturesque poses of these girls, as, standing on their wooden balconies or terraced roofs, they deftly send the spindle whirling down into courtyard or street while twisting the thread for knitting. To the old women is generally relegated the last of these home industries, and swiftly plying their five fine curved and hooked needles, the "feed" of the yarn, regulated by a pin fastened to their bodices, they sit in their doorways for hours together, gossiping with neighbours, or telling *paramythia* (fairy tales) and crooning nursery rhymes to the little ones of the household.

In some districts the silk industry keeps the women fully occupied during the spring months. In Crete, for instance, this constitutes the chief domestic industry, for each family cultivates its own little crop. Cyprus is also famous for its industries in linen, cotton, silk, and wool, and the Cypriote women of to-day maintain the renown for cunning needlework which pertained of old to the island more especially associated with the Queen of Beauty.

The numerous holidays observed by the Bulgarians in common with other members of the Eastern Church make it necessary for them to work doubly hard on other days, in order to accomplish the year's work in twelve months. Consequently, during the spring and summer more especially, the women and girls, as soon as their household duties are finished, go out to assist the men and boys in the field. The work of cutting the grain is accompanied by these simple people with observances quite Arcadian, enlivened by the notes of the *gaida*, or bagpipe, and by song. After the corn harvest comes the vintage, when the grapes are gathered and pressed in the same light-hearted fashion. Besides wine and the spirit called *raki*, or *mastica*, a kind of treacle is also made from the juice of the grape and stored with the oil, grain, and other provisions for winter use. In some districts the culture of the roses, of which the famous "otto" and rose-water are made, forms an important branch of industry. Gathering the blossoms is quite a festal affair for which the women

A GREEK WOMAN.

don their picturesque gala costumes. The children run to and fro, emptying the baskets of roses as they are collected into larger receptacles presided over by the matrons, who, seated under the trees, sort the blossoms according to their quality, the whole forming a picture of happy toil, amid harmonious surroundings, in the highest degree fascinating and idyllic.

THE WESTERN BALKAN PENINSULA

By M. EDITH DURHAM

The Slavonic Invasion—Modern Influences—The Turkish Conquest—The Slavs—Montenegrin Marriages—Woman's Work and Position—Childhood—The Art of Weaving—Dress—Balkan Cookery—Agriculture—Women's Privileges—Dances and Songs—Mourning Customs—Slavonic Moslem Women—Albania—Albanian Weddings—Dress—Position of Albanian Women—"Men" Women—Albanian Characteristics

The Slavonic Invasion.

WHEN we first hear of the Balkan peninsula it was inhabited by wild tribes—not Greek—who were known by various names and were always fighting one another. Nevertheless they appear to have been closely allied by blood. From them are descended the modern Albanians. These still speak a language which is possibly the oldest Aryan tongue in Europe. They are massed in what is called Albania, but are also spread in large numbers throughout Macedonia and, indeed, through all the Balkan lands. They claim, and with justice, to be Alexander the Great's Macedonians.

In such a short article as this it is impossible to deal with more than a very general view of the races that have poured into and influenced the Balkan peninsula. The Romans, the Huns, the Celts, though all have doubtless left their mark, must be passed over. The one event of superlative importance was the great Slavonic invasion.

This began, perhaps, as early as the fourth century A.D. By the sixth century the Slavs had poured in from the north, beyond the Danube, in resistless thousands, and in the seventh were settled in vast numbers on the plains, having largely displaced the former inhabitants and driven them to the mountains.

Those that withdrew to the mountains retained their language and customs. Intermarriage to a great extent must, however, have taken place between the invaders and invaded, as the same types and peculiarities often occur in people who call themselves of different nationalities. Slavonic and Albanian customs merge into one another, and it is almost impossible to draw a definite line between them.

Modern Influences.

Circumstances are changing rapidly in the Balkan peninsula. Modern ideas and systems of education are spreading. In Servia, and also in Bosnia and Dalmatia, schools quite up to modern Western standards are sweeping away old customs and traditional modes of living.

It is only in the outlying villages and more inaccessible mountains that life still goes on much as it did in the Middle Ages.

Till the end of the fourteenth century the Servian peoples were making steady progress, and do not seem, in general culture, to have been much behind the rest of Europe in general civilisation. But they had one fatal weakness. Like the people they had displaced, they were still in the tribal stage of a nation's development.

The coming of the Turks found them divided and weakened by rival chieftains, and though in the end they united and made a gallant stand, they were finally overpowered at the fatal battle of Kosovo in 1389. From that time till the beginning of the nineteenth century the bulk of them were crushed under Turkish rule. Turkish rule acts, and has always acted, as a withering blight. Under it nothing develops. As things are, so they remain till they fall and die and rot. So it has come to pass that many of the conquered people preserved mediæval and even quite primitive customs right up to the twentieth century. For many were not freed until 1877, many are still under Turkish rule, and all were completely cut off from the rest of the world.

The Turkish Conquest.

There are, of course, very many local customs, and costumes differ in detail from village to village. But into this we have not space to enter. We can only indicate the general customs, and will take the Slavophil peoples first. These are the Servians, the Bosniaks, the Herzegovinians, the Montenegrins, and a large number of the people of Old Servia and Macedonia. There are also the Dalmatians, many of whom are of very mixed blood. Except in Macedonia, where the language forms a link between Servian and Bulgar, and is considerably mixed with Albanian words, these people all speak Servian. The local differences are merely those of dialects, not more marked than the difference between Cockney and broad Yorkshire.

The Slavs.

The people have also great physical resemblances. There are two marked types, a fair and a dark type. Among the upper class of women in Servia and Montenegro the average of good looks is very high, but the peasant women are worked extremely hard, and age rapidly.

Among all these people there is a striking disparity between the height of the men and women.

Servia is by far the most advanced of the West Balkan peoples. Old customs are fast passing away. Modern methods of work and cultivation are spreading. And the nation desires to learn.

Photograph by M. Edith Durham.

SLAV PEASANT WOMEN, OCHRIDA, MACEDONIA.

In Bosnia and Herzegovina, on the contrary, the people cling closely to their old customs and adopt new ones with the greatest reluctance. For the new methods are introduced by the hated Austrians, who have "annexed" the territory, and are looked on askance as the ways of the foe.

In Montenegro, too, old customs have remained intact till quite recent days. By incessant fighting the Turks were kept at bay, and the Montenegrins in their

Photograph by M. Edith Durham.

SERVIAN PEASANT WOMAN, OBRENOVAC, NORTH SERVIA.

mountain fastnesses were quite isolated from the outer world, and lived on primitive tribal lines. The tribes were and are divided into large groups of cousins, called "Bratstvos." Each Bratstvo was made up of several large household communities, each with its head man and head woman, who directed all the work of the men and women of the household. A man can marry within his clan, but not within his Bratstvo.

Montenegrin Marriages.

All the South Slavs are exogamous, as are also the Albanians, and there are Bratstvos still existing that boast that they have never married into a drop of their own blood.

As it was desirable to obtain strong allies, and as all a woman's relations were classed as the blood relations of her husband's relations, it was customary for all marriages to be arranged by the men of the Bratstvo. Indeed, until modern days, it was a frequent occurrence for the bride and bridegroom never to have seen one another till they met in church. Infant marriages or betrothals were common, and children were sometimes betrothed before they were born.

The preliminaries, a matter of much ceremony, are concluded by the elders of the two Bratstvos and the parents of the young couple. The bridegroom's father hands the bride's father an apple with a golden ducat stuck in it. This is possibly symbolic of a previous custom of marriage by purchase.

The bride is busy for weeks preparing presents (garments and stockings gaily knitted in patterns) as gifts for her new relations. Then, on the appointed day, the bridegroom's relatives, a perfect army of men, all in full gala costume, go to fetch the bride. At the feast that then ensues at the bride's house a very elaborate etiquette is observed. Mistakes on such points have led not infrequently to violent quarrelling — for Balkan honour was, and is, sensitive—and bloodshed might result.

"'How did the wedding go off?' my mother asked my father," says Vuk Vrchevich in one of his books on local custom in the Bocche de Cattaro and Herzegovina. "'Oh, quite quietly,' says my father. 'Bah!' says mother. 'What a very effeminate wedding!'"

The feast being satisfactorily finished, the groomsmen then take the bride back with them. No woman, and no relation of her own, goes with her. It is most unlucky should she look back on leaving her father's house. Should she have to travel for more than one day, she has to pass the night between two of the bridegroom's brothers, or such other relatives as have been appointed to the post of "Djever." On arriving she is taken straight to the church and married. The bridegroom leaves her at the church and hurries home to be ready to receive her there. It is his parents' home, and he and the bride will probably share one room with his parents and two or three married brothers. The bride, on entering, is given a boy baby to hold, and a sword or knife is hidden under the rug which is laid at the entrance, in such a manner that she must step on it. This is to cause her to bear a male child. The groomsmen all accompany her to the house and more feasting takes place. Next morning she must rise early and fetch water from the well, enough for the whole party to wash in. As she pours the water for each groomsman he drops a coin into the basin for her. Until recent years, girls were married as young as thirteen or fourteen.

All the work, both domestic and agricultural, fell to the lot of the women. Men were occupied almost entirely in repelling, and making, frontier raids, and in guarding the flocks on the mountains. Custom in this respect changes very slowly, and all the heavy work of carrying wood and water and luggage is still performed by women. Nor will they often accept help from a man, for they consider that such work would degrade him.

Women sitting by the roadside, however tired, will scramble to their feet and stand respectfully when a man passes. Nor do the women in the up-country parts ever think of sitting down to table with the men. The women of the household eat up what is left after the men have finished.

Woman's Work and Position.

It was not etiquette for a man to speak to his wife before strangers. If he were obliged to do so, he spoke over his shoulder, with his back to her. Husband and wife, in many parts, never called one another by name, but addressed one another as "he" and "she," a custom that is not yet quite extinct.

In spite of the manner in which marriages were arranged, or because of it, as the old people will tell you, they were by no means loveless. There are many romantic tales. Women often displayed great valour in following their husbands to the front, taking water to the wounded and carrying ammunition. And there is many a grisly tale of a woman crawling at night across the Turkish frontier at great risk, to fetch the head of her slain husband from the pole on which

Photograph by M. Edith Durham.

BOSNIAN WOMEN BEING CHURCHED AT CHURCH DOOR, LAJNICA.

it was stuck as a trophy, in order to bury it with his body in his own land.

All tribal business was strictly masculine. No woman was supposed to give an opinion on any but domestic affairs, nor, indeed, to offer an opinion on anything at all unless she were asked.

It has frequently happened to me when asking a woman a question that the master of the house has roared at her, "Hold your tongue, woman! I will tell it." "Long hair, short wits, a woman's head," is a very favourite proverb.

As the existence of a tribe depended on the strength of its fighting men, it was naturally the ambition of everyone to have as many sons as possible, and the birth of a daughter was and is still regarded as a calamity. "You feed a boy for your own Bratstvo, and a girl for someone else's Bratstvo." "You can marry your son where you will; you must marry your daughter where you can," are popular sayings.

Childhood.

It is a woman's duty to provide the cradle for her daughter's first child, and to make the cradle cover. These cradle covers are woven of wool, and are so thick and heavy that they would seem more fitted to suffocate the child. All through the Balkan peninsula, so far as I have seen, the peasant women spread this thick and heavy cover completely over the cradle, and take great care that the child shall never have a breath of fresh air. When a woman has to go out to work she slings the heavy wooden cradle on her back and takes the child in it, still covered.

Servian women, when working in the fields, often hang their babies on the branches of trees, slung hammock-wise in a shawl or blanket.

Three days after childbirth a woman, in most of the country districts, is supposed to be fit to fetch and carry wood and water, as usual. She is not allowed to make bread until she has been churched. This takes place at the church door.

The Art of Weaving.

Until recent years, every family group throughout the South Slavonic peoples made practically everything at home. The wool was spun on a distaff with no wheel or other aid (*see* the photograph of a Herzegovinian woman of the neighbourhood of Mostar on p. 678). It was then woven on hand looms, and dyed with native dyes, many of them very stable and very beautiful.

Particularly in Servia, the art of weaving rugs and carpets has been carried to great perfection. Native traditional designs are used, many of them of high decorative quality. Bosnia also has a native carpet industry.

For ordinary garments the wool is woven undyed and taken to a fulling-mill and beaten into a hard felt by wooden hammers worked by water power. This felt, or thick flannel, still forms the chief wear of the peasants of the larger part of the Balkan peninsula. In the mountainous parts, cotton and linen were until recent times very scarce. In the plains where the mulberries flourish, silk is cultivated and woven.

Dress.

The garments, both men's and women's, are often very beautifully embroidered. Every district has its own patterns, and it is to be hoped they will be preserved, as they show great originality and decorative quality. The South Slavonic women excel in cross-stitch designs, and in North Bosnia men work in the fields in shirts that are most elaborately worked over the whole of the breast and sleeve in dark blue worsted.

Most wonderful of all are the shirts of the women in parts of Old Servia and Macedonia. The whole of the breast, sleeve end, and edge of the skirt are a mass of the finest stitchery in two tones of red or orange, or in dull red, dull blue and dull green. The work is extraordinarily minute and takes many months to execute. The patterns are all worked entirely from memory, and have names, such as the "frog," the "pear," and so forth.

The dress of most South Slavonic women consists of the long shirt, which is worn both by day and night (night-gowns are quite unknown to the peasant), an em-

Photograph by M. Edith Durham.

PEASANT WOMEN FROM HERZEGOVINA, THE SANDJAK OF NOVI BAZAR, AND BOSNIA ON PILGRIMAGE AT CAJNICA.

Photograph by M. Edith Durham.

HERZEGOVINIAN PEASANT WOMAN.
She carries a distaff in her hand.

broidered waistcoat, with or without sleeves, and a long sleeveless coat, the *koret* (*see* illustration on p. 679), which is open in front.

Many districts have characteristic aprons which are woven in bright colours, and a great variety of designs. They are of solid wool, and often very heavy.

In Bosnia and parts of Herzegovina, many women, both orthodox and Moslem, wear the large Turkish "bloomers," but with these they do not, as a rule, wear the *koret*.

In parts of Herzegovina the women wear trousers; when on the march, or working in the fields, they turn back the *koret* and apron, and at a distance are often not distinguishable from men.

The making of the *opanke*, or native sandals, is also woman's work. These are of raw hide, dried and rendered supple afterwards by oil. They are laced over the instep with leathern thongs, twisted gut, or often nowadays with string, and are extremely well suited to rough tracks and rocks.

Balkan Cookery.

Houses, of course, differ somewhat in type and structure, according to the district, for they are influenced by the local material. In the greater number of native houses throughout the Balkans the fire is lit in a square hole on the stone floor, often near the middle, and the smoke makes its way as best it can through the thatched roof. A large cauldron hangs by a chain from the rafters above, and in this most of the cooking is done.

To bake bread or meat, a large tile—roughly made of clay moulded by hand—is heated in the fire. A large iron cover is heated at the same time. The bread is laid on the tile, the cover placed over it, and hot wood ashes piled on top. Bread and meat are cooked excellently in this way. Nor are the stews and soups from the cauldron at all to be despised. Milk forms a very large part of the diet of all the people in the high pasture lands. Maize is greatly preferred to wheat by very many of the South Slavonic peasants. In many parts the corn is still ground by women with hand-mills.

Where there is a stream, water-mills with little turbine wheels are used. Some of these little mills are not much bigger than a large dog-kennel. They are, in fact, only a little cover built over the two millstones.

Agriculture.

Hoeing the fields is also woman's work, and in many parts is still mainly done by women. They also plough, but under the altered circumstances of life men are now taking more and more to agriculture, which is, in most Balkan lands, being scientifically developed, more especially in Servia.

In all parts where the winter is severe, and it is impossible to feed more sheep than will be required for breeding, there is a great making of dried meat in the autumn. Every household slaughters sheep and goats. The joints are hung up in the roof, and large wood fires are lighted on the floor. The family, if it possesses but one room, sleeps out of doors and gives up the house for four days or a week, until the winter supply of food is prepared. Cabbages are preserved from the frost by burying them in deep pits.

Woman's Privileges.

The Balkan woman, whether she be Servian, Bosniak, Montenegrin or Macedonian, has plenty to do. But it must not be supposed that she regards herself as a slave, or that she has no privileges. Women, for example, were exempt from blood vengeance, and in the parts where the vendetta still prevails it is considered very wrong to kill a woman. Thus it may happen that most of the marketing is done by women, as they

Photograph by M. Edith Durham.

A PEASANT WOMAN FROM THE NEIGHBOURHOOD OF TREBINJE.

can pass freely to the bazaar when the man of the family would run the risk of being waylaid and shot.

The Bratstvo arranged a woman's marriage, but in marrying her away did not

Photograph by M. Edith Durham.
ORTHODOX MONTENEGRIN PEASANT GIRLS.

give up responsibility for her. A woman's brother in Montenegro is considered by the country people as her nearest and dearest relative, and it is thought, therefore, more likely that her children will resemble her brother than her husband. When a woman's husband treated her cruelly she could flee for protection to her own family, and if the brethren considered her complaints justified they would refuse to give her up. In this case the husband came with his brethren and fought for her. It is said that in some of these battles as many as twenty or thirty were killed.

Women throughout the South Slavonic lands, though they are worked hard, are not without holidays and amusements. On the principal feast days large gatherings of peasants take place, when the women appear gorgeous in their best clothes, gay with embroidery, and glittering with coins and ornaments. Many of these dresses are immensely heavy and very hot, but this does not deter the sturdy Balkan maiden from dancing the national dance, the *kolo*. The dancers, men and women, form a long chain by holding each other's hands or belts, and serpentine and circle round with great energy, singing lustily the while. Each district has its own *kolo* song.

Dances and Songs.

Women also throughout the Balkan peninsula have songs with which they enliven their work: spinning songs, harvest songs, and so forth.

Women play an important part at funerals, as it falls to them to sing the death songs that celebrate the virtues of the deceased. The women who thus sing are called *Pokajnitza*. When —as is the case with the funeral of a celebrated man—there is a very large assembly, the wailing all takes place out of doors. The guests sit in a large circle. Two women of the tribe then walk quickly back and forth within the circle, chanting in a loud wailing voice. One corroborates the statements of the other, and they lament together. Many stock phrases are used, but many women are well known for their power of improvising, and their recitals are very dramatic. When two are exhausted two others take their place. Only married women perform this duty.

Mourning Customs.

Until recent years women cut off their hair in sign of mourning, and hung it on the grave of the deceased. In some districts they still tear their faces with their nails.

Customs similar to these prevail also in Old Servia and Macedonia.

Medicine is largely practised by wise women who possess herbal remedies in great variety. "Every disease has its herb," they say. They also employ many charms. The belief in the evil eye is still prevalent in many parts. Witches were formerly stoned to death by the whole community, but this terrible punishment has, I believe, been extinct for over a century.

Immorality was also sometimes punished in a similar manner.

It was usual to punish a wife's infidelity by cutting off her nose previous to divorcing her, and this practice is not yet quite extinct.

There are throughout Bosnia and the Herzegovina a number of Moslems. These must not be mistaken for Turks. They are Servian-speaking, and are the descendants of people who found it expedient to become Mohammedan after the Turkish invasion. For the most part they have preserved their national customs with but slight modifications. The women are veiled, but not universally so.

Slavonic Moslem Women.

At weddings the bridegroom's male relatives go to fetch the bride in the same manner as in the case of the Christians, but two women go with them to be her escort.

Moslem women in some ways have an easier life than the Christian. They do not have to do such severe labour. Except in the case of the very poor, they do not do heavy field work or carry burdens. This holds good throughout the Balkan Peninsula. Of work that is done at home they do a great deal, and especially excel at embroidery and weaving fine silk gauze.

It is rare for a Mohammedan Slav to have more than one wife. The Moslems in Bosnia who are not veiled are said to be descended from the heretical sect of Bogomils, who were persecuted by both the Roman Catholic and the Orthodox Churches, and turned Mohammedan in large numbers. The majority are not only veiled but heavily cloaked as well. The continual covering of the face when out of doors renders it very white, and these ladies, when in full dress, are therefore in the habit of rouging very freely. The Moslem women smoke tobacco. Among the Christian peasants this is considered a very low and degrading thing to do.

In type the Albanians are more slightly built than the Slavs. The typical Albanian nose is aquiline, and often very finely cut. Albanian peculiarities of type are spread far beyond the strip of coast land known as Albania, and are scattered throughout Macedonia and

Albania.

ALBANIAN WOMEN, PODGORICA.

Montenegro, and in other South Slavonic lands. The blood in many districts is extremely mixed.

In North Albania are pre-eminently preserved the primitive modes of life. The same tribal system prevails as in Montenegro. Many of the tribes are semi-independent, and are governed by the traditional tribe law.

The women do all the heavy work. The burdens which they can, and do, carry are enormous. They trudge for two days' march down from the mountains to Scutari, the capital, so loaded with faggots and hides that the woman herself is almost invisible, and then return again equally loaded with sacks of maize, tin pots, and other things that cannot be obtained in the mountains. The men, if they come at all, carry only their weapons. A man may often be seen riding, while his wife carries the luggage and the baby.

Albanian Weddings.

At weddings the bride is fetched in the same manner as with the Slavs. It is correct for the bride to weep and show great reluctance to leave her home. As most frequently she is going out to quite a strange house, it is probable that this reluctance

VEILED ALBANIAN MOSLEM WOMAN, DULCIGNO, MONTENEGRO.

is not always feigned. The bridegroom has to present the bride with a handsome dress for the marriage. I am told that among the northern tribes there are now fewer women than men, and that brides therefore demand, and obtain, very handsome presents.

In the south of Albania the girl is expected to bring a "dot." In one place I was told as much as a hundred pounds is expected, and that the richer families of the village subscribe to the marriage portions of the poorer.

The majority of Albanians are Moslem, but for the most part very lax. In many villages where the people call themselves Moslem, the women are all unveiled, and go about freely among the men.

Dress.

On the other hand, the Roman Catholic women of Scutari wear huge "bloomers," and are closely veiled. Over the veil they wear a great scarlet cloak with a flap to cover the head, and make a gorgeous spot of colour in the street. The veil is pinned over the nose. The woman withdraws the pin and lets the veil fall open as she goes into church. Otherwise she always goes closely veiled. The Catholic girls of Scutari are also kept in great seclusion.

The women of Scutari, both Catholic and Moslem, do a great deal of weaving in cotton and silk, and produce some beautiful textures.

The Moslem women of Scutari and the neighbourhood very often dye their hair a deep red. Both Christian and Moslem wear a great number of ornaments, strings of coins, quantities of necklaces, etc. Many of them sew cowries and coins to a plait of hair on either side of the face. Most of the children wear blue beads, or some amulet, to protect them from the evil eye.

When Moslem women are veiled they are often most effectually veiled—completely hidden, in fact, under a huge hooded cloak—as the accompanying illustration shows.

Position of Albanian Women.

In spite of the wild and primitive life of the mountain tribes, it is their proud boast that women can always travel among them in safety, and to kill a woman is accounted a great crime. Here again, therefore, women act as messengers, and can pass freely to market when their men are unable to do so.

I remember when visiting one of the semi-independent villages of Shpata, near Elbasan, we had to halt on the frontier and shout for permission to advance. A woman was sent to reconnoitre and to ask our business. She was told I had come from England, and wished to visit them. She retired, and we waited till she returned with permission for us to advance, on condition that all was peace, and that my two men

MORLACH WOMEN, ZARA, DALMATIA.

laid down their rifles. She then led us to the village, and we were nobly entertained. All the men who "owed blood" had in the meantime hidden themselves, but lurked in the bushes around, with their rifles ready in case we displayed hostilities. Men from such villages rarely visit the larger towns, but the necessary business is carried on by the women.

Photograph by Clive Holland.

SERVIAN WOMEN GOSSIPING AT A WELL.

Women are exempt from blood feuds and vendettas. Among the northern tribes, however, a woman can, if she please, rank as a man. She must take a vow of celibacy. She can then dress as a man, have her head shaved as a man, carry arms, and inherit property. When a man has several daughters and no son, he can allow one of his daughters to rank as a son. In case of the father's decease, she is then the head of the family, and has to make suitable marriages for her sisters. I am told these "men" women are not uncommon. I heard of one who served for many years in the Turkish army. They are not allowed to become women again and marry. Should one of them bear a child I am told that both woman and child are killed by the tribe, and the child's father too if he can be discovered. Such a woman can carry on the blood feuds of the family. In cases where all the men of the family have been killed, they have often been avenged by a woman.

"Men" Women.

The North Albanian is superstitious beyond belief. Witchcraft, magic, and divinations are all believed in. The life is as wild and rough as in the most primitive days. Nevertheless, even in quite out-of-the-way places, many of the houses are surprisingly clean. As for the South Albanians, I think their cottages are some of the cleanest I have seen anywhere. Even the highly polished, speckless Dutch houses can hardly beat those of South Albania. The "spring clean" is a real Easter purification. Every

Albanian Characteristics.

house is re-whitewashed, within and without. Gipsy women are for the most part the house-painters. All is scoured and cleaned to the highest pitch; and as the Albanians have not our dirty habit of coming into a carpeted room with boots on, their homewoven carpets are clean and gay. As a race the Albanians are strong and healthy. And the women, when not prematurely aged by toil, are often very handsome. The women of the south are not severely worked like the women of the north. The south is in every way more cultured and advanced. Were it not that the Turkish government prohibits schools in the Albanian language, and thereby greatly and intentionally impedes the advance of civilisation, the Albanian people would make rapid progress.

The tribal system does not exist in the south, and life is not so primitive as it is in the north. Koritza, one of the chief towns in South Albania, is the cleanest and best built town that I know on Turkish territory. Women are here playing an advanced part. An excellent girls' school exists under the protection of the American mission, and the teaching can, therefore, be carried out in Albanian. It is the only school of its kind. Thus the girls get instruction that is denied their brothers. This is a singular fact. Albania is the most neglected and oppressed of all the countries of Europe, but it is one that has great possibilities.

UNVEILED MOSLEM ALBANIAN PEASANT,
SHPATA, CENTRAL ALBANIA.

From "Red Russia," by permission of J. Foster Fraser.

GREETING A BRIDE AND BRIDEGROOM IN RUSSIA.

RUSSIA

By ANNETTE M. B. MEAKIN

Mighty Russia—Old Customs—Sanctity of Marriage—Russian Lace—"Little" Russia—Middle-class Russia—Women Doctors—Democratic Russia—Employments Open to Women—The Superiority of Russian Gentlewomen—Russian Convents—Emigration to Siberia

A RUSSIAN PEASANT WOMAN.

ENGLISH people find it hard to realise how vast is the extent of the Russian Empire.

Mighty Russia.

The Tsar's dominions stretch from the Arctic Ocean to within a hundred miles of British India, and from Poland to the Sea of Japan. Siberia is Russia's Canada, and Turkestan is Russia's India; but no sea separates them from their mother country.

For three centuries Russia lay under the cruel yoke of her Tartar conquerors, and when at last she became a free country she still retained many Tartar customs.

Old Customs.

Two hundred years ago the women of Russia lived in as much seclusion as if they had been Mohammedans. It was Peter the Great who first commanded them to lay aside their veils. Every house had its women's apartments quite separate from those of the men, and girls were prisoners until their marriage. In Russian villages there are still old women who act as professional matchmakers, and the peasant women still keep their heads covered out-of-doors, even in the warmest weather. But in the towns and in the vicinity of factories, modern ways have taken the place of old customs, and, discarding the neat handkerchief, girls now exhibit elaborate puffs and coils of hair stuck all over

AN OSTIAK WOMAN, SIBERIA.
DRAWN BY NORMAN H. HARDY.

Facing on page 686

with combs of imitation tortoise-shell. It is to the rural parts of Russia that we must look for the remnants of ancient Slav customs, and when we find them they are so mixed up with traces of Mohammedanism and with the ceremonies and laws introduced by the Greek Church that wide study is required before we can separate one from the other.

Sanctity of Marriage.

To the peasants of Great Russia marriage is a tie that death alone can dissolve, and divorce by the help of the law courts is practically unknown to them. If a husband and wife cannot get on together they simply agree between themselves to live apart, the husband taking the boys and the wife the girls in cases where there are children. The wife's dowry remains her own as long as she lives, and after her death it goes to the nearest female descendant. Money earned by the wife is her own, and she is free to do what she likes with it. When a widow is left without children she usually returns to her own people; she has the right to marry again as soon as her husband has been dead six months.

The Greek Church forbids cousins to marry until the fourth degree, and marriage with a deceased wife's sister is still unlawful. When small groups of peasants live far out in the country, separated as if by the sea from their nearest neighbours, this strictness of the marriage laws is beneficial, for, as in our own Hebrides, where the young people have so little choice, near marriages have to be carefully guarded against, or frequent cases of insanity result.

THE ABBESS OF EKATERINBURG.

One of the chief industries among the peasant women of Great Russia is lace-making. Girls begin to learn it at the age of seven, and at nine they can almost support themselves with their earnings.

Russian Lace.

Children may be seen working at cushions large enough to conceal them; but a good deal of lace is made by the needle. This is the lace *par excellence* of the aristocracy, while cushion lace is worn by all classes. Russia got her lace-making from Asia long before the industry was known to the rest of Europe. I saw very fine specimens in some of the provincial museums. In the Middle Ages pearls and lace were worn profusely by all classes of society; the pearls were usually stitched into the lace when it was made. The high head-dresses, still worn by the great ladies of Russia, and even by the Empress on State occasions, are mostly of lace covered with pearls. Chasubles and stoles of velvet, covered with pearl-stitched lace, are still presented to the monasteries by royal visitors. There are now only two districts where purely national lace is still made—in the governments of Riazan and Minsk. But a great deal of the so-called German lace is made in other parts of Great Russia, and there are in every centre a number of women who make a living as lace agents, and act as "middlemen" between the peasant workers and the large firms in Moscow and St. Petersburg.

RUSSIAN RED CROSS NURSE.

Some fifty years ago the women used to spin and weave most of the clothing worn by their families, but since factories have sprung up they find it cheaper to buy their material. The wives of artisans in Western Russia still do a good deal of embroidery on frames, and by its sale help to support their households.

"Little" Russia.

The women of Little Russia have many customs quite different from those of Great Russia, and, indeed, they might belong to a different nation. They wear much brighter colours, and clothes of quite a different cut. On important occasions they don velvet tunics without sleeves, embroidered at the neck and arm-holes. The young girls, who are often very handsome, wear the hair in a plait tied by long ribbons, and generally have several necklaces of glass beads or coral. A girl's wedding dress is got ready for her as soon as she is thought old enough to be married, and in the event of her early death it becomes her shroud. So great is the love of the Little Russians for bright colours that they decorate the walls of their rooms with red and white towels, sometimes in checks, sometimes in stripes. Even the *ikon* in the corner of the room is swathed in these bright-coloured towels.

If a woman of Little Russia is found leading an immoral life, her neighbours paint her door with tar to make her feel her disgrace. On the whole, women are more respected in this part of Russia than elsewhere; the Little Russians have a proverb to the effect that when the mistress is absent the house weeps.

Middle-class Russia.

A few years ago we used to hear that there was no middle class in Russia, but to-day there is a large and increasing middle class. It is to this section of society that the numerous Hebrew and German families belong, and those once wealthy Russian families who were ruined by the freeing of the serfs in 1861. It is from this class that the Russian girl students at foreign universities come.

Women Doctors.

Medicine is one of the most popular professions among Russian women, and we must not forget that, after Miss Blackwell, the first pioneer to take up that calling was a Russian, Miss Souslova. The Russian medical woman generally crops her hair short, and cares not a straw about her personal appearance. She is often the mother of a large family, and supports by her earnings a lazy husband. On one occasion when visiting a hospital I mistook the medical officer for a servant, on account of her neglected appearance. After an introduction had taken place I expressed my surprise to the gentleman at my side that the lady doctor did not even wear a collar.

"*Que voulez-vous?*" he replied. "Is it not better to have brought ten children into the world than to wear a collar?"

On another occasion, when I remarked to a lady doctor that I thought she would look better with long hair, she replied, "Very likely; but I could not wash it so easily."

Democratic Russia.

Russia, like America, is a democratic country at heart, and in spite of Peter the Great's attempts to introduce primogeniture, the nobility, as Miss Zebriakoff has pointed out, clung to the democratic custom of dividing the property equally among the sons; consequently widows and orphan daughters are not handed about as part of the property as is the case in our great houses.

Employments Open to Women.

The Russian women are taking up nearly all the callings formerly occupied only by men. Although they are not yet allowed to practise at the Bar, numbers are studying for that profession in the full assurance that they will, ere long, be allowed to follow it.

I found women as clerks in many of the largest banking houses of St. Petersburg and Moscow—in the customs houses, and in the post offices. They are said to be more reliable than the men, not because they are more honest, but because they are less daring. But the real reason why they get these posts is that they are satisfied with a lower salary.

The Superiority of Russian Gentlewomen.

The women of the upper classes in Russia are among the most thoroughly educated, the most intelligent, and the most charming women that it has ever been my lot to meet. Their knowledge of three, four, and five languages, and their wide reading in those languages, have broadened their sympathies and given them a wider outlook than is often the case with English and German women. They are quite womanly, but added to their womanliness there is a virility that gives a backbone to their character. They do not over-dress or put on "side" like so many of the Americans, but move and act with a quiet dignity, while their conversation exhibits not mere flashes of wit, but common-sense and intellectual and consecutive thought.

Russian women of the upper classes do not feel that their interests are separate from those of their men, nor do they think their sex inferior and imagine that submissive self-effacement is their highest ornament, yet no country in the world has given us more beautiful examples of wifely devotion and self-sacrifice than Russia. The story of those noble women who followed the Decabrists into exile has been immortalised by poets, and will ever remain fresh in the hearts of the Russian people.

Convents for women are to be found in every part of Russia. I have visited many

From "Red Russia," by permission of J. Foster Fraser.

A TYPICAL RUSSIAN FAMILY.

of them, and invariably found the nuns engaged in some kind of useful work. I have seen them embroidering military and naval uniforms with gold thread, lace-making, painting *ikons*, candle-making, embroidering linen, gardening, cooking, and so on. Many of the nuns are very good-looking, and they are generally happy and contented. The convent at Tver particularly attracted me. It consists of a number of pretty little detached villas built in a circle and enclosed by a high wall, with an imposing entrance. In the centre stands a church with a graveyard and a tall campanile. Each villa has its own garden, which is tended by the nuns in their spare time. There are four nuns in each villa, but each nun has her own sitting-room and bedroom, divided by a comfortable screen.

Russian Convents.

At Ekaterinburg, in the Ural Mountains, I visited a convent containing six hundred nuns, besides a hundred novices and fifty orphan girls who were destined to become nuns. The Lady Superior who received us was young, graceful, and dignified; there was a tranquillity and serenity about her movements and her speech which greatly attracted me, and I was much pleased when, on taking leave of me, she presented me with her photograph as a souvenir of my visit (*see* p. 687).

Emigration to Siberia.

Russia is making great efforts to colonise Siberia with Russian peasants, and every train on the Siberian railway carries numbers of emigrants. Land is given to the colonists, and they are free from taxes for the first three years. Both the men and the women improve greatly in their new home; they leave behind their Slav indolence and become industrious and thriving. Many of them soon make comfortable little fortunes, and are able to give their children a much better education than they themselves enjoyed. Much of the butter sold in London as "Danish" has really travelled all the way from Siberia, and was made by Russian peasant women.

A GROUP OF COLONISTS (MINUSINSK, SIBERIA).

Photograph by Clive Holland.

UPPER MIDDLE CLASS VIENNESE ON THE WAY TO CHURCH.

AUSTRIA

By AMY A. LOCKE

A Slavonic Empire—Slavonic Traditions—Position of Slavonic Women—Slav Marriage—Dress—Slav Morality—The Slav Gift of Song—The Hungarian Woman: A Contrast—Hungarian Marriage Customs—Hungarian Dress—Hungarian Characteristics—Roumanians—The Future of Woman in Austria

IN spite of the fact that Austria-Hungary, in its history as the battlefield between Teuton and Slav, has come to exist politically as a Germanic centre, and a Germanic force in Europe, it is in the main ethnographically, if not politically, an empire of the Slavonic races.

A Slavonic Empire.

The German element among the women of Austria can soon be dismissed, since the Austrian German, whether Saxon or Swabian, generally preserves her native characteristics. It is rather the women of the Slavonic races, together with the Magyars or Hungarians, and the Roumanians or Wallachians, who have most claim to be considered as the women of Austria.

The Slavonic type in its many variations exists over all the empire, but mainly in two sweeping groups north and south of Hungary. In the northern group are Czechs, Moravians, Slovaks, Poles, and Ruthenes, forming the main bulk of the population of Bohemia, Moravia, Galicia, Bukownia, and the northern part of Hungary. In the southern group are Slovenes, Croatians, Servians, and Bulgarians, who occupy Croatia, Dalmatia, and parts of Transylvania.

Varieties of custom, individual taste, and character, exist among the numerous subdivisions of the Slavonic race, but on the whole the main characteristics are the same.

Slavonic Traditions.

The Slavonic woman first appears in Bohemian history, as represented by early tradition, with all the beauty of character, and power, and wisdom, which an heroic age always ascribed to its women. The poem of "The Judgment of Libusa," retold in the eleventh century by the chronicler Cosmas, relates how a certain people scattered by the failure of the Tower of Babel, found their way into Germany, and finding a plain between the rivers Ogra (Eger), and Wlitawa (Moldan), settled there and called the plain Bohemia, after the eldest of their party, named Boemus. At first the settlement was peaceable and communistic, but the idea of private property having once been grasped a judge was necessary to settle disputes. Crocco, who was the chosen judge, had three daughters, the eldest of whom was skilled in medicine, the second was a religious teacher, instructing the people in the worship of the Oreads and Dryads, the third, Libusa, was full of political wisdom and foresight. On the death of Crocco, Libusa was chosen judge in his stead, but her position was a difficult one. Like the Israelites, the people of Bohemia wanted a military chief, and found the peaceable rule of a woman too sane and just for the carrying out of the ideas of private property with its motto that "might is right." They began to say that Bohemia should not submit any longer to women "who were fitter to receive the advances of wooers than to dictate laws to soldiers." Physical force was to be the determinant factor, and woman, whose true power rests on a very different basis, was gradually to be forced into the dependent and subordinate position which she holds to-day among the Slavonic races. For Libusa, although, like Samuel, she tried to warn her people of the dangers of a military monarchy, and set before them the proverb of the frogs and Jupiter, was forced to submit to the popular

Photograph by Clive Holland.

TYPES OF AUSTRIAN MARKET WOMEN.

demand, and take a husband who should be king.

"Let us sing and dance," says one of the popular songs of the women, "as long as we have no husbands, for as soon as we have one, we must forget our songs and only mend his shirts and trousers." Indeed, the fate of the woman in Slav-land is to work and suffer and obey in silence. Beautiful though she is in her youth, with her finely formed figure, regular features, and rich complexion, she quickly becomes old when she is married. It is she who has to carry the heaviest loads, and do the roughest work. She becomes the mere slave and drudge of her husband, and treats him as her lord and master, receiving his blows and rough words silently, eating out of his plate, standing behind him, waiting on him, and only drinking when he offers her something from his glass.

Position of Slavonic Women.

"Women," says a man-made Slav proverb, "have long hair and short judgments; they are like the grass, man is their head." So a man may sin as he likes against his wife, and, if he imagines he is not satisfied with her, being blessed by the gods with such a marvellous power of judgment, he may send her away; but if she is violent to him in any way he may punish her with death. The Slavs of southern Austria regard the birth of a girl as a punishment from heaven, and a Montenegrin, on whom such a calamity has fallen, if asked the sex of his child will answer apologetically and shamefacedly, "Pardon me, it is only a girl."

Needless to say, a daughter has no part in the paternal inheritance. The most she has is a dowry of a cow on her marriage, and the cow, of course, goes to the husband, who probably would not marry her without it.

Photograph by Clive Holland.

WOMEN OF CARINTHIA (SOUTHERN AUSTRIA).

Their aprons and head-dresses are very costly and valuable. The latter are of filigree silver work and satins. They are valued at from £40 to £50.

As for the marriage itself the whole ceremony is symbolic. The would-be bridegroom presents the girl with a bunch of flowers as she comes out from mass on Sunday, and if she accepts it he calls a few days afterwards at her home with a friend, has food and drink, makes sure that the girl is healthy, and a month afterwards the wedding takes place. Her trousseau consists of at least five white garments, two pairs of boots, if possible, a cloak, and seven or eight silk handkerchiefs to tie round her head and

Slav Marriage.

waist, some coloured ribbons, and a table-cloth for grand occasions. On the wedding-day the bridegroom comes to the house, with friends and musicians, to fetch his bride, who is supposed to come out of the house alone, and walk last in the train of the friends around the bridegroom. Even at the wedding feast she begins her submission and service, since it is her part to serve the guests. When a girl is married she is called *sneha*, when she has a child *gena*, when she is forty *baba* (*i.e.* grandmother) and when she is over fifty *starababa* (*i.e.* old decrepit one).

Photograph by Clive Holland.

HUNGARIAN WOMAN WITH EMBROIDERED APRON.

Among the doubtful privileges of being a married woman is the right to drink *raki*, the Slav peasants' absinthe. It is sold even before the doors of the churches, and as the women come and go from mass they toss off large glasses of it at a draught.

Dress.

In matters of dress the married woman also has her distinction. The dress of both married and single is eminently simple, consisting of one garment or chemise, supplemented sometimes in winter by a short sheepskin jacket called *Cabanitza*, coloured and decorated with pieces of pointed leather, stamped out into flowers and arabesques. The married woman alone may wear sleeves in her jacket, and there is a tale that a young unmarried Croatian girl, being advised to wear sleeves for her health's sake, refused in case she should incur scandal thereby. The head-dress is a silk handkerchief tied over the head, under which the young girl's hair flows loose or in plaits, whereas the married woman wears "horns," her hair being twisted up the day after the wedding, and rolled round little sticks called "horns," on which the handkerchief is supported. Both married and unmarried wear a silk handkerchief, the *Pojas*, of a bright colour, round the waist, and a second of vivid scarlet, knotted under the breasts like the *Strophion* of nymphs and goddesses. A pair of boots on festal occasions, a coral necklace, and a few little mirrors hung round the waist complete the normal best dress of the Slav woman. Boots are very precious; often the women carry them to church, put them on at the threshold of the church, and take them off on leaving it. When not in full dress they generally go barefooted or wear a kind of sandal called *opanka*.

Slav Morality.

The young Slav girl has a strong sense of morality, good character being held in great respect. A girl who has lost her good name is disgraced and called *Kuca*, and all the young people insult her publicly. If any proof of lightness of character is discovered in a bride on her wedding day, the wedding guests are plunged into sadness, and the father is forced to take back his daughter or pay an indemnity to the husband.

The Slav Gift of Song.

Uneducated and subdued though she is the Slav woman has one great gift, and that is the gift of song. "Wherever you find a Slav woman," says a native poet, "you will hear singing." She sings in the morning as she dresses, she sings at her work, she sings in the evening coming home from work in the fields, at feasts, at meetings, at dances,

A HUNGARIAN PEASANT GIRL
DRAWN BY NORMAN H. HARDY.

Facing on page 694

everywhere, improvising as she goes both words and music. It may be a glad song, it may be a sad song, it may be a love song, it may be a death song, but so long as there is a spark of youth left in her she sings.

The Hungarian Woman: A Contrast.

It is suggestive to turn from the Slav proverb, "That household is threatened with ruin in which the distaff rules, and the sword obeys," to the Magyar saying, "It is the chignon that must rule." For though both are exaggerated, and the truth lies between the two, the note of contrast is struck between the position of the Slav and the Hungarian woman. The Hungarian is the companion of her husband, not the servant or slave, and she retains in her married life much of her gaiety and youth.

Hungarian Marriage Customs.

Though it is said that love does not play much part in the marriage of the Hungarian peasants, and that the woman who does not possess two acres of land, and the man who does not possess a large cloak or *bunda* ornamented with heavy embroidery, will never marry, the marriages in the country especially seem in most cases to be very happy, and a distinctly high standard of morality is preserved.

The Hungarian peasant who would a-wooing go comes at night to the house of his beloved, and knocks at the door until the girl's mother says, "He has knocked so long, open the door to him." The girl obeys, and the young man then enters the kitchen wrapped in his long cloak, which envelops them both. The evening before the wedding the bridegroom comes in a carriage with his friends to inspect the trousseau of his future wife. This consists of a painted wooden chest, filled with household linen, clothing, and bedding. On the wedding-day the bride walks to the church accompanied by two of her friends already married, and six young girls in white carrying crowns. The bride's crown sparkles with spangles, and is ornamented in the middle with a little mirror, and the national colours, red, white and green.

At the wedding feast each guest dances with the bride, giving her a few kreutzers in exchange for a kiss, and a present in kind, a fowl, pigeon, or some fruit.

Hungarian Dress.

The Hungarian women of all classes are generally brunettes, with slender supple figures, and are strong, healthy and graceful, and noted for their physical beauty. Unlike the Slav women, who are content to wear one garment, the Hungarian peasant who wears less than three petticoats imagines herself half naked. The chief garment of the national costume is the *rekli*, or jacket embroidered with braid and silver buttons, and ornamented with flowers and lined with sheep skin with its soft warm wool. In summer the *rekli* is often packed away, and replaced by a chemisette, with short embroidered sleeves, which leaves the arms bare. The petticoats fastened over the *rekli*, or the chemisette, are puffed out into a thousand pleats, and reach nearly to the ankles. A black apron trimmed with lace, and a handkerchief of

Photograph by Clive Holland.

TYROLESE GIRL IN FESTIVAL DRESS.

Photograph by Clive Holland.

DALMATIAN GIRL AT THE FOUNTAIN.

some bright colour twisted round the neck, with well-fitting stockings and boots, complete the ordinary costume. The hair is usually divided into plaits fastened with red or green ribbons, and light silver chains. The unmarried girls go bareheaded even under the hottest sun and in the cold of winter. The married women always wear their hair carefully covered with a handkerchief, or among the richer classes with a sort of hood or cap, fixed at the back of the head.

Hungarian Characteristics.

The Hungarian women, especially among the aristocracy, are reputed to be gay, quick-witted, and light-hearted, fond of dancing and frivolity, ease and luxury, but they are good mothers, and through the dark ages of the history of their country they proved once and for all that they could lay all else aside, smile under suffering, and be sublime in their courage and self-denial. "My wife and my sword," exclaimed the soldier poet Alexander Petöfi, and added prophetically, "If my country has ever need of my arm, my wife herself would buckle on my sabre, and blessing us both would say, 'Go, be faithful each to the other!'" In the revolution of 1848 wives followed their husbands into battle, fighting by their sides, sisters fought by their brothers, girls by their lovers. When a town was besieged, the women mingled with the men in the ranks of the besieged, and "they were only to be distinguished from the men by their blind and impetuous courage."

The Gipsies.

One word of the Gipsies of Hungary, those lazy kings and queens of solitude whom the Hungarians alone welcomed when in the rest of Austria they were reckoned among "Turks and infidels." Free and wayward as the wind, the women of the gipsies keep their "splendid vices," and are untouched by the manners and customs of the Hungarians. Unspoilt by civilisation the women of the purely nomadic tribes feel no need for the shelter of clothes so long as they are in the country, and are content with the most scanty covering, even in the villages and towns. They are the fortune tellers, the jugglers, the dancing girls of the country, and whether nomads or settlers are full of the language which the Hungarians have caught from them, the language of music.

Hated by the Hungarians as a lower and despised race, the Roumanians of Transylvania threaten by their increasing birth rate to Roumanise Transylvania. They are an Italic race, dark-skinned, black-haired, black-eyed, indolent in temperament and thriftless, the poorer classes being generally forced by the extravagance of a moment to a monotony of severe frugality. Among the aristocracy the women are said to pass their time lounging on a sofa, dressing and adorning themselves, or driving in the public promenades. The peasant women are the chief workers on the fields, and are far more industrious than the men. They are commonly employed as navvies and road-menders, and often a gang of women can be seen working on excavations, etc., on equal terms with the men. Like the women of the Slav races they are beautiful in their youth, but are worn out before middle age comes by the overstrain of being both child-bearers and field-workers.

Roumanians.

A loosely fitting jacket, a skirt of the same colour or some bright material, and a kerchief folded over the head and tied under the chin, is the normal working costume. The Roumanian gala dress is often very handsome; not only are the dresses and decorations made by the women, but the cloth itself is spun by them.

The Future of Woman in Austria.

Whether Slav or Roumanian, German or Hungarian, the women of Austria have the same need to awaken to the meaning and dignity of their womanhood, not as greater or less than manhood, but as a thing equal though different; the same need to find a voice which shall free them from the oriental ideas still undermining men's and their own conception of themselves, and if that voice is to prevail it will utter a cry not of political rights, but of social, moral, and intellectual freedom.

Photograph by O. Kramer, Vienna.

THE MARKET PLACE, VIENNA.

GERMAN PEASANT GIRLS OF BADEN-BADEN.

These girls are "Sisters of the Red Rose," a society formed among the recipients of the bounty of Frau Huebsch, a wealthy widow, who sits in their midst. She provides marriage *dots* each year for seven peasant girls of good character who are unable to marry from lack of means.

GERMANY

By AMY A. LOCKE

German Types—Characteristics—How the German Peasant Woman Works—Absence of "Middle-Age"—Peasant Dress—Betrothal and Marriage Customs—Position of the German Woman

IT is necessarily difficult to generalise as to the women of Germany, since the connotation of the word "German" covers such varying types as Prussian, Saxon, Bavarian, and Rhinelander. But, properly speaking, Germany divides itself into two large groupings of Swabians and Saxons, or High and Low Germans. The Saxons, the fair-skinned, flaxen-haired Germans, occupy the plains of the north, which are here and there encroached on by mountain ranges such as the Harz. The Swabians, the swarthier dark-haired type, occupy the mountainous tracts of the south, mostly in Bavaria.

German Types.

For the most part the people living on either side of the Elbe are the fairest types; in farther Pomerania also flaxen hair predominates, though in the frontier lands west and east in the Rhine provinces and Silesia the dark types increase. The three frontier rivers, the Rhine, the Danube, and the Oder, mark the limits of the darker races.

In the mixed communities of the towns both dark and fair are met, but it is among the peasant women more particularly that the distinctive types are seen. The fairer type is generally square set, with the proverbial German hips, good, slow, lymphatic; the darker type is characteristically of slighter build, more energetic, and more temperamental.

Characteristics.

But whether Saxon or Swabian, there is no race of women more thrifty, more frugal, more hard-working, than the German peasants. However poor or hard-worked they may be, their own clothes are scrupulously clean and mended, their children's stockings are darned and their clothes patched, and their cottages are clean and tidy. Very early one morning I went to see a woman of a little village near Dresden—the mother of a large family—before she started to her work in the fields. I found her sitting mending an old skirt; one of the boys, already dressed in old but carefully patched clothes, his hair brushed, his face and hands and feet clean, was sitting near her rocking the perambulator in which the youngest child lay; the room was neat and dustless, and sheets of newspaper were spread over the spotless boards. Her husband and the other children were still asleep in the one other room they had. Everything would be ready for them when they appeared, but she would be gone to work. And she is only one of many. "We are not proud of our peasants," a German said to me one day. I can well believe they are not of the men, or of the way the men treat the women, but, loving thrift and frugality as every German does, I cannot well believe they are not proud of the women.

Then, beside their thrift and cleanliness in their homes and persons, the way the women work! The barefooted carrier women, old and young, bent under their heavy baskets, tramping in and out from the neighbouring towns or larger villages; the gangs of road-menders; the workers in the fields, threshing, ploughing, yoked with oxen, digging

How the German Peasant Woman Works.

TYPICAL GERMANS OF THE BAVARIAN TYROL.

potatoes or harvesting, are familiar sights throughout Germany. And another frequent sight is to see a girl or woman yoked with a dog to a cart of milkcans. Or again, to see a woman and a milch cow, both unfitted for the task, yoked together in the struggle to drag a heavy burden of milkcans uphill while a man, maybe, slouches by, busily lighting his suffocating pipe.

In former years women were still more terribly overworked in the fields than they are now; they used to begin at four in the morning, and work on until nine—seventeen hours of solid work. When the family at the manor house had a half-yearly wash the village women were called in to help, and were kept at the wash-tub from the midnight of one day to eight o'clock the next evening. In 1880 the working-day was shortened, and the normal hours now are from five in the morning to seven at night, with two hours for dinner and shorter pauses for breakfast and vespers.

Absence of "Middle-age."

It is little wonder, under the strain of heavy work indoors and out of doors, added generally to the bearing of children in quick succession, that the women grow old terribly soon. Indeed, it is remarkable how little "middle-age" one sees among the poorer peasants; they are either young unmarried girls or old women. Among the richer peasants, those who have their own farms and bit of forest, as well as a vineyard or hop garden, and possess a horse or horses to save the labour of the women and the cows, the women look less old and overworked, although even in these cases they work equally with their husbands in the fields, and are glad to get an extra day's work of washing, ironing, or charing.

Peasant Dress.

The ordinary working dress of a German peasant woman consists of a loose jacket and short skirt, often brightly coloured, and a coloured handkerchief tied picturesquely over the head and fastened under the chin. Generally speaking, the poorer women make little difference in their costume in winter and summer, except that sometimes in the summer they have cotton jackets, and sometimes short cotton skirts. They rarely wear shoes or stockings, except on festal occasions. The picturesque costumes of the richer peasants, donned only on Sundays, were originally worn universally, and, as in Holland, one could tell what village a peasant came from by some distinctive feature of the costume he or she wore. But the custom is gradually dying out, and modernity is creeping into the Sunday dress of the German Bauer and his wife, who were formerly content to put on their picturesque mediæval costume and march solemnly to church and give thanks that they were not as other men. It is certainly a pity, for Germans generally, whether middle-class or peasant, do not seem to be fortunate in their choice of modern clothes.

Betrothal and Marriage Customs.

Among all classes in Germany the betrothal ceremony is of great importance, and among the upper classes the event is announced on silver-printed notices, sent round to friends and acquaintances. Between the betrothal and the wedding the bride and bridegroom—for they are bride and bridegroom in Germany as soon as they are betrothed—are royally entertained among their friends if they both happen to be living in the same place. If, however, the bridegroom lives far away the bride is invited to no parties, and is expected to join in no dances, but to live quietly and in retirement until he comes again. A few days before the wedding the young friends of the bride and bridegroom portray in scenes and dialogues, composed for the occasion, all the events they know of the past lives of the two, before a large gathering of friends and relatives. Laurel leaves and bouquets are brought in abundance to the bride, and in some districts bunches of flowers are brought by her friends and relatives on the day the *Aussteuer* is hung on the line for good luck's sake. The bridal wreath of myrtle is woven by two or three of the bride's best girl friends. The bride herself gives a bride "chocolate" or "bean coffee" to all her girl friends. At this function the cake of honour has a bean in it, and the girl who gets the bean in her slice is supposed to be destined for a *Braut* herself before the year is out.

For the civil marriage the bride was in former days attired in a black silk dress, and she still wears a dark, plain costume. In the religious ceremony the bride wears the conventional white silk or satin, and white veil, with a wreath of myrtle. The wedding guests wear evening dress, and no hats.

A familiar sight among the peasantry is to see the *brautwagen*, an open cart, in which the bride herself often sits among her furniture and wedding presents, going to the new home.

The *Hochzeitsmahl*, the feast and dance after the wedding, is a great institution among the peasantry. Dancing is in fact a great feature of their every gathering. Singing is also one of their forms of enjoyment, especially among the young girls of the richer peasantry, who often ramble about the fields and hills arm in arm, singing part-songs that they have learnt at the village school. The poorer peasants are too often silent.

A TYPICAL GERMAN LADY.

According to Tacitus the Germans esteemed something sacred and prophetic in woman, followed her counsels, and exalted her as a goddess. But the stern evidence of the early laws shows another side. Woman was treated as a household slave, bought and sold, and let and lent. Her life was given her, as it has been said, "by the capricious generosity of her father, and when her husband died she was expected to burn herself on his body as of no more use in the world." And this, with the semi-refined moderations that necessarily came with later civilisation, has been the typical attitude of the Germans to woman. She has been the wise angel and goddess of the poem, the submissive *hausfrau* of real life. "German marriage," cried Heine, "is no true marriage. The husband still goes on living his intellectually isolated life even in the midst of his family." In the higher and middle classes, of which Heine was then speaking, this is changing with the awakening of the women of the twentieth century, and the growth of their moral and intellectual independence. Yet even so it is rare in Germany to find a man who has not some sneaking, if not open, sympathy, with the attitude expressed in Herr Riehl's *Die Familie* in 1854. The family, he says, is all-important, the individual, if a woman, is of no importance at all. As long as a woman is working for the family all well and good, but she must not enter any profession which would make her independent of the family. Even Goethe, in spite of his spiritual insight, and in spite of ten years of intellectual companionship with Frau von Stein, has the typical German ideal for woman, that of service, self-sacrifice, and submission. "Let woman learn betimes to serve," he says, "for by service only shall she attain to the command and authority *in the house* that is her due."

Position of the German Woman.

As for woman's education, Herr Riehl would concede her the right to such provided it be "womanly." What he meant by "womanly" only men who think like him, and perhaps our grandmothers, know, but for the women of this century its true meaning is a broad and liberal education that will give an insight into and knowledge of life, practical as well as theoretical, and fit them above all for the responsibility of being the mothers of a future generation. Some of the women who are working for the cause of freedom in Germany at the present day are inclined in their over-enthusiasm to lose the historic sense, simply because their education has not carried them far enough. They are, as it has been well put by a modern writer, "drunk with a freedom which they claim in a country where women are not allowed to attend a political meeting except with the consent of the police," and have not the knowledge or training to see themselves historically, and their part in the perspective of the past and the future. They see all the failures and errors of civilisation as the result of the enforced ignorance and helplessness of women, and imagine that all will be swept away with the coming of the golden age of the supremacy of women. It is this unhistorically conceived fallacy that is a real danger to the woman's movement in modern Germany, splendid and hopeful though it be.

Turning again from the women of the higher and middle classes—the women for the most part of the towns and intellectual centres—to the peasant women of Germany, one finds that they carry out both in letter and spirit the ideal of Herr Riehl, and those who think like him. The sight of a peasant woman yoked to a plough does not sicken them—she is doing her duty to her family and husband. It does not matter that she is her husband's slave indoors, and his beast of burden out of doors, that she is old before her time, or that she patiently suffers—it is her duty to sacrifice herself body and soul to the family. She is her husband's equal in

Photograph by Dr. Kotzsch.

SAXON PEASANT GIRL IN WORK-DAY COSTUME.

nothing except in the amount of work she does, and he probably married her not for herself, her beauty or character, but for the hard cash she possessed and the work she could do. And as yet these women are practically untouched by the thought of freedom. Sooner or later the movement must work downwards and reach them, but for the present they submit unquestioningly. I have heard them praised for their faithfulness and patience, long-suffering, and unselfishness, and though these are attributes of which all of us would be glad to be possessors, one realises sometimes how undesirable and illogical virtues become when carried too far. A case in point recently came before me. A Saxon peasant woman of the poorer class (her photograph in her best dress is on this page) came to a friend of mine in great trouble, saying she felt like hanging herself. Her husband for the last three or four years had been suffering from a *maladie imaginaire*, and kept his bed. She worked in the fields and supported the whole family of five or six children. In spite of his supposed illness he had strength enough to beat her. Now he was getting more violent, and the children were getting more and more depressed with living in such surroundings, and she was utterly worn out. My friend did all that was possible to get the husband into a home. The only one where he could be taken was some distance from the village where they lived. Immediately the woman said : "Oh, that is too far away, he couldn't come home if he wanted to. He shall not go there." So the case was left. She goes on slaving for him and being cruelly treated by him ; the children's lives are being ruined. Such is her faithfulness and her fatuous idea of her duty !

Side by side with the women of unconquerable energy who are fighting for the cause of freedom in Germany are those who cling to the old conventions and the old ideals, and these peasant women belong to the latter class. The new will prevail, not to-day perhaps, and not to-morrow, but in a sure near future.

SAXON PEASANT GIRLS IN FESTIVE COSTUME.

HOLLAND

By N. PEACOCK

Position of Dutch Women—Women as their Country's Defenders—Racial Variations—Characteristics of Dutch Women—Quaint Head-dresses—Home Life—Employments for Women—The Servant Question—Domestic Ceremonies—The Significance of the Pipe—A Haarlem Custom—Home Industries—Girl Life

In Holland, more than any other country, women have found their Earthly Paradise. There woman's influence and activity meet with full appreciation and she reigns paramount over all matters which fall within her sphere. "The Daughter of the Sea," as their country is so appropriately named, may well be proud of these her children. Unlike the spoilt and selfish yet brilliant American, without the charm and the attractive dependence of the Spaniard or Italian, not a managing partner in the family household in the same way as the Frenchwoman, nor a comrade to her men-folk like the Russian, the Dutchwoman is a citizen with the welfare of her country at heart, her husband's trusted helpmate, and her children's best friend. Critics may say that the modern Dutchman has lost the ambition necessary to progress because he is too fond of his home. It is true, indeed, that club-life has not developed to any great extent, and that the great national sport—skating—is one in which men or women indifferently may hope to excel; it is a pastime which both can enjoy in common, but men there, as everywhere else in the civilised world, find plenty of interests outside the four walls of their home, interests that tend to separate the sexes without being allowed to encroach at all seriously upon domestic unity.

Position of Dutch Women.

ZEELAND FARMER'S DAUGHTER.

Women as their Country's Defenders.

In olden days, in face of the perpetual menace to personal safety and property of flood and fire, the men were brave and enterprising enough in all conscience, and the women were strong. Kenau Hasselaer, the heroine of Haarlem, who, with three hundred women, helped to hold its walls against the Spaniards during one of the finest and fiercest struggles for freedom from foreign domination ever witnessed, must always be remembered whenever woman's courage or patriotism is under discussion. Yet it must be said that in spite of their critics the Dutch are not so easy-going as they seem;

A DUTCH GIRL.
DRAWN BY NORMAN H. HARDY.

Facing on page 704

are an Italic race, dark-skinned, black-haired, black-eyed, indolent in temperament and thriftless, the poorer classes being generally forced by the extravagance of a moment to a monotony of severe frugality. Among the aristocracy the women are said to pass their time lounging on a sofa, dressing and adorning themselves, or driving in the public promenades. The peasant women are the chief workers on the fields, and are far more industrious than the men. They are commonly employed as navvies and road-menders, and often a gang of women can be seen working on excavations, etc., on equal terms with the men. Like the women of the Slav races they are beautiful in their youth, but are worn out before middle age comes by the overstrain of being both child-bearers and field-workers.

Roumanians.

A loosely fitting jacket, a skirt of the same colour or some bright material, and a kerchief folded over the head and tied under the chin, is the normal working costume. The Roumanian gala dress is often very handsome; not only are the dresses and decorations made by the women, but the cloth itself is spun by them.

Whether Slav or Roumanian, German or Hungarian, the women of Austria have the same need to awaken to the meaning and dignity of their womanhood, not as greater or less than manhood, but as a thing equal though different; the same need to find a voice which shall free them from the oriental ideas still undermining men's and their own conception of themselves, and if that voice is to prevail it will utter a cry not of political rights, but of social, moral, and intellectual freedom.

The Future of Woman in Austria.

Photograph by O. Kramer, Vienna.

THE MARKET PLACE, VIENNA.

GERMAN PEASANT GIRLS OF BADEN-BADEN.

These girls are "Sisters of the Red Rose," a society formed among the recipients of the bounty of Frau Huebsch, a wealthy widow, who sits in their midst. She provides marriage *dots* each year for seven peasant girls of good character who are unable to marry from lack of means.

GERMANY

By AMY A. LOCKE

German Types—Characteristics—How the German Peasant Woman Works—Absence of "Middle-Age"—Peasant Dress—Betrothal and Marriage Customs—Position of the German Woman

German Types.

IT is necessarily difficult to generalise as to the women of Germany, since the connotation of the word "German" covers such varying types as Prussian, Saxon, Bavarian, and Rhinelander. But, properly speaking, Germany divides itself into two large groupings of Swabians and Saxons, or High and Low Germans. The Saxons, the fair-skinned, flaxen-haired Germans, occupy the plains of the north, which are here and there encroached on by mountain ranges such as the Harz. The Swabians, the swarthier dark-haired type, occupy the mountainous tracts of the south, mostly in Bavaria.

For the most part the people living on either side of the Elbe are the fairest types; in farther Pomerania also flaxen hair predominates, though in the frontier lands west and east in the Rhine provinces and Silesia the dark types increase. The three frontier rivers, the Rhine, the Danube, and the Oder, mark the limits of the darker races.

In the mixed communities of the towns both dark and fair are met, but it is among the peasant women more particularly that the distinctive types are seen. The fairer type is generally square set, with the proverbial German hips, good, slow, lymphatic; the darker type is characteristically of slighter build, more energetic, and more temperamental.

Characteristics.

But whether Saxon or Swabian, there is no race of women more thrifty, more frugal, more hard-working, than the German peasants. However poor or hard-worked they may be, their own clothes are scrupulously clean and mended, their children's stockings are darned and their clothes patched, and their cottages are clean and tidy. Very early one morning I went to see a woman of a little village near Dresden—the mother of a large family—before she started to her work in the fields. I found her sitting mending an old skirt; one of the boys, already dressed in old but carefully patched clothes, his hair brushed, his face and hands and feet clean, was sitting near her rocking the perambulator in which the youngest child lay; the room was neat and dustless, and sheets of newspaper were spread over the spotless boards. Her husband and the other children were still asleep in the one other room they had. Everything would be ready for them when they appeared, but she would be gone to work. And she is only one of many. "We are not proud of our peasants," a German said to me one day. I can well believe they are not of the men, or of the way the men treat the women, but, loving thrift and frugality as every German does, I cannot well believe they are not proud of the women.

Then, beside their thrift and cleanliness in their homes and persons, the way the women work! The barefooted carrier women, old and young, bent under their heavy baskets, tramping in and out from the neighbouring towns or larger villages; the gangs of road-menders; the workers in the fields, threshing, ploughing, yoked with oxen, digging

How the German Peasant Woman Works.

TYPICAL GERMANS OF THE BAVARIAN TYROL.

potatoes or harvesting, are familiar sights throughout Germany. And another frequent sight is to see a girl or woman yoked with a dog to a cart of milkcans. Or again, to see a woman and a milch cow, both unfitted for the task, yoked together in the struggle to drag a heavy burden of milkcans uphill while a man, maybe, slouches by, busily lighting his suffocating pipe.

In former years women were still more terribly overworked in the fields than they are now; they used to begin at four in the morning, and work on until nine—seventeen hours of solid work. When the family at the manor house had a half-yearly wash the village women were called in to help, and were kept at the wash-tub from the midnight of one day to eight o'clock the next evening. In 1880 the working-day was shortened, and the normal hours now are from five in the morning to seven at night, with two hours for dinner and shorter pauses for breakfast and vespers.

Absence of "Middle-age."

It is little wonder, under the strain of heavy work indoors and out of doors, added generally to the bearing of children in quick succession, that the women grow old terribly soon. Indeed, it is remarkable how little "middle-age" one sees among the poorer peasants; they are either young unmarried girls or old women. Among the richer peasants, those who have their own farms and bit of forest, as well as a vineyard or hop garden, and possess a horse or horses to save the labour of the women and the cows, the women look less old and overworked, although even in these cases they work equally with their husbands in the fields, and are glad to get an extra day's work of washing, ironing, or charing.

Peasant Dress.

The ordinary working dress of a German peasant woman consists of a loose jacket and short skirt, often brightly coloured, and a coloured handkerchief tied picturesquely over the head and fastened under the chin. Generally speaking, the poorer women make little difference in their costume in winter and summer, except that sometimes in the summer they have cotton jackets, and sometimes short cotton skirts. They rarely wear shoes or stockings, except on festal occasions. The picturesque costumes of the richer peasants, donned only on Sundays, were originally worn universally, and, as in Holland, one could tell what village a peasant came from by some distinctive feature of the costume he or she wore. But the custom is gradually dying out, and modernity is creeping into the Sunday dress of the German Bauer and his wife, who were formerly content to put on their picturesque mediæval costume and march solemnly to church and give thanks that they were not as other men. It is certainly a pity, for Germans generally, whether middle-class or peasant, do not seem to be fortunate in their choice of modern clothes.

Betrothal and Marriage Customs.

Among all classes in Germany the betrothal ceremony is of great importance, and among the upper classes the event is announced on silver-printed notices, sent round to friends and acquaintances. Between the betrothal and the wedding the bride and bridegroom—for they are bride and bridegroom in Germany as soon as they are betrothed—are royally entertained among their friends if they both happen to be living in the same place. If, however, the bridegroom lives far away the bride is invited to no parties, and is expected to join in no dances, but to live quietly and in retirement until he comes again. A few days before the wedding the young friends of the bride and bridegroom portray in scenes and dialogues, composed for the occasion, all the events they know of the past lives of the two, before a large gathering of friends and relatives. Laurel leaves and bouquets are brought in abundance to the bride, and in some districts bunches of flowers are brought by her friends and relatives on the day the *Aussteuer* is hung on the line for good luck's sake. The bridal wreath of myrtle is woven by two or three of the bride's best girl friends. The bride herself gives a bride "chocolate" or "bean coffee" to all her girl friends. At this function the cake of honour has a bean in it, and the girl who gets the bean in her slice is supposed to be destined for a *Braut* herself before the year is out.

For the civil marriage the bride was in former days attired in a black silk dress, and she still wears a dark, plain costume. In the religious ceremony the bride wears the conventional white silk or satin, and white veil, with a wreath of myrtle. The wedding guests wear evening dress, and no hats.

A familiar sight among the peasantry is to see the *brautwagen*, an open cart, in which the bride herself often sits among her furniture and wedding presents, going to the new home.

The *Hochzeitsmahl*, the feast and dance after the wedding, is a great institution among the peasantry. Dancing is in fact a great feature of their every gathering. Singing is also one of their forms of enjoyment, especially among the young girls of the richer peasantry, who often ramble about the fields and hills arm in arm, singing part-songs that they have learnt at the village school. The poorer peasants are too often silent.

A TYPICAL GERMAN LADY.

According to Tacitus the Germans esteemed something sacred and prophetic in woman, followed her counsels, and exalted her as a goddess. But the stern evidence of the early laws shows another side. Woman was treated as a household slave, bought and sold, and let and lent. Her life was given her, as it has been said, "by the capricious generosity of her father, and when her husband died she was expected to burn herself on his body as of no more use in the world." And this, with the semi-refined moderations that necessarily came with later civilisation, has been the typical attitude of the Germans to woman. She has been the wise angel and goddess of the poem, the submissive *hausfrau* of real life. "German marriage," cried Heine, "is no true marriage. The husband still goes on living his intellectually isolated life even in the midst of his family." In the higher and middle classes, of which Heine was then speaking, this is changing with the awakening of the women of the twentieth century, and the growth of their moral and intellectual independence. Yet even so it is rare in Germany to find a man who has not some sneaking, if not open, sympathy, with the attitude expressed in Herr Riehl's *Die Familie* in 1854. The family, he says, is all-important, the individual, if a woman, is of no importance at all. As long as a woman is working for the family all well and good, but she must not enter any profession which would make her independent of the family. Even Goethe, in spite of his spiritual insight, and in spite of ten years of intellectual companionship with Frau von Stein, has the typical German ideal for woman, that of service, self-sacrifice, and submission. "Let woman learn betimes to serve," he says, "for by service only shall she attain to the command and authority *in the house* that is her due."

Position of the German Woman.

As for woman's education, Herr Riehl would concede her the right to such provided it be "womanly." What he meant by "womanly" only men who think like him, and perhaps our grandmothers, know, but for the women of this century its true meaning is a broad and liberal education that will give an insight into and knowledge of life, practical as well as theoretical, and fit them above all for the responsibility of being the mothers of a future generation. Some of the women who are working for the cause of freedom in Germany at the present day are inclined in their over-enthusiasm to lose the historic sense, simply because their education has not carried them far enough. They are, as it has been well put by a modern writer, "drunk with a freedom which they claim in a country where women are not allowed to attend a political meeting except with the consent of the police," and have not the knowledge or training to see themselves historically, and their part in the perspective of the past and the future. They see all the failures and errors of civilisation as the result of the enforced ignorance and helplessness of women, and imagine that all will be swept away with the coming of the golden age of the supremacy of women. It is this unhistorically conceived fallacy that is a real danger to the woman's movement in modern Germany, splendid and hopeful though it be.

Photograph by Dr. Kotzsch.

SAXON PEASANT GIRL IN WORK-DAY COSTUME.

Turning again from the women of the higher and middle classes—the women for the most part of the towns and intellectual centres—to the peasant women of Germany, one finds that they carry out both in letter and spirit the ideal of Herr Riehl, and those who think like him. The sight of a peasant woman yoked to a plough does not sicken them—she is doing her duty to her family and husband. It does not matter that she is her husband's slave indoors, and his beast of burden out of doors, that she is old before her time, or that she patiently suffers—it is her duty to sacrifice herself body and soul to the family. She is her husband's equal in nothing except in the amount of work she does, and he probably married her not for herself, her beauty or character, but for the hard cash she possessed and the work she could do. And as yet these women are practically untouched by the thought of freedom. Sooner or later the movement must work downwards and reach them, but for the present they submit unquestioningly. I have heard them praised for their faithfulness and patience, long-suffering, and unselfishness, and though these are attributes of which all of us would be glad to be possessors, one realises sometimes how undesirable and illogical virtues become when carried too far. A case in point recently came before me. A Saxon peasant woman of the poorer class (her photograph in her best dress is on this page) came to a friend of mine in great trouble, saying she felt like hanging herself. Her husband for the last three or four years had been suffering from a *maladie imaginaire*, and kept his bed. She worked in the fields and supported the whole family of five or six children. In spite of his supposed illness he had strength enough to beat her. Now he was getting more violent, and the children were getting more and more depressed with living in such surroundings, and she was utterly worn out. My friend did all that was possible to get the husband into a home. The only one where he could be taken was some distance from the village where they lived. Immediately the woman said: "Oh, that is too far away, he couldn't come home if he wanted to. He shall not go there." So the case was left. She goes on slaving for him and being cruelly treated by him; the children's lives are being ruined. Such is her faithfulness and her fatuous idea of her duty!

Side by side with the women of unconquerable energy who are fighting for the cause of freedom in Germany are those who cling to the old conventions and the old ideals, and these peasant women belong to the latter class. The new will prevail, not to-day perhaps, and not to-morrow, but in a sure near future.

SAXON PEASANT GIRLS IN FESTIVE COSTUME.

HOLLAND

By N. PEACOCK

Position of Dutch Women—Women as their Country's Defenders—Racial Variations—Characteristics of Dutch Women—Quaint Head-dresses—Home Life—Employments for Women—The Servant Question—Domestic Ceremonies—The Significance of the Pipe—A Haarlem Custom—Home Industries—Girl Life

Position of Dutch Women.

In Holland, more than any other country, women have found their Earthly Paradise. There woman's influence and activity meet with full appreciation and she reigns paramount over all matters which fall within her sphere. "The Daughter of the Sea," as their country is so appropriately named, may well be proud of these her children. Unlike the spoilt and selfish yet brilliant American, without the charm and the attractive dependence of the Spaniard or Italian, not a managing partner in the family household in the same way as the Frenchwoman, nor a comrade to her men-folk like the Russian, the Dutchwoman is a citizen with the welfare of her country at heart, her husband's trusted helpmate, and her children's best friend. Critics may say that the modern Dutchman has lost the ambition necessary to progress because he is too fond of his home. It is true, indeed, that club-life has not developed to any great extent, and that the great national sport—skating—is one in which men or women indifferently may hope to excel; it is a pastime which both can enjoy in common, but men there, as everywhere else in the civilised world, find plenty of interests outside the four walls of their home, interests that tend to separate the sexes without being allowed to encroach at all seriously upon domestic unity.

ZEELAND FARMER'S DAUGHTER.

Women as their Country's Defenders.

In olden days, in face of the perpetual menace to personal safety and property of flood and fire, the men were brave and enterprising enough in all conscience, and the women were strong. Kenau Hasselaer, the heroine of Haarlem, who, with three hundred women, helped to hold its walls against the Spaniards during one of the finest and fiercest struggles for freedom from foreign domination ever witnessed, must always be remembered whenever woman's courage or patriotism is under discussion. Yet it must be said that in spite of their critics the Dutch are not so easy-going as they seem;

A DUTCH GIRL.
DRAWN BY NORMAN H. HARDY.

Facing on page 704

men and women still regard religion as the important factor in their daily life, and any encroachment upon their liberties, whether civil or religious, is immediately resented. A visit to the dykes, the

WEST FRISIAN WOMAN.

only protection of Holland from complete destruction, affords a glimpse of the stern side of Dutch life. Free, as we are, from the constant menace of the sea, nothing can help us to realise the horror and anguish of the people when the cry "Come out! Come out!" goes up from the watchers on the dykes. Man, woman, or child, all who hear must instantly obey the summons to lend a hand at the pumps, for the call means that the sea threatens to overwhelm the land. The fisher-folk maintain that when the waters rise the sirens of the North Sea may be heard singing:—

"Beware, Beware! Ye doomed on land,
Above the watch-towers the water shall stand!"

At the same time they never fail to do their utmost to prove the sirens' prophecy false. Women owning land in the coast and polder districts are admitted to vote by proxy for the *water-schappen* (water-districts boards), whose members are responsible for the maintenance of the dykes and pumps in a state of efficiency.

Racial Variations. The eleven provinces which compose the Netherlands vary very considerably in scenery, race, dialect, and religion, and naturally great differences are to be noticed in the features and character of the people. The difference between the Southern and the Northern Provinces is most marked, and depends on the geographical situation of the former. Lying round the mouth of the Rhine, the great waterway which connects Central Europe with the ocean, alien races very early in their history settled among them alternately as conquerors and guests, attracted by the wealth of commerce, while the freedom-loving races of the North, devoted to fishing and agriculture, were preserved from contamination by their comparative poverty and isolation. The Frisian differs from the Zeelander, and both differ from the Hollander. More especially does this difference show in their women-folk. The tall, graceful, fair-haired, blue-eyed Frisian girl in no way resembles the laughter-

WOMAN OF SOUTH HOLLAND.

loving brunette of North Brabant; the vivacious, *petite* Amsterdammer who has the blood of the French Huguenot in her veins is with difficulty recognised as a fellow-countrywoman of the stolid, flaxen-haired, pink-cheeked, dumpy Hollander. It was of the latter that the stranger who made the following polite remark must have been thinking—"The Dutchman has no legs, his wife no waist, and his daughter no ankles." In Zeeland, velvety brown eyes and clear, dark complexions testify to the long Spanish occupation.

Characteristics of Dutch Women.

Throughout the land, however, we find the same simplicity of manner, the same love of the *gezellig* (cosy, sociable) home; the wife a thrifty housekeeper and a devoted companion, trim and tidy in her person, zealously —even hypercritically—clean in her surroundings. The weekly washing of the outside of the houses with a big brass squirt amazes the tourist, more especially when he sees the servant carrying on the operation in a heavy rain-shower, and holding an umbrella in one hand to keep herself dry. Every self-respecting matron carries a key-basket. Her store of provisions is always kept under lock and key, and it is the first of her morning duties to hand over to the servants the exact quantity of everything required for the daily needs of the household. We are not to think of her as mean or sparing; there is no lack of good cheer in the home, but waste is an abomination to every Dutchwoman, and her "man's" hard-earned pence must be looked after. An imposing linen-press, with piles of snowy linen, exactly folded and placed with mathematical precision on the deep oak shelves, is a valued and highly necessary possession in the home, for it is the custom to have the family washing done once a month, or it may be once in three months. In spite of her domestic capability the Dutchwoman must not be considered a mere household drudge; she is, like the Frenchwoman, a very important person in her home, and, unlike the average Frenchwoman, she invariably takes an active part in some branch of public work. She visits or nurses the sick poor, inspects and controls the Cottage Hospitals, free Schools of Needlework, etc., and is an energetic worker in one of the many philanthropic institutions which are admitted models of practical administration and efficient help. As a rule a Dutchwoman does not take any part in a discussion on politics in a mixed gathering, however strong may be her opinions, though there are indications that this custom will soon have become quite old-fashioned. The recent movement in favour of woman suffrage is well supported, but the demand is confined to the vote for unmarried women.

Quaint Head-dresses.

The helmets of Friesland, the imposing caps of Brabant, the gay kerchiefs, and voluminous petticoats of the Islanders of South Holland are known all over Europe. The best opportunity for seeing a collection of national costumes is market-day in a busy town. Women from the outlying villages, little girls like walking barrels, and boys with their full trousers and wooden *sabots*, mingle with the townsfolk intent on bargains, this being the one occasion upon which town and village meet in a friendly way. Caps of every sort, shape and size may be seen, the wide flaps of the "cornet" caps standing out like the snow-white sails of a diminutive windmill. The exquisite golden haze which envelops Dutch landscape softens the quaintly shaped outlines and gay colours of the dresses, while it enriches the simplicity of the white lace head-coverings. Caps, varying in shape according to the locality, are worn over metal head-irons (to use the old name)—close-fitting helmets of gold, silver, or copper which gleam through the lace—or placed upon the tightly bound and almost hidden hair. The Frisian woman with her dignified, upright carriage and fine features has been compared to the Swan-Maiden of the Scandinavian Ballads or the Chooser of the Slain of the Sagas. The "free Frisian" prides himself on never having been in bondage, and certainly the queenly bearing of his women-folk confirms this ancient tradition. Their present head-dress is a modification of the crown or head-ring worn ten centuries ago by their ancestors. The story of its gradual transformation from a plain split metal ring or circle is full of interest, but would take up too much space in these pages. The head-dress is still worn by all classes in the Northern Province, contrary to the custom in other parts of the Netherlands. There are distinctions, of course, and the helmets vary considerably in value, but even among the peasants the gold casque is a cherished heirloom, and real lace caps are a matter of family pride. The aristocrat is distinguished by the pin with its long end coming down over the forehead, against which it fits closely. A glance at the photograph of the Queen of Holland in Frisian costume will make this clear.

H.M. THE QUEEN OF HOLLAND IN FRISIAN COSTUME.

The women of the Islands of South Holland and Zeeland pay particular attention to the knobs of their head-irons. These knobs, often of exquisite workmanship, form the two ends of the closely fitting metal band they wear round the head ending just above the temples. In Zeeland a Protestant may be recognised by her round knobs; a Roman Catholic's are square. Buttons or conical spiral extensions upon which long ear-rings are hung also serve to finish off the rough edges of the head-band. In North Brabant, Limburg, South and East Guelderland, the metal head-coverings are no longer worn, though caps have not been discarded. In Amsterdam only the girls from the Orphan Asylum wear them. They have quaint, tight-fitting (and certainly unbecoming) caps, their dresses are made half of red and half of black woollen material, and never fail to attract attention.

The comfort of the home is the Dutchwoman's triumph and certainly the sense of repose and orderliness one feels there is very refreshing in this age of rush and worry.

Home Life.

The after-dinner tea-hour is the time of all others for a visit to one's friends, when the sight that meets the eye is more like an interior by one of the seventeenth-century Dutch Masters than a glimpse of a twentieth-century home. The family will be found gathered round a large, well-polished mahogany table upon which the weekly portfolio of illustrated papers and magazines from the circulating library has been put; the mother busy with her knitting, the father contentedly smoking his cigar, the children reading or looking at pictures, the bronze pail with its glowing peat (which does duty for our spirit-lamp), the soothing song of the bronze kettle, the dainty East Indian

A MARKEN GIRL MENDING NETS.

The side curls are only worn by girls. The *huive* is a very old form of cap.

handleless cups and saucers—all combine to make an ideal picture of home-life. The peasant's or fisher's cottage is invariably clean and neat, while the shiny blue and white tiles, and the much-rubbed brass and copper offer innumerable surfaces for the reflection of every animate and inanimate object. A well-to-do peasant's home always has a *pronk-kamer* (a "best parlour" for show), the huge Family Bible with its big brass clasps in the place of honour, and the pipe of "mastership" smoked on the wedding-day in a small glazed cupboard. The *pronk-kamer* in the Hindeloopen farmhouse contains one or two *pronk-bedden*, decked out with fine lace-edged linen sheets and embroidered pillow-slips, the curtains of which are opened during the day and closed at night to keep out the dust. It is hardly necessary to say these beds are never slept in. They are the pride and delight of their owner, and they are also the envy of the poorer neighbour.

Employment for Women.

Of the 2,819,000 women in Holland 80,000 are engaged in husbandry and agriculture, their average wages being one shilling a day in summer, and from eightpence to tenpence in winter. During the harvest they take their full share of labour, the lighter tasks falling to their lot throughout the rest of the year. In the central provinces of South Holland and Utrecht the women attend to the vegetable gardens, and only go into the fields for the hay-making. Robust-looking women may be seen towing barges, at work in the brickfields, in the peat-beds of Drenthe, and in the Zeeland oyster-pits dressed like men. Sturdy Dutch *fraus* unload sugar-cane at the quays, load and unload bullet-like cheeses and tubs of butter at the landing-stages along the canals, throwing them about with a fine indifference to their weight and unwieldiness. At Hoorn, women otherwise unemployed devote their energies to weeding the streets, and throughout Brabant wood-carving is a favourite occupation.

The Servant Question.

The servant problem has not yet reached the acute stage it presents to housewives in England. Young girls are carefully trained in well-to-do houses, where they are not much interfered with when they know—and can be trusted to perform—their duties. They go to market with their mistresses and learn to get good value for their money. On the whole Dutch servants are capable, independent and friendly, and they make thrifty industrious wives, having comfortable homes in spite of low wages. An amusing story is told by Sir William Temple, when Ambassador in Holland, of a magnate who, when paying a call on a muddy day, found himself, to his great surprise, picked up in the arms of a strong North Holland servant girl, and put down on a chair in the hall. Here she proceeded to take off the visitor's boots, which were exchanged for a pair of slippers; then, satisfied that the floor would run no risk of being dirtied, she solemnly ushered the bewildered Englishman into the drawing-room where the mistress of the house was sitting, quite oblivious of the shock her visitor had received.

Domestic Ceremonies.

The various ceremonies attendant upon every domestic event, great and small, in Holland are the very breath of life to the women of the country. Does a neighbour expect the welcome stork, general excitement reigns in the village, and preparations are made long beforehand for the inevitable reception to be held after the birth. Has a neighbour been married two or three years without doing her duty to her country, the wise women take the matter in hand, and good advice is plentifully given to the guilty couple. A wedding provides occupation for leisure hours for months ahead, and a funeral means indulgence in regret tempered by the prospect of substantial refreshment. "Eat as much as you can, my girl; you'll get nothing more from Uncle Klaas," is a straightforward expression of the general feeling at a peasant funeral. Cakes and drinks of many different kinds figure at the birth, wedding, and funeral feasts, also at the *kermesses* or fairs still held, in spite of much opposition, throughout the land.

In Groningen, at *kermesse* time it is the custom for an engaged couple to eat *ellekoek* together. Face to face at either end of this fancy bread an ell long they both begin to eat, and continue to do so without a stop until their lips meet. If either *vrijer* or *vrijster* is unable or unwilling to swallow his or her share it is a proof that the marriage would be unsuitable.

Gingerbread made with honey instead of treacle, and called by different names according to the quantity and quality of spices used, is the favourite cake of both rich and poor. It figures prominently in the *Joen-piezl* or "night-sitting." When a suitor is approved by the parents, he is invited to spend an evening alone with the daughter. The young man makes his appearance carrying a large cake, and is shown in by the expectant maiden, who watches him put the gingerbread on a table, often without saying a word. If she is favourably disposed the girl goes at once and puts more peat on the fire; the question thus decided, the cake is cut, and the couple proceed to discuss the future. If, however, the fire is neglected, the rejected suitor picks up his cake and retires with as good a grace as possible. In some parts of Holland the young couple are deprived of the excitement

A FISH-WIFE OF SCHEVENINGEN.

of sharing a cake. Seated at either side of the table with a lighted candle between them, they must decide whether they really love each other before the light gives its final splutter and dies. The offer of a Gouda pipe on arrival is decidedly encouraging, but if the maiden complains of headache and takes off her cap and head-iron, the would-be lover must begone. As the girls like an eager lover the time of arrival is an important point when courting. "He who comes after eight may leave before nine," "When in earnest, lovers come before ten and don't leave before one," are favourite sayings among Dutch peasant girls.

The Significance of the Pipe.

A long clay pipe is generally offered by the *fiancée* to her lover on the wedding eve, and a many mile walk to Gouda (where the best clay pipes are made) is gaily undertaken to fetch the symbol of man's authority in his home. In winter, groups of girls go to the busy town in North Holland on skates, and buy a provision of pipes; the return journey is an exciting one, for a broken pipe brings ill-luck, and the grief-stricken maiden is considered thoroughly incapable by her friends. The pipe of "the master" is decorated with coloured ribbons, and must be smoked on the wedding-day, a difficult and even dangerous proceeding, as the ribbons flutter about and catch fire; it must be confessed that after lighting the pipe the bridegroom often disappears, and is only seen again when his smoke is over. The pipe is never used again, but serves to decorate the *pronkkamer*.

A Haarlem Custom.

In Haarlem the pretty custom of hanging lace at the door of a house where the stork is expected is still preserved. This is said to have originated during the siege in the sixteenth century, when a Spanish general received a deputation of matrons of the town and promised protection to all women in childbed who had a piece of lace nailed to the door of their house.

Home Industries.

Spinning is still practised in the province of Overijssel. Parties of women, with their wheels, meet together at each others' houses in the evening, beguiling the time with song and gossip. Once a year a weaver with his loom goes from house to house, and the linen, when woven, is rolled up, tied with coloured ribbons, and carefully put away in the linen press for future use and for the daughter's dowry. The wool, when woven, is made into thick petticoats—of which most peasant women wear six or seven, a modest number compared with the fourteen or sixteen worn by the fish-wives of Scheveningen. Fortunately for the appearance of the latter, the breadth round the waist is balanced by the hats with enormous brims well raised at the back and front (which serve them, too, as carriers for as many as three baskets of fish), and their short red-lined full capes.

Girl Life.

In the villages and towns little girls are not seen playing about so much as the boys, for they are useful in the home, and even when sent out they must look after the little ones of the family, and go on with their knitting. Skipping is occasionally indulged in, and, naturally, skating in the winter. These miniature women are admirable sempstresses, and a visit to any of the free sewing-schools to be found all over Holland, where plain sewing, patching, knitting, and all kinds of darning are taught, will fill the breast of any fastidious Englishwoman with envy. On the whole, there is little song or dance among the Dutch country-folk; the fun of the *kermesse* is apt to degenerate into rough horseplay, and careful mothers see that their daughters go home early when the fair is on. The art of growing old gracefully is not yet a lost art in Holland—the old ladies depicted for us by Rembrandt still remain the best portraits of their descendants of to-day.

Photograph by Emilia, Bologna.

ITALIAN PEASANT WOMEN.

ITALY

By LUCY M. J. GARNETT

A Land of Contrasts—Italian Women's Rights—Importance of Marriage—Restrictions in South Italy—Educational Facilities—Lack of "Home Sentiment"—Woman and Agriculture—The Olive Harvest—The Lace-makers—Other Industries for Women

A Land of Contrasts.

MODERN Italy may be said to be pre-eminently a land of contrasts and anomalies, and in no respect, perhaps, are these contrasts more marked than in the social usages determining the position of women in the various Provinces which have since 1860 formed a united kingdom. The legal code is now, of course, uniform for the whole country; but as each Province still tenaciously adheres to its own ancient customary law in all matters connected with domestic and social economy, the status of women, determined by these customary laws, in the industrial and progressive Provinces of the North may be said to differ almost as much from that obtaining in Sicily and Sardinia as the status of English women differs from that of Chinese.

By statute law a married woman's property is absolutely her own, and is immune from any interference or abuse on the part of her husband. She has a right to the guardianship of her children and, as a daughter, to an equal share with her brothers in any patrimonial inheritance in case of intestacy; and only in a few instances are woman's legal rights inferior to those of a man. In localities, however, where these enactments conflict with time-honoured usage, a father will defeat their provisions by bequeathing all his property to his son. A dowry, however small, is almost indispensable to marriage, and the usufruct of this remains in the husband's hands, being settled upon the children, and in default of offspring it reverts to the donor or his heirs.

Italian Women's Rights.

Photograph by C. Naya, Venice.

GIRLS OF CHIOGGIA BATHING.

In Italy, as in other countries where few careers are open to women, marriage is looked upon as the end and aim of their existence, and old-maidism as something of a disgrace. It is also only as a wife that a woman obtains any degree of personal liberty, as custom does not allow a spinster to traverse the public thoroughfares without a duenna, even if she have attained the respectable age of forty.

Importance of Marriage.

In Southern Italy—and especially in Sicily—even married women are subjected to many restrictions, and, indeed, to a quite Oriental seclusion from intercourse with the other sex; for in some districts of this island, a man may have lived for twenty years on intimate terms with a neighbour without even having exchanged a word with his wife or daughter. In these localities, when a husband goes abroad, he leaves his wife, should she be young, under lock and key; and, far from resenting such usage, these women appear to be gratified by this exceeding care for their safety, as its neglect would imply want of regard.

Restrictions in South Italy.

In the great industrial centres of the North, however, and generally in localities frequented by foreigners, native customs in this respect have been considerably modified, and girls and young women are allowed greater freedom. Such changes in manners are the natural concomitants not only of changed social conditions, but also of higher education; and facilities for this in Italy are not inconsiderable.

The law makes little or no difference, in matters educational, between the sexes, for though special schools and colleges for girls are provided, the classical and technical courses in all the State-provided institutions are open to women, as are also the

Educational Facilities.

Universities. The number who avail themselves of these advantages is as yet, however, but small, and in the Universities the faculties most frequented are those of literature, natural science, and medicine. The women graduates comprise several lady doctors in good practice, and a certain number of professors and lecturers on literature and science.

Although no woman artist of any great merit has as yet emerged from the schools now existing in all the great art centres of Italy, in the domain of literature may be mentioned such names as Grazia Deledda, who in her novels has graphically depicted the strange and still half-savage population of Sardinia; and Matilde Serao, whose stories present the seamy side of Neapolitan life. This enterprising woman, herself of humble origin, is the founder and editress of a successful daily paper, *Il Mattino* (*The Morning*), which is devoted to the interests of the labouring classes. As actresses, Italian women have also attained a high level of excellence, while in the domain of opera, it need hardly be said, they stand in the foremost rank.

The intellectual attainments of middle-class women generally are, however, especially in the provinces, by no means on a level with those of men of the same social standing; while the vast mass of the female population of Italy may be said to be wholly illiterate. This state of affairs is largely due to the still surviving prejudice against female education, not a few men, though themselves well educated, preferring wives—to use their own phrase—"all Church and children."

The Italian language contains no equivalent for our English word "home," and the sentiment appears to be equally lacking. The only home to which an expatriated Italian desires to return is his

Photograph by Brogi, Florence.

AN OLD PEASANT WOMAN.

or her *paese*—native town or village. The men spend all their leisure time in the cafés and market-places, and as much of their money as possible on dress and amusements for themselves and their families, who are content to live meagrely in order to dress well and "make a figure," as they term it, on Sundays and *festas*. An Italian dwelling—which is generally a "flat"—is consequently, as a rule, bare and

Lack of "Home" Sentiment.

comfortless; and even the wealthy usually succeed in combining in their houses a maximum of magnificence with a minimum of taste, comfort, or convenience. In winter both sexes wrap themselves up warmly when out of doors in furs and great-coats; but at home they are content to shiver in their vast uncarpeted saloons over absurd little charcoal braziers. These *scaldini* are commonly mere earthenware bowls eight or ten inches in diameter, with a handle across the top; and market women, and others whose occupation takes them much abroad, carry with them this primitive heating apparatus, over which they warm alternately their chilblained hands and feet.

Notwithstanding, however, this craze for "making a figure" in public, the sanctity of Italian family life is jealously guarded. Deaths only are publicly announced, births, betrothals, and marriages being ignored save by relatives or intimate friends. Nor are "interviews" ever published in the Press, save occasionally with a political man, and even then neither his family nor his home would be described for the benefit of a curious public. Indeed, to an Italian, the publication in an illustrated journal of a portrait of his mother, wife, or sister would be an outrage rather than an honour.

Women and Agriculture.

The manifold favours bestowed by Nature upon Italy have made of her an essentially agricultural country. Even the industrial towns and cities of the north, in which life now presents many features common to other countries, are mere isolated spots surrounded by great pastoral or agricultural regions. It is in these vast rural districts that the Italian woman can best be studied. The major portion of agricultural land is owned by large proprietors, and tilled for the most part by peasants who hold their farms by various forms of tenure, some paying a definite money rent, and others sharing the produce with the landlord in varying proportion, according to whether or not he pays the taxes, provides the cattle, seed, etc. The system which is held to produce the best results, especially in its effect on the peasants, is that under which the landlord supplies a dwelling-house, farm buildings, and the cattle, pays the taxes, and gives a sum annually for seed, etc., receiving in return half the produce. Nominally it is an annual tenancy, but practically an hereditary one. A peasant family often continues to occupy the same farm for centuries, the married sons living with the house-father, and, with their wives and children, assisting in the farm work. As it appears to be a traditional creed that each family must produce every necessity of life on the farm, the system of mixed culture is the result which gives to the hills and valleys of Tuscany and Umbria especially the appearance of a vast garden. Maize, barley, and wheat are sown under the olive and orchard trees, and vegetables of every kind planted between the vine-garlanded maples. In addition to spinning and weaving, many rural home industries are carried on in which the women have often the most considerable share.

The silkworm culture, for instance, is undertaken almost entirely by the women and children of a family. It occupies less than two months of the year before the beginning of harvest, and forms one of Italy's most lucrative exports. To ensure a successful crop, constant care and attention are demanded by the voracious *bachi*, which must be kept at an even temperature, in a good atmosphere, and fed and tidied several times daily. It is consequently not unusual for a peasant family, who possess no sufficiently spacious and well ventilated outhouse, to camp out during the early summer months in order to accommodate this lucrative crop. During the last week or so of the caterpillars' lives the women and girls watch and tend them day and night. As soon as the worms show signs of spinning, branches of dried broom are laid on the trays, and on these the cocoons are spun, and afterwards picked off one by one and sold by weight to the dealers.

Where this Arcadian system of mixed culture is followed, and each crop is small, the grain harvest is reaped by hand in primitive fashion. The women and girls follow the men and bind up the golden sheaves, singing meanwhile their strange plaintive *stornelli* or *ripetti*, in which they appear to find a measure of jubilation, but which, to a northern ear, seem to express a human misery immeasurable and unending.

Gleaning is quite a passion with the Italian *contadina*, but can, of course, be indulged in only on the great estates cultivated by the landowners themselves. Harvest is pre-eminently the period of courtship; and, as it is customary to glean on Sundays, the girls may be seen on Saturday evenings seated at their doors dressing each other's abundant glossy dark hair in which, on the morrow, a clove carnation or crimson rose will nestle. Clad in their close-fitting bodices, white *camicie*, and skirts and aprons of red, yellow, and blue, but barefooted, these daughters of Italy move over the stubbles with an easy grace, each vying with her companions in her efforts to amass as many as possible of the scattered ears, for the most successful gleaner has the best matrimonial chances. The resulting sheaves are hung from the maiden's chamber window, or displayed on the roof of her dwelling, so that he who runs may read. Nor is this labour unenlivened by song, for the possession of robust lungs is as much a desideratum in a wife as a sturdy ankle or nimble fingers.

Photograph by Brogi, Florence.

ITALIAN GIRLS,
Showing the National Costume.

Probably the very day after the corn has been carried the stubbles will be turned for a new crop, for as much is got out of the land by these thrifty peasants as it can be made to yield. While the husbandman and his sons guide the plough drawn by a yoke of long-horned white oxen—calm and beautiful beasts, patient and dignified, and untiring in their toil for man — the women and children follow, collecting into little heaps for burning the weeds and roots turned up by the primitive plough, while around them frolic their domestic pets, the cat, the dog, and the pig—the last generally a half-grown animal which follows the good-wife everywhere. The grain harvest is generally over quite early in July, and the golden patches which have lighted up the valleys and hill-slopes again give place for awhile to the bare, red-brown earth. But now comes the fruit harvest. The daughters of the soil, with wide circular baskets poised securely on their heads, carry into the historic market-place of the ancient hill towns their figs, plums, and pears, their peaches, pomegranates, and apples, or, it may be, Nature's wild crop of strange fungi, unknown in our isles, but much appreciated by the Tuscan and Umbrian housewife. In September comes the vintage. Festooned from tree to tree in an unending vista hangs the fruit, white and purple, which men and women, boys and girls, busily transfer to great baskets. These in their turn are carried on primitive carts drawn by oxen to the family winepress, or, it may be, to the little walled town hard by, where the wine industry is in full swing; the long, narrow, winding main street is thronged from gate to gate with heavily laden vehicles, and reeks with the pungent odour of the grapes which are being trodden in dark-vaulted basements on either hand.

ITALIAN WOMAN OF THE AGRICULTURAL DISTRICTS

Showing the baskets used for carrying dried grass, fruit, &c.

The Olive Harvest.

Gathering the olives is essentially a winter industry, which lasts from November till February. In this tedious and laborious work the women and girls take their full share. Olive trees may be seen growing at intervals all over the plains and valleys, but the lower slopes of the hills are generally covered with olive yards rising one above another in stone-banked terraces which represent untold centuries of hereditary toil. The ripe olives are picked either directly from the branches into a deep basket strung round the waist of the picker, or beaten from the trees with long switches. Sometimes cloths or mats are spread to catch the fruit as it falls; but most usually every berry is picked by hand from the ground. As the crop is gathered, the olives are carefully sorted by the elder women into three categories, as on this depends the quality of the oil they will produce. The first, according to a Tuscan saying, "is gold, the second silver, the rest nothing." The olives are then conveyed to the mill to be crushed, and after undergoing some further processes, the oil is stored for household use, or sale, in *orci*—great earthenware jars of classic shape which recall the Oriental tale of "The Forty Thieves."

The Lace-makers.

On the Italian Riviera the large flower farms afford occupation in winter and spring to considerable numbers of women and girls; but the chief female industry of these regions is lace-making, in which almost every woman is an adept; even quite young girls may be seen seated in their doorways, or by the roadside, pillow in lap, diligently plying their numerous bobbins. Lace-making is, indeed, a home industry more or less generally carried on throughout the peninsula, though only at Venice has it been systematised. Here, under the patronage of Queen Margherita, the making of both "pillow" and point lace has become an important industry. ever increasing in beauty of design and execution, and in quantity of output.

Other Industries for Women.

In certain localities embroidery, artistic bookbinding and leather-work, as also the manufacture of beads, mosaics, etc., afford employment to women and girls, either at home or under direction in workshops.

The chief industry of the women of Tuscany, however, is straw-plaiting. The straw-market of Florence, held twice a week under the Loggie of the Mercato Nuovo, is the great centre of the trade. Whether standing at their doorways gossiping, or walking along the country roads with their burdens poised on their heads, the fingers of the Tuscan women and girls are ever busy mechanically weaving the yellow straws; for so small is now the return for their labour—owing to Japanese competition—that it is only by ceaseless industry that a living wage can be earned.

SPAIN AND PORTUGAL

By A. DE ALBERTI

The Charm of Spanish Women—Spanish Characteristics—Decline of the Mantilla—The Cult of the Black Silk Dress—The Spanish "Young Person"—Influence of Religion—The Awakening of Spanish Women—Woman's Employments—A Land of Courtesies—The Pride of Birth—The Position of Spanish Women—Portugal—Portuguese Characteristics—No National Costume—Woman's Work

THERE is a legend current in Spain that at the creation of the world the Spaniards begged three boons of Heaven, a beautiful country, beautiful women, and a good government, but the last boon was denied by Providence lest that happy land should prove a serious rival to Paradise. Therefore the unfortunate government is proverbially bad and to be held responsible for every evil, from an army revolt to an earthquake; but the most censorious of travellers would be hard put to it to find the smallest stone of criticism to hurl at the country or the women. The beauty of both is a point upon which travellers, novelists, poets, and painters are unanimous.

The Charm of Spanish Women.

The chief charm of the Spanish woman is her absolute femininity: she is the apotheosis of the eternal feminine, unconscious, as yet, that to be just a woman is no longer the highest ideal of the civilised contemporary female. A gracious softness is her dominant note; softness in the modelling of her features, in the liquid glance of her dark eyes, in the rounded curves of her figure; and softness in the gentle dignity and beautiful simplicity of her manners.

Physically the women of Spain are long-lived, healthy, vigorous, and well developed; obviously intended by Nature to be the joyful mothers of many children. They are generally about middle height, and are renowned for their graceful carriage and the beauty of their feet and ankles. Black hair and eyes are not nearly so general as is commonly supposed; soft brown eyes, which close inspection proves to be hazel, and hair of a rich glossy brown are much more common. Grey and green hazel eyes are also numerous; there are Spanish women with eyes of this colour who might easily be mistaken for Irish beauties. Blondes, whose soft fair hair is easily distinguishable from the bright gold of the English girl, are fairly numerous, especially in the northern provinces.

Spanish Characteristics.

The complexion of the Spanish woman is one of her greatest beauties, the transparent texture of her creamy skin through which the red blood glows brilliantly, defies the heat of the climate, and is often retained long after indolence, child-bearing, and advancing years have spoiled the beauty of her figure.

> "How much
> Hath Phœbus woo'd in vain to spoil her cheek,
> Which glows yet smoother from his amorous clutch!"

Sings Byron, ever loud in his praises of "Spain's dark glancing daughters."

It has sometimes been suggested that the high standard of beauty in Spain was due to the charming national costume, and that a basquiña and mantilla would make

SPANISH PEASANTS FROM SEGOVIA.

For many centuries Spanish women were happily free from the tyranny of the Sunday hat and bonnet, and the temptation to mingle devotion with a study of the latest fashions. A dress of sober black, and a black lace mantilla were considered the only reverent wear in the house of God. This costume is still seen at the early Masses, though at High Mass Parisian hats and fashions prevail, for the idea of irreverence attached to receiving Holy Communion in a coloured dress is not easily overcome. For this reason the wedding dress of the Spanish bride is still of black satin with a mantilla of black lace, even among the upper classes, though the aristocracy and all those who aspire to the ranks of high fashion have adopted the conventional white and orange blossom. In Holy Week no lady would dream of appearing in anything but a black dress and mantilla, either at church or in the streets.

The Cult of the Black Silk Dress.

a plain woman pretty, and a pretty one irresistible; but though the basquiña has practically vanished, and the mantilla is relegated to special occasions, the beauty is still conspicuous. Women of the upper and middle classes now wear the ordinary Paris fashions. The lower classes and the peasantry are still faithful to the picturesque costumes of the different provinces, some of which are shown in our illustrations. As her waving feather to the English coster girl is the bright flower in her hair to the Spanish work-girl. The wearing of a hat is the badge of the upper and middle classes: I have heard a man-servant proving the superior station of his promised bride by calling her a *señorita de sombrero*—a young lady with a hat.

Decline of the Mantilla.

It is when attending the performance in the bull ring that the Spanish woman now appears in her most national aspect. A white lace mantilla draped over a high comb, and a flower in the hair, are seen on every head, flowers are in the bosom of every dress; and in every hand a fan opens and shuts like a hovering butterfly, emphasising every word and gesture as only Spanish fingers can make it.

The Spanish girl develops early, and escapes the awkward age; the English high-school girl with her hockey-stick or tennis-racket, scorning sentiment, adopting her brother's slang, and eager to shine in some

The Spanish "Young Person."

impending examination, has no prototype in Spain. We have instead a little woman ripe for marriage, but of an engaging innocence, who begins to attend social functions in her early teens, and displays a keen interest in her own possible *novios* and those of her friends. No frank good-fellowship is possible between the young people, owing to the disastrous notion that a girl cannot be alone with a man, however old a friend or near relation, without being compromised. Even an engaged couple, though they may whisper in corners or dance together all the evening, are never allowed out of sight of their elders. Yet the Spanish woman is unconscious of her thraldom; she does not look forward to marriage as emancipation as is often the case in France. After marriage she is generally quite content with domestic cares, and makes an exemplary wife and mother. Naturally of good intelligence, she has never been taught to use her brain; centuries of mental apathy lie behind her; she is untroubled by the mysteries of life, and accepts the solutions offered by her religion with an unquestioning faith.

Influence of Religion.

The high standard of morality among married women in Spain is partly due to this strong sense of religion, and partly to the fact that the marriages are generally love-matches. The tyranny of the *dot* as it prevails in France is unknown: the young people are allowed to choose for themselves, and the idea of allowing commercial considerations to weigh in such a matter would be abhorrent to the average Spaniard, who is generally free from the snobbishness of valuing his friends according to their fortunes.

The Awakening of Spanish Women.

Unconscious of undue subjection in one sex and of undue dominance in the other has hitherto prevented friction between them—both are persuaded that all is as it should be, but there are already signs that the day of awakening is at hand. An apostle of the Feminist movement has arisen in the person of Doña Emilia Pardo Bazán, a distinguished novelist, who has laboured zealously for years to arouse her countrywomen from their apathy, and has translated John Stuart Mill's "Subjection of Women" for their benefit.

Speaking at the Paris Conference in 1899 she said: "The customs are completely unfavourable to woman, the universities and classes of the Faculties are open to her; but those who avail themselves of them are

SPANISH PEASANTS OF THE PYRENNEAN DISTRICTS.

blamed and ridiculed; families dare not brave public opinion and women are left with no resource but marriage, and, in the lower classes, domestic service, prostitution, or mendicity."

Woman's Employments.

As regards the lower classes this seems an exaggerated statement, for, though the field of woman's labour is more restricted than in other countries, she has still many ways of earning an honest livelihood. Women are largely employed in agricultural labours; bronzed daughters of the soil, pictures of vigorous health and beauty, are to be seen throughout the length and breadth of Spain. Numbers of women are employed in factories, notably in the celebrated cigarette factory of Seville and in the lace and other factories of Barcelona. Many women earn a living as street vendors of fruit, flowers, etc., and the *aguadoras* with their cry of "*Agua! agua fresca! Quien quiere agua?*" sell cool drinking water in the streets and railway stations. There is also the resource of sewing and laundry work—the Spanish needlewoman is a mistress of her craft and the laundresses are unsurpassed in any country. Domestic service is not unpopular in Spain, for it can be undertaken without loss of personal dignity. No undue servility is shown or expected; the servants treat their mistresses as "even Christians," speak their minds freely, and identify themselves with the family interests.

A Land of Courtesies.

Strangely enough in a country where difference of station is so sharply defined, Spain has achieved *liberté, egalité, fraternité* in human intercourse in a greater degree than any other civilised country. Difference of rank is admitted, but personal superiority not at all. The noblest gentleman in the land will doff his hat to his charwoman as though she were a duchess. Before the young King's marriage, peasants working by the roadside have been heard to call out an affectionate remonstrance to him on his recklessness, as he started off in his motor-car, bidding him be careful not to break his neck before he had an heir. A smile and a merry word of reassurance would be given in reply. Beggars in the streets demand alms with a "Brother, for the love of God," and expect a "Pardon, brother," in return. If this courtesy, at least, is not forthcoming the Christian brother or sister is liable to burst into quaint and original invective: "May you have swollen feet and be made a postman," was the inhuman wish hurled by an old gipsy woman after some such offender.

The Pride of Birth.

If Doña Emilia Pardo Bazán has overstated her case as regards the lower classes, her reproach is deplorably true as regards the rest of her countrywomen. That a woman of gentle birth should make the least effort to earn a penny is considered quite out of the question. She may be as poor as she likes and still retain her social standing, but let her grow weary of existing on a miserable pittance, and use her brains and energy to increase her income, and she will lose caste at once. Inconceivable as it may appear, the Spaniard considers it preferable for intelligent and able-bodied young women to live upon the charity of relations or friends than that they should endeavour to provide for themselves even by intellectual or artistic pursuits.

The Position of Spanish Women.

In his treatment of women the Spaniard mixes the tyranny of the Turk with the exaggerated reverence of the knight-errant, a combination unfavourable to the evolution of the perfect woman nobly planned. He is thoroughly persuaded that the sole aim of woman is and should be to please man; but he does acknowledge that he owes her a debt of gratitude in return. This is certainly the underlying motive of the Spanish habit of paying women compliments in the streets, which is so often misunderstood by foreigners. The Spaniard considers it part of the duty of man to thank every pretty woman for contributing to the beauty of the landscape. Not the

A SPANISH WOMAN.
Drawn by Norman H. Hardy.

Facing on page 720

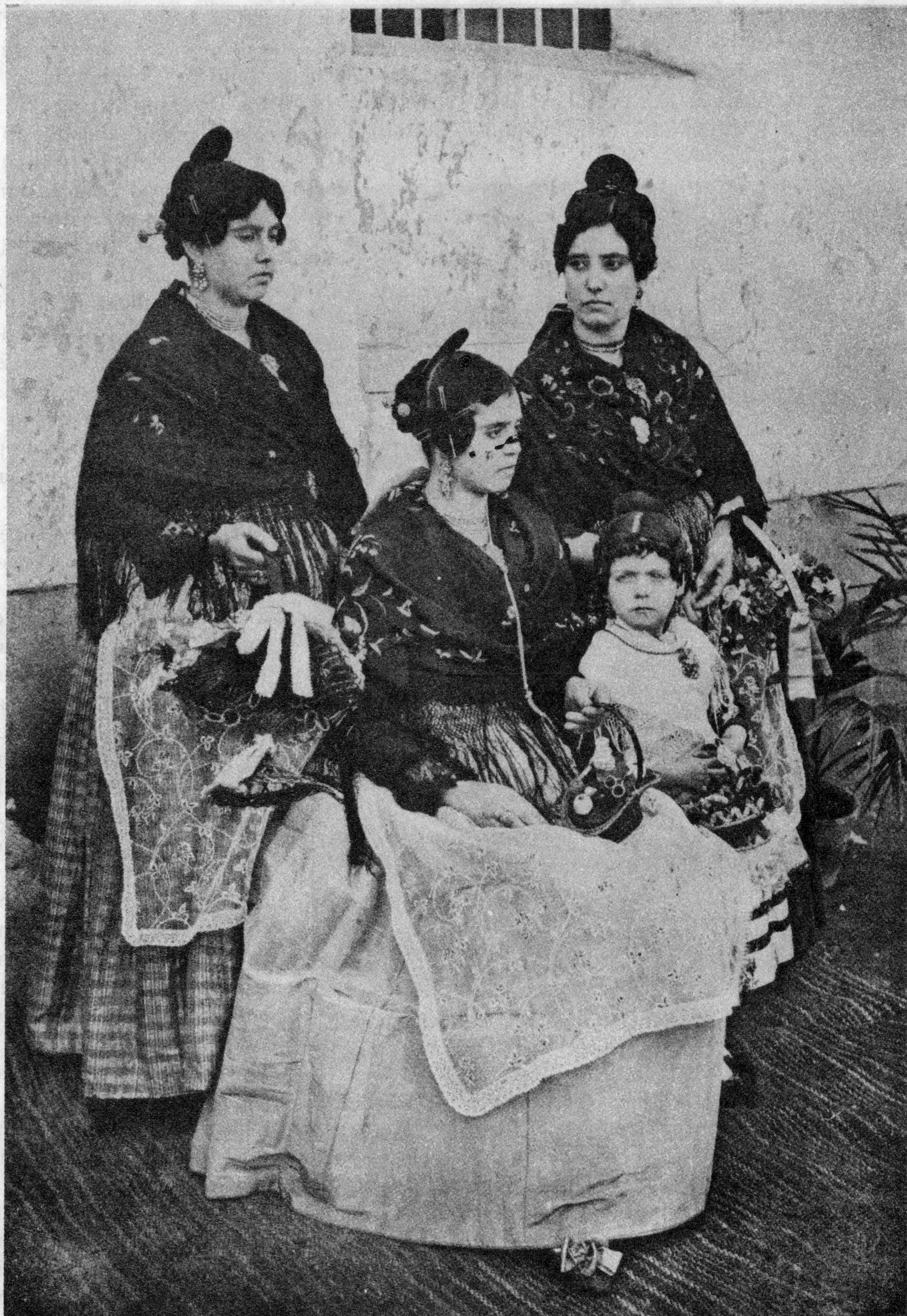

WOMEN OF VALENCIA.

least offence is intended, nor does any Spanish woman dream of taking any; this is clearly proved by the fact that the habit is called *echando flores* (throwing flowers), and the pretty girl as she takes her walks abroad expects to collect a large bouquet of these flowers of speech. I have seen staid business men stop in the middle of their conversation to hum the refrain of some popular love song to a passing damsel, and then resume their talk with the utmost gravity. This idea of paying homage to beauty gave birth to the following charming incident witnessed on the quay at Cadiz. A party of young people were crossing the quay to a pleasure yacht, when a very beautiful girl hesitated for a moment before a patch of mud; quick as lightning one of a group of common men who were standing by flung his gaudily lined *capa* over the muddy spot, and dropped on one knee with a grace which would have done credit to the blood of all the Howards, saying: "Let Beauty pass dry-shod." And Beauty, after a moment of pretty hesitation, tripped over the improvised carpet with a bow of gracious acknowledgment, amid the plaudits of the bystanders. The girl was a society *belle*, her humble Raleigh the Spanish equivalent of an English navvy. I believe Spain is the only country in Europe where such an incident could possibly occur.

GIRLS AT A FOUNTAIN IN THE COURT OF NARANJOS, CORDOVA.

This attitude of superficial homage, however charming to read about, is a very poor substitute for human liberty, and an intelligent woman on whom its true significance has once dawned might well be goaded into expressing herself still more forcibly than Doña Emilia Pardo Bazán. It is a trite saying that the civilisation of a country may be gauged by the status of its women; and many hold that the regeneration of Spain will be brought about by the awakening of her daughters. There is magnificent material in the Spanish woman; she is a creature of great natural intelligence, capable of the utmost strength and fortitude in adversity, and has often given proof of a high physical courage, and strong individuality. There can be no doubt that when she has succeeded in overthrowing the artificial restrictions by which she is hemmed in on every side, the ultimate result will be a great national advantage.

No country can bear such witness as

Portugal to the truth of the adage that comparisons are odious. Rarely is that unfortunate country considered apart from Spain. It is generally approached through Spain, dealt with after Spain, and judged with eyes blinded by the Spanish prejudice against all things Portuguese. The racial hatred between the two nations is deep-rooted, and enshrined in many popular jests and sayings which have just the spice of truth that makes the worst calumny. The close neighbourhood of the two countries and the similarity of customs and language make it difficult to put aside the idea of comparison in dealing with them, yet this is not always so detrimental to Portugal as is commonly supposed. The Portuguese women of the upper classes labour under the same disadvantages of education as the Spaniard, and as the raw material is not nearly so good the comparison is always greatly in favour of the latter; but the Portuguese peasantry can triumphantly stand the test of comparison with that of Spain or any other country.

Portugal.

Portuguese Characteristics.

The Portuguese, especially in the central and southern parts, are of a very mixed race; there is a strong semitic element, and a strain of negro blood that has not tended to beauty. During the sixteenth century the negro population of Lisbon almost equalled the whites in number, and at the end of the eighteenth century was still a fifth of the whole. Traces of the negro characteristics are often plainly visible in the Portuguese national type, excepting in the north, where the race is purer. The standard of female beauty is not nearly so high as in Spain. The women are vigorous and well developed: coarse black hair and black eyes are the most common. The healthy open air life of the peasant women gives them a brown and ruddy comeliness of complexion, but the women of the upper and middle classes who take no exercise and lounge their lives away in vapid idleness are far behind them in good looks. It would hardly be too much to say that all the beauties in Portugal are to be found among the lower classes. Some of the Ovarinas, the barefooted women from the port of Ovar, who sell fish in the streets of Lisbon, are strikingly handsome, with straight black hair, dark eyes, and strongly marked features. These are almost a race apart, and are said to be of Phœnician origin.

PORTUGUESE WOMAN.

Mr. Oswald Crawfurd has pointed out that the beauty of the women increases with every degree of northerly latitude, and pays the following tribute to the looks of the peasant women of Avintes, a parish in the neighbourhood of Oporto: "In the southern portion of this wide district the children at the cottage doors, boys and girls, are strikingly pretty, and every third or fourth girl one meets is nothing less than lovely; taller and more slender and graceful than the average peasant women, with delicate transparent complexions in place of the healthy brown ruddiness that is common elsewhere, large expressive eyes, and features full of a pleasant intelligence. The Avintes type is not un-Portuguese, but it is the national type at its highest expression, refined and idealised."

At the other end of the scale we have squat figures, sallow complexions, and thick lips, upon which the slight down of early youth too often develops into an unsightly moustache in middle age.

No National Costume in Portugal.

There is no national characteristic in dress among the upper classes, such as the mantilla in Spain; Parisian fashions are worn, and the women of Portugal are accused of being more extravagant than those of Spain in matters of dress.

The costume of the peasant women varies slightly in the different districts. They generally go barefoot, their heavy skirts drawn up through a girdle below the hips for better convenience in walking. A bright coloured kerchief is worn over the shoulders and another twisted round the head under a soft round black hat, very unbecoming but convenient for the carrying of heavily-laden market baskets. Nearly all the peasant women possess chains and pendants of fine gold, which are handed down from generation to generation.

There is comparatively little distinction among the Portuguese peasantry between the work of men and women. The women even act as porters, carry passengers' luggage on their heads with the greatest ease, and help to unload vessels. Every kind of commodity is carried to market on the heads of the women. They work in field and vineyard, in factories and railway stations, and even assist in road-making.

Woman's Work.

The climate is so beautiful, the necessities of life so cheap, and the women so thrifty and industrious, that dire poverty is hardly ever to be seen. Though the women work hard, they find leisure on Sundays and holidays for many simple open air amusements, and are generally pictures of health and contentment. Mr. Oswald Crawfurd, the best of all English authorities on Portugal, sums up the position of the Portuguese peasant women as follows: "I have noticed that among the Portuguese peasant class women hold a very independent position. They work very hard, they are active and cheerful, very helpful in any trouble, very genial and sympathetic, and yet full of quick answers and mother wit. They know well their value in the economy of life, and without any clamour for impossible rights, take their full share of all that is attainable in that way. Their suitors in love are very humble and persevering, but the women know well what is due to their dignity."

PORTUGUESE WOMAN MILK-SELLER.

Truly the contrast between the Portuguese women of the upper and lower class is a most perfect object lesson against the blind prejudice which would keep womankind in a parasitic dependence upon the work of men.

Photograph by Clive Holland.

BRETON GIRLS.

FRANCE

By CLIVE HOLLAND

A Conglomerate Race—Physical and Mental Characteristics of the Women—A Conventional People—The Parisienne—Street Types—The French Peasant—Thriftiness of the Peasant Woman

THE French, though differing very materially from the Italians, are nevertheless connected to a considerable degree with Italy, both geographically and linguistically. Who the original or very early inhabitants of France were is still a matter of some dispute, but many credible authorities incline to the view that they came from an Iberian stock, represented nowadays in some measure by the Basques, and that the race from which the modern French may be said to have descended were the Gauls, who sprang from a Celtic stock.

A Conglomerate Race.

In the present-day Frenchwoman one may trace the influences and strains of blood which were brought to bear after the Romans had abandoned the country to work out its own civilisation, and to be overrun by various Teutonic tribes, the Goths, Burgundians, and then the Franks, who, amongst other things, gave their name to the land they annexed. The conquering Normans, who were of Scandinavian stock, came later still. Thus it will be seen that the French are a conglomerate race, having the blood of Celts, Scandinavians, and Teutons in their veins, and characteristics of all three (and perhaps in a small measure of other races) in their physique and mental qualities. In language they are chiefly Latin.

Speaking roughly, one may say that so far as physical types are concerned, the French are divided very sharply into at least two — those of the North and those of the South. Frenchwomen—say of Brittany and Provençe—differ fully as much as those of two distinct nations, just as the Channel climate and that of the Mediterranean are entirely dissimilar. The Bretons are taller of stature, generally light-haired, with blue or grey eyes, and an oval-shaped head; they possess a finer physique, and are more Teutonic or stolid in disposition, less susceptible to outside influences, retaining even in this twentieth century their ancient dress and customs in a marked degree, with less refinement and beauty of feature. Whilst south of the Loire in Provençe there is a race of women of smaller build, less height, possessing softer contours, rounder heads, and generally both dark hair and dark eyes. The Provencal women are, indeed, not only smaller but are more often pretty, and have not fair but dark and rich complexions. There are, of course, several modifications of these two types in different parts of France, but on the whole the differences are well marked, and serve the purpose of division. The smaller, softer type of the Provençal is said by some authorities to be traceable to the Iberian strain; but this is difficult to prove, owing to the number of racial factors which at various times have been brought to bear.

Physical and Mental Characteristics.

Photograph by Clive Holland.

A PARISIENNE OF THE *BOURGEOISIE.*

"The Frenchwoman of to-day is the product of many influences, some of which have been antagonistic, and by reason of this she has many contradictions of character as well as not a few excellencies." Thus are his countrywomen summed up by a modern French writer of some distinction. One characteristic which cannot, however, fail to impress itself upon the mind of even a casual observer is the vivacity and mercurial nature of the Frenchwoman's intellect. She is quick-witted, possessed of the gift of repartee, and in conversation brilliant rather than solid. But withal as a housekeeper—rather than as a home-maker—she shines, and as a business woman she has probably, take her all in all, few feminine equals and scarcely a superior. Whether she be one of the beautiful daughters of Arles, the passionate, hot-blooded Provençale, the ***chic*** Parisienne, or the phlegmatic Normande or Bretonne, there is the same underlying instinct of economy, the same desire to avoid waste. Except with those exotics of the *demi-monde*, or the wives and daughters of *les nouveaux riches*, there is, too, the same underlying simplicity of life which has done much to make the French the wealthiest of Continental peoples, although not by any means a nation of many huge fortunes.

This same uniformity in a measure afflicts all classes in their various walks of life. By the changes which France has undergone since the Revolution of 1789 the aristocracy as such has practically disappeared, and left remaining only the great class known as the *bourgeoisie*—which comprise the professional, mercantile, trading, and public official classes—and the

A Conventional People.

peasantry. The *bourgeoisie* form the great backbone of the nation in the towns; the peasantry in the country; and whether they be men or women of those classes, their lives are much more conventional, and more closely hedged round with *les convenances* than are ours. In a word, the Frenchwoman has much less freedom than her English sister, and is more a slave to custom, more subject to the opinions of her relatives, friends, and neighbours.

But a long and somewhat wide experience of French life and character leads us to think that few women have greater powers of fascination than the well-bred Parisienne; and few a more gracious frankness and more charming spirit of hospitality than the French peasant woman whose confidence has been successfully won.

There is even a greater contrast between the Parisienne and the provincial than that which exists between the Londoner and the countrywoman. It is a mistake to consider the French as a nation of artists, as some writers appear to assume; for, as a matter of fact, except by a few côteries in provincial cities, little is known of art and less interest is evinced for it. Paris, however, yet remains the great art centre of Europe. It is not merely a place where the works of artists are exhibited, sold, and talked about, but is truly artistic in the wider sense of the term.

It may also be said that the French as a nation are not intellectual as are the Germans or English. The French brain is quicker and cleverer over small things; but life in the provinces and small provincial towns is, generally speaking, so dull and uniform that brilliance of intellect is neither required nor looked for, and life there is at a far less high intellectual level than with us. The type of mind found in Paris and that of the centres of population in the provinces is totally different. In the former the question is rather what one is and what one may attain; than (as is the case in the latter) who one's grandfather and ancestry were, and what the family's past history has been, and what one possesses.

Almost all great provincial towns of France have their own individuality, which has arisen from either an historic past, or peculiarities of situation, or from a combination of both. In the commercial towns all the life and energy and ambitions are deeply centred in material prosperity, and the inhabitants esteem one another chiefly according to their wealth. In these towns religion will be somewhat of a dead letter, or at

Photograph by Clive Holland.

A PARIS ART STUDENT AT WORK.

least the public exercise of it be left chiefly to the womenfolk. On the other hand, one still finds here and there clerical towns in which traces of the exclusiveness of the old *régime* of the aristocracy has yet a certain power; where women of the commercial classes, even though the wives or daughters of well-to-do people and those of public officials, would have little or no chance of getting into "Society." In such places no one appears to trouble much about modern ideas or progress, but to be eternally dwelling upon the often vanished greatness of certain distinguished families.

The Parisienne.

Perhaps the provinces are chiefly dull because most ambitious, and intellectually gifted or artistic people gravitate towards Paris. For this reason it is possible, with certain limitations, of course, to gain a fairly accurate idea of Frenchwomen as a whole from a knowledge of the Parisienne. Not the typical Parisienne of the illustrated papers, the caricaturists, and the fashion journals, but the conglomerate mass of feminine humanity which makes up the women of the French capital. Examples of almost all types are to be met within the confines of the city, though the character of Paris itself is strangely local rather than national.

At pilgrimage time, on the Place in front of the Église du Sacré Cœur on the heights of Montmartre, and in the streets leading up to it, one meets the white-coifed bronze-cheeked Breton woman, the stalwart, white-capped Norman peasant with hard, honest face, side by side with the women of Arles with picturesque head-dresses and beautiful features. These introduce a note of "costume" into the streets of Paris, and remind one of days in misty, charming Brittany, the apple orchards of Normandy, or the fierce, insistent sunshine of Provençe.

It is the Parisienne proper, however, with her air of *chic*, whether she be a "Society" woman, spending annually a large fortune on dress, or a work-girl earning ten to fifteen francs a week, who may be considered typical of the women of France as a whole. Of her there are, of course, many types; but through most run those elements of character and disposition which go to make the woman in her count for so much. Let us consider for a moment the woman who is well off, is married, and has an assured position in "Society." Her life, provided she enjoys good health and is of an even temperament, is not far from ideal. She has been trained for her ultimate place in the world at the convent school, or at one of the fashionable "finishing" schools which are yearly becoming more numerous and esteemed; and then she is launched on the sea of married life to sink or swim as her fate or temperament ordains. She becomes, as a rule, a finished woman of fashion in an astonishingly short time.

Her marriage, though it has been arranged for her in the most matter-of-fact way, has emancipated her; it seldom (as often happens with us) enslaves her. She now dines with her husband or a friend at smart restaurants. She thinks much more of the *menu* than does her English sister. After dining she goes to the play, not so much to see the actors as to show herself and her toilette to admiring and envious friends. The Parisienne dresses well not only from innate good taste, but because she has been taught to recognise the fact that dress is a potent weapon in the defeat or discomfiture of other women. In the afternoon she will drive in the Bois. Her eyes on the *qui vive* for equipages smarter than her own, her mind intent upon solving the genesis of them so that she may gossip with her friends on the subject at "five o'clock."

There are distinct variants of this type, such as the "sportif," who is seen at all the race meetings in the neighbourhood of the capital, and follows the guns in tastefully adapted male attire when the shooting season causes her to desert Paris for *la campagne*. And later in the year she will be seen flying over the ice in the Bois de Boulogne at the Cercle des Patineurs in a costume sensibly short and plain to severity. The athletic Frenchwoman has also become a common type. With her, in recent years, physical recreations have become almost a religion. She always enters with enthusiasm into new things; continuing or abandoning them as she ultimately discovers their suitability or otherwise to her temperament.

The types of the street—which are met in most large provincial towns as well as in Paris itself—how many there are! First there is the superior *demoiselle de magasin*, or shop girl, who trips along with a huge paper *carton* slung over her arm. One hand manages her skirts if the day be wet and muddy, and the other carries an umbrella, and perhaps also a tiny reticule for *mouchoir*, powder puff, and smelling salts. Not less picturesque is her sister the little milliner, who, in a neatly-fitting dress and as often as not hatless, with *carton* also on arm, comes smiling along the broad Boulevard St. Germain or St. Michel from some tiny slip of a shop where skill in designing and trimming fascinating hats makes up for lack of plate glass display.

Street Types.

The flower girls of Paris are another well-known type. And in their ranks one finds not only Parisians born, but many provincial types also. Dark-eyed girls and women who have gravitated to the capital from far-off l'Orient and the Basque country; Normandes with fairer skins and sometimes flaxen hair; dark-eyed, dark-complexioned and dark-haired women from the land of the Mistral; and oval-faced, olive-tinted beauties from the Italian frontier villages of the far south-east. They stand, with their trays or baskets of buttonholes and posies, violets, lilac, lilies of the valley, carnations and roses according to the season, almost always neat and smiling, and in sharp contrast to their frowsy sisters of the London streets and pavements.

Another type of the city is the *bonne*, or servant, neat as her mistress, generally wearing a spotless linen cap with goffered frill and equally snowy-white apron. Basket in hand or on her arm, she purchases the day's supplies for the family—for personal marketing is an outstanding feature of French domestic life—with a keen eye for economy: a thrifty housewife, whose only extravagance (*if* so it can be called) will probably be a four-*sous* bunch of flowers, which her love of beauty and artistic sense will prompt her to buy.

In the gardens of Paris one finds many types, some of which are common to all France. Such are the *bonnes des enfants*, with their neat distinctive dress and wide ribbon streamers to their close-fitting caps; the Sisters of Charity (the "little Sisters of the Poor" they are not inappropriately named), sometimes in pairs on some mission of mercy bent, or at the head or end of a procession of schoolgirls. Then in the garden of the Luxembourg one finds the artists' models, foreign and native types, indigenous to Paris, sitting idly waiting for artist or student friends, or promenading beneath the giant chestnuts, dressed less neatly and more smartly than most women of the *bourgeoisie*.

But one could multiply almost endlessly the types of the Parisienne, and one well-known type must close our list. The *blanchisseuse* is truly national: she of the spotless cuffs, apron, and cap, trim of figure even though stout, making her way along the street with her basket of snow-white starched linen, with lace underskirts often tied, so as to prevent crushing, to the handle and fluttering in the wind.

These are types of the women of France, it is true, but somehow or other, although their prototypes are to be found in most large towns, those of the capital have one and all the indefinable *cachet* of the Parisienne.

The Peasant Woman.

The French peasant woman forms a very distinct type, whether she lives in the south, the east, the west, or the north. She has, notwithstanding all that has been written to the contrary, a certain air of dignity and a charm of manner somewhat similar to that which distinguishes so many of the women of Ireland; and the former characteristic is probably chiefly traceable to the independence which has been developed in the last two or three generations of the French peasantry, and was brought about by the radical changes which were created in the social order of things by the Revolution. Taken as a whole, she is religious even in the towns, and certainly deeply so, and even superstitious, in far-off western Brittany. Possibly she may be more so because her men-folk as a general rule are apt to leave such observances, except at special times and seasons, almost entirely to her.

Photograph by Clive Holland.

A LACE-MAKER OF SOUTH-EASTERN FRANCE.

The French peasant proprietor and his women-folk are probably the most independent and self-respecting class of toilers in Europe. With them one seldom finds any apeing of their social superiors in either dress, pretensions, or ambitions. Few of the women or girls waste money, thought or time upon finery; and, indeed, to do so would be esteemed, at least by the older women, to indicate the reverse of respectability. It is only, indeed, when the peasant girl, who has entered service and has migrated to the larger towns or Paris itself, returns to her old home and village that one finds any jarring note in the costumes seen in the streets. The ambition of most peasant women and girls appears to be to dress as their mothers and grandmothers did before them, and the returned wanderer who wears a gown or a hat of recent fashion is looked upon much as a canary would be in a cage of hedge sparrows.

As a general rule domestic service is not a favourite occupation or refuge as employment for the average peasant. The French girl looks forward with some degree of confidence to ultimate marriage, and her brother's ideal is not to work for someone else, but to become a peasant proprietor under a system which has been so enormously developed and answers so admirably in France.

Thriftiness of the Peasant Woman.

The French peasant woman, like her husband, has been accused of meanness and of having a miserly nature; and there is some ground for the accusation. Doubtless as a general rule she is close-fisted and keen at a bargain. A person to be reckoned with, who would rather part with some of her own blood than loosen her fingers which have clasped themselves tightly over a franc. But however much miserliness is to be condemned, there can be no doubt whatever that the peasant's frugality and stern economy, with the love of saving the pence that they may grow into pounds, has largely made France what she is. In addition, these things not only materially helped her after the terrible national tragedy of the years 1870 and 1871 to regain her financial status, but assists her to-day to occupy the proud position which she does among the nations.

Saving in all departments of the household is the one guiding spirit of the women-folk of France, whether they be the wives and daughters of peasants, artisans, or *bourgeoisie*. To enable economies to be practised many a housewife makes not only her jams, jellies, bread, vinegar, and essences, and dries the herbs which play so important a part in French cookery and are grown in her own garden; but also makes wine, spirits, and liqueurs, and not seldom also the household linen. Everything that can be turned to useful account is husbanded and applied, with the result that the French housewife is one of the most hard-working and industrious of women. Most peasants and countryfolk have their own fruit and vegetables in abundance, for almost every Frenchman and every Frenchwoman in the country is a gardener at heart, and amongst the peasant class meat is a luxury, the need for which their frugal tastes make unnecessary as a general rule. In their fields they can grow, in addition to the usual crops, flax, hemp, beans, cloves, and maize and the variety of dishes that a French peasant woman can make on a strictly vegetable basis is astonishing.

Amongst the peasants and artisan classes in the country districts honesty and sobriety are of a high standard. There is very little extreme poverty or drunkenness; and although marriages are very frequently contracted early, thrift and industry prevent the disastrous results that so often follow such unions in our own and other lands. Those who know the peasants of France will agree that they are singularly human and lovable, and this in spite of the fact that their thrift often is but another name for the parsimony, and "eye to the main chance," which generally distinguishes all their dealings with their neighbours.

Photograph by Clive Holland.

WOMEN OF FINISTERRE.

SWITZERLAND

By CHARLES E. ROCHE

Ethnology—World-famed Embroidery—Guardians of the Home—Education and Intellectuality—Native Dress Disappearing

As is the case with most other nationalities, the Swiss are not a homogeneous people. When Cæsar invaded the country it was inhabited chiefly by two tribes, known as the Rhæti and the Helvetii, who were of Celtic origin, and who were so decimated by their Roman foes that they were never again able to raise their heads as a separate people. Their conquerors remained for over 300 years in the country. As the Empire began to totter to its fall, Helvetia was overrun by hordes of Alemanni and Burgundians, who thenceforward became the permanent occupiers of the land. The former appear to have been the sturdier and fiercer people, and they it probably was who gave those tougher and more enduring elements to the character which we associate with the Swiss. They preserved their ancient tongue, while the Burgundians, a milder race, adopted the language of the conquered people. Hence it arose that we have to-day the two broadly defined limits of the French and German-speaking cantons, or districts, for the dividing line does not always coincide with cantonal boundaries.

Ethnology.

French and German are not, however, the only languages in use among the Swiss. Italian is spoken in the canton of Tessin (or Ticino), while in parts of the Grisons (or Graubünden), another offshoot of the ancient Latin tongue, called the Romansch, is spoken.

Taking them as a whole, the Swiss are a strong and healthy race. As a rule, they are well built and remarkably tough of fibre, especially those engaged in agriculture. The average length of life is 40.6 years, and the proportion of males to females is 49 per cent. to 51 per cent.

The canton of St. Gall may be said to be the headquarters of the Swiss embroidery industry, which occupies thousands of female workers in this part of Switzerland. Much of the embroidery work is done by machinery, but there is still a very large quantity turned out by hand. Appenzell is especially noted for its productiveness in this respect, its women being gifted above almost all others for their deftness and taste in this delicate art. The picture of the fields about St. Gall and along the Toggenburg Valley, white with the webs spread out to bleach, is not more common nor more surprising to the stranger than that of the Appenzellerin seated before her embroidery frame in the shade and amid the flowers of her garden.

World-famed Embroidery.

Embroidery is to East Switzerland very much what watchmaking is to West Switzerland, and it employs probably an equal number of the population. Fifty thousand persons are said to be so engaged, chiefly in St. Gall, Appenzell, and parts of the canton of Zurich. The Swiss find it worth their while to establish schools for instruction in the art of embroidery, in order that there may be no fatal lagging behind the fashion. There is also a museum of embroidery in St. Gall. Apart from any mere industrial value, it need hardly be pointed out how all this tends in the direction of artistic culture and general refinement. In Zurich, power-loom weaving is largely in vogue, but 20,000 to 30,000 hand-looms are at work in the villages round the lake. A considerable amount of linen-weaving is also done—for home use—in the Alpine valleys, where the pleasant hum of the spinning wheel may yet be heard in many of the mountain cottages.

Swiss women are, as a rule, of medium stature, stoutly built, and generally plain.

Guardians of the Home.

The reason for this general unattractiveness of type is doubtless the terrible hardness of the life lived by them in the past. By way of compensation, the Swiss woman shines most in all the qualities that are best and most lovable in woman. The one ideal of duty prevails. The Swiss woman's place is in her home, and here she lives and works. Not only does she have the care of the children and of the house, but she frequently aids in the bread-winning by embroidery, lace-making, and weaving.

Marriage customs vary in different parts of the country, but, essentially, they are all the same in one respect, for the law, regarding marriage as a civil contract, requires it to be performed by a magistrate.

Swiss women of the better class are noted for the general tone of intellectuality which prevails among them. They can, as a rule, talk intelligently not only on politics, but on literature, science, and education.

Education and Intellectuality.

The latter is a favourite topic. This is natural among a people who have played so important a part in the mission of education, and whose daughters, from necessity as well as predilection, devote themselves to the art of teaching. No country in the world produces better governesses than Switzerland, and it must be recorded that they speak the purest of French, untainted with any provincial intonation or accentuation.

The educational system of Switzerland is very near perfection—all children must go to school, but their curriculum may be settled by the canton which saw their

Photograph, Copyright, 1897, by Underwood & Underwood, London.

SOME SWISS TYPES.

birth. Geneva enacts that three hours a week shall be devoted to manual work. The girls are instructed in the occupation which will surely be theirs, whatever be their individual destiny. In most of the cantons dressmaking is a compulsory subject, and from two to eight hours a week are devoted to "cutting out," a work of no little artistic importance.

Many of the Swiss cantons boast of normal schools for the training of teachers, both male and female. The age of entry into these establishments is fixed at fourteen in the Grisons, at sixteen in Schwyz and at Lausanne, and fifteen in other cantons. The course of instruction lasts two years in Valais, and in the canton of Vaud the same period is fixed for young women; but in most of the other cantons it extends to three or four years. There is a strong tendency towards the co-education of the sexes. At Lausanne a girl who leaves her high school with a diploma may, on that evidence, continue her studies at the university.

Photograph, Copyright, 1897, by Underwood & Underwood, London.

SWISS PEASANT GIRL.

"In wandering through the Forest cantons, one may find the distinctive dress now and then, though even in the more conservative of the cantons, such as Unterwald and Schwyz, it is not often you will get a glimpse of the cantonal costume, except for the head-dress of the women. In Schwyz, the maidens who keep up the old fashion wear a black cap, the married women a white one," observes Mr. Clarence Rook.

Native Dress Disappearing.

In his observations of "Swiss Life in Town and Country," Mr. Alfred Story writes thus of the Swiss costumes as surviving in the Forest cantons. As to the maids and matrons of Schwyz, in their caps "are two slips of upright lace, which, coming from behind over the head, meet on the forehead, the whole having the appearance of a butterfly with wings half-spread. Between these the girls' tresses are puffed and held back by a silver pin called a 'Rosenadel,' from its head resembling a partially opened rose. The hair of the married women is treated in a similar way, but is covered with a piece of richly embroidered silk. The old cantonal costume holds its own as strongly in Catholic Appenzell as anywhere, and, as it is very picturesque, it is worth a few words of description. The dress consists of skirt, bodice, and head-dress. The skirt is of a rather heavy material, black and dark red in colour, and is folded longitudinally into a number of narrow pleats. The bodice consists of black velvet, and is worked back and front with silver cord. The breast, shoulders, and arms to the elbows are clad in white. A fancy bonnet, with a pair of black, semi-circular wings, constitutes the head-dress. The wings are large, and are attached on each side of the head. They are lined with a soft, white material, which is brought to a point over the forehead. The bonnet, worn at the back of the head, is usually adorned with streamers of pink ribbons. The bonnet is often discarded for comfort's sake, both by girls and married women, but the wings never. A good deal of chain-ware and jewellery is worn to complete the costume. It must be said that the fashion suits the plump, blue-eyed, fair-haired daughters of Appenzell."

Generally speaking, the girls wear short skirts and elaborate bodices. The mountain maid of the Bavarian Tyrol still treasures her "Tracht," the national dress for gala occasions, and more particularly her wedding day, but in Switzerland the traditional costume is worn by few but waitresses and itinerant musicians, who have to dress the part.

BELGIUM

By CLIVE HOLLAND

Geographical Position — The Ancient Belgæ — Two Distinct Races Living in Unity — A Common Religion, but Two Languages — The Walloons — Differences between Walloon and Flemish Women — A "Homely" People — Costume — National Prosperity Largely Traceable to the Women

BELGIUM, which has been independent of Holland since 1830, is approximately bounded on the north by Holland and the North Sea, on the west and south by France, and on the east and south by Rhenish Prussia, and has an area of only 11,373 square miles, or about one-seventh of that of Great Britain. The smallest of independent European kingdoms, it has the distinction of being the most thickly inhabited, with a population numbering slightly over 7,000,000.

Geographical Position.

Originally the country formed a portion of what is known as Gallia Belgica, a district inhabited in the days of the Roman Empire by a race known as the Belgæ, who, ethnologists tell us, differed not only in dialect, but also in their institutions, customs, and code of laws from the Celtic inhabitants of other portions of Gaul. Indeed, not a few authorities are inclined to the view that these fair-hued Celts came of a German stock, and may be regarded as a Celtic-speaking though originally a Germanic tribe.

The Ancient Belgæ.

The present-day inhabitants of the country are undoubtedly a mixed Celtic and German stock. The Celtic ancestry is traceable chiefly in the Walloons, who are thought by many to have descended from the ancient Belgæ; whilst the Flemings, who form the other part of the population, are as Teutonic to-day as they were many centuries ago. Thus in Belgium we still have two distinct races living side by side, though differing entirely the one from the other in blood and language, forming a single nation, and even a united one. Probably this latter somewhat curious circumstance is mainly attributable to the fact that they have for nearly five hundred years shared a common political destiny and evolution under successive foreign and native-born rulers. This political fusion has doubtless served to remove many causes of friction which otherwise might have arisen between the Walloons and Flemings, and has given rise to a feeling in both races that their political independence and material progress largely depends upon unity. At all events, it is significant that neither race during its long term of combined existence, which commenced at the time the feudal system came to an end, has been in any way actively or racially antagonistic one to the other. It is undoubtedly this absence of internecine strife during past ages which has made possible the continued independent existence of so small a State, though it has more than once formed "the battlefield of Europe."

Two Distinct Races Living in Unity.

Probably one of the reasons, and not the least potent, for the absence of racial antagonism has been the fact that both Walloons and Flemings have a common religious belief — Roman Catholicism. This circumstance has removed one very fruitful and frequent source of the

A Common Religion, but Two Languages.

differences that arise between distinct races inhabiting one country.

But although they have a common religion, the Belgians, as we have said, speak two quite distinct languages. The Flemings speak Flemish, of a kind which has scarcely changed since the Middle Ages; whilst the great majority of the Walloons speak French, although those of the Ardennes and a portion of the province of Liége still use the old Romance tongue, Walloon. A few of the inhabitants who dwell on the German frontier in the province of Liége have adopted the German tongue.

Photograph by Clive Holland.

SOME BELGIAN TYPES AT OSTEND.

One would have supposed that nowadays, at least, some attempt would have been made towards the unification of the language by making it either French or Flemish; but, although the former is the official language, nearly half of the inhabitants still speak Flemish, about 43 per cent. French, whilst the remainder retain either the Walloon language, or French and Flemish combined. Thus rather less than 10 per cent. are bilinguists, and most of this small proportion are dwellers in Brussels or in the province of Brabant, which forms, as it were, a "buffer" state between Flanders, with its Flemish influence, and the Walloon districts.

The Walloons.

As we have mentioned, the Walloons are by some ethnological authorities considered to be the real descendants of the original tribes of the Belgæ, or at least of such of them as survived the very drastic measures of Cæsar and the one-time Roman occupiers of the country. The effects of the intermarriage of their women with the conquerors in those far-off centuries, and of a similar practice with the Spanish occupiers of the sixteenth and seventeenth centuries, can yet be traced in the Roman and Spanish types often to be found, more especially in the provinces of Luxembourg, Liége, and Namur, where there are to be met many handsome girls and women with patrician and Southern features and colouring. Even at the present day Roman names are found among the Walloons. The latter people, too, have far less jealously preserved their own language than have the Flemings, the vast majority of whom, indeed, are only acquainted with their own tongue, and are quite at a loss when visiting French-speaking districts in the western portions of the country.

Belgian Characteristics.

The history of Belgium contains many historic episodes and events which well illustrate the chief national characteristics of a people who in ancient times were distinguished for the boldness of their undertakings, both commercial and adventurous, their generosity to Mother Church (which has made Belgium a country of cathedrals and magnificent churches), and the people's love of freedom, by which they have in past centuries gained distinction when the sword was one of the most speedy and acceptable means to secure fortune. Nowadays the Belgians may be said chiefly to excel in commerce and the arts of peace. By reason of this the country has to-day become prosperous, peaceful, and, on the whole, contented, with many valuable manufactures, including that of machinery, iron, steel, linen, cotton, and glass, whilst it still remains noted for the manufacture of lace which earned it fame in the olden times.

Differences between Walloon and Flemish Women.

As regards physical differences existing beween the Walloon and Flemish women, it may be pointed out that the former are of stouter build and greater stature than the latter, who are fairer and usually possess fresh complexions and good colouring. The Walloon women are not only bigger and taller, but usually present a distinct contrast to the Flemings by reason of their darker hair, and pale—though often swarthy—complexions. In Liége and Luxembourg and in some other districts one finds fair-haired Walloon women, but as a general rule they are dark, whilst the Flemings are the opposite. The women of the latter race are more actively industrious and energetic; whilst the former have better heads for business, and are also better cooks and housekeepers. Both races of women are fond of bright clothing, although the Walloons have the credit for better taste, and of wearing their garments with greater effect and distinction. To see the lower classes of both races at their smartest it is necessary to wait for a Sunday or *fête*. Then women, who may have seemed on ordinary occasions quite dowdy, will appear startlingly smart, but on the whole dressed in excellent taste.

The life of the Belgian people, and more especially of the women, can best be seen in the capital or in one of the larger towns. There is, however, very little difference in the general domestic life which is led by that large class which comes between what is commonly known as "Society" and the working classes proper. Whether the household be that of a professional man, or a

A Homely People.

Photograph by Clive Holland.

A BELGIAN WORKING WOMAN AND HER DOG-CART.

manufacturer, or shopkeeper, who is prosperous enough to live away from his office or business premises, there is probably less difference to be noticed as far as daily routine of life is concerned than there is in that of any other European country. One chief reason for this is the fact that *au fond* the Belgians are a simple people, who have learnt the lesson of thrift in a hard school, and who now practise it as a matter of course. There is certainly in Brussels itself—though it is called "Paris in little"—a notable absence of the lavish display one finds in the French capital. It is always difficult to estimate a man's income at all accurately from the appearance of his women-folk, from himself, or from the furnishing of his house.

Photograph by Clive Holland.

BELGIAN GIRLS OF THE LOWER MIDDLE CLASS.

Costume.

There is little, except in certain districts of the Ardennes and less frequented parts of the country, in the now prevailing costume of the Belgian women to distinguish them from women of the same class of any large town in Eastern France, or even of Paris itself, although fashions and customs in the larger country towns of Belgium do not change very rapidly.

In Antwerp, however, and in several other towns on the German and Dutch frontiers, one still sees many, of the older women more especially, wearing the deep white collars of former times, velvet bodices, and "coif"-like caps with lace wings.

But if what is known to artists as "costume" is not nowadays very apparent or distinctive, there are many characteristic types of Belgian women. As a whole, it may be said that the women of Belgium as regards physique may be considered to be of a mixed French and German type. The Bruxelloise differs little from the Parisienne as regards figure and appearance; and we have certainly noticed a marked resemblance between the Parisian and Brussels *midinettes*, work-girls, and school-girls. The Belgian farmer's wife and daughters are very like their sisters of Alsace and Lorraine, and in some cases are almost indistinguishable from Normandy peasants; whilst the familiar milkwoman, with her little cart drawn by dogs, is not very markedly differentiated from the "comfortable" and elderly *blanchisseuse* of the French capital and large provincial towns. The famous bathing-women of Ostend and Blankenberge could be paralleled in either Germany or France, though many of them are fairer and more Teutonic than French in build.

Characteristics of Belgian Women.

But there are some distinguishing characteristics of Belgian women of almost all classes—more especially noticeable, however, in those of the lower—which mark them out from those of our own land. Tidiness in dress and absence of cheap finery is one of their most prominent virtues. The Belgian women of the working classes might indeed well be held up as an example to those of our own land in this respect. That they are singularly bright, cheerful, and contented in disposition is obvious to all who have spent any considerable time in the country, just as their industry and thrift cannot be gainsaid. Indeed, so many of the businesses appear to be in the hands of women that it would at first sight tempt one to say that Belgium is a nation of feminine shopkeepers. Most of the " milkmen " are women, and a large proportion of all " light " businesses—such as groceries, greengroceries, haberdashery, floral, and similar undertakings—are managed by women. Often, indeed, the husbands have occupations quite apart, and find that their women-folk are capable of controlling and making good incomes in commercial undertakings of considerable size. Many of the cafés and café-restaurants even in the large towns have women, known as *patronnes*, as their presiding geniuses, who are often the widows or the wives of the proprietors.

In the home the Belgian woman is literally a host in herself. She is frequently a good cook, can usually make most of her own clothes, and except in the richest families usually does so, with or without the help of a sewing-maid or a hired sempstress. But this is with the exception of the two or three good dresses which almost every Belgian woman—save the very poorest—expects her father or husband to give her each year. These dresses will be the best that can be afforded, in the last of " latest fashions," and in excellent taste. Indeed, the Brussels dressmakers are little if anything behind their more famous sisters of Paris save in their charges, which are decidedly less extravagant.

Even a cursory survey of the position and distinguishing characteristics of Belgian women must lead one to the conclusion that they are usually excellent housewives, cheerful in disposition, thrifty, tidy, religious, charitable, and industrious, and that they do their fair share in all stations

Photograph by Clive Holland.

A WELL-KNOWN BELGIAN (FLEMISH TYPE).

of life towards the prosperity and comfort of the home. Indeed, one might venture to assert that the national prosperity of a small and not, otherwise than politically, very important nation is largely owing to its women and their many excellent qualities.

DENMARK

By EMMY DRACHMANN

High Attainments of Danish Women—Institutions for Women—Danish Characteristics—The Influence of the High School—Danish Hospitality—Feasts for all Events—The National Dress—Position of Danish Women

THE Danish woman usually stands on a high intellectual plane; as a rule she is more the equal of man than in other civilised countries. In the course of the last twenty or thirty years she has developed with astonishing rapidity, and it must be confessed that man, so far from hindering her, has even assisted her to her new position. When in 1877 the University opened its doors to women students, the other colleges in the country followed suit. It was not only in academical studies, however, that the young woman sought to advance, but in all branches of practical life she tried to obtain independent occupation. Nowadays it is considered almost reprehensible for a young girl, even if she be rich or belong to the higher circles, to have no occupation by which she can earn a living, and this not only in the higher professions but in book-keeping or general office work. These workers have organised themselves with remarkable ability, and have formed their own unions and clubs. Intercourse between the well-educated women and their less fortunate sisters has had a wonderful effect in improving the position of women generally.

High Attainments of Danish Women.

Among the institutions organised for women in Copenhagen must be mentioned the Women's Reading Club, the library of which contains nearly 40,000 volumes. In connection with it are spacious and well-furnished rooms for reading and social purposes, where, in winter, there are frequently concerts and lectures. Amongst others Bjornstjerne Bjornson and Fritdiof Nansen have lectured here. This institution was founded by Miss Sophie Alberti. The subscription is very modest, consisting only of 12 kroner (about 13s.) a year. The School of Art Needlework for Women is supported by the Government, and provides instruction for girls in all sorts of national embroidery and weaving, free, or on very moderate terms. The school was founded and is directed by Mrs. Gad, wife of an Admiral in the Danish Navy. The Women's Kitchen, an excellent institution, was started by two ladies as a private undertaking; here women of all classes can obtain their meals served at a well-laid table for a very small sum, two well-cooked and substantial courses costing 45 öre (6d.). The Women's Commercial Club, originally founded merely for social gatherings and lectures, was soon able to provide for its members in old age and sickness. It is worthy of mention that the intercourse between the sexes at colleges, in offices and clubs, is quite free and natural, but marked by sound tact: there is no idle flirtation. This fact has contributed much to the advancement and development of women. On the other hand it is said that since the admission of women to these institutions drinking and gambling in clubs have decreased, and the only habit which the fair sex shows a tendency to adopt is that of smoking.

Institutions for Women.

Danish women, as indeed Danes generally, are of a gay and bright temperament, quick of comprehension, and with a well developed æsthetic sense.

Danish Characteristics.

In no other country is there such a sale for works of *belles lettres* as compared with the number of the population. However, the Danes are not exactly hard-working, they like to take life easily, and it would be better if the English proverb "Time is Money" were more widely recognised.

The High School, founded by the famous bishop N. F. S. Grundtvig, exerts great influence in the country, and almost every young man or young girl has attended for one or two terms. Great stress is there laid on national history, political economy, the study of the old folk-songs and national literature. Grundtvig called his school "A school for life." There are at present about ninety high schools in Denmark, of which Askov Hojskole is the most celebrated, and many strangers, especially English, come to see it. Much as the high schools have raised the status of the rural population, they have also contributed in part to the deplorable fact that manual help on the farms is becoming more and more difficult to obtain: in many cases the daughters and sons of the wealthier peasants who are studying in towns are called home to work, most unwillingly, on the parental farms.

The Influence of the High School.

Farm-work is much lightened nowadays by the presence of co-operative dairies, which are found in each village, and by machinery. The women, nevertheless, find plenty to do with housekeeping, cooking, and attending to the poultry, for eggs are an important article of export.

Danish Hospitality.

Food is rich and rather heavy; butter is used in great quantities, though in later years, owing to the increased exportation to England, it is in many cases replaced by margarine. Danish "sandwiches" (*smorrebrod*) form a noteworthy item of the national diet. Big loaves are cut into slices which are thickly buttered and covered with dainty slices of meat, sausage, ham, egg, or cheese; these are always prepared by the women with the greatest care, and are served three or four times a day. Dinner is the only hot meal. In some places, however, barley porridge is served in the morning, or a kind of soup prepared from rye-bread and beer.

A WOMAN OF THE ISLAND OF FANO

Baking and brewing on the farms have nearly died out; the bakers' and brewers' carts call at nearly every cottage door and provide the inmates with what they require. Only on the larger farms fine bread and cakes are made to eat with tea and coffee, and they are in great request, for the old hospitality still exists to a certain degree.

When a guest arrives the table is immediately laid for him with an abundance unequalled in any other country. This hospitality is carried to such lengths that, in some parts, an extra and substantial meal will be prepared late at night. When the neighbours drop in after supper, coffee and cakes are brought at once, and later when the guests commence leave-taking the hostess presses

WEDDING COSTUME WORN ON THE ISLAND OF AMAC.

them to resume their seats, saying "You won't refuse to take a bit of bread?" and at once the table is laid with meat, ham, cheese, sweets, beer, brandy, schnapps and coffee. The latter is much drunk, and is to the women what schnapps is to the men; in many kitchens the coffee-kettle is never off the fire, and is continually being replenished.

The celebration of weddings on the large farms in many parts of the country lasts for two d s or more. The ceremony takes place on the first day, and is followed by the great wedding dinner at which the clergyman and his wife are present. The men and women—groom and bride excepted—sit apart, arranged according to rank and degree of relationship to the bridal couple.

Feasts for all Events.

Funeral ceremonies last only one day, and are also accompanied by much eating and drinking. The coffin rests in the middle of the state-room, surrounded by the nearest female relatives clad in black and with prayer-book and handkerchief in hand. Their head-dresses are covered with black veils. The chief among them stands at the head of the coffin and removes the "eye-cloth" (*ojenkladet*) every time a fresh guest approaches.

When a baby is born the female neighbours, dressed in their best, bring the young mother all sorts of dainties, and are regaled with coffee. A religious ceremony worthy of mention is the churching of women. The mother waits in the porch until the clergyman advances to receive her; after having spoken a few words to her and blessed her, he leads her into the church.

As the old customs are gradually disappearing, so is the national dress. Of this, originally, there were many varieties, for each district had its own.

The National Dress.

Common to all is the heavy gathered skirt of home-spun wool, and the large apron of black wool or ilk, with broad, flowing ribbons. The head-dress, which entirely covers the hair, is usually richly embroidered with gold, silver or linen thread, and bears long bows of coloured ribbon. The costumes are now only found in occasional use, but in most places at festivals the elder women may be seen in them. Strangely enough most of the women in two villages quite close to the metropolis, Amager — called the Kitchen-garden of Copenhagen—and Skovshoved—a fishing village—retain them and so dressed bring their goods to market. In the little isle of Fano in the North Sea, near Esbjerg, and in parts of the west coast of Jutland, the women when working in the fields wear masks of black satin, to protect them from the sharp sea breeze.

In the numerous fishing villages along the Danish coast the women help the men to mend the fishing-nets, a task which involves considerable labour. They also sell the fish not suitable for export or for the great markets; they carry it in baskets on their backs, and go from house to house, often for long distances.

Position of Danish Women.

Danish women, in the country as well as in the towns, are greatly interested in political and social matters, and now that they have obtained electoral rights their influence is sure to be felt in many ways. The next step will doubtless be their admission to the great political elections, and as important men, as well as women, are working for this end, it is only a question of time.

DANISH COSTUMES.

SWEDISH WOMEN AGRICULTURISTS. *Photograph by Ad. Stähre, Kisa.*

SWEDEN

By MARY T. NATHHORST

Characteristics—The Position of Swedish Women—Work and Wages—Higher Education—The Peasantry —Town Workers—The Arts in Sweden—The Growing Influence of "Mam'selle"

THE Swedish woman shares her chief characteristics with other branches of the Germanic race, and her nearest relative is undoubtedly the Finn. Both Finn and Swede are honest and fair-dealing, frank and loyal; perhaps rather phlegmatic in temperament, but at the same time of a lively fancy, and gifted with a great propensity for dreaming. If there is a difference between the two, it lies in the more earnest nature of the Finn, in her more serious view of life, and in her deep interest in social questions; while the Swede is more refined, more highly cultured, and takes broader views of things in general.

Characteristics.

If we compare the Swede with the women of less closely related races, we may say that while both she and the Norwegian are industrious and independent, the woman of Norway is more wide-awake mentally, and has a more breezy manner; while the Swede has more natural tact and a finer feeling of modesty. The Swede shares with the women of Germany the love of home, but not the delight in daily work; she resembles the Englishwoman in her love of sport and the open air, though she lacks her endurance, her patriotism, and her interest in politics.

The hair of a Swedish woman is generally brown, her eyes are grey or blue, and her active love of sport gives her a fresh complexion and a well-developed figure above medium height. What she lacks in classical beauty she makes up by her temperament, which gives brilliance to her eyes, an ever-changing colour to her cheeks, and deep soft tones to her voice. To this must be added that the Swedish woman dresses well—better, indeed, than any other daughter of the Germanic race.

The Position of Swedish Women.

The Swedish woman was one of the first whose position was improved by the emancipatory movement of the last century. Fredrike Bremer put an axe to the root of those prejudices which hindered the poor but educated woman from doing anything better for her living than working as a governess. Much has already been accomplished, and the unseemly strife, which comes to the fore in other countries when the woman question first makes its appearance, is a thing of the past in Sweden. True, the suffrage, which was the first question to unite the majority of Swedish women under the standard of emancipation, is still before us; but, thanks to the assistance of the men, we are not compelled to use such aggressive means as some Englishwomen consider necessary. This is well, for we earnestly desire the end of the conflict, and we desire, moreover, that the attitude of the emancipated woman may not divide the sex but so preserve the subtle bouquet of womanhood that a suffragist will only differ from another woman in her profounder conception of life, in her deeper realisation of its responsibilities, in her wider interests, and in her more tolerant views.

Work and Wages.

What we lack, above all, is a feeling of solidarity, not so much as a protection against man as against each other; the question of wages is the dark side of woman's life in Sweden. She is paid starvation wages, and there are few instances of women receiving as good a salary as men.

When Ellen Key some fifteen years ago declared that woman would be happier in more womanly occupations, the dictum was received with a storm of resentment; she, so it was declared, "was in the pay of man—she was betraying her own sex." But years and experience have made our warlike words more mild, and taught us that woman should know her own resources before she applies herself to new work: taught us, above all, that to woman belongs the care of the children — the nation's wealth and hope for the future.

Photograph by Granbergs Konstindustrie-Aktiebolags Förlag, Stockholm.

SWEDISH GIRLS OF RÄTTVIK.

A society has been formed which aims at giving practical training to young women of all classes in the rational treatment of children. After three months' instruction in the care of children, the young women utilise their knowledge either in their own homes or act as instructors themselves. Schools have also been founded for training in domestic economy and practical housekeeping.

Reform in housekeeping is one of the questions of the day, as a natural result of the servant famine. The servants are recruited from the ignorant and irresponsible classes; domestic work is not held in honour, and the mistress has to face ever-increasing demands on the part of the servant. The Swedish woman is in some things absurdly conservative, but a refreshing breeze of practicality has blown over the girls of Sweden, and every year she has new openings for wage-earning occupations.

The Peasantry.

should. In places where home "sloyd" has begun to blossom again, there is some dawning of prosperity. Weaving or lace-making brings in a welcome addition to the pittance to be earned by agriculture. But in some places the soil is so poor that the

Photograph by Ad. Stähre, Kisa.

A CLASS OF INSTRUCTION IN HOME "SLOYD."

married women have to leave their home and children in winter under the care of the old women, and themselves go away to richer parts to earn money, returning in spring to till and sow the land.

Higher Education.

Higher education for women is a reality in Sweden; at the age of eighteen or twenty a girl passes the high school examination and goes to the University. The philosophical faculty counts the greatest number of female students, then comes medicine, then law, and last of all, with very few, theology. The university course finished, girls pass on to their work in life, some as teachers, some as midwives, some as instructors of home "sloyd," and so on.

I know few beings more pitiable than our poor peasant women; their whole existence is children and cooking, children and mending, children and children without end; and withal not the shadow of a notion of how to care for children or household as they

Town Workers.

Poor girls who earn their livings as sempstresses, nurses, shop-girls, and so on, as a rule, lead respectable lives. Waitresses have not a specially bad reputation, and even the "bath-women," whose offices are, to the just astonishment of foreigners, available for both sexes, give no cause for scandal.

Sweden, by the way, is not rich in women of distinction: a few authors and singers are known outside our frontiers, but most enjoy at best a home reputation only.

Such artistic ability as we have is utilised mainly in our arts and crafts, especially the textile industries. Many women devote their lives to art embroidery, lace-making, tapestry-weaving, and so on. Another field of work in which the Swedish woman stands first is gymnastics and massage.

The Arts. in Sweden.

The married woman of means leads, if possible, a more industrious life than the unmarried woman; true she seldom has an occupation outside her home, but the Swedish woman does not marry in order that she may have more leisure. Marriage is, as a rule, fairly happy, owing to the freedom with which the youth of both sexes can associate before the fateful knot is tied.

The Growing Influence of "Mam'selle."

In middle-class families the number of children seldom exceeds four; the working classes often exceed this, but just now the "two-children" movement is gaining ground in Sweden. If woman is over-burdened with household duties, it is not because she has too many children, but because of the unpractical way in which she arranges her life; her spheres of interest become limited, and in social life she has a dangerous rival in the wide-awake, interesting young spinster. There is nothing more characteristic of Sweden at the present day than the growing influence of the "mam'selle."

Photograph by Granbergs Konstindustrie-Aktiebolags Förlag, Stockholm.

SWEDISH GIRL OF FLODA, DALARNE.

NORWAY

By GINA KROG

Norwegian Characteristics—Women and Out-door Life—Ski-ing—Women in Civil Life—Enfranchisement of Women—The Dignity of the Peasantry—Women and Weaving—The National Costume—Bridal Costumes and Customs—Mountain Life—Fisher-women—The Laplanders

THE Norwegian women who take part in the social life of the towns are not very different from the women of other civilised countries: their manners, dress, and general behaviour are in accordance with the rules set down by European custom, although it is by no means unusual to hear foreigners comment upon their happy temperament and the absence of conventionality which they frequently display.

Norwegian Characteristics.

A free, untrammelled comradeship between the two sexes has always been a distinctive feature of Norwegian life, and this, together with the newly-won social independence and out-door life of women, has set its mark upon the younger generation.

Those who visit Christiania in winter will see a sporting life in which the young women share to an extent that is unknown in other countries. They are to be seen going out in troops, accompanied by friends and brothers, or women by themselves, as the case may be. Two or three together, sitting on the long, sleigh-like toboggan called a *kjælke*, steering with a stick fifteen feet in length, they rush down the steep roads and round the neck-breaking curves, while the sound of their laughter penetrates the clear winter air.

Women and Out-door Life.

But ski-ing is the favourite amusement; it was first introduced into the towns from the outlying country districts, where skis are often necessary as a means of getting about, and it has won the chief place among winter sports. Thirty years ago it was considered a mark of eccentricity when a lady went out on skis, but now it has become the universal custom amongst the younger women in all classes of society. On Saturday evenings, or as soon as the day's work is over, the working clothes are cast aside and a ski costume is adopted in its place. This consists of an ordinary coat, or a bolero, and short skirt of tweed or thick woollen homespun, a soft woollen cap with or without ear-lappets, and a pair of long knitted gloves reaching half-way to the elbow, and often embroidered. In addition to these, some people wear Lapp boots. Light grey or blue are the usual colours worn, and sometimes the dress is enlivened with bright-coloured borders copied from the national costume, but upon the whole there is great variety, both as regards colour and style.

Ski-ing.

With skis on their feet and staff in hand, off they go. Many women are excellent ski-runners, but as a rule they are not ambitious from a sporting point of view; they look upon it more as a means of enjoyment than as an end in itself, and they often go with their friends for a trip lasting several days to ski huts on the hills, and then a small knapsack becomes a necessary part of the outfit.

Norwegian women occupy posts in the civil life of the country which are not open

A WOMAN OF HARDANGER, NORWAY.
DRAWN BY R. B. M. PAXTON.

Facing on page 748

to their sisters in other lands. In a local court of justice it is not uncommon to find women there, not merely as plaintiffs, witnesses, or listeners, but also as jurors chosen by the people, and doing their share of the work with thoroughness. In many of the town and county councils women may be seen sitting side by side with men, and the same is the case on school boards, workhouse committees, and other municipal bodies.

Women in Civil Life.

The Woman's Cause has advanced with great strides during the last generation. The way for it was prepared in literature by the greatest writers of the nation, and twenty-five years ago it had become a practical question among women themselves. One reform after another was passed with increasing energy, and the women who are leaders of the movement have gradually gained the support of the foremost lawyers and politicians. In 1901 women obtained the municipal franchise and the right of election to local boards, and on June 14th, 1907, they gained the political franchise, with the right to election as members of the *Storthing* (Parliament), but they have not got it on the same terms as men, who have universal franchise. For this reason there is still cause for agitation in the women's camp. Meetings and lectures are being held with the object of keeping the question to the fore, but, although the proceedings are conducted with great enthusiasm, they are not lacking in dignity.

Enfranchisement of Women.

In 1909 women will take part in the political elections for the first time; they have already voted at municipal elections. In towns, where it is merely a question of walking to one of the many polling booths and delivering a voting paper, women are to be met in crowds on election days. Husbands and wives are seen going together, generally to vote for the same candidate, but sometimes for opposite parties. In the country, where distances are great and the

Photograph by E. Enger, Christiania.

A MARRIED WOMAN FROM THE PARISH OF FANE, NEAR BER.

roads often bad, fewer women use their right; yet there are some districts where the women make every effort to record their votes: mothers carrying young children are often seen at the polling booths. There is no harm in accustoming them in good time to the public duties which now await the girls no less than the boys.

On the other hand there are a few outlying districts where not a single woman is to be seen at the poll; but it is safe to prophesy that in a few years' time these ideas will have penetrated to the remotest

Photograph by A. B. Wilse, Christiania.

A NORWEGIAN GIRL SKI-ING.

village, and the women will come forward in the interests of society.

The Dignity of the Peasantry.

Although in these and in many other ways women are taking their share in the pulsating life of modern times, we dare to hope that they will not lose that part of their old habits and customs which is most valuable. All who are acquainted with the historical development of Norway know that there is a great deal of the old aristocratic culture retained among the Norwegian peasantry,* not least noticeable among the women. Even superficial observers cannot help being aware of the dignity and nobility of bearing which characterise the peasant women in some of the remotest valleys of Norway.

When the railways forced their way up the valleys it seemed probable that they would wipe out all that was most characteristic of Norway. Tourists and collectors invaded the country, purchasing for ridiculously small sums all the home-made articles they could find in the way of clothes, furniture and jewellery, many of which were genuine masterpieces. But at present there is a national renaissance which is doing all that is possible to encourage home industries, to raise the standard of language

* The meaning attached to the Norwegian word "bonde" is not exactly what we mean by "peasant." A "bonde" is a landowner, not an ordinary labourer. —TRANSLATOR'S NOTE.

Photograph by S. Lund, Christiania.

A PEASANT BRIDE FROM SOGN (NEIGHBOURHOOD OF BERGEN).

and architecture, and to preserve many of the good old customs. Some of the mountain districts and places near the sea have remained almost untouched by the levelling tendencies of modern times.

Women and Weaving.

The art of weaving has always held a high place among the women of the country, some of whom have shown remarkable powers of invention, imagination, and good taste in their work. By this means they have given fresh impulse to modern art, and a revival of the industry has been brought about throughout the country, thanks to the patronage of rich people and the encouragement received from museums in the towns. The women in the farmhouses look forward with pleasure to the quiet hours when they can lay aside their household work and sit at their looms.

They also embroider trimmings for their dresses in coloured wool or in white linen. The celebrated linen embroideries, known as Hardanger, are done on the west coast, and are very fine and artistic.

The National Costume.

There is great variety in the national costume which is still worn in Norway, both on week-days and holidays. Of the two principal types of women's dress, the first may be described as a short skirt, sewn on to a low bodice without sleeves, worn over a loose blouse of white or coloured material. In some west country districts the married women wear a folded white handkerchief, called a "skant," on the head. The second type of dress resembles the Empire style, and the women who wear it have beautiful trousseaus. The skirt reaches up close under the arms, and is worn short on week-days when it is gathered up round the waist with a broad leather belt and trimmed with braid. But the best dress has a long skirt, trimmed with coloured embroideries of great beauty. With regard to the minor details there are many variations of these two types in the different districts. The costume worn by the women of Sætersdal is an artistic example of the Empire style. It consists of two frieze skirts gathered round the waist and attached to braces, so that the weight is equally distributed. The underneath skirt is white, of undyed wool, with a black border round the hem, while the upper skirt is black with a red border. The white skirt is the longer of the two, and its black border is allowed to show below the other. Both these skirts are short, the longer does not reach very far below the knees. On Sundays and holidays a black frieze jacket with long sleeves is worn, and in addition to this a pretty homespun shawl, which is very long, and gives an Oriental touch to the costume. When all these are worn together the costume is naturally very heavy, and it requires no little skill to wear it gracefully, but to those who are tall and have well-developed figures, it can be very becoming. Many of the women of Sætersdal have a very graceful walk.

Bridal Costumes and Customs.

In some of the west country districts the bridal costumes are very beautiful indeed; they are trimmed with silk ribbons woven in colours or in gold and silver, with long chains and other ornaments round the neck and a crown upon the head. It is quite an art to adorn a bride in this manner.

In olden times there were numerous customs connected with courtship and marriage, of which only a few remain, but the marriage ceremonies still occupy several days, and the evenings are spent in dance and merriment. The modern international dances are to be seen as well as the old ones, and some of the latter are very intricate.

It generally happens that the bride enters upon a life of hard work, for during the last few years it has become more difficult to procure labourers to do the farm work, and the women are kept hard at it from morning to night to prepare the food necessary for man and beast.

As St. John's Eve draws nigh, the mountain districts are filled with life and merriment. The cattle have to be driven up to the mountain pastures, and the girls are delighted when it falls to their lot to live at the *sæters*, where their voices can be heard echoing among the hills as they call the cows.

Mountain Life.

Sometimes a girl is obliged to live quite alone in one of these *sæter* huts, but she does not mind it in the least; she enjoys the mountains and the solitude. Saturday evening is a holiday for her, and she takes pride in seeing that everything is tidy and in good order; then if the right man comes he is sure to be well received. Strangers, however, are also welcomed, and treated to cream and porridge and other good things. The young women in these mountain districts are very honest and reliable, as well as pleasant and hospitable in their manners.

In summer-time the women take part in the out-of-door work on the farms, but as a rule there is an arbitrary division between men's work and women's work.

Women lead a very different life on the sea-coast among the fisher folk from that passed at the farms and *sæters*. When the herring fishing is in progress the women take their share of the work, and crowds of them may be seen standing in their yellow oilskins and cutting up the herrings with a speed that is almost incredible.

Fisher-women.

In Nordland, when the annual fishing takes place, which lasts until early spring, the men leave their homes to go to the big fishing "stations," as they are called, and the women are overburdened with work. No sooner have they equipped their husbands for their long absence from home than they have not only their own work to do, but the men's also; they have to go out in the boats and to attend to the farm work as well.

Further inland, in Nordland and Finmarken, we come upon a different race of people who are not troubled with work of this kind. These are the nomadic Laplanders whose whole occupation consists in looking after the reindeer, and preparing all with which the deer provide them for food and clothing. During the short summer months the little Lapp women may be seen, dressed in their practical and picturesque cloth garments, busily employed round about their tents, with their babies on their backs in small cradles manufactured out of bark. During the long winter season they are obliged to clothe themselves in reindeer fur, and when they go out they either drive in a *pulkha*, a sleigh drawn by reindeer, or they go on skis over the endless expanse of snow, lit by the flames of the Northern Lights.

The Laplanders.

ICELAND

By EMMY DRACHMANN

A Primitive Land—Woman's Work—National Dress—A Democratic People

A Primitive Land.

THIS great island affords an inhospitable lodging for the sparse population scattered along its coasts. The inhabitable portion consists of a strip of ground between the foot of the glaciers and the coast, and those parts of the narrow valleys which are nearest to the ocean; the remainder is one huge ice-plateau.

The inhabitants live principally by sheep-rearing and fishing, and the women, as well as the men, must labour hard to gain their modest livelihood.

A WOMAN OF ICELAND.

Life is very primitive, the houses, except in the towns—of which there are but four in the island—are built mainly of turf and wood. The rooms are constructed separately, each under its own roof, and are connected by corridors. Along the wall of the principal room are arranged the beds, which serve as seats during the day. Two individuals sleep in each bed, the men on one side of the room, the women on the other: for the head of the family and his wife a corner of the room is screened off. Statistics show that these conditions have no prejudicial effect on morality.

Woman's Work.

The food is prepared in the apartment called the *ildhuset* (*ild* fire, *huset* house), and the women, who eat by themselves in the kitchen, serve the meals in wooden bowls to the men as they sit on their bedsteads in the *badstofa*. The fare is very plain, consisting of porridge or milk-soup, fish, and sometimes meat, which is nearly always dried, salted or smoked. The Icelanders are very modest in their ideas of luxury, and by no means *gourmands;* in fact, meat and fish is often eaten when not quite fresh, and found delicious. Coffee is drunk in great quantities, though not, of course, to the same extent in the poorer households, where it is considered a great luxury. Cows are found on every farm, and these are milked by the women, who also make the butter and cheese. From the sheeps' milk they prepare, during summer, the national dish called *skyr;* the whey is separated from the curd and the latter stored for the winter when milk is scarce. The work of a woman is very hard in winter; she often has to fetch water for the cattle from long distances, she must assist the men with their fishing-implements, and dry and mend their clothes. In the evenings and in her spare time she is busy spinning, weaving and embroidering in gold and silver; for the state-room is decorated with woven carpets, and the woman's dress on festal occasions is richly ornamented.

National Dress.

In distinction from the men, the women wear national costume, of which there are two separate varieties, one for every day, and one for times of festivity. The first consists of a full, gathered skirt of home-spun wool, a large coloured apron, a tight-fitting bodice with a broad velvet border round the sleeves and down the front, which is open, showing the white chemisette. The head-dress is quite characteristic. It consists of a small circular piece of black cloth (formerly tightly knitted), six or eight inches in diameter, which is fastened with pins to the crown; in the centre of this is fastened a projection of cloth, like a glove-finger, ending in a brass or silver tube, which terminates in a black silk tassel, about twelve inches long, hanging down over the ear.

The festal garb consists of skirt and bodice decorated with gold and silver embroidery on velvet ribbons; the chemisette is an exquisite piece of needle-work; the girdle consists of oblong silver plates of fine filigree. The head-dress is helmet-shaped, of white linen stretched over a cardboard frame filled with cotton, and covered with a long embroidered veil. This is secured by means of a tiara, also of rich filigree. A dark blue velvet cap, trimmed with sable, is used for outdoor wear.

Common to all Icelanders, men and women alike, is a strongly-developed, independent nature. They have a natural antipathy to subordination and but little respect for authority; they are remarkably democratic, and cling to their individual rights.

ICELANDIC WEDDING COSTUME.

A Democratic People.

The old Sagas still play an important part in their mental life, and they love to dwell on the former glorious days of their country. Although there are but thirty established schools in the island—instruction in the country is obtained from wandering teachers—yet every Icelander reads and knows the Sagas, and even the poorest home possesses one or more volumes of the national poetry.

THE BRITISH ISLES

By M. H. MORRISON

The Era of Enlightenment—As to Numbers—The New Generation—The Initiative Power—Woman in Sport—Influence in Politics—The "Home" Influence—As Wife and Mother—The "Bachelor Woman"—The Power of the Middle Class—The Lower Rank—The Aristocracy—Characteristics of the Scotswoman—Types—The Irish "Mary"—No Middle Class—Influence of the Priest—The Celtic Temperament—"The Gentry"—Welsh Characteristics—Education—The Possibilities of the Welsh Woman

The Era of Enlightenment.

THE English woman, it has been said, lags behind her husband, the American woman strides ahead, the French woman walks beside him. Of the American and the French woman the reflection remains true. Of the English woman it is becoming less true, and of the Welsh woman apparently scarcely true at all. For this thanks is due to the era of enlightenment through which the sex is passing, and for which we need a word as neatly comprehensive as *Meiji* is of the present era of enlightenment in Japan, which, by the way, closely corresponds in number of years with the Woman Movement here.

As to Numbers.

The women of England, especially as seen in our too-absorbing London, are taken, by foreign observers at any rate, as the type of the women of the whole kingdom. And from the point of view of numbers there is much to be said for that assumption.

Whereas, according to the last census, the people of Ireland number 4,458,775, of whom 2,258,735 are women; and Scotland 4,472,103 of whom 2,298,348 are women, the people of England and Wales number 32,527,843, of whom, in round figures, 17,000,000 are women and 16,000,000 men. Curiously enough, women emigrate in larger numbers than men from the country places, perhaps because of the demand for domestic servants. In the record of 259,400 marriages the brides were made of 240,807 spinsters and 18,593 widows—enough to justify old Weller's remark, "Be wery careful o' widders!" The most recent returns show that of women under the age of forty-five years 4,133,322 were unmarried, and the wives and widows together numbered 3,987,525. The spinsters are greatly in excess of the bachelors in the Home Counties and in those districts where women take a large part in the staple industry. In Surrey the unmarried women of twenty-five and upwards are nearly 12,000 in excess of the bachelors; but in South Wales the bachelors of corresponding age are 18,429 in excess of the spinsters.

The New Generation.

As the John Bull of caricature has given place to a John Bull not yet delineated—the hard-headed, keen, city man of wide-world interests; so the extremely beautiful, but rather characterless, type of English beauty published some months ago by an illustrated daily is giving place to a young womanhood of distinctive personality, liberal education, many interests, wide sympathies.

Our men to-day are not very different from what we would wish them to be. Those of our women who have the interests at heart of nation and of sex try to bring our girls into line. This is conspicuously so among the upper middle classes, whose influence is specially dominant amongst us and is telling in the ranks below and above.

AN ENGLISH GIRL.
DRAWN BY NORMAN H. HARDY.

Facing on page 756

Taunts that had the sting of truth some years ago, that women could not initiate, could not organise, could not hold together, now fall impotent to the ground. Not to mention the women's colleges of Oxford and Cambridge, the High Schools for Girls have revealed a wealth of private enterprise on the part of women that is the constant theme of praise. Proof also of this can be found in the ladies' clubs that have been inaugurated; in the professions of which, despite opposition and sometimes obloquy, they have pushed open the door; and in the many occupations which thev have entered or have actually created.

The Initiative Power.

Turning to the realm of sport, they now take an increasing part in otter-hunting, in bloodhound trials, hare-hunting, whippet-racing, spaniel and pointer field trials, yachting, angling, in deer-stalking and big-game shooting—in mountaineering, ballooning, curling, tobogganing, fencing, *jiu-jitsu!* And there has just been started a school where they can learn motoring as a profession.

Woman in Sport.

As to politics, there is not an organisation in this country among men but has its keenly alert counterpart, quite as far-reaching, amongst women, And the militant Suffrage Societies, acting on the principle laid down by Coke that Ministers only yield when goaded, have let loose explosive forces unsuspected in the women of the country, to which there are no exact parallels in history unless it be certain episodes in the French Revolution.

Influence in Politics.

But the background to all this intensity of life is the same as in the past. Not to mention our lovely park-like country with hedge-divided fields and dreamy villages, there is the English Home; and "the comfort, the organisation, and the unbroken peace of a well-managed English household are not surpassed, in some details not equalled, anywhere in the world," which is as one would expect in the country of "Home, Sweet Home." In material things, too, its charm is not easily matched. In winter our open fire-places are the most æsthetic thing we have; in summer our gardens are a delight we take for granted till we miss them elsewhere, especially in Scotland.

The "Home" Influence.

As to the heart and soul of the Home, the wife and mother, these two apparently opposing observations are made of her. One foreign critic amongst us says the Englishwoman is a better friend of her husband than of her children; that Englishmen take themselves far more seriously than their women-folk, who, instead of retaliating, yield a largely unsolicited loyalty, whilst the children are left far too much to the care of nurses and of schools. Max O'Rell, too, has pointed out—though the picture is almost out of date—that the woman here is to man a necessary evil, and her submission lies at the basis of the social system; that when the Frenchwoman marries her good time begins; when an Englishwoman marries her good time, which might include flirting, ends; her function is to give *des enfants*, not *des conseils*. She knows nothing of her husband's business: when he fails he simply says, "We must go to Australia." "Yes, John," she replies submissively; "just give me time to get my hat!" On the other hand, a well-known woman worker amongst us, who is constantly moving amongst the mothers, rich and poor, of our land, declares they are "better as mothers than as wives; they are good at making nets to catch husbands, but not cages to keep them; whereas they can best serve their children by humouring him to be a good father; that a man, in other words, ought to be able to say of his wife, as of Cleopatra, 'Nothing can stale her infinite variety.' A wife, then, should not let her husband tire of her by letting him be too sure he has got her; the guile of the serpent is as useful as the innocency of the dove." Another criticism she utters is that women are now far too sentimental in

As Wife and Mother.

the up-bringing of children; that a return to Spartan-like hardness is necessary.

The "Bachelor Woman."

As to the unmarried women of the country, apart from the pity of it that there should be so much waste motherhood, their preponderance is a good thing for the woman movement, for it is they who give continuity to every great cause; it is they who show what women can do in any career they seriously take up; it is they also who screw salaries up to a higher level. However, the bachelor woman has done much to lengthen the prime of women's life. Formerly the maiden was "finished" at seventeen, and old at thirty; now the University woman of twenty-two or twenty-three is as fresh and callow as her brother undergraduate and as full of revolutionary ideas. At the other end of the scale the grandmother is no more.

The Power of the Middle Class.

To sum up: the change in type has been most marked in, as it has certainly been pioneered by, the upper middle or professional classes, who have had the advantage of a good secondary education, leading in many cases to the University. It is worth while emphasising this fact, because the influence of these women is spreading to the class above, and in a more organised degree to the classes below.

But the limits of such influence are soon reached. It has been declared that the lower middle, or tradesmen, classes do not command respect because they do not respect themselves, a condition very different from that obtaining among the corresponding class in France; and that they betray especially the national trait of snobbery.

The Lower Rank.

It is from this class are recruited the ranks of County Council teachers, dressmakers, shop-girls, tea-room waitresses, barmaids, the last-named including some of the best-looking women in the country. The affectation of the past in the girl of this class has given way, if not to an effort to imitate the voice aristocratic, at any rate to a voice that is fuller and not so loud. The vocabulary, too, has improved; but, leaving out of account the teachers, the novel and the novelette is with this type an intoxication that gives nothing in return save a silly view of life. Her dress (also that of the factory girl who goes to evening club) has improved from frills and furbelows to trimness. But, speaking generally, she spends a far larger sum, actual and proportional, on dress than, say, the High School mistress and her friends in the class above. She is also prettier, and her carriage finer, attributable, doubtless, to her emancipation from tight lacing and tight boots, and to the physical training got at school.

The Aristocracy.

Among the aristocracy one feels that change has been less marked. The type of high-born woman to-day is not very dissimilar from the type of high-born women painted by Sir Joshua Reynolds and by Romney. There has been less change, it may be, because less was needed. As in the past, the home governess is in requisition; foreign travel and thorough training in modern languages have been easily available; and companionship with statesmen, leaders, men of affairs, with those who make history was, and is, even more inspiriting than a University education. But the line of demarcation between this class and the professional is becoming blurred; for a certain number of girls belonging to the upper ten thousand have been educated at such schools as Cheltenham Ladies' College.

Coming to the apex of society, it is significant of much else as well as of our warm loyalty to the throne that we feel closer in sympathy to our Queen and Royal Family than we do even to the aristocracy.

Characteristics of the Scotswoman.

"Does the Scotswoman lag further behind her husband than the Englishwoman?" asked the writer of a distinguished Scotsman? "No," he replied, "she sits at his feet!" The Scotch family, then, retains a certain patriarchal atmosphere.

This in turn is not unconnected with the idea of clanship expressed now, not in warfare, but on festive occasions in the rivalry of the tartan, and in thoughts of romance, no small element in the make-up of the cautious Scot. At the same time the enormous share the Scotswoman has taken for ages in agriculture and in fishing, and for many years in the textile industries, has been not without influence in placing her on terms of equality with men. Her separate personality has also been marked by the custom of a married woman being known to her neighbours by her maiden name. "Margaret Ogilvy" stands as proof of it.

Types.

Glasgow, Edinburgh, Aberdeen, St. Andrews, each with a character of its own, together have done much to build up the professional woman as we know her to-day; but her footprints are usually found on the road south, where she mingles with her kind.

For other strong types, not newly evolved but old, one must turn to the smaller towns, to the fishing villages, to the farms. The towns-wife is proud, self-respecting, exclusive, keeps herself to herself; and is reserved beyond the reserve of an Englishwoman, who, distant at the outset, will, once the barrier is removed, reveal everything. The Englishwoman on the whole is freer in manner with her husband, where the Scotswoman would defer to him. In dress and *coiffure* she is not so attractive as the Englishwoman, who generally manages to be trim in the afternoon. Though thrifty in many things like the Frenchwoman, yet, unlike her, her culinary acquisitions leave much to be desired. The "halesome parritch," no longer "chief of Scotia's food," is too often supplanted, not by a variety of wholesome dishes, but by innutritious baker's confectionery; for the teaching of cookery in the schools and the improved type of stove being introduced have not yet fulfilled their promise.

The fish-wife is always picturesque with her short winsey petticoat, plaid "shawlie," mutch, or hood cap, and her creel suspended by a broad band from the top of the head. Physically big, muscular, healthy in character, she is the soul of honour, of truthfulness, of fine emotions; but she is unprogressive, and her outlook limited.

Photograph by W. Reid.

SCOTCH FARM GIRLS.

On the other hand the farmer's wife has her horizon bounded only by the ends of the earth. She is a woman of affairs. Not only does she bake, cook, wash, sew, knit, but will take a turn in the field and help stack the peat; her influence also is felt in Church work, in business, and even in local government. A voracious reader, not of novels, but of the weekly paper, she is always well informed. Above all, she is a mother who has given to the Empire many of her ablest sons.

The Scots have many of the fine qualities of the English—only more so.

Husband and wife are on excellent terms, and equally enjoy the joke that the best Englishman is a Scotsman! The women north of the Tweed are more serious, more tender, and more religious than their sisters on this side. They are slower to take up any new thing; but once converted are more full of zeal, of fire, and of staying power.

Photograph by W. Lawrence, Dublin.

IRISH PEASANT GIRLS.

British women as a race are hospitable; but the educated, refined Scotswoman is the most charming hostess in the world. The American woman may excel her in the technical details of entertaining; but ere long will forget. The Scotswoman on the other hand puts her whole soul into the task. She gives you not only the hospitality of her home, but the hospitality of her heart!

The Irish "Mary."

How can one express more delicately the difference between the Irish and the English woman than by recalling once more the story of the Sisters of Bethany? Martha the Englishwoman is cumbered about much serving; Mary the Irishwoman leaves her to serve alone while she sits at the feet of the Master! The Englishwoman worships the great god Common Sense; the Irishwoman sits brooding at the altar of Might-have-been. Ireland is the skeleton in the cupboard of England—the thorn in her side, pricking her to remembrance of sad, unutterable things; and all she can utter in self-defence is the witticism: "The Irish don't know what they want, and won't be happy till they get it." They for ever pray "God save ould Ireland," forgetting that God only helps those who help themselves.

No Middle Class.

The poise in English society is found in the great progressive middle class, the hyphen between lower and upper. In Ireland there is practically no middle class. The small tradespeople approximate to the peasantry; the professional and gentlefolk approximate to, and in many parts form, the only aristocracy. The lower classes of Ireland, always omitting Ulster, are almost solidly Celtic, Roman Catholic, Nationalist—terms that for long, if not for ever, will there be almost interchangeable. Meanwhile there are 20,000 speaking Irish only. The upper classes, sprinkled with Protestantism, are less solidly Roman Catholic; also, being largely of English or Scotch descent, they are less solidly Irish. It follows then that as a class they are partly Nationalist and partly Royalist. And in matters social, where formerly they foregathered at Dublin, they now look too often above and beyond the Viceregal Lodge to London itself.

Worst of all there is not throughout the British Empire any poverty more intense, or, this side of the grave, more hopeless than that of an Irish cabin—the virility of the country has been sapped by excessive emigration; the residue is stagnating below the line of reason and even of sanity.

No country in Christendom reveals a higher standard of chastity, which must be put to the credit of the priest. A young man and woman show signs of being drawn to each other. "Now, Pat and Molly," says the priest, "you must get married." They obey, and start another homestead of indescribable dirt and untidiness, a fresh breeding-place for consumption, the curse of Ireland. Manure, hen, and piggery litter take the place of the English garden, not garnered in stacks at the dictation of thrift as in Eastern France, but because nothing matters "wan way or the other." These faults they reveal also as servants, but their good humour and unfailing kindliness atone. They are not easily "put upon," and their adaptability is wonderful.

Influence of the Priest.

As they share with the Church a portion of all they earn, so they will share literally anything with their neighbours in sickness and trouble —even a general pardon for inability to tell the truth! "I niver see anny harrm tellin' a lie, providid 'twas for a good purrpose," which good purpose their imagination always supplies.

The Celtic Temperament.

Turning to the gentry, a word common enough in Ireland, though like many other words and prejudices—political and religious—out of date in England, one finds their condition too characterised by poverty which, in face of public opinion, they are unable to mitigate. A professional man, for instance, would in many cases lose as much as he gained, by letting his daughters take up a career. You are supposed to lose caste by engaging in any but certain old-fashioned, over-stocked employments such as companion housekeeper, or invalid attendant; hence the Irish Central Bureau a year or two ago found itself unable to find ladies qualified to fill posts, the aggregate salaries of which totalled £3,000.

"The Gentry."

Yet educated Irishwomen are not without enterprise. But to find the necessary social conditions in which to exercise the quality they must leave the country. For Protestant girls the number of public secondary schools is very small. For Roman Catholics the higher education is carried on by the religious Orders, chiefly the Loretto, Dominican and Ursuline Sisterhoods. Taking the finer examples of educated women, they have, perhaps, a greater quickness of perception, a wider versatility of interest, keener love of argument, and more highly developed sense of humour than is revealed by the non-Celtic. Like the Irish climate of brilliant sunshine alternating with clouds and showers they, too, reveal the grave and gay; for underlying their mental alertness, vivacity, conversational power, there is a strain of sensitiveness and melancholy making a sum total that is not rightly comprehended by the less imaginative and comparatively unemotional Englishwomen.

JUST a supplementary note concerning the Welsh, for the details of which one is indebted to a distinguished Welsh lady. The races of mankind, it has been said, can be divided into masculine and feminine. The Welsh, then, with their delicacy of feeling, their adaptable and tractable ways, and their shy sensitiveness, are obviously feminine; and, as in other races where the feminine virtues are emphasised, the woman counts for very much. In a third-class carriage in England, crowded with working men and their wives, the former would talk together about politics, trade, etc., whilst the latter would remain silent or would talk apart. In Wales they would all talk together on terms of equality, for women take a very ample share in the life of the country. George Meredith, then, is true to his race in revealing the equality of men and women and in setting forth the characteristics of women as at once very charming and very clever.

Welsh Characteristics.

Geographically, by their mountains and valleys, historically and in language, the Welsh—who have not the slightest intention of becoming English — have been isolated from the other peoples of these islands, and in consequence have been much misunderstood. In passing, one might remark that the Welsh are shorter than the English, although there is a tall, dark variety; they have often small, beautiful hands and feet. Again, they are not clannish like the Scotch, nor aggressively nationalistic like the English. But with no Sir Walter Scott, no Barrie to portray them, they have, hitherto, been a dumb people. The very language they have been forced to learn at school has been to them a foreign tongue; and in examinations no allowance has been made for that fact. But now wiser counsels prevail. It is characteristic that the privileges and responsibilities of the Welsh University and colleges are open to women equally with men, who together reveal a perfect passion for secondary and higher education.

Education.

Thus the Welsh are beginning to believe in themselves and their possibilities: in future, then, let others, and especially the Scotch, beware. Meanwhile, it must be understood that the self-praise of a Welsh woman or man is really caused by lack of self-confidence, by surprised delight in the success achieved. They seem to think, says an English critic, that if one feels good what one does is not of much importance; and that in telling a story one need not be trammelled by facts. Certainly they find it difficult to tell the truth against friends towards whom they are intensely loyal and sympathetic. Democratic and intensely individualistic, it is difficult to maintain amongst them any combination or *esprit de corps*.

The Possibilities of the Welsh Woman.

The Welsh singer, of whom Mrs. Mary Davies is an excellent example, and the Welsh preacher—the woman preacher is in Wales no novelty—are the fullest expressions of Welsh life, but each depends very much upon his or her audience. If it is Welsh, they together see visions which do not appear to a colder race. It is worth mentioning that the women, like the men, discuss with keenest intellectual alertness the gravest theological, ethical, and philosophical problems. It is not, then, without significance that G. F. Watts, the artist preacher, true to his race, made earthly things symbols and stepping-stones by which to pass to things eternal, and represented Death not as a fierce man or skeleton of a man, but as a tender, loving woman.

Photograph by The Excelsior Photograph Company, Carmarthen.

SOME TYPICAL WELSH WOMEN.

THE UNITED STATES AND CANADA

By CHARLES E. ROCHE

The American Spirit—Foreign Opinion—An American Woman on American Women—The American Mother—Education—Girls' Colleges—Women in Politics—"Miss Mapleleaf"

THE American woman has, perhaps, been written about more critically, not to say, occasionally, savagely, and again admiringly or appreciatively than any other of her sex. A single specimen has oftentimes been selected, pinned down to a card, and psychologically dissected from a physiological standard, as if she were truly an emotional insect, and not a woman. And yet, this woman of the United States is very much a woman, and, from whatever State of the Union she may hail, she is all in all very American, in the sense that her men are American. "Americanism is not of birth, ancestry, or creed, but of the spirit within a man's soul," President Roosevelt has truly said, and that spirit is within the soul of the American woman, from Maine to California, and from the shores of the Great Lakes to the delta of the Mississippi. The same restless energy, the same thoroughness, the same perseverance in prosperity, and more especially in adversity, the same generous spirit, constitute the hall-mark of the woman of the Northern New Hemisphere. But it is impossible in her case, to make of her a type, for she represents, owing to her mixed ancestry, a great variety. The descendant of the old Knickerbockers who built Nieuw Amsterdam, nowadays New York, the New Englanders of English ancestry, the soft-voiced Floridan, in whose veins courses a strain of Spanish blood, the fair, or perhaps we should say dark Louisianan of French origin, the woman from the North-West, the daughter of vikings or men of the wicks, and she of the Pacific Slope, who, like her Floridan sister, owes something of herself to Spain, one and all may have their special temperaments and characteristics, but all possess the spirit of Americanism; in heart and mind they are Americans.

The American Spirit.

Writers of various nationalities have attempted to describe or analyse the American woman, but few there are who have been able to form a correct opinion of her or to make a judicial pronouncement in her case, as their knowledge of her has most often been of a fleeting kind. The French novelist's view of her may be treated as a negligible quantity, and cast aside with a smile. To him she is always the daughter of a *milliardaire*—a *millionnaire* would not suffice to gild the fair creature—and, according to him, she is little more than *un flirt*. It must be admitted that she does indulge in that pastime—it is a pleasure to her, though it cannot be said that it gives the man much, if any, pain; nay, it may be added that it gives him great pleasure while it lasts. After all, there is a good deal to be said in defence of the American girl's "flirtation." She has not, like girls of some other nations, been taught to look upon man as something vastly superior to herself; she has been brought up with him to a greater extent than her European sisters; she has never had the idea ingrained in her that she must get married early, and, consequently, jump at

Foreign Opinion.

Stereograph Copyright by Underwood & Underwood, London & New York.

MRS. ROOSEVELT AND MISS ETHEL ROOSEVELT.

the first man she meets. She prefers judging for herself. She never flirts with a man for whom she has a thorough respect.

In speaking of her, the late Sir Edwin Arnold was most complimentary. "Affrin!" (the Persian for "O Allah, make many more of them!") was the prayer he breathed, nor would he add another word about her.

His Excellency the Chinese Ambassador at Washington, Wu-Ting-fang, has thus put himself on record over his own signature: "The most pronounced mental characteristic of the American woman which I have observed is her quickness of understanding. To me her sense of perception is remarkable. When you tell her anything, however complicated, she grasps the idea at once. I hardly know how to analyse the origin of this sense. It is a trait very marked in all Americans, and developed to a high degree in the American women. Perhaps it is due to the fact that the United States was settled by pioneers. Women as well as men came over as pilgrims in the *Mayflower;* women as well as men settled at Jamestown, and other historic places, nearly three centuries ago; and, in later days, the wives and sisters of the frontiersmen made their way with their husbands and brothers across the continent until they reached the shores of the Pacific ocean. The American woman is the product of evolution. She comes by her sense of quick perception as a natural inheritance." Further on, the Ambassador remarks: "Very few of the American women are victims of *ennui*. They are always busy," and he concludes by saying: "When I speak of the American woman, I cannot say that there is really a prevailing type. It is a composite—a mixture of all types. The American type is a combination of all that is good in the types of the world."

Max O'Rell had this to say of the American women: "All are not handsome, but all are intelligent and beaming with activity."

An American Woman on American Women.

Mrs. Gertrude Atherton, herself a Californian, has pointed out wherein American and English girls differ, in the following terms: "Perhaps the greatest point of difference between the American and the English girl is the encouragement which the former receives, from the earliest possible period, to form and express her own opinions. This she does with a thoroughness which makes her a pest in the land as a child, but unquestionably contributes to the rapid development of her intelligence." In regard to the oft-made remark that the American girl "often buys titles," the well-known novelist has this to say: "The American girl who prefers a foreigner to one of her own countrymen is the exception, as can easily be proved by an examination of marriage records in the United States. Where one rich girl buys a title, hundreds marry in their own set."

The American mother is venerated by her children to the same extent as is the

French mother, and she is always reverenced by them in after life. Like all good mothers, she is a mother to the fullest extent of the word. The education and mental and moral training of the children devolves almost entirely upon her, since the head of the family is too actively engaged in business pursuits, in his unwearying chase after that dollar which represents so much to one who has others for whom to provide. Above all things, the American mother is a close student of her child's mentality, and it is with kindly sympathy, and not by resorting to physical correction, that she rules her household. As her children grow up, she who knows them, she who has closely watched over their mental growth and their idiosyncrasies, is in a position to talk to them with authority, and with a full knowledge of their minds. Seldom, if ever, does she delegate the bringing up of her children to servants — the nursery is practically unknown in the United States, except for children of the tenderest age. And, when the time comes for the selection of a college, the mother has generally as much to say in the matter as the father, who would not dream of taking so important a step in the career of his children without consulting her, and listening with affectionate respect to her counsels. And, from college, boy and girl write to their mother as to their best and most trusted friend, and so it is that she still keeps abreast of their mentality during the years they spend there.

The American Mother.

The educational system in the United States is one which has been held up as a model by many authorities. Space will not permit a detailed review of it, but a word of praise must be meted out to that well-known type the "schoolmarm" to whom many a novelist has paid a tribute well deserved. At an early age boys and girls are brought together in the common schools, and pursue their studies together on a footing of friendly rivalry and emulation. The training in the

Education.

Stereograph Copyright, 1907, by Underwood & Underwood, London & New York.

A GIRL OF TEXAS.

primary schools is admirable, the teaching is intelligent, and the result is that the pupils are well fitted, in the case of those who are not to enjoy the advantages of a college education, to face the battle of life and to earn their living in the capacity which suits them best. From their very childhood American youngsters are told that they will have to earn their livelihood; and, however wealthy the father may be,

Stereograph Copyright by Underwood & Underwood, London & New York.

COLLEGE GRADUATES IN PROCESSION.

he is determined, although he may himself have had but a poor education in matters scholastic, that his children shall enjoy the fullest benefits of what has been denied him. The American system of co-education eliminates affectation from the character of the American girl, and makes her more direct in manner, but it is an open question whether or not it tends to destroy good healthy sentiment. It certainly gives her some insight into the character of man, for it affords her the opportunity of noticing his faults and weak points, as well as his virtues, some of which she absorbs unconsciously, and to her great advantage.

Many are the colleges for girls in the United States, the principal being Vassar, an annexe of Harvard, Wellesley, Bryn Mawr, Smith, Radcliffe, and Barnard. These six have taken the lead in giving a quite special tone to the educa-

Girls' Colleges.

tion of women, but there are others scattered about the several States of the Union which have attained a remarkable degree of excellence, and the "sweet girl graduates" who emerge from them are thoroughly equipped to hold their own in circles of culture and refinement, and, if they do not intend to marry, they are free and able to pursue any career they may select. Yet, to quote the figures of Professor Münsterberg of Harvard University, only 5,319,000 are engaged in paid employment, where there are 23,319,000 men. Still, the proportion is here greater than in other countries. Teaching absorbs the largest number of women; female physicians number 7,399; 8,000 female officials are employed by the State; in this connection, it may be mentioned that there is such a thing as a woman marshal or sheriff in one of the Western counties, and she is reported to accomplish her duties with the unflinching nerve and courage of a man. The biggest desperado will hesitate before "drawing a gun" on a woman, but the lady has no compunction in the methods she employs when demanding his surrender. To continue the enumeration: there are 1,000 architects, 3,405 ministers of the Gospel, 45 locomotive engineers, 5 pilots, 167 masons, 196 blacksmiths, 3 auctioneers, and 1,320 "professional huntresses"—these last-named doubtless include the many girls who have "taken up land," and who are engaged in cattle-ranching and wheat-growing. Many of them are college-bred, and the same girl who during the day has been milking her cows will be heard playing the piano in her cosy cabin on the prairie, or be found perusing the latest interesting book published in New York. She enjoys to the fullest extent the advantages of mental and physical culture.

Mr. Burroughs, a well-known American scholar and observer, expressed the opinion some ten years ago that the American college girl of the day was not up to the average of the ten previous years. Then girls sought the higher education, and studied for the acquirement of knowledge. Now they go because they are sent, and their diploma looms larger in their ambition than what it formerly represented. He attributed this deterioration to the rapid increase of wealth, which begets idleness and indolence. "But," writes Mrs. Gertrude Atherton, in commenting upon this statement, "all countries have their tides which rise and recede with almost mathematical regularity. The English girl is just 'finding' herself. The American girl is resting on her laurels, a bit bored. The English girl, in her brief fling, has done much to antagonise man. So far, the American girl has stopped short of embittering the American man. The relative positions of the two phenomena a half-century hence will doubtless give rise to a literature in itself."

Photograph Copyright by the Illustrations Bureau.

THE WORK-GIRLS' LUNCHEON-HOUR IN ST. PAUL'S CHURCHYARD, NEW YORK.

The American woman takes a keen and active interest in the politics of her country, although she has so far not shown any particular anxiety to secure the right to drop a ballot into the "electoral urn." Four States, it is true, have enfranchised women, but the result has not been to stimulate to any extent the women of other States to demand the right to vote. Be this as it may, the voting of women in the States quoted has not made any perceptible difference in the "reformation" of their citizens, and the ladies are credited with being "as politically corrupt as the men." However, American women, when striving for their admission to the franchise, have disdained to have recourse to tactics unworthy of their sex, on which they would shrink from trading, and in so acting they have retained the respect of men. There are, of course, women whose enthusiasm for reform has carried them to absurd lengths, but their influence has proved to be merely fleeting; it has not commanded the respect, even of their own sex, and it has had no lasting result. On the other hand, there are those who have won undying fame in the cause of temperance, and one has but to mention

Women in Politics.

the late Frances Willard, a name well-known on both sides of the Atlantic, to confirm this assertion.

By way of conclusion to this article, it cannot be amiss to say a word or two about the Canadian girl, who is separated from her sister in the United States by an imaginary boundary line. The type of the former is not of so composite a nature as that of the latter. Two nationalities are mainly responsible for the Canadian woman's

"Miss Mapleleaf."

" Skating as gracefully as a Canadian girl " Charles Reade has written. The French-Canadian girl has jealously preserved the traits and virtues of her forerunners, famed among whom in the history of the Province are Madame de la Peltrie and the Mère Marie Guyart de l'Incarnation, who, with their faithful companions, first inculcated womanly virtues into French-Canadian girlhood. And, if the need arose, many a girl born and bred on the banks of the St. Lawrence would be prepared to emulate the heroic Madeleine de Verchères. The blood

Photograph Copyright by the Illustrations Bureau.

A SCENE AT ATLANTIC CITY.

being—the British and the French. The French-Canadian type shall be the first to occupy our attention, for reasons of seniority. The national song of Canada " Vive la Canadienne ! " has immortalised her in the line " Avec ses beaux yeux doux," those black lustrous eyes of the woman of the Province of Quebec. She has preserved all the characteristics of the *ancien régime*, and has generally been educated in one of the three famed convents of the Province. She is of a sturdy and dark type, and is the embodiment of grace and old-time courtesy. With her British sister, she is fond of outdoor exercise, and is an expert at skating.

of the hardy French pioneers would stand her in good stead. The girl of the Province of Ontario represents the best features of the British character. She has pluck, endurance, and " grit," and leads a very active outdoor life, taking part in all Canadian winter sports, such as skating, tobogganing, and snow-shoeing with all the skill and zest of her male relatives. And, whether she dwells in one of the palaces of Montreal's or Toronto's merchant princes, or on a farm in Manitoba or Alberta, she can hold her own, not only with her sex of other nations, but with the hardy men of her race. She is a fine type of Britain's colonial womanhood.

INDEX

ERRATUM

P. 335, for Grandi read Gbandi.